5,000 Open Salts
A Collector's Guide

By William Heacock and Patricia Johnson

Dedication
To the loving memory
of the author's husband, Ralph L. Johnson

Additional copies may be ordered from:
THE GLASS PRESS, INC.
DBA ANTIQUE PUBLICATIONS
POST OFFICE BOX 553
MARIETTA, OHIO 45750
1-800-533-3433

TABLE OF CONTENTS

William Heacock was just 34 years old when he co-authored this book. By then, he had already established his reputation as a leading authority on America's "Golden Age" of glass production from 1880 to 1910.

Born in Dallas, Texas, Mr. Heacock attended Dallas Community College, entering the antique business in 1971 as a dealer. His interest in research outweighed all other objectives and he became a full-time writer and lecturer in 1976.

For several years Mr. Heacock was a regular columnist for *The Antique Trader Weekly* and *Glass Review*. He also launched three glass research journals in the early 1980s, and served as Senior Advisor for *Glass Collector's Digest* when it began in 1987.

He was an honorary member of more than a dozen national glass clubs, a supporter of several glass museums, and lectured extensively from coast to coast. In 1975 he appeared on ABC-Closeup to discuss the problems posed by glass reproductions.

Before his untimely death on August 14, 1988 at the age of 41, Mr. Heacock had published more than 15 books on Victorian glass. He is remembered today not only as a pioneer in glass research, but as a warm, generous, and dynamic personality. He is greatly missed in glass circles.

A native Iowan, Patricia Johnson spent many years with her folks as an executive secretary at Little Giant Crane & Shovel, Inc. in Des Moines. Married to an airline pilot, she and her husband traveled extensively in the States and abroad. They moved to Torrance, California in 1957. Mrs. Johnson was employed in the real estate business until her semi-retirement in the early 1980s.

In addition to her passion for collecting open salts, Mrs. Johnson's interests included a study of metaphysics and a special affection for poodles, the culinary arts, music, fishing and gardening. Widowed in 1975, she spent much of her free time researching her collection. Mrs. Johnson became acquainted with William Heacock in 1980, and their cooperative efforts made this book possible.

Mrs. Johnson maintained an active interest in open salts throughout the 1980s and early '90s. She was grateful for her book's acceptance in the collecting community and lived to see the first edition sell out. On the way to a national open salts convention, Mrs. Johnson was involved in an automobile accident in 1994. She died from these injuries several months later.

In reprinting this work, Antique Publications hopes to provide collectors and dealers with an important reference book, while perpetuating the memory of William Heacock and Patricia Johnson.

INTRODUCTION
By
William Heacock

Tiny but mighty! Good things come in small packages. The meek shall inherit the Earth. Man through the ages has always held a natural appreciation for the small and meek.

This appreciation within myself was reflected in my own collection of small toothpick holders—the subject of my very first book in 1974. Eight years and a dozen books later, I am "working my way down" to something even smaller—open salts. These tiny little charmers, designed to serve salt at the dining table, have been a constant source of delight to thousands of collectors across the country. The original, and then practical function, has been lost to recent generations familiar only with the late 19th Century salt shaker, a creation considered more practical for simplified and hurried modern dining habits.

Fortunately for today's open salt collector, literally thousands upon thousands of different salts were produced for centuries, in such materials as glass, china, pottery, silver and other metals, even natural materials like wood, bone and shell.

There is no secret that my particular field of expertise is glass and in fact the majority of examples shown in this book are made in glass. This is why I was contacted by my co-author, Patricia Johnson. She had spent many years accumulating her superb collection of open salts, and her dream was to see them captured between the covers of a major, well-researched book. She offered her collection to me as a subject for one of my books. During one of my speaking engagements on the West Coast I visited with Mrs. Johnson to discuss this project and see her collection for the first time. To say I was overwhelmed is an understatement. The diversity of her collection, which consisted of much more than glass, made the project much more than that of which I felt capable. I knew nothing about the field of antique silver and silver-plate, and very little about early porcelains and china. However, Mrs. Johnson had already spent hundreds of hours researching the marks on her silver and china, and I felt a mutual compilation of our findings would make a fascinating record as a "guide" for collectors.

The distance between California and my base state of Ohio made the project somewhat prohibitive. We worked out many of the details, including the ominous task of properly photographing such a massive collection. My photographer, Chuck Smetana, was flown in from Ohio. For ten days we gathered, catalogued, measured, arranged, polished and photographed all the salts shown in this book. The job was much too big for the three of us, and with the incredibly generous help of Betty Odom and Sara Jane Hunt (salt collectors from the area who provided us with hundreds of additional rarities) we managed to photograph over 4,000 salts in this brief period.

This experience was not without its share of problems. The special light table we built on which to photograph the clear glass salts was, in many cases, too small for the larger individual and all the master salts. We did not forsee the problem of inventory stickers or old price tags still remaining on the salts, which had to be scraped off with razors and alcohol in some cases, eating up valuable time. The color shots had to be approved after each day's shooting, as the film was flown overnight back to Ohio for processing the next morning. On the more than 100 black and white shots we could only "hope for the best". Some of them did not turn out as well as we had expected, but it was impossible to reshoot them later. Because of the intensity and pace required to complete the photography in the alloted time, an occasional duplicate salt was pictured. We have tried to note this accordingly in the text. Unfortunately, also due to haste, some minute errors in measurement may have occurred. In some cases we took shortcuts by measuring only the height of the salt. Most of the measurements are offered in diameters or lengths.

It is important that the readers of this book realize right up front that not everything in this volume is OLD, nor is everything illustrated a confirmed open salt. We have included several items which are frequently confused for salts, or are sometimes misrepresented as salts by a few unscrupulous dealers (most are honest). We have made a concerted effort to identify those items which we do not believe are salts, but occasionally a sponge cup, nut cup, almond dish, butter pat, individual ash tray, ink well insert, or egg cup may get through unrecognized. We have labelled all recently produced salts as "new", even though some may be ten to twenty years old, or were produced by recently disbanded companies (Degenhart). In a few cases it was impossible for us to determine if the example we picture is new or old, so please bear with us on these limitations.

While this giant book is a mutual co-authorship between Mrs. Johnson and myself, we beg your indulgence with our different writing styles. My responsibilities were limited entirely to the glass salts—the others were covered by her. We both collaborated on final editing stages, where we tried to smooth over any noticeable differences.

A final word is warranted on the dates offered for each of the salts. Providing an exact date of production on each of almost 5,000 salts is as risky as setting an exact value to all of them. The overwhelming majority of the salts in this book are from the "Victorian" era, which technically means 1837-1901. However, the difference between "Early" and "Late" Victorian can be substantial To call a salt Victorian simply because it falls into this 64 year period is rather vague. In the case of pattern glass we can trace production years through old trade journals and original catalogues. Silver can be dated by precise Hallmarks. Some salts are dated according to design (the era to which it is condusive), the material in which it is made, and sometimes the color. However, most salts are dated "circa", and must be considered an estimate to the best of our abilities. Some salts were kept in production for decades. Others were revived and reproduced at later dates by the same factory. Always bear this in mind on the dates.

FROM THE COLLECTOR'S POINT OF VIEW

An Introduction by Patricia Johnson

With all due respect and appreciation for previously published books on open salts, it seemed the desire and need to know more about these salt dips has prompted me to delve into another book, my own. I studied every salt I purchased for my collection, and felt the research I turned up needed to be documented. We all want to know as much about these precious little charmers as possible. When an individual salt can sell today anywhere from $1.00 to hundreds of dollars, I felt we collectors really needed to know what we were buying and about value received.

One of the most interesting facets of collecting open salts is the wide variety of types—art glass, cut glass, pressed glass, blown glass, china, fine porcelain, figurals and animals in all forms, sterling and old silver-plated metals, even reproductions from all parts of the world. It is sometimes frustrating to salt collectors when so many good and rare salts end up in collections of 17th and 18th Century silver, porcelain and early glass. This is probably the result of a heretofore lack of knowledge concerning these finer antiquities.

I started collecting salts about 15 years ago as I retired and it has been the most rewarding hobby I ever thought possible. I believe there must be more then 10,000 different examples available to the more discriminating, dedicated (and unfortunately wealthy) collectors. We have tried to cover as many different types as possible in the variety presented in this book.

I have never been much interested in history until I had acquired several salts from the 18th and 19th centuries. Now I am continually confronted with an overwhelming interest in how they were originally used, in what type of dining atmosphere, what foods were served, seating arrangements, etc. With a little knowledge of the furniture, politics, clothing, social customs and manners of the period, together with a vivid imagination, one can easily visualize some gay and elegant dining affairs. It is surprising to me that these salts are in as good a shape as they are found today. Undoubtedly they were as highly revered when new as they are today as antiques.

Even though salts are more commonly used in Europe today than in our country, I'm certain a few homes in America have retained the custom of serving salt, "open", and do not just let them set idly in china closets or in cabinet drawers. I have spoken to several elderly people who remember using their set of salts, and some still own them.

I'm certainly not in favor of buying damaged salts, but in some cases a damaged "find" may be the only way you can ever hope to own one. Just as old chipped, flaked and cracked Sandwich glass is collectible, other forms will soon follow suit. This is a part of our social history and culture which will never be repeated, since salt shakers are so much more practical.

Advanced and beginner collectors alike literally speak of "love" when referring to their salts. Periodically I tire of collecting and all the hassles involved—then a day or two later these precious little things all look so charming again.

One of the most frequently asked questions is "How do I display my salts?". Most of mine are in custom built cabinets of various heights and widths, 5 to 6 inches deep with glass shelves, mirrored backs and lights. Others are displayed in French or Oriental curio cabinets.

I am told that just about any book takes at least twice as long to publish as planned, and I realize how patiently many of you have waited for this book. I sincerely hope that you are pleased and delighted as I am. If you have additional comments or research which you would like to share with us, we will be happy to hear from you. All of the latest research will be integrated into the price guides as they are revised from time to time.

My sincerest thanks to William Heacock, a tremendous individual with uncanny knowledge, a photographic memory and intuitive perception about these salts. He is a young and energetic person who will accomplish many lifetimes of research in his years. I feel fortunate to have had his help with this book and will always be grateful for this. My thanks to Chuck Smetana, our photographer from Richardson Printing Corp., whose superb work will let us all treasure this book for many years to come. My thanks also to Betty and Sara, who have both given so much of their time and continued efforts to make this book a success—as well as the loan of many of their salts. A final thanks to the printer and most helpful staff of Richardson Printing Corp., who have all been a delight to work with, directly guiding many phases of this book.

To all fellow collectors of salts—Happy Hunting!

PATRICIA JOHNSON

ACKNOWLEDGMENTS

So many people gave so much to the production of this book that we two co-authors do not know where to begin. Certainly the two people which first come to mind are the wonderful friends Betty Odom and Sara Jane Hunt, both of whom worked diligently with us during the arduous two-week photography session. Betty and Sara Jane also loaned us many of their rare salts and donated literally hundreds of volunteer hours to this project. There are no words to express our appreciation. We all worked very hard for very little, knowing full-well that the "book" would be our final reward. Salts had to be unpacked, markings noted, arranged by categories, cleaned, labels removed, and measurements taken. With every shot taken and catalogued we all felt a sense of pride and accomplishment which could not be weighed against the sacrifices. Betty and Sara Jane helped keep Mrs. Johnson and me free of all these tasks so we could concentrate on the setups, lighting and photography. Both of these wonderful ladies are equally as responsible for the beautiful pictures as we co-authors.

An additional important contribution to this book were the dozens of double salts from the collection of Frank and Rosanne Nehlig. Only a small portion of their extensive collection of doubles, gathered all over the world, could be included in this book. We are especially grateful for their generosity.

For her help in the preparation of the price guide on this book, as well as other suggestions and contributions, we must thank Mimi Rudnick.

Additional appreciation is extended to Bill and Helene Applegate for their photographic and printing contributions to the section of late additions.

For his advice and aid in identifying some of the pattern glass salts, we are most grateful to Tom Klopp, Editorial Advisor to the research magazine The Glass Collector.

A special thanks to several other collectors who made additional important contributions to this book, including Milli Dean, Irene Bobrowicz, Al Turner, Heather Long, Ardis Slater, Mr. & Mrs. Paul Klosterman, Oleta Whitecotton and Cyril Manley.

For permission to reprint portions of rare early catalogues picturing salts, our unlimited appreciation to The Corning Museum of Glass, The National Art Library, London, The Carnegie Library, Pittsburgh, Pa., London-based antique dealers Ronald Inch and Michael Blicque, Everett & Addie Miller, the National Cambridge Collectors, Inc., Fred Bickenheuser, Raymond Notley, Berry Wiggins and Kamm Publications.

RESEARCHING GLASS SALTS

This book was a distinct challenge to this researcher and definitely an aid in expanding my interests in the field of glass. I was not only faced with identifying and documenting hundreds of pattern glass salts, but many hundreds more in other forms of glass of which I was not as familiar. This book taught me to understand and appreciate even more the fields of art glass, cut glass, novelty glass, foreign glass, new glass and even very early glass usually found only in museums.

Dozens and dozens of books were referenced in my search for origin and identification. Most are listed in the bibliography. Frequently these cross-references are listed by abbreviation in the text on the more questionable or theoretical listings.

Pattern glass alone is a complicated enough field in itself, one which has become a specialty of this researcher. The three standards for identifying pattern glass are the substantive works of Ruth Webb Lee, Minnie Kamm and Alice Metz. However, there are scores of other lesser used reference books on glass, more specific in content, which provide much of the documentation available to the modern historian. Some of these books are no longer in print, probably due to the limited market for specialized works.

Sometimes the pattern design on a pressed glass salt is not easy to recognize. Frequently the pattern detail is reduced to a point that it looks very little like the "mother" tableware line. The YUTEC salt by McKee looks absolutely nothing like the table pieces in the same design. The hundreds of hours poring over reference books for pattern names was an educational experience in itself. Sometimes a salt that appeared to be pattern glass would end being another novelty or "specialty" salt with no matching tableware counterparts. These do not qualify as pattern glass, even though sometimes original catalogues gave them names like "Cog", "Octagon", "Diamond", etc.

Further explanation is necessary to clear this problem. There are dozens of pressed glass salts in this book which look like pattern glass designs, but to qualify as pattern glass, they **must** be part of a matching table line. Pattern Glass is usually pressed glass, but pressed glass (a manufacturing technique) is **not always** pattern glass. Thousands of novelties, candlesticks, bread plates, commemoratives, etc. were pressed into form, but the over-abused term pattern glass must be reserved for matched lines of tableware. A "specialty" or "novelty" salt, even though it may be pressed, should not be called pattern glass. It is quite possible that we may have missed a few patterns previously listed in other works for pattern glass salts in this book. If so, we will update the information in future editions of the price guide.

On the other hand, occasionally a salt that looked like a novelty or "specialty" item would turn out to be part of a table setting (i.e. HOMESTEAD).

Pattern glass names are listed in ALL CAPS. Names of Novelty salts are listed in quotation marks, if their original factory name is known.

Occasionally a salt will appear to be a certain pattern, only to discover later that it is another. This was one of the frustrating practices undergone by glass factories of the Victorian "golden age" of glass production. If a pattern was popular, it was bound to be copied by one of the competing factories to capture part of that market. Usually the copied tableware lines had different shapes, sizes and finials, but the basic design is the same (**Daisy & Button, Colonial, Honeycomb**, etc.). The same is true of open salts. There are many varieties of salts in varying designs of honeycomb, ribbing, panelling, swirl, zippers, blocks, etc. More than likely some of these common designs were meant to accompany a "mother" tableware line, but it is virtually impossible to match these much-copied basic designs to the exact pattern. Without original catalogues, we can only guess.

Many original catalogues from 1860 to 1910 are reprinted in this book to substantiate many of the attributions in this book. The problem of copies is easy recognized after a careful study of these reprints. The "Octagon" footed rectangular salt was made by several different companies, even at the same time. This explains why the same salt will be found in slightly different sizes. We trust that you will bear with us of the possibility of error concerning "copies" by competing companies.

Indeed, errors are bound to be made. The dates provided are not meant to be exact years of production, only estimates to the best of our ability. Popular patterns and salt dips remained in production for years, sometimes decades. On occasion a newly opened factory would acquire molds from one which closed down earlier. The modern glass historian not only has to deal with copies, but also mold transfers. Any errors which we discover will, again, be corrected in revised editions of the price guide.

I must admit my **Achilles Heel** when discussing cut glass salts, especially the numerous individual sizes. Shortcuts were definitely taken here. It is important that we accept cut glass as a form of art glass. It begins as a piece of plain, quality pressed crystal. It is then turned into a work of art by a talented glass cutter on a cutting wheel. Certainly there are hundreds, even thousands, of different "patterns" in cut glass, but we have made no attempt to locate their names. A popular "pattern" or design in cut glass could easily be copied by a competitor. There were over 260 cutting shops, small and large, in America at the turn-of-the-Century. The simple addition of a slash, groove or curve would prevent lawsuits, but retain the basic look of the original idea. Cutters relocated from factory to factory, taking their ideas and talent with them. Perhaps we could have spent hundreds of hours studying the many fine books on cut glass, comparing the patterns to these tiny salts for a matchup, but this seemed a futile and time-consuming endeavor. Most of these salts were sold as gift sets and not necessarily as part of a large comprehensive table setting. In fact most cut glass was sold "by the piece" or in a limited set (creamer and sugar), as it was expensive. In 1918 a good set of cut glass salts costs from $4.00 for a dozen. Compare this to the cost of $3.30 for 144 pressed glass salts (wholesale). This figures to about 4¢ each pressed, 35¢ each cut.

Thus, the many cut glass salts are described as motifs, not patterns. Only measurements are provided and occasionally a brief description or personal observation.

—William Heacock

RESEARCHING SILVER AND SILVER-PLATED SALTS

As with the fields of glass and china, there are a number of books written regarding the marks found on silver and the makers. The ones I used have been listed in the bibliography. The research on silver and "plate" is a specialized field all its own. Local dealers have been extremely generous with their time and knowledge during the last few years, at first with the common or ordinary, later with some more difficult attributions. Without their help this part of the book would not have been possible.

In Europe, the term "800" silver is known as Continental Silver. Here in the states, it is frequently confused for Sterling because it is solid and not plated. The prices on "800" silver are often questioned, when it should be pointed out that it is the quality of the workmanship as well as the silver content and age which will determine the value. An ornate "800" silver salt can be worth much more than a plain "solid" silver. This "800" classification was started in the mid-19th Century.

Occasionally the term "hallmarks" is used throughout the book for American marks. Perhaps a more appropriate term would be "trademarks" or maker's marks. In cases where there are no markings at all, the design and style of the salt are studied to determine the period of production. These are merely estimates of origin and age. There are a few cases where a trademark has been copied or imitated, but these are easily detected by the trained eye.

—Patricia Johnson

RESEARCHING CHINA SALTS

The term "china" can be interpreted two different ways. Literally it is a term reserved for high-quality porcelain. Colloquially it is ANY porcelain or high-glaze ceramic ware. Thousands of open salts were produced in the 1800's and early 1900's in china and porcelain. The overwhelming majority were imported from 1890 to 1920, mostly from Europe and Japan. In 1891 government import regulations required that all imports be clearly marked with the country of origin. Some of these were marked in English, clearly designed for the American market. Others can be found in foreign languages.

Exact dates on these china salts is not always possible. A few handpainted examples were dated by the artist, usually the case on "home-decorated" European "blanks". But care should be taken here not to confuse a factory decoration number (i.e., 1623) for the year 1623. These numbers have nothing to do with the date of production.

Sometimes it is difficult to determine exactly what material a particular salt is made from. It is a fine line indeed which separates the categories of china, porcelain, bisque, clay, pottery and other earthenwares.

FREQUENTLY ASKED QUESTIONS ABOUT OPEN SALTS

WHAT IS THE PROPER NAME BY WHICH TO CALL THESE OPEN SALTS?

Open salts have been called many different names, including salt dips, salt cellars, salters, trencher salts, celery dips, and just plain "salts". The term "open salt" is the most popular colloquial name used today, helping differentiate between the equally popular and highly collectable salt shakers.

HOW OLD A CUSTOM IS THE USE OF OPEN SALTS AT THE DINING TABLE?

Probably due to its scarcity and high cost in ancient times, the earliest recorded salts date back to pre-Christianity 1st Century, A.D. The high regard held for salt was a direct result of many traditions and even superstitions surrounding it. It was considered bad luck to spill salt, a curious superstition we continue even today, and in fact an overturned salt dish is shown in front of Judas in de Vinci's famed "The Last Supper" painting. Because salt was revered and considered unique, the earliest salts were usually created with great care—made of silver, gold, carved wood, etc. King Edward III reportedly owned more than five hundred trencher salts in 1329, mostly silver. Charles I records one of his salts in his personal diary in 1625, made of gold and studded with precious gems, weighing more than 150 ounces.

The salt "server" generally dates back as early as the first recorded use of salt as a flavoring agent. As salt became more readily available and the price more realistic, open salts were produced in more massive quantities for the general public.

WHY DIDN'T PEOPLE USE SALT SHAKERS INSTEAD?

Before table salt was successfully treated or mixed with moisture abosrbing agents in the early 1900's, it tended to lump and harden inside salt shakers. A few early salt shakers had "agitators" attached to the lids or laying loose inside to disperse the lump before each use. Many early patents were issued to inventors claiming to have solved the lumping problem with varying moisture absorbing materials inside the shaker or lid, with unique air-tight tops, or with other unusual features like coils. The open salt remained the most realistic, albeit less convenient, method of serving freshly ground salt. After the lumping problem was solved, the salt shaker became a permanent table fixture, replaced only occasionally on the more elegant table set in a nostaligic "old world" atmosphere.

WHY ARE THERE SO FEW PATTERN GLASS SALTS IN COLOR?

The popular period of open salt production was phasing out as colored tableware was becoming more popular. A number of pattern glass salts are available in color, but these generally tend to be the table size (masters). Only a fraction of the patterns made after 1905 had a salt dip made to match, as glass companies were cutting mold production costs by limiting the number of table items made in each design. Colored tableware was popular after 1890, reaching it's production peak about 1905-10.

It should also be noted that occasionally a pattern glass salt can be found in color in a pattern which is not generally known in color. These were probably colored sets made up from existing salt molds, and not sold as part of a line of colored tableware.

HOW DO YOU TELL THE DIFFERENCE BETWEEN OLD AND REPRODUCTIONS SALTS?

This book will help you get a start. Many so-called "reproduction" salts were never made originally in the shapes and colors you find at flea markets. The **Wildflower** rectangular salt is a new mold, never made before 1960. The **Moon & Star** salt was made before 1900 only in clear, so all colored examples you find are reproductions. Learning these simple basic rules on the handful of patterns which HAVE been reproduced (less than .1% of the total number available) will save you valuable collecting dollars in the future.

On clear salts it becomes more difficult telling new from old. Salts are so small that they seldom show signs of age wear on the base (tiny hairline multi-directional scratches). Look for tiny chips or scratches on the sides. Ask the dealer where he got the salt, and if his story is convincing ask for a guarantee of age in writing on the receipt. Sometimes this is not terribly convenient, as in the case of travelling flea market dealers. If the dealer refuses to guarantee the product they are selling, then do not buy. They know something they are not telling you. If you get that guarantee, take the salt to another collector or trusted dealer for their opinion immediately, and act accordingly on the guarantee if you are told it is probably not old.

WHY ARE SOME PRESSED GLASS SALTS LESS THAN $5 AND SOME MORE THAN $50?

It is not age which determines value, it is buyer demand. Salts are not bought only by salt collectors—many are bought by Sandwich glass collectors, pattern glass collectors and by collectors of a particular company's glass (Heisey, Higbee, Cambridge, etc.) If a particular pressed glass salt is in demand AND rare, the prices will skyrocket. Some pattern glass salts are common, and thus less in demand. Others were made by companies of limited collectability, and thus are only sought after by salt collectors. Condition is also important when determining the value—a crack or big chip limits the value considerably. If you see a salt and the price seems high, ask the dealer why it is expensive. There is probably a very good reason.

CATALOGUE REPRINTS

Unquestionably, the easiest method of determining the origin of the salts shown in this book is through finding them pictured in original glass company catalogues. There were hundreds of glass factories operating in America and Europe between 1850 and 1910, the major production period of open salts, but only a limited number of original catalogues have been preserved for the historical record. Reprinted on the next several pages are a wide variety of salts which were found in these available catalogues. A serious study will reveal that several salts were copied by competing companies, or the molds were purchased or transferred at a later date. This practice has proven to be a constant source of confusion to researchers and collectors today, as we gradually realize that even the most precise attributions can be questioned.

The American catalogue reprints are labelled A through Z. The European catalogue reprints starting on page 21 are labelled AA through SS.

Many of these reprints are through the courtesy of Museums, authors and collectors nationwide (listed in the acknowledgments), and we wish to thank them again for sharing these historical documents with us.

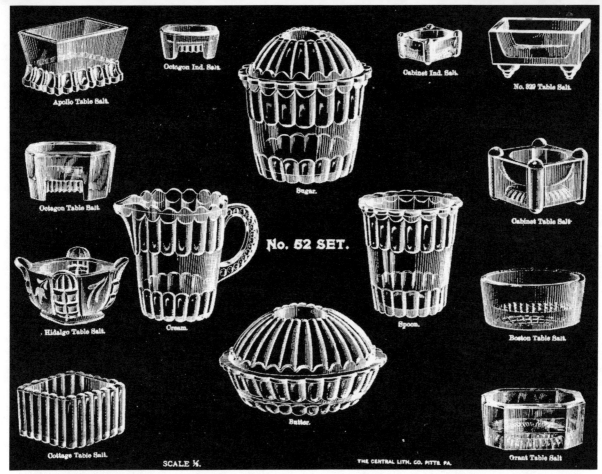

(Reprint A) Assortment of salts shown in Adams & Co., Pittsburgh, Pa. catalogue (while part of U.S. Glass) circa 1891

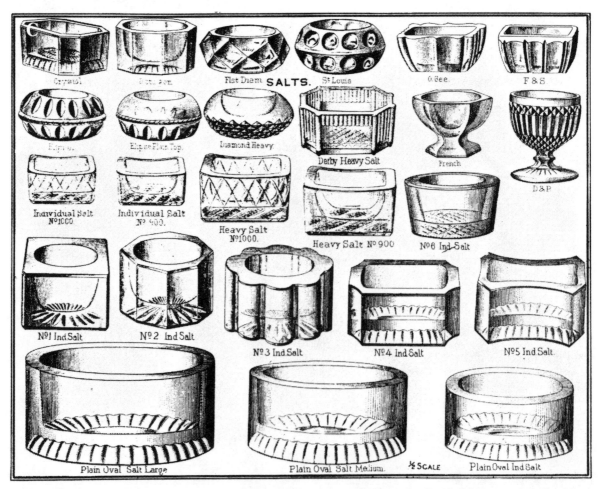

(Reprint B) Assortment of salts from Bryce Brothers, Pittsburgh, Pa. (while associated with U.S. Glass) circa 1891

(Reprint C) Wide assortment of salts shown in catalogue of Central Glass Co., Wheeling, W. Va., circa 1880

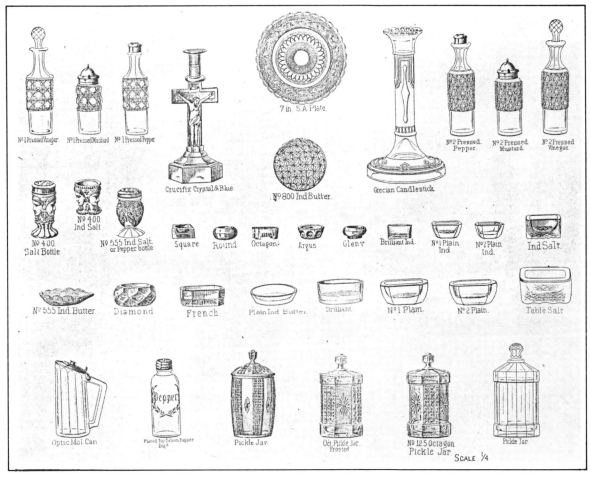

(Reprint D) Seventeen different salts by George Duncan Sons & Co., Pittsburgh, Pa., circa 1891 (while part of U.S. Glass)

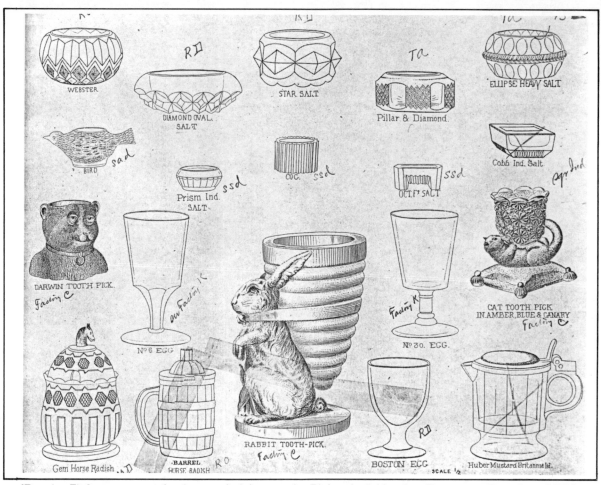

(Reprint E) Assortment of salts, toothpicks, etc. by Richards & Hartley, Tarentum, Pa., circa 1891 (while part of U.S. Glass)

(Reprint F) A few salts shown on page from Challinor, Taylor & Co., Pittsburgh, Pa. catalogue (while associated with U.S. Glass)

(Reprint G) Assortment of salts and celery vases from Bakewall, Pears & Co., Pittsburgh, Pa., circa 1875

(Reprint H) Assortment of salts, egg cups and caster bottles from Hobbs, Brockunier & Co. catalogue, Wheeling, W. Va., circa 1891 (while part of U.S. Glass)

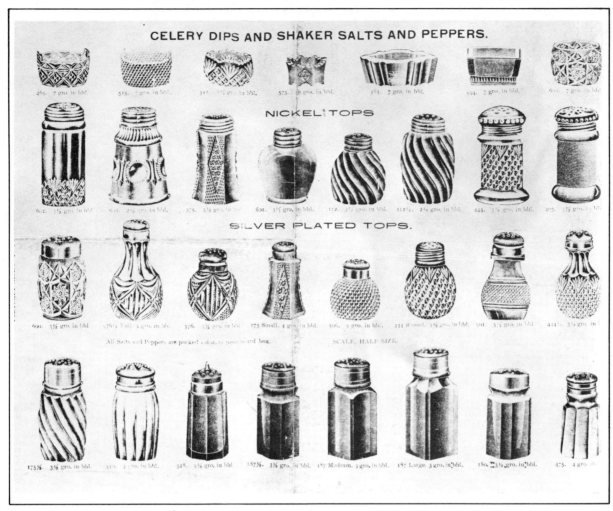

(Reprint I) Assortment of salts and salt shakers from 1901 Fostoria Glass catalogue

Open Salt Dishes, Salt and Pepper Shakers
Imported Cut Glass

E76521
Dozen 1.30

E76524
Dozen 1.70

E76541
Dozen 2.00

E76560
Dozen 2.30

E76562
Dozen 2.50

E76550
Dozen 2.50

E76542
Dozen 2.70

E76557
Dozen 3.00

E76567
Dozen 3.00

E76558
Dozen 3.30

E76552
Dozen 3.30

E76559
Dozen 3.50

E76569
Dozen 3.50

E76584
Dozen 4.00

(Reprint J) Variety of cut glass salts from 1913 Marshall Field & Co. retail catalogue (Chicago)—
Reprint courtesy Dorothy Prior

14

(Reprint K) Wide assortment of salts by King, Son & Co., circa 1880—also shown are two rare early salt shakers, a pepper shaker, and a setting of Argus pattern

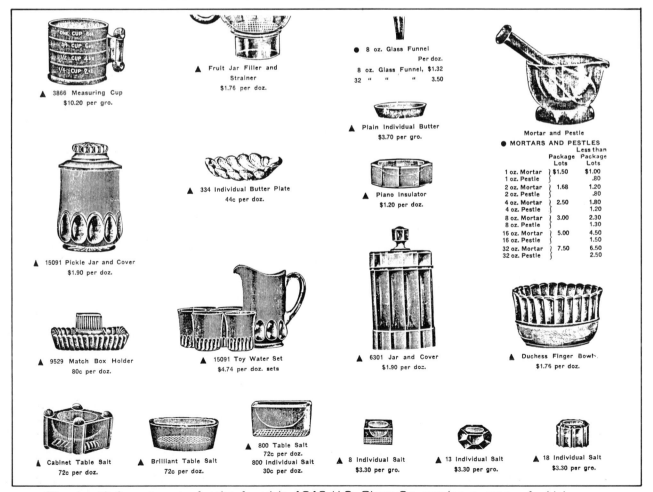

(Reprint L) Assortment of salts found in 1910 U.S. Glass Co. catalogue, many of which were made by member factories as early as 1885

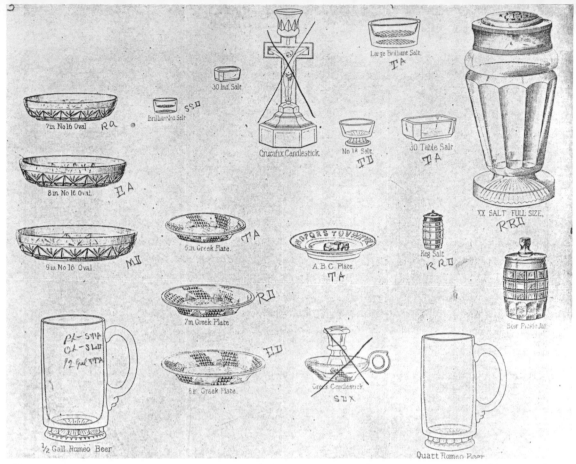

(Reprint M) A few salts by Ripley & Co. (Factory F of U.S. Glass) are shown in this page from an 1891 catalogue

(Reprint N) An unusual "Toboggan" celery, olive dish and open salt are shown in this page from an 1891 O'Hara Glass catalogue, while part of U.S. Glass (Courtesy The Corning Museum of Glass)

(Reprint O) Assortment of salts, including No. 99 Horseshoe, by O'Hara Glass, while part of U.S. Glass, circa 1891 (Courtesy The Corning Museum of Glass)

Shaker Salts and Peppers. Table and Individual Salts and Sugar Shakers.

Illustrations One-third Actual Size.
For Prices See 1904 List Page No. 106.

(Reprint P) Assortment of salts and salt shakers from 1898 U.S. Glass catalogue (Courtesy The Corning Museum of Glass)

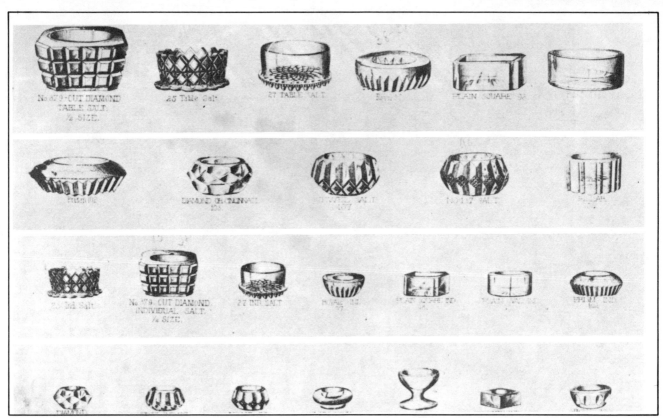

(Reprint Q) Assortment of salts from King Glass Co. catalogue, circa 1890 (Courtesy The Corning Museum of Glass)

(Reprint R) Assortment of salts and salt shakers from Co-Operative Flint Glass Co., circa 1910. The "Basket Salt" was also used as a holder for shakers. Many of these salts are identical to some made by other companies. (Courtesy The Corning Museum of Glass)

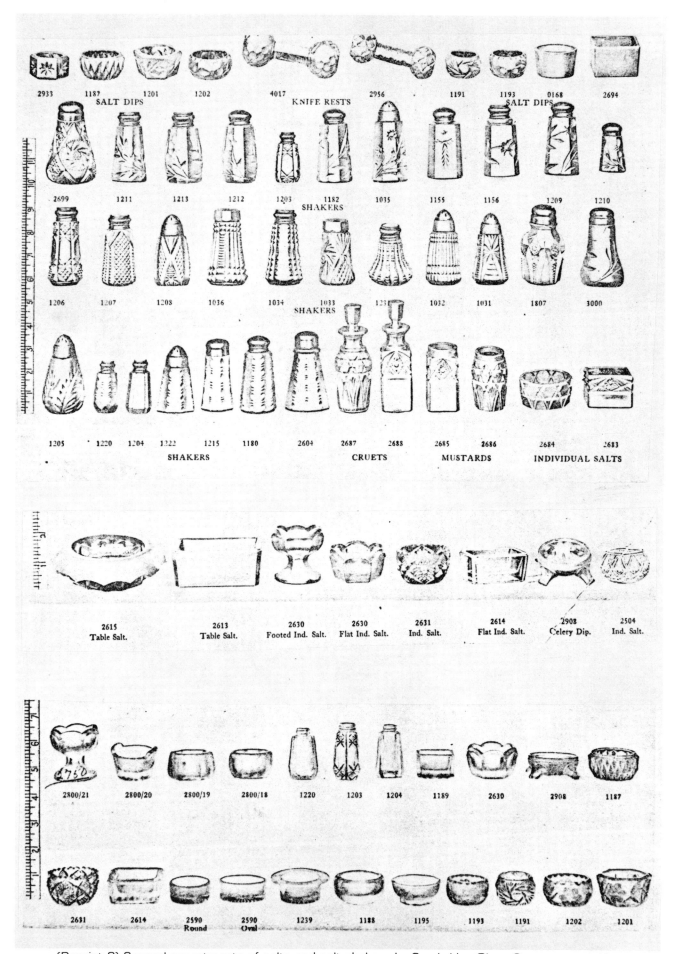

| 2933 | 1187 | 1201 | 1202 | | 4017 | | | 2956 | | 1191 | | 1193 | 0168 | 2694 |
| | SALT DIPS | | | | KNIFE RESTS | | | | | | | SALT DIPS | | |

| 2699 | 1211 | 1213 | 1212 | 1203 | 1182 | 1035 | 1155 | 1156 | 1209 | 1210 |
| | | | | | SHAKERS | | | | | |

| 1206 | 1207 | 1208 | 1036 | 1034 | 1033 | 123? | 1032 | 1031 | 1807 | 3000 |
| | | | | | SHAKERS | | | | | |

| 1205 | 1220 | 1204 | 1222 | 1215 | 1180 | 2604 | 2687 | 2688 | 2685 | 2686 | 2684 | 2683 |
| | | SHAKERS | | | | | CRUETS | | MUSTARDS | | INDIVIDUAL SALTS | |

| 2615 | 2613 | 2630 | 2630 | 2631 | 2614 | 2908 | 2504 |
| Table Salt. | Table Salt. | Footed Ind. Salt. | Flat Ind. Salt. | Ind. Salt. | Flat Ind. Salt. | Celery Dip. | Ind. Salt. |

| 2800/21 | 2800/20 | 2800/19 | 2800/18 | 1220 | 1203 | 1204 | 1189 | 2630 | 2908 | 1187 |

| 2631 | 2614 | 2590 Round | 2590 Oval | 1239 | 1188 | 1195 | 1193 | 1191 | 1202 | 1201 |

(Reprint S) Several assortments of salts and salt shakers by Cambridge Glass Co. appear on this page, composed of several different catalogue pages dating circa 1910-20 (Courtesy National Cambridge Collectors, Inc.)

INDIVIDUAL SALT DIPS

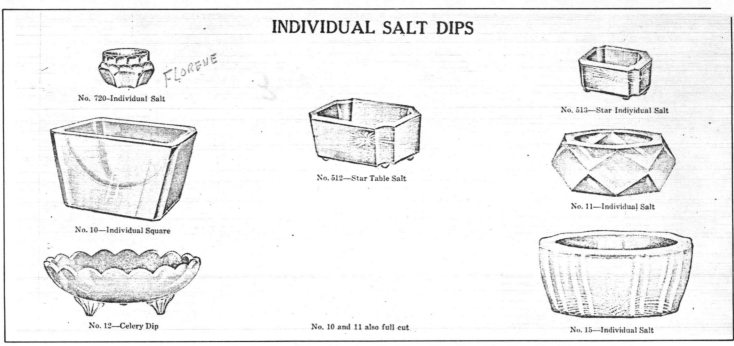

FLORENE

No. 720—Individual Salt

No. 10—Individual Square

No. 512—Star Table Salt

No. 513—Star Individual Salt

No. 11—Individual Salt

No. 12—Celery Dip

No. 10 and 11 also full cut.

No. 15—Individual Salt

(Reprint T) Assortment of salts from New Martinsville Glass Co., New Martinsville, W. Va., circa 1910-15. Only the No. 720 Florene qualified as pattern glass. (Courtesy Everett & Addie Miller)

11 Salt Dip.

113 Salt Dip.

100 Salt and Pepper Shakers

121 Salt and Pepper Catalin Top

120 Salt Dip.

112 Oval Salt Dip.

(Reprint U) A few salts appeared in a Viking Glass catalogue from the 1940's (with glass salt spoons). This firm was the same as New Martinsville Glass Co.

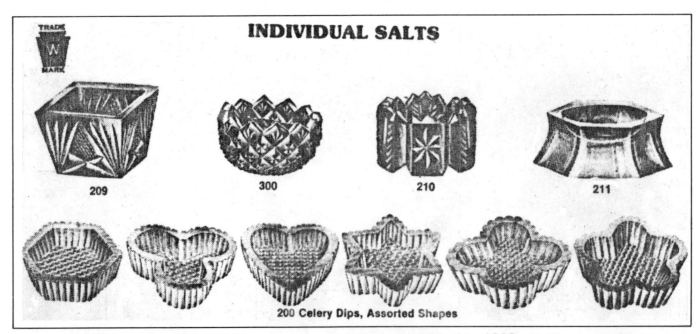

INDIVIDUAL SALTS

209

300

210

211

200 Celery Dips, Assorted Shapes

(REPRINT W) Assortment of salts from Westmoreland catalogue, circa 1920, showing the set of "Euchre" salts in assorted shapes

20

ABBREVIATION KEY

aka — also known as
circa — estimated date of production
D & B → Daisy & Button
diam. — diameter
diff. — different
EPNS — Electro-plate over Nickel Silver
Fig. or # — Figure number
HM — Hallmarks
Ind. — individual
Info. — information
IVT — Inverted Thumbprint
NMT — no measurements taken
NPG — not pattern glass (part of a table service)
PG — pattern glass
Prod. — production
Reg. — registered or registration
Repro — reproduction or reproduced

SEE PRICE GUIDE FOR LATEST RESEARCH FINDINGS AND CORRECTIONS.

INDEX FOR EXAMPLES OF SOME MAKERS AND TYPES

PATTERN INDEX BY NUMBER

ART GLASS

ART & COLORED GLASS

35 36 37 38 39 40

41 42 43 44 45 46

47 48 49 50 51

52 53 54 55 56

57 58 59 60 61 62

63 64 65 66

67

68

69

70

71

72

73

74

75

76

77

78

79

80

81

82

83

84

85

86

87

88

89

90

ENGLISH ART GLASS

91   92   93   94

95   96   97   98

99   100   101   102

103   104   105

EUROPEAN ART GLASS

106

107

108

109

110

111

112

113

114

115

116

117

118

119

120

121

122

EUROPEAN ART AND COLORED GLASS

123

124

125

126

127

128

129

130

131

132

133

134

135

136

137

138

139

140

141

142

143

144

145

146

147

148

149

150

151

152

153

154

155

156

157

158

159

160

161

162

163

164

165

166

167

168

169

170

171

172

173

174

175

176

177

178

179

180

181

ASSORTED GLASS, SHELLS, ETC.

182

183

184

185

186

187

188

189

190

191

192

193

194

195

196

197

198

199

200

201

202

203

204

205

206

207

208

EARLY 20TH CENTURY INTAGLIO SALTS

209   210   211   212   213

214   215   216   217   218

219   220   221   222

223   224   225   226

227   228   229   230

231   232   233   234

34

EARLY 20TH CENTURY INTAGLIO SALTS

235 236 237 238 239

240 241 242 243

244 245 246 247 248

249 250 251 252 253

254 255 256 257

258 259 260 261

CRANBERRY GLASS

262   263   264   265   266

267   268   269   270   271

272   273   274   275   276

277   278   279   280   281   282

283   284   285   286   287

288   289   290   291

CRANBERRY, RUBY & OTHER "REDS"

292

293

294

295

296

297

298

299

300

301

302

303

304

305

306

307

308

309

310

311

312

313

314

CRANBERRY & SILVER

315

316

317

318

319

320

321

322

323

324

325

326

ASSORTED GREENS

327 328 329 330 331

332 333 334 335 336 337

338 339 340 341 342 343

344 345 346 347 348 349

350 351 352 353 354

355 356 357 358

ASSORTED GREENS

359

360

361

362

363

364

365

366

367

368

369

370

371

372

373

374

375

376

377

378

379

380

381

382

383

384

AMETHYST & PURPLE SLAG

385
386
387
388
389
390
391
392
393
394
395
396
397
398
399
400
401
402
403
404
405
406
407
408
409
410
411
412
413
414
415
416

BLUE GLASS (PRESSED & BLOWN)

417

418

419

420

421

422

423

424

425

426

427

428

429

430

431

432

433

434

435

436

437

438

439

440

441

442

443

444

445

446

447

448

449

450

451

452

453

454

455

456

457

458

459

460

461

462

463

464

465

466

467

468

469

470

471

472

473

474

475

ASSORTED OPAQUE COLORS

476

477

478

479

480

481

482

483

484

485

486

487

488

489

490

491

492

493

494

495

496

497

498

499

500

501

502

503

504

AMBER SALTS

505
506
507
508
509

510
511
512
513
514
515

516
517
518
519
520
521

522
523
524
525
526
527

528
529
530
531
532

533
534
535
536

AMBER & CANARY YELLOW

537

538

539

540

541

542

543

544

545

546

547

548

549

550

551

552

553

554

555

556

557

558

559

560

561

562

563

564

565

566

ROSE PINK & AMBER

567   568   569   570   571   572

573   574   575   576   577   578

579   580   581   582   583

584   585   586   587

588   589   590   591   592   593

594   595   596   597   598

ASSORTED COLORED GLASS

599

600

601

602

603

604

605

606

607

608

609

610

611

612

613

614

615

616

617

618

619

620

621

622

623

624

COBALT BLUE GLASS & COBALT WITH SILVER

625

626

627

628

629

630

631

632

633

634

635

636

637

638

639

640

641

642

643

644

645

646

647

648

649

650

651

652

653

654

655

656

657

SILVER WITH COBALT LINERS

658   659   660   661   662

663   664   665   666   667

668   669   670   671   672

673   674   675   676   677

678   679   680   681

682   683   684   685

686

687

688

689

690

691

692

693

694

695

696

697

698

699

700

701

702

703

704

705

706

707

708

709

710

711

712

713

714

715   716   717   718

719   720   721   722

723   724   725   726

727   728   729   730

731   732   733

SILVER WITH COBALT LINERS

734   735   736   737

738   739   740   741

742   743   744

745   746   747

SILVER WITH COBALT LINERS

748

749

750

751

752

753

754

755

756

757

758

759

ASSORTED COLORS   IN SILVER HOLDERS

760

761

762

763

764

765

766

767

768

769

770

771

772

INDIVIDUAL NUT CUPS

774

775

776

777

778

779

780

781

782

783

784

785

786

787

788

789

790

791

56

COLORED GLASS DOUBLE SALTS

792

793

794

795

796

797

798

799

800

801

802

803

804

805

806

807

ASSORTED COLORED GLASS

808

809

810

811

812

813

814

815

816

817

818

819

820

821

822

823

824

825

826

827

828

829

830

831

832

833

834

835

836

837

838

ASSORTED PRESSED NOVELTY SALTS—OLD & NEW

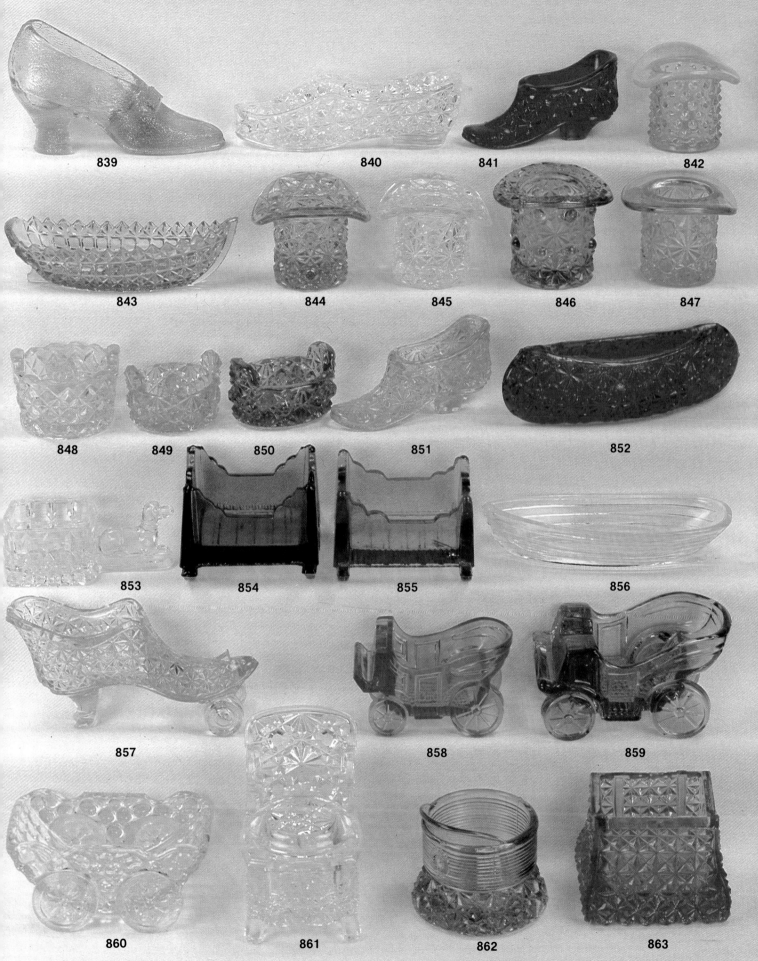

839

840

841

842

843

844

845

846

847

848

849

850

851

852

853

854

855

856

857

858

859

860

861

862

863

REPRODUCTIONS AND CONTEMPORARY SALTS

864

865

866

867

868

869

870

871

872

873

874

875

876

877

878

879

880

881

882

883

884

885

886

887

888

889

890

891

892

REPRODUCTIONS AND CONTEMPORARY SALTS

893

894

895

896

897

898

899

900

901

902

903

904

905

906

907

908

909

910

911

912

913

914

915

916

917

918

919

920

921

922

923

924

925

SWANS, CHICKS AND OTHER BIRDS

926

927

928

929

930

931

932

933

934

935

936

937

938

939

940

941

942

943

944

945

946

947

948

HENS & CHICKS

949

950

951

952

953

954

955

956

957

958

959

960

961

962

963

964

965

966

967

968

969

970

971

972

973

974

975

976

977

BIRDS AND ANIMALS—GLASS & CHINA

978

979

980

981

982

983

984

985

986

987

988

989

990

991

992

993

994

995

996

997

998

999

1000

1001

1002

1003

1004

GLASS & CHINA DUCKS, SWANS & CHICKENS

1005

1006

1007

1008

1009

1010

1011

1012

1013

1014

1015

1016

1017

1018

1019

1020

1021

1022

1023

1024

1025

1026

1027

1028

1029

CHINA SWANS

1030

1031

1032

1033

1034

1035

1036

1037

1038

1039

1040

1041

1042

1043

1044

1045

1046

1047

1048

1049

1050

1051

1052

1053

1054

1055

1056

1057

1058

FIGURAL CHINA

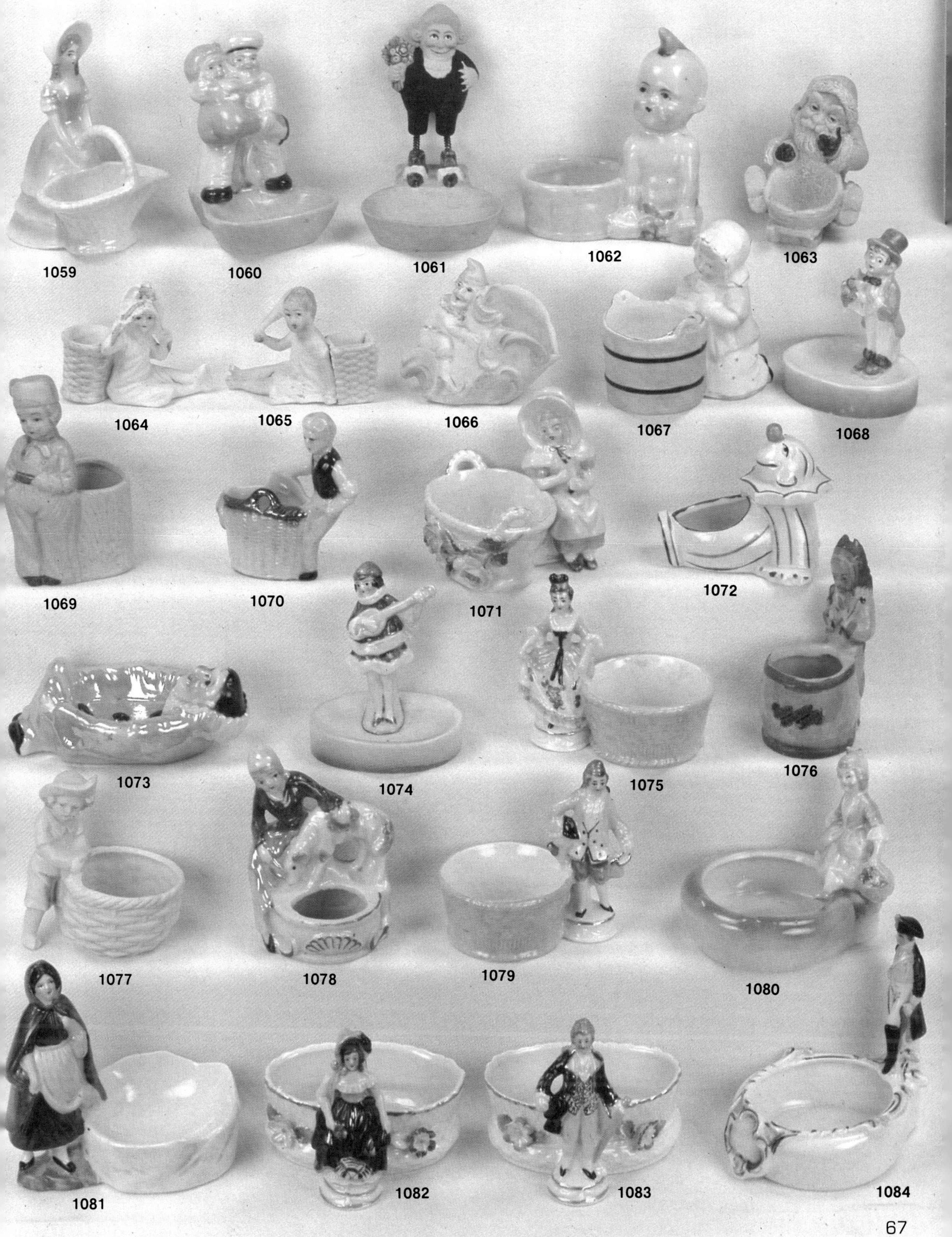
1059
1060
1061
1062
1063
1064
1065
1066
1067
1068
1069
1070
1071
1072
1073
1074
1075
1076
1077
1078
1079
1080
1081
1082
1083
1084

FIGURAL CHINA

1085

1086

1087

1088

1089

1090

1091

1092

1093

1094

1095

1096

1097

1098

1099

1100

1101

1102

1103

1104

1105

68

UNUSUAL CHINA

1106

1107

1108

1109

1110

1111

1112

1113

1114

1115

1116

CHINA SALT & PEPPER SETS

1117

1118

1119

1120

1121

1122

1123

1124

1125

1126

1127

1128

CHINA & POTTERY DOUBLE SALTS

1129

1130

1131

1132

1133

1134

1135

1136

1137

1138

1139

1140

CHINA & POTTERY DOUBLE SALTS

1141

1142

1143

1144

1145

1146

1147

1148

1149

1150

1151

1152

CHINA & POTTERY DOUBLE SALTS

1153

1154

1155

1156

1157

1158

1159

1160

1161

1162

1163

1164

1165

1166

1167

1168

1169

1170

1171

1172

OPEN SALT & PEPPER SETS—CHINA & SILVER

1173

1174

1175

1176

1177

1178

1179

1180

1181

1182

1183

1184

1185

1186

MISCELLANEOUS CHINA SALTS

1187

1188

1189

1190

1191

1192

1193

1194

1195

1196

1197

1198

1199

1200

1201

1202

1203

1204

1205

1206

1207

1208

1209

1210

1211

BASKETS & SHELLS—GLASS, CHINA & POTTERY

1212

1213

1214

1215

1216

1217

1218

1219

1220

1221

1222

1223

1224

1225

1226

1227

1228

1229

1230

1231

1232

1233

1234

1235

1236

1237

1238

1239

1240

ELFINWARE CHINA

1241

1242

1243

1244

1245

1246

1247

1248

1249

1250

1251

1252

1253

1254

1255

1256

1257

1258

1259

1260

1261

1262

1263

1264

1265

1266

1267

1268

1269

1270

77

DECORATED CHINA

1271   1272   1273   1274   1275   1276   1277

1278   1279   1280   1281   1282   1283   1284

1285   1286   1287   1288   1289   1290   1291

1292   1293   1294   1295   1296   1297   1298

1299   1300   1301   1302   1303   1304

1305   1306   1307   1308   1309   1310

DECORATED CHINA

1311   1312   1313   1314   1315   1316

1317   1318   1319   1320   1321   1322   1323

1324   1325   1326   1327   1328   1329

1330   1331   1332   1333   1334   1335

1336   1337   1338   1339   1340   1341

1342   1343   1344   1345   1346

DECORATED CHINA

1347 1348 1349 1350 1351

1352 1353 1354 1355 1356 1357

1358 1359 1360 1361 1362 1363 1364

1365 1366 1367 1368 1369 1370 1371

1372 1373 1374 1375 1376

1377 1378 1379 1380 1381

CHINA—FOOTED & SCALLOP BASED

1382

1383

1384

1385

1386

1387

1388

1389

1390

1391

1392

1393

1394

1395

1396

1397

1398

1399

1400

1401

1402

1403

1404

1405

1406

1407

1408

1409

1410

81

HAND PAINTED CHINA—FOOTED

1411   1412   1413   1414   1415   1416

1417   1418   1419   1420   1421   1422

1423   1424   1425   1426   1427   1428

1429   1430   1431   1432   1433   1434   1435

1436   1437   1438   1439   1440   1441

1442   1443   1444   1445

HAND PAINTED CHINA WITH HANDLES

1446   1447   1448   1449   1450

1451

1452   1453   1454   1455   1456   1457

1458   1459   1460   1461   1462

1463   1464   1465   1466   1467

1468   1469   1470   1471   1472   1473

1474   1475   1476   1477   1478

HAND PAINTED CHINA—PEDESTAL BASED

1479   1480   1481   1482   1483

1484   1485   1486   1487   1488

1489   1490   1491   1492   1493   1494

1495   1496   1497   1498   1499

1500   1501   1502   1503   1504

1505   1506   1507   1508   1509

CHINA—PEDESTAL, FOOTED & PLAIN

1510   1511   1512   1513   1514   1515

1516   1517   1518   1519   1520   1521

1522   1523   1524   1525   1526   1527

1528   1529   1530   1531   1532   1533

1534   1535   1536   1537   1538   1539

1540   1541   1542   1543   1544

GOLD DECORATED CHINA

1545

1546

1547

1548

1549   1550   1551   1552   1553   1554   1555

1556   1557   1558   1559   1560   1561

1562   1563   1564   1565   1566   1567

1568   1569   1570   1571   1572   1573

1574   1575   1576   1577   1578

CHINA—ASSORTED UNUSUAL SHAPES

1579   1580   1581   1582   1583

1584   1585   1586   1587   1588

1589   1590   1591   1592   1593   1594

1595   1596   1597   1598   1599

1600   1601   1602   1603   1604

1605   1606   1607   1608   1609

CHINA—ASSORTED UNUSUAL SHAPES

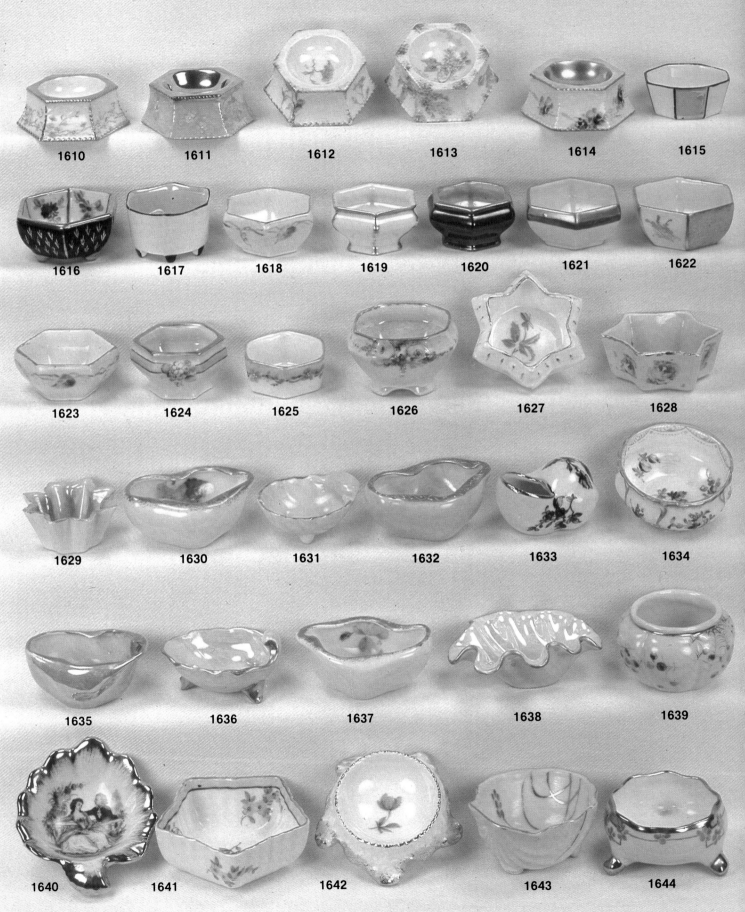

1610   1611   1612   1613   1614   1615

1616   1617   1618   1619   1620   1621   1622

1623   1624   1625   1626   1627   1628

1629   1630   1631   1632   1633   1634

1635   1636   1637   1638   1639

1640   1641   1642   1643   1644

CHINA—PEDESTAL, FOOTED & PLAIN

1645

1646

1647

1648

1649

1650

1651

1652

1653

1654

1655

1656

1657

1658

1659

1660

1661

1662

1663

1664

1665

1666

1667

1668

1669

1670

89

ASSORTED CHINA

1671

1672

1673

1674

1675

1676

1677

Capucin gourmand

1678

1679

1680

1681

1682

1683

1684

1685

1686

1687

1688

1689

1690

1691

1692

1693

1694

1695

1696

1697

ASSORTED CHINA

1699

1700

1698

1701

1702

1703

1704

1705

1706

1707

1708

1709

1710

1711

1712

1713

1714

1715

1716

1717

1718

1719

1720

1721

1722

MISCELLANEOUS CHINA

1723

1724

1725

1726

1727

1728

1729

1730

1731

1732

1733

1734

1735

1736

1737

1738

1739

1740

1741

1742

1743

1744

1745

1746

1747

1748

1749

1750

1751

1752

1753

1754

1755

1756

MISCELLANEOUS CHINA

1757

1758

1759

1760

1761

1762

1763

1764

1765

1766

1767

1768

1769

1770

1771

1772

1773

1774

1775

1776

1777

1778

1779

1780

1781

1782

1783

1784

MISCELLANEOUS CHINA & GLASS

1785

1786

1787

1788

1789

1790

1791

1792

1793

1794

1795

1796

1797

1798

1799

1800

1801

1802

1803

1804

1805

1806

1807

1808

1809

1810

1811

1812

1813

1814

MISCELLANEOUS CHINA

1815

1816

1817

1818

1819

1820

1821

1822

1823

1824

1825

1826

1827

1828

1829

1830

1831

1832

1833

1834

1835

1836

1837

1838

1839

1840

1841

1842

1843

1844

ENGLISH POTTERY & PORCELAIN

1845

1846

1847

1848

1849

1850

1851

1852

1853

1854

1855

1856

1857

1858

1859

1860

1861

1862

1863

1864

1865

1866

1867

1868

1869

1870

1871

1872   1873   1874   1875   1876

1877   1878   1879   1880   1881   1882

1883   1884   1885   1886   1887   1888

1889   1890   1891   1892   1893

1894   1895   1896   1897   1898   1899   1900   1901

1902   1903   1904   1905   1906

MISCELLANEOUS ORIENTAL SALTS & NOVELTY ITEMS

1907

1908

1909

1920

1921

1922

1923

1924

1925

1926

1927

1928

1929

1930

1931

1932

1933

1934

1935

1936

1937

1938

1939

1940

1941

1942

1943

1944

1945

1946

1947

1948

1949

1950

1951

1952

1953

1954

1955

1956

1957

1958

1959

1960

1961

1962

1963

1964

1965

1966

1967

1968

1969

1970

1971

1972

CLOISONNE & ENAMELS

1973   1974   1975   1976   1977   1978

1979   1980   1981   1982   1983   1984

1985   1986   1987

1988   1989   1990   1991   1992   1993

1994   1995   1996

1997   1998   1999   2000   2001

2002   2003   2004   2005

2006   2007   2008   2009   2010   2011

2012   2013   2014   2015

16   2017   2018   2019   2020

2021   2022   2023   2024

2024   2026   2027   2028

LATE ADDITIONS IN CHINA, GLASS & SILVER

2029

2030

2031

2032

2033

2034

2035

2036

2037

2038

2039

2040

2041

2042

2043

2044

2045

2046

2047

2048

2049

2050

2051

2052

2053

2054

2055

2056

2057

2058

LATE ADDITIONS IN COLORED GLASS

2059

2060

2061

2062

2063

2064

2065

2066

2067

2068

2069

2070

2071

2072

2073

2074

2075

2076

2077

2078

2079

2080

2081

2082

2083

2084

2085

2086

2087

2088

2089

LATE ADDITIONS IN COLORED GLASS

2090

2091

2092

2093

2094

2095

2096

2097

2098

2099

2100

2101

2102

2103

2104

2105

2106

2107

2108

2109

2110

2111

2112

2113

2114

2115

2116

2117

2118

2119

2120

2121

OPEN SALTS IN COLOR

On the next 28 pages are brief descriptions, attributions, and measurements for Figures 1 through 2121, the salts shown in color on pages 25 through 104. Only the more colorful examples could be shared with you in color, due to the prohibitive costs of color printing. How we wish we could have shown you more than 80 pages in color.

This section of text is grouped according to the order in which they appear. If you see a salt which you would like to know more about, simply note the number and turn to this section, also in numerical order, for essential data.

The old expression "a picture tells a thousand words" is our basic rule on limiting the amount of words we provide in this section. We felt there was no need to describe the details which are easily recognizable in the quality photographs.

As this book goes to press, research continues daily on finding more and more information. If additional data or important attributions become available, we will be adding them to a special section at the rear of this book near the index. After the book is complete, a special page will be included in the price guide for further additions and corrections. The accuracy of this book is as important to us as we are sure it is to you, and the authors would be pleased to learn of any errors for future consideration.

The original idea was to have these brief notes placed conveniently at the bottom of each color plate in small type, but upon seeing how difficult this could be for some to read, a larger type was chosen to match the layout and style of **1000 Toothpick Holders—A Collector's Guide.** We understand the occasional flipping of pages between illustrations and data can be frustrating at times, but feel that once you become accustomed to the format, each search will become easier. A numerical system of identification is an important addition to the field of salt collecting, making it much simpler to advertise salts for sale with a Heacock-Johnson Figure number to which to refer.

ART GLASS

1—Signed L.C.T., Favrille, 4-footed, 2⅛" diam., circa 1910

2—Unsigned, appears to be Tiffany, four feet, too short to be a toothpick holder, 2⅜" diam.

3—Signed L.C.T., in gold Favrille, 1¾" round

4—Similar to Fig. 1, except shorter and unsigned, 2⅛" diam., 1⅛" high, four feet

5—Signed L.C.T., two tiny handles, 1⅞" diam. at top

6—Signed Aurene 260, 1¾" high, too short for a toothpick holder

7—Signed Daum Nancy, almost 2" diam. oval, early 1900's, France

8—Signed Daum Nancy, French, circa 1900, just under 2" diam. round

9—Signed Daum Nancy, almost 2" diam. oval, French circa 1900

10—Signed Daum Nancy, just over 2" round, turn-of-the-century French, Windmill scene

11—Daum Nancy cameo glass, signed, just over 2" round, late 19th century, France

12—Signed Gallé on attached gold over sterling base, Hallmark 950 S, 1⅝" diam. in tub-shape, French, circa 1880

13—Signed Steuben Aurene, possibly nut cup, 1⅝" diam., early 1900's, New York

14—Signed Aurene, blue, made by Steuben, early 1900's, 2" diam.

15—Signed L.C.T. "X 355", perhaps a code for experimental run, similar to Fig. 3, except taller, 1⅜" high, circa 1900

16—Signed Quezal, 1¼" high, round panelled, after 1900, American

17—Signed L.C.T., gold with blue highlights (sometimes incorrectly called blue Tiffany), round shape, 1⅜" high, circa 1900

18—Signed Quezal, 1¼" high, round with crimped top, American, after 1900

19-25—All seven of these opalized and iridized salts are French art glass by Monot-Stumpf, which can be identified by a small round paper label which can sometimes be found still intact, late 19th century

26—Outstanding cased "rainbow" type art glass, probably English, circa 1890, 1⅜" high

27—Signed Webb cameo glass, exceptionally beautiful layered and carved floral design, circa 1885-1890, 1⅜" high

28—No mark, probably foreign, pinched opening possibly too small for a salt (toothpick?), circa 1910, maker unknown, 1¾" high

29—Millefiori, two-handled, Italian, circa 1900, 1¾" high, much-reproduced but not in salts

30—Signed L.C.T. Favrille, just over 1" high, in choice blue color, circa 1900

31—Signed L.C.T., similar to No. 30 except tighter crimp, same height, circa 1900

32—Signed L.C.T. Favrille, gold with pale blue highlights, same height, circa 1900

33—Signed Daum Nancy, 1½" tall, scenic design, French, circa 1890's

34—Steuben Calcite, possibly a nut cup, American, circa 1905-1910, 1¾" high

ART AND COLORED GLASS

35-44—Wide variety of hand decorations on satin opal glass by Smith Brothers, New Bedford, Mass., circa 1890-1894, melon-rib mold, 1⅜" high, Fig. 38 is signed with "Rampant Lion" trademark of this firm

45—A different melon-rib mold, shiny finish opal, possible Wavecrest, circa 1900, 1⅜" high

46—Unusual footed fancy mold with hand-painted decoration, possibly Mt. Washington or Smith Brothers, rare in satin finish, 1⅜" high

47—Wavecrest, "tulip" mold, hand-decorated, satin finish, made by C.F. Monroe Co., Meriden, Conn., circa 1903

48—English or French decorated white bristol, circa 1890's, possibly bottom to a small covered pomade, 1⅜" high

49—Rare Nakara salt or open pin box, signed C.F. Monroe Co., attached ornate brass-plated rim and handles, circa 1900-05, 1½" high

50-51—Two more examples of Wavecrest line by C.F. Monroe Co., "tulip"

mold with beaded enamel top, circa 1903

52 —French crystal with decorated enamel and engraving, rectangular shape, circa 1890, 1 3/8" high

53 —English bristol with enamel decoration, attached silver rim and handle, circa 1895, 1 1/2" high

54 —Bohemian decorated crystal, similar in workmanship to Fig. 52, circa 1895, 1 1/2" high, exceptional

55 —Blown crystal with gold and enamel decoration, Austrian, circa 1900, 1 3/8" high

56 —Not exactly art glass, but an unusual decorated milk glass example, 1" high, maker unknown

57 —Gorgeous English salt with gold decoration, attached silver rim, 1 1/4" high, circa 1890, possible Webb

58 —French "Lacy Enamel", decorated to simulate fine lace, circa 1900-1910, 1" high

59 —Same as Fig. 58, circa 1905, France, 1 1/4" high

60 —Amber Inverted Thumbprint with enamel decoration, probably American but maker unknown, about 1 1/2" high, beware of similar reproductions, Fig. 877

61 —Exquisite enamel-decorated crystal, probably French or Austrian, circa 1900, outstanding detail, 1 1/2" tall

62 —French scenic decorated glass, circa 1910, similar to but not the quality of decorated Daum Nancy, 1 1/4" high

63-64 —Master salt in melon rib mold by Smith Brothers (shown at top of page in individual sizes), circa 1890, unsigned, 1 1/2" high

65 —Probably Austrian decorated cranberry with applied curled crystal feet, circa 1900, some gold on feet, 1 1/4" high

66 —Either German or Austrian enamel-decorated crystal, pedestalled shape similar to nut cups, circa 1895, 1 1/2" high

ART AND COLORED GLASS

67 —Probably German cobalt cut to clear stemmed salt, 3 1/4" diam. at top, 3 1/2" high, circa 1870

68 —French white opaline double salt, sterling handle, circa 1850

69 —Yellow opalescent WILLIAM & MARY pattern salt, circa 1903, 2 3/4" diam. oval, by Davidson & Co., England

70 —Yellow opalescent CHIPPENDALE pattern salt, Davidson & Co., 2 1/2" diam. round, circa 1885, pressed, English

71 —French Monot Stumpf iridized art glass, circa 1890, 5 scallops, 2 3/8" diam. round

72 —Yellow opalescent blown with applied rigaree and feet, 2 3/8" diam., circa 1890, English

73 —Tiffany Favrille, unsigned, very heavy (6 oz. compared to 2 1/4 oz. on Fig. 15 & 17), 1900, 2 1/4" diam. round

74 —Stevens & Williams cased white over pink with applied amber rigaree, 2 3/4" diam., circa 1890

75 —Very rare Burmese, deep color typical of "Queen's Burmese" by Webb, circa 1890, English, 1 3/4" diam.

76 —French or English blue opaline, hand decorated, 2 3/4" diam., circa 1890

77 —Same as Fig. 46, probably Mt. Washington, sometimes called "shiny" Crown Milano, which I don't believe it is, 2 1/4" diam., circa 1890

78 —Cranberry opalescent, English blown, circa 1885, also known in yellow, 1 7/8" diam.

79 —Opaque lilac, English, applied London Silver rim with trademarks from 1925, 2 1/8" diam.

80 —Guernsey Glass Co. reproduction iridized by Robert Hansen (signed), trademarked with B-in-a-Circle (Bennett, owner of Guernsey), 1970's, 2 1/2" diam., 3" high

81 —Ice blue iridescent, heavy, almost 2" square, maker unknown, circa 1920

82 —Plique de Jour, 930-S silver, enamel detailed with rows of butterflies around top edge, Norway, circa 1885

83 —Plique de Jour, 930-S silver, outstanding enamel detail, almost 4" diam., circa 1880, from Norway

84 —Webb cameo, hand carved overlay, London silver rim from 1885, matching acorn spoon, choice olive green color 2 1/4" round

85 —Webb cameo, Birmingham silver rim from 1893, rare individual size, 1 1/4" diam., blue with white carved overlay, original spoon with matching hallmarks

86 —Intaglio with gold decoration, crystal, probably Czechoslovakia, early 1900's, 2 3/8" diam.

87 —Intaglio, amethyst with frosted floral design, Czech, circa 1910, 2 5/8" diam.

88 —Stack of clear Intaglio salts (ash receivers?) in original brass-plated holder, European (English, French or Czech), from early 1900's (1900-1920), pseudo butterfly mark, holder 5" high

89 —Early black amethyst master, pressed with cutting, circa 1840, probably English

90 —Another original holder for 2 1/8" salt-ash (?), 5" high, jewelled frame of brass-plate dates from early 1900's, European origin unknown

ENGLISH ART GLASS
All Stourbridge area glass factories

91 —Canary with opalescent applied rigaree around center, cranberry rim, 3-footed metal holder, 3 1/2" round

92 —Canary opalescent blown insert with 3-footed metal frame, see Figure 78 for similar salt insert, 2" round

93 —Canary opalescent with applied rigaree and feet, 3" round

94 —Blown clear with light opalescent rim, applied amber rigaree, 4-footed frame, 3 1/4" round

95 —Blown cranberry with opalescent swirling, applied clear rigaree, 3-footed metal frame, 2 3/4" diam. insert

96 —Clear blown with much white swirling, applied canary rigaree and ruffled rim, pontil scar covered by a splash of same glass, 3-footed metal frame, insert 2 3/4" diam.

97 —Clear blown with applied amber rigaree, no pontil (polished at top), 3" diameter

98 —Canary opalescent with touch of blue in glass at top, applied canary rigaree, 3-footed metal frame, insert 3 1/8" round

99 —Cranberry with white threading effect in opalescence, applied clear feet, 3 3/4" diameter

100 —Cased yellow with white spatter, swirled mold, applied clear rigaree, polished top, 3 3/4" diameter round

101 —Amber with applied blue feet and ornamentation, polished top, 2" diameter round.

102 —Cranberry with clear applied rigaree and feet, pontil scar, 3 1/2" round

103 —Clear blown with white and pink wide stripes, applied clear rigaree, 3-footed metal frame, insert 3 1/2" diameter

104 —Cased canary opalescent with rubina (note two layers on rim), applied canary yellow rigaree and feet, 3 3/4" diameter

105 —Blown emerald green with double rows of applied clear rigaree, polished top, 3 1/2" diameter

EUROPEAN ART GLASS

106 —Exceptional cut glass with two-color flashing, ornate plated stem, Austria-Hungary, 1880's, 3" high

107 —Free-blown yellow-green opaline with applied fancy rim, circa 1900, 3" diameter, 2 1/4" high

108 —Bohemian ruby-overlay cutback, very early, circa 1875, 3 1/8" high, 2 3/4" diameter

109 —Blue overlay cutback on ornate plated stem, Austria-Hungary, circa 1850, 3 1/2" high, 3 1/2" diameter

110 —Rectangular blue overlay cut, European, early 1900's, 2 3/4" long, almost 2" wide

111 —Venetian glass with matching spoon, age unknown, 3 1/2" diameter

112 —Cased white on cobalt base, European, circa 1910, 3 1/2" diameter

113 —Clear stemmed salt with blue threading, signed Steuben, circa 1920, 2 1/4" diameter, 2" high

114 —Delicate stemmed salt combine black with opalescent threading, early 1900's 3" diameter

115 —Clear with blue swirling, Venetian type, age unknown, 3 1/2" diameter

116 —Another Venetian salt with applied glass leaves and spun edges, age unknown, 2" diameter

117 —Blue with white stripes and attached coral spoon rest, Venetian type, age unknown, almost 2" diameter

118 —Six-sided salt on sterling stem, delicate etching in panels, unique, 2 1/4" diam., 2" high, Austria-Hungary, circa 1866

119—Pink Venetian ruffled salt with white base, European, early 1900's, almost 3" diameter

120—Unusual red opaque cased salt, polished top, early 1900's probably Czech, 2" diameter

121—Amber with blue striping in ornate sterling footed and handled frame, 4½" oval shape, circa 1890

122—Modern looking bubble air-trap in pink, paper label "Made in Italy", age unknown, 2½" diameter

EUROPEAN ART AND COLORED GLASS

123—Ruby Bohemian etched grape design, scalloped top, circa 1885, 2½" high, 2¾" diameter

124—Outstanding Victorian double with frosted pressed inserts decorated in blue in a Greek key design, circa 1890, holder 6" long and 5" tall

125—Another Bohemian etched salt with grape design, polished base, circa 1890, 2¾" round

126—Cased pink over white, double crimped edge, possibly Webb, 3¼" diam.

127—Blue opalescent English, made by Davidson in 1891, a pattern I call LADY CAROLINE, as it was made in other matching items, 4¼" diam. handle to handle

128—Pink and white swirling opaque, mold blown, circa 1920, 2¼" round

129—Ruby Venetian salt with spun white edge, two tiny free-blown dolphin handles, age unknown (may be recent), 3" diam.

130—French green opaline ribbed oval salt in brass-plated metal frame, 3¼" diam. circa 1885

131—Pink opaline insert attached to jewelled holder, European, circa 1910, 2½" round

132—Ruby-flashed insert with silver-plated holder, no marks, circa 1900

133—Venetian type salt in blue with tiny red "handles", age unknown, 2⅞" round

134—English, "spatter" glass with clear applied rigaree and feet, 3⅛" diameter oval shape, circa 1895, unusual

135—Pink cut insert on plated frame, English, circa 1900, frame is 3½" square

136—Charming Venetian type ind. salt with three tiny applied feet, clear with alternating swirls of white and black, Victorian, 1¼" diam., almost 2" high

137—Canary opalescent salt in LORDS AND LADIES pattern, made in other table items, English from 1890, 2¼" round

EUROPEAN ART & COLORED GLASS

138—Bohemian overlay cutback on ornate plated stem, white over clear, circa 1880, 2¾" diam.

139—Sowerby's #1328, made at their Ellison Glass Works, Gateshead-on-Tyne, England, appeared in 1882 catalogue, green opaque, 5⅛" long

140—White opaline (clambroth) cornucopia on stem, French, circa 1890, faded gold decoration, 4¾" tall

141—German pedestal salt, clear decorated top on amber stem, gold decorated with "Sand/Schnarzmald" (meaning unknown) spelled on bowl, 2¾" high

142—Beautifully decorated crystal, hand-painted with minute detail, 3¼" round, 2½" tall, circa 1900, probably French

143—Cased "Tortoise Shell" over white, probably English, circa 1885, 1¾" round

144—Blue milk glass divided pedestalled double, French, circa 1910, almost 3" diameter

145—Green blown Venetian type pedestal salt with applied leaves, age unknown, 1¾" round

146—English cranberry oval salt with applied clear rigaree and feet, polished top, circa 1885, 4½" diameter oval, 2" high

147—Amethyst with jewelled rim, circa 1910, 2¾" round

148—Blown clear glass with applied green ball feet, hallmarked Sterling rim dates this from 1901, Birmingham, 2" round

149—French white opaque decorated salt, circa 1850, six-sided with three animal feet (see Reprint), 3" diam.

150—Venetian "Ribbon" glass with applied flower, age unknown, 3½" diam.

151—Frosted crystal with unusual red border decoration, circa 1915, Foreign, 2½" round

GOLD ON CRYSTAL

152—TWO FLOWER pattern by U.S. Glass, circa 1915 (H5, 170), also in clear, oval shape, almost 5" diam. handle to handle

153—BIG PANSY, name by author, previously unnamed, probably Westmoreland, also known in carnival glass, circa 1910-1915, almost 3" diam., 2½" high

154—Etched crystal (some gold) in gold-plated frame and spoon, European, circa 1910, insert is 2" diam. round

155—KEYSTONE COLONIAL by Westmoreland Specialty, circa 1910, previously unlisted, toothpick in this found with W-in-a-Keystone trademark, similar to "Chippendale" and "Evangeline", 4½" diam.

156-160—Assortment of "Intaglio" salts (ash trays) in clear with decoration, all are "signed" with a small impressed butterfly, reportedly attributable to Webb (England), all are 2¾" diam., date circa 1910

161—Pressed salt with hand-painted flower in base, European imitation cut, circa 1915

162—Etched crystal with touch of gold, square shape, just over 1" long

163—Blown clear with applied gold decorated feet and original blown spoon, 1½" diam. round

164—Solid gold decorated pressed crystal, No. 211 salt by Westmoreland (Reprint W), circa 1910-20, just over 1½" diam.

165—Another "Intaglio" decorated salt with butterfly mark, red poppies, 2¾" long

166—Blown gold-decorated cut, 2" round, circa 1910, European

167—Pedestal salt with gold-decorated cutting, also European, circa 1900, almost 2¼" diam.

168—Three-footed blown with applied feet, light cutting with gold, almost 2" diam.

169—Crystal with detailed cutting, gold decorated, circa 1900, almost 2¾" diam.

170—Heart-shaped crystal with applied handle, light etching, circa 1900, 2⅝" tip to hdl

171—Imitation cut pressed, gold decorated, circa 1910, American, 2" round

172—Blown and lightly cut, with gold, three applied feet, European, circa 1900, 2" round

173—European cut with gold, pedestal shape circa 1905, 2¾" round

174—Boat shaped, blown crystal with gold on light cutting, 3½" long, European

175—Blown crystal with light cutting, European, circa 1900, almost 2¼" diam.

176—Heavy etched and cut, gold banding, European, circa 1910, almost 2" diam. round

177—Blown crystal with light gold decorated cutting, 3 applied feet, circa 1900, 2" round

178-180—Three VERY early salts, circa 1840, decorated on bottom with portraits, floral designs, etc., to be viewed from the top, frequently found with decoration worn considerably, probably German, 3⅛" diam. at longest point

181—Square-shaped etched crystal with touches of gold, European, circa 1910, 2" diam.

ASSORTED GLASS, SHELLS, ETC.

182—Looks like a nut cup (see Fig. 780), similar to one by Fenton, but this one is typical of Steuben's Verre de Soi, frosty iridescence, circa 1920's, 2½" round

183—Blown clear glass with gold-decorated cutting, French, circa 1900, about 2½" diam.

184—Gold-decorated cut crystal, European, circa 1910, almost 2" square

185—PATTEE CROSS variant pattern by U.S. Glass, toy berry dish in pressed gold-decorated crystal, circa 1910, 2" round

186—Venetian gold-flecked blown crystal, age unknown, shell shaped, 3⅝" diam., 1¾" high

187—Pressed clear glass with gold decoration, foreign, circa 1925 (?), 2½" round at top

188—Tiny individual blown salt, touch of gold decoration, crimped top, circa

1900, just over 1½″ diam., origin unknown

189 — Blown crystal with gold-decorated light cutting, French, circa 1910, 1½″ diam.

190 — Clear with gold-band, three applied feet, Foreign, circa 1910, 1½″ diam.

191 — Clear with "dripping" applied glass, English, circa 1900, unusual, 2″ diam. round

192 — Clear with gold-decorated engraving, three applied feet, French, circa 1905, scalloped top, 2⅝″ diam.

193 — Unusual free-form crystal, rather modern, age unknown, probably foreign, almost 3″ long, oval

194 — Clear with color-decorated bands, Depression era, circa 1925-35, American, 1½″ diam.

195 — Unusual figural salt or ash tray in frosted crystal, marked with Registry marks dating it from about 1893, probably French (not all registry marks are English), 3¾″ long, oval

196 — BEATTY RIB salt in white opalescent, A. J. Beatty Glass, circa 1890, 2″ diam.

197 — SQUARE HOBNAIL in white opalescent, possibly to accompany "Four-Foot Hobnail" (H2, Fig. 156), maker unknown, circa 1895, almost 2″ diam.

198 — Round HOBNAIL salt in white opalescent, possibly to go with NORTHWOOD HOBNAIL (H2, Fig. 163), but would accompany almost any other pressed opalescent pattern in this popular line, 2″ round diam.

199 — Blown shell-figured salt or ash tray. European, age unknown, similar to Verre de Soi lustred glass, 3¼″ oval

200-206 — An assortment of salts made from actual sea shells, dating much earlier than most of us would realize. Figures 200 and 202 have sterling hallmarked bases which date them from about 1908-09, London Silver. These shells were polished and sometimes carved (Fig. 201) into other shapes. See also Figure 208, with three attached feet.

207 — Ivory colored celluloid salt and pepper (see also Fig. 302) by William Thoreson and Co., Chicago — probably an importing company. Dates from about 1920's salt is 2″ long

208 — See notes Fig. 200

EARLY 20TH CENTURY INTAGLIO SALTS

Shown on page 34 and page 35 are a varied assortment of small, flat receptacles which have become known as "Intaglio Salts". There is evidence that these were originally intended to be small individual ash trays, but their small size and incredible charm has made them especially sought after by salt collectors. The many varied impressed designs you see are on the underside of the glass, usually with a delicate acid treatment to create a frosted effect. Sometimes the same impression can be found on different shapes (Figures 217, 252). The designs range from the masculine to the sublimely feminine. Figures 236 and 244 on the next page picture women smoking, validating somewhat the ash tray theory. Figures 237 and 250 indicate that these may have been designed as a "bridge set" of ash trays for card players.

Most of these can be traced to European origins, primarily Czechoslovakia (a few are signed), France, and possibly England. However, Fig. 217 can be attributed to the New Martinsville Glass Co., New Martinsville, W. Va. circa 1915-1920. The Rugby players are most decidedly English in nature (Fig. 228). The style of clothing and hair in Figures 214, 236 and 228 appear to date these "salts" from the 1920's.

Occasionally you will find this type of receptacle attached to an ornate brass frame, or a set which is stored in a brass holder. These are much harder to find, but add to the delight of the search for what is fast becoming a collectable sub-chapter within itself.

209 — Pink crystal with classic figures, almost 2½″ long

210 — Teal blue with Isadora Duncan "Greek Dancer", just over 2½″ long

211 — Pink crystal with fox hunt scene, 2½″ square, "butterfly" marked

212 — Electric blue with classic figures, just over 2½″ square

213 — Pink cut crystal with Olympic discus thrower, almost 3″ long

214 — Sapphire blue with bathing beauties, 2⅛″ oval

215 — Emerald green with Cupid, about 2½″ oval

216 — Teal blue with Elephant (note tiny butterfly — Webb?), just over 2½″ diam.

217 — Pink crystal with classic figures, same as one by New Martinsville Glass (Miller, 17), "butterfly" mark

218 — Amber with horse head, 2¼″ square

219 — Amber with circle of playing children, just over 2½″ diam.

220 — Emerald green with naked girl blowing bubbles, "butterfly" mark, just over 2½″ diam.

221 — Amber with classic scene, just over 2½″ diam.

222 — Amethyst cut moose in forest, almost 3″ diam.

223 — Blue cut with cat in a hat, almost 3″ diam.

224 — Amber with polo players, 2¾″ diam.

225 — Sapphire blue with flowers in vase, 2½″ oval

226 — Pink crystal with classic figure playing harp, 2⅛″ diam.

227 — Pink crystal with Cupid, cut bevelled edge, 3″ oval

228 — Emerald green with rugby players, 2¾″ diam.

229 — Same as Fig. 221, except teal blue color, 2¾″ diam.

230 — Amethyst with classic scene, just over 2¼″ diam.

231 — Emerald green with boy and dog, 2⅛″ square

232 — Same as Fig. 232, except amethyst, 2½″ oval

233 — Amber with two "love birds" with hanging hearts, 3⅛″ diam.

234 — Blue with winged figure blowing bubbles, 2¾″ diam.

MORE INTAGLIO SALTS

235 — Dark amber oval shape with classic figures, 2¾″ long

236 — Light green with cigarette smoking woman, 2″ square, note butterfly

237 — Amber with heart in center, part of a bridge set, note butterfly, 2½″ square

238 — Sapphire blue with classic musicians, 2¾″ long

239 — Amber with classic figure, 2½″ long

240 — Crystal with ship, 2¾″ long, ribbed edge

241 — Deep amber with two birds, somewhat different from most, almost 3″ long

242 — Amber with classic figures, 2½″ long

243 — Light green with courting scene, 2¼″ long

244 — Emerald green with smoking woman, 2⅛″ long

245 — Deep amber with Oriental figures, 1¾″ diam.

246 — Teal blue with rose sprig, 2¾″ diam.

247 — Clear with basket of flowers, 2½″ diam.

248 — Emerald green with spray of roses, jewelled rim, 2⅝″ diam.

249 — Olive green with classic figures, 2¼″ round

250 — Clear with King of Hearts, part of bridge set, 2⅝″ long

251 — Light blue with pair of roses, 2⅛″ round

252 — Amber with classic figures, 2¾″ diam. oval

253 — Sapphire blue with classic figures, just over 2¼″ long

254 — Clear with goldfish, scaled edge, note it is marked "Japan", after 1921, 3″ long

255 — Teal blue with classic figures, just over 2½″ long

256 — Clear with unknown vegetation, almost 3″ long

257 — Teal blue with classic figures, 2¼″ long

258-261 — Four different clear examples with dogs featured, 2½″ square, 2⅝″ long, 2⅛″ square and 3½″ long respectively, 259 signed Libby

CRANBERRY GLASS

The pale pink crystal known as cranberry is always blown or mold-blown. Any pressed piece found in this color is cranberry-flashed, a light coating of color on crystal. The formula for ruby glass was not perfected until the 1920's, so if the salt you find is a deeper shade of red, it can be an especially "rich" cranberry, or a ruby-stained piece of crystal. The depth of the color often depends on the thickness of the glass. Most of the salts on this page (except 277, 285) are English, so this will not be repeated over and over below. Unfortunately, only the height was noted on this early shot.

262 — Round shape in wire frame with handle, ¾" high, circa 1890
263 — Plated frame double salt with polished cranberry inserts, 4½" tall to top of frame, 1900
264 — Cranberry over clear, "nut cup" shape, 1920's, 2½" tall
265 — Cranberry over clear, light cutting, crimped top, 1¾" tall
266 — Three-footed silver-plate frame, applied rigaree on insert, 1880's 1¾" tall
267 — Polished top, applied clear rigaree, unusual to find on smaller salts, 1" tall, 1890's
268 — Plain round with applied clear feet, over 1½" tall, circa 1900
269 — Plain round with polished bottom, 1¼" tall, circa 1900
270 — Ornate silver-plate frame with oval insert, circa 1890, 1¼" tall
271 — Sterling overlay, may be French, circa 1915, 1¼" tall
272 — Mold blown and cut fluting, tub-shaped, 1¾" to tip handle, circa 1920, has matching pepper
273 — Round in threaded mold, polished top, circa 1900, 1" tall
274 — Round with Diamond Optic in blow-mold, polished top, circa 1890, 1" tall
275 — Oval with Honeycomb cutting, circa 1900, 1" tall
276 — Round with thin bands of silver decoration, circa 1910, 1" tall
277 — Colonial type salt, cranberry-stained, Westmoreland, circa 1920's just under 1" tall
278 — Plain round, may be insert, circa 1890, ⅝" tall
279 — Round insert in charming footed silver-plate frame, circa 1885, 1" tall
280 — Round with applied clear feet, circa 1890, 1¼" tall
281 — Mold-Blown round with flared top, not an insert, circa 1910, 1" tall
282 — Oval insert in silver-plated frame, circa 1895, 1" tall
283 — Light cranberry with polished flutes, flared shape, circa 1910, 1⅛" tall
284 — Round ind. size with applied clear rigaree, ¾" tall, circa 1890
285 — Candlewick pattern by Imperial, dating after 1940, cranberry-stained, 1" tall

286 — Oval shape, may be insert, circa 1890, 1⅛" tall
287 — Round and beautifully cut honeycomb design, thick glass, circa 1900, 1⅜" tall
288 — Round, bulging midsection, with fancy applied clear feet, circa 1890, 1½" tall
289-291 — Three more round shapes, master size, with applied clear rigaree and feet, circa 1890

CRANBERRY, RUBY AND OTHER "REDS"

292 — Cranberry with applied rigaree and feet, English, 1890, 3" diam. round
293 — Ruby-overlay, cut-back, European, after 1900, 4¼" long, oval shape
294 — Deep cranberry pedestal salt or nut cup, delicately enamelled decoration on inside, Moser type, Austria, circa 1900, 2¼" high and 2¼" diam.
295 — Deep cranberry blown into a gold-over-sterling ornate "frame", inseparably molded together, hallmarks from Whiting, American, circa 1910-20
296 — New ruby salt by Imperial, circa 1972, 2" diam.
297 — Rare ruby-stained SCALLOPED SIX-POINT salt by Duncan, circa 1895-1900, shown on cover, 2" diam.
298 — Ruby-stained ILLINOIS state pattern salt, U.S. Glass, 1903-1910, 2" diam.
299 — Shell shaped salt in ruby glass, circa 1930's similar to a larger version by Fenton, this one here is 2¼" diam. (Fenton, 3½"), may be Cambridge
300-301 — Two identical shapes in ruby glass, with Fig. 301 having a thicker "base". This difference in base depth can vary, depending on how deep the "plunger" was pushed in the pressing process, age unknown, 2" diam., oval
302 — Not glass, but celluloid (an early type of plastic), age uncertain (1920's), labelled "William Thoresen & Co. — Chicago", possibly an importer
303 — New Guernsey Glass salt, 1970's in red "slag", repro of old Duncan pattern, 2" round
304 — Cranberry flashed with cutting, English, 1900, 2½" round
305 — Enamel and gold decorated cranberry, Austrian, circa 1905, 2" diam.
306 — Clear with flashed color, 2" square, circa 1930's, possibly Fostoria
307 — Clear CANDLEWICK with flashed beading, Imperial glass, 1940's, still being made, 2¾" diam.
308 — Cranberry overlay cut-back, European, after 1900, 3½" long, 1½" high
309 — Depression era salt or small liqueur in ruby, probably American, 1½" diam., 1½" tall, also known in cobalt and clear
310 — Deep cranberry with polished bottom, European, circa 1900, almost 3" diam.

311 — Beautiful gold and enamel decorated salt or shot glass, Austrian, circa 1900, 2" diam.
312 — English cranberry with applied clear rigaree and feet, circa 1890, crimped top, 3¾" diam.
313 — Round shaped cranberry with cutting, European, after 1900, polished top, 3" diam.
314 — Cranberry with silver-plated ornate frame, no markings, probably American, circa 1895, 2½" round

CRANBERRY AND SILVER

315 — English silver-plated handled frame, insert with crimped applied rigaree, insert is 2½" diam., frame 4" high, circa 1890
316 — Another English example with clear applied edge and rigaree, plated frame, 2½" diam. round, 3-footed frame, circa 1890
317 — Four-footed silver-plate frame with oval insert, circa 1885, 3¼" long, 2" high, no markings but probably American
318 — Ornate handled and footed Victorian silver on brass frame, no markings, French or English, circa 1885, exceptional, 4¼" diam.
319 — Plated frame marked Derby Silver Co., American, circa 1905, 3¼" long, oval
320 — Fancy silver-plated frame in oval shape, 4-footed, no markings, circa 1885, 3" long
321 — Three-footed silver-plate frame, 2¾" round at top, circa 1900, probably English
322 — Reed & Barton silver-plate holder with foxes heads, may have had a handle like Fig. 315 at one time attached to discs on each end, insert has deep color, circa 1890, 2½" round
323 — Ornate sterling silver frame, with hallmarks, Gorham silver, circa 1890, American
324 — Another silver-plate frame by Derby Silver Co., oval shape, circa 1900, 3½" long
325 — Outstanding example of cranberry with applied rigaree, claw-foot plated frame, English, circa 1885, 3" round
326 — Sterling silver frame with scalloped insert, oval shape, circa 1890, 3½" long

ASSORTED GREENS

327 — This "Octagon" salt was made by McKee, Duncan, Adams, Richards & Hartley and probably others from about 1880 to just after 1900 (see Reprints), 1" high
328 — Apple green TWO PANEL by Richards & Hartley, Tarentum, Pa., 1880's-1890's, 1" tall
329 — ENGLISH HOBNAIL by Westmoreland Glass, 1920's with continued productions, 2" tall

330—Foreign pressed Hobnail salt, possibly German, circa 1890, 1¾" tall

331—Blown English example with clear applied rigaree, circa 1890, 1½" tall

332—FLEMISH pattern by Fostoria Glass, circa 1910, rare in color, 1" tall

333—Fostoria No. 95 (Weatherman Fostoria, pg. 22), circa 1900-10, 1" tall

334—Multi-sided pedestal salt in plain fluted pattern, maker unknown, circa 1910-20, 1¼" tall

335—BRAZILIAN pattern by Fostoria, circa 1899-1905, rare salt in color, 1½" tall

336—Cambridge No. 2933 (Welker 1, 110), novelty salt, circa 1910 with lengthy production, 1" tall

337—Westmoreland's LOTUS pattern (WDG2, pg. 378), circa 1920's with continued production into recent years, 1⅛" tall

338—Plain fluted pattern, maker unknown, circa 1915, 1" tall

339—Another round plain fluted salt in somewhat better glass, circa 1925-35, probably Cambridge, about 1" tall

340—Round with scalloped top, cut panels, probably foreign, circa 1895, 1⅛" tall

341—Mold-blown, polished top, circa 1890 foreign

342—Same as Fig. 339, except with wider flare at top rim, the result of different "finishing", possibly Cambridge, from 20's to 40's

343—Finely ribbed pressed salt, probably American, circa 1920's, round 1" tall

344—Finely polished with cut panels, six-sided, probably English, circa 1895, under 1" tall

345—Three-footed round example with Greek Key design, foreign (Mexican?), circa 1910, 1" tall

346—Square shape with plain sides and CANE pattern in base, this one by Duncan (see Reprint D), hard to find in color, circa 1890, under 1" tall

347—Square shape with bevelled sides, DIAMOND POINT design on base, maker undetermined, circa 1890, under 1" tall

348—Multi-sided colored cut with star design in base, circa 1900, maker unknown, ¾" tall

349—Triangular shape with bevelled edges, maker unknown, circa 1905, may be English, ½" tall

350—Low round scalloped edge with tiny nubbed feet, foreign, circa 1910, ½" tall

351—Toy berry dish to child's set in LACY DAISY, Westmoreland Glass, 1920's, 1" tall

352—Appears to be D & M No. 54 (H6,83), but this is not generally known in color, probably Cambridge, circa 1930's, 1" tall

353—Green with gold band, mold-blown with applied feet, probably American, circa 1925, just over 1" tall

354—Clear and green combined, mold-blown, circa 1930, probably an almond cup, 1¾" tall

355—Threaded and swirled, European, age unknown, 1¼" tall

356—Beautiful colored cut glass master salt, English, circa 1900, 1½" tall

357—Green pressed glass, foreign, feet appear to be blown but are part of mold, dates from about 1915, almost 2" tall

358—French or English blown glass with applied gold decoration, circa 1900, round shape, 1¼" tall

ASSORTED GREENS

359—Fenton's No. 923 nut cup with unusual flared top (see also page 56), in Jade Green color, circa 1925-1930, 3" diam., almost 1¾" high

360—Unusual green opaline early French salt, six-sided circular mold, circa 1885-90, this one is signed Baccarat, almost 3" diam.

361—Early opaque green master salt, diamond-point design, probably unmarked Sowerby, circa 1885 (color matches Fig. 139), 2½" diam. round

362—Green milk glass in pedestalled swirl design, French, circa 1900-1910 (see also Fig. 480), unmarked, almost 2" high, 2½" diam.

363—Large oval master with a panelled herringbone design, unusual aqua-green color, probably foreign, circa 1900, about 4½" long

364—Apple green WILDFLOWER salt, turtle base hard to find in perfect condition, Adams & Co., Pittsburgh (continued by U.S. Glass), circa 1885-1895, reproduced—but not with turtle, 3¾" long, 2⅛" high, oval

365—Deep blue-green canoe novelty, foreign, circa 1900, 4⅝" long

366—Green master salt, plain, round with a large Daisy & Button type pattern on bottom, maker unknown, circa 1890, 2¾" diam.

367—Common master salt dating about 1890-1900, made in all colors, maker unknown but probably American, shown here in emerald green, rectangular and slightly oval, 2¾". Also reproduced in the 1970's, watch when buying, they look old

368—Same as Fig. 421 in light green of the 1920-30 period, pedestalled flute pattern, Cambridge Glass, 2" high

369—Mold-blown, light green top with amber base, this was purchased as Steuben, called "Turkey Tracks" (accuracy undetermined), probably a nut cup from about 1925-30, 2¾" diam.

370—Tiny ind. pressed salt, foreign, looks Mexican, circa 1910, under 1½" diam.

371—Low, square salt, cut and bevelled, maker unknown, circa 1905, 1½" square

372—Central Glass No. 439 PANEL WITH DIAMOND POINT ind. salt, circa 1880 (see Reprint C) in scarce apple green color, similar to one made by Bryce Bros. (Reprint B), 2" diam. round

373—Emerald green blown, silver deposit decoration, probably foreign, circa 1910, 2" round

374—Light green tub-shape, cut bottom, may be Heisey, circa 1930, 2" diam.

375—Mold blown with polished top, notch on rim identifies this as an ind. ash receiver, oval shape 2⅛" long

376—Green insert with Sterling Birmingham silver frame, hallmarks date this from 1902, oval shape about 2" long, English

377—Threaded glass with plated rim, clearly identified as to its purpose, English from about 1895, 2¼" diam. at widest, round shape

378—Large oval shape in marked Derby Silver Co. frame, marks date this about 1900, about 3½" long

379—Oval ind. Birmingham silver frame, hallmarks date this from about 1902, 2" long

380—Pressed insert on silver-plate frame by Wallace Bros., circa 1879

381—Silver-plate ornate footed frame with original insert, Fleur-de-Lis open-work design on frame, no marks, circa 1900, 3" diam.

382—Plated frame with pressed glass insert, probably foreign, no marks, circa 1910

383—Plated oval frame, no marks, with green opaline insert, probably French, circa 1895, 3½" long

384—Unmarked ornate plated frame (silver over copper), green opaline insert, French circa 1890's, 3½" long, oval, quite rare

AMETHYST AND PURPLE SLAG

385—Boat-shaped, handled and pedestalled with Sowerby mark (Peacock head), registry marks date from about 1880, 2" tall, 4¼" long

386—Tiny slag salt with Sowerby mark, same as Fig. 392 except handles have been ground off (shown to alert collectors), 2½" long, oval

387—Pedestalled purple slag master salt, with Lion trademark of George Davidson and Co., Gateshead, England, circa 1880, 2½" tall, 3" diam.

388—Rectangular slag salt, no trademarks so may be American, lighter slag color is usually not English, circa 1890, 1" tall, almost 3" long

389—Early Cambridge glass salt, deep color typical of 1920's production, notice slight difference in size from Fig. 336, 1½" diam.

390—French "Lacy" pressed glass salt of undetermined age, may be a reproduction, original made in France circa 1870's but not in color, non-flint, 3¾" long, oval, 2⅛" high

391—Tiny pedestal salt, American, circa 1930, almost 2" tall, 1½" diam.

392—Same as Fig. 386 except with handles still intact, circa 1885, 3¼" long, oval

393—Square shape with polished edges pressed design in base, maker unknown, circa 1890, American, about 1 1/2" square

394—Low, multi-sided salt which is of unknown age or origin, 1 3/4" long, oval

395—Sun-turned crystal (chemical reaction in early glass causes clear glass to change when exposed to sunlight), Duncan's SCALLOPED SIX-POINT (# 30 line), 1890's 1 1/2" diam.

396—Light amethyst, octagonal salt, highly polished, probably foreign, circa 1910, 1" diam.

397—Unusual pedestal salt in light amethyst, may be sun-turned, appears to be foreign, circa 1915, 2 1/8" tall, 1 3/4" square top

398—Central's No. 178 salt in sun-turned amethyst (See Reprint C), circa 1880, 1" round

399—Salt to toy cruet set (Weatherman DG2, 380) in ENGLISH HOBNAIL by Westmoreland, this is probably sun-turned, circa 1900-10 (lengthy production into recent years), 1" round

400—Either Duncan or Cambridge Glass, circa 1905-10, in sun-turned color, 2" tall

401—Reproduction of early Duncan salt by Guernsey Glass (signed with Bennet's B) in "Alexandrite" type color, 1970's, 1 1/8" diam. round

402—Low, semi-oval salt or ash tray, foreign, circa 1910, 2 3/4" long

403—Unusual frosted camphor glass with pink staining, probably French, early 1900's may have been polished, creating color change at top, 1" round

404—Sun-turned early Honeycomb salt, popular design used by several firms (see catalogue Reprints), circa 1880, 1 1/4" diam.

405—Venetian type salt with spun edge and applied dots, clear with color-staining, age undetermined, 1 1/2" diam. round

406—Mold-blown crystal with faded amethyst flashing, gold decoration, European, circa 1900, may be an insert, almost 2" diam. at top

407—Chinese polished amethyst stone on wooden pedestal, age unknown, 1 3/4" tall combined

408—Sun-turned amethyst square salt, American, maker unknown, circa 1880, 1 1/2" square

409—Imitation cut, sun-turned, possibly a pomade, maker unknown, circa 1905, just over 1 1/2" diameter

410—Round deep amethyst on sterling base, purchased new in Switzerland in 1970, 1 1/4" round

411—Cambridge glass amethyst footed nut cup, circa 1930's, almost 3" diam.

412—Sun-turned "Octagon" master salt, made by several companies, this one probably by Central (see Reprint C), circa 1880, 3 3/8" long

413—English purple slag Sowerby trademarked open bucket or washtub

registry marks date it from 1877, 2 3/8" round

414—Another slag salt with Lion trademark of George Davidson and Co., Gateshead, England, circa 1880, 2 1/8" diam.

415—Leaf-shaped amethyst salt with original Fostoria paper label showing, dates from about 1940, rare in color, see Fig. 605, 1" high

416—Deep amethyst boat-shaped oval salt on pedestal, origin unknown, circa 1920's, 3 3/8" long at top

BLUE GLASS (PRESSED AND BLOWN)

417—Central's No. 16 "Coach" ind. salt, circa 1880-85, see Reprint C, 1 1/2" tall

418—Oval master salt with tiny ribbed star peg feet, plain sides, maker unknown, circa 1890, 1 1/4" tall

419—Pedestalled blown salt with blue bowl and mercury-lined stem, origin unknown, circa 1880-1900, 3 1/8" tall

420—Blue panelled salt by U.S. Glass, also used with PORTLAND pattern in clear, circa 1910

421—Fluted salt in pedestal shape, made by Cambridge, circa 1920, 2" tall

422—Sapphire blue blown salt with clear applied rigaree, English, circa 1890, 1 1/2" tall

423—Periwinkle blue DIAMOND QUILTED salt, U.S. Glass, 1891-1910, made in full table setting, presed pattern, (Lee PG, 104), also other colors, 1 1/4" tall

424—Paden City No. 12 salt (Barnett, 75), deep sapphire blue is a rare color for this company (molds may have been acquired from earlier factory), circa 1916-20, less than 1" tall

425—Cut honeycomb design with ribbed, base, foreign, circa 1900, 1" tall

426—Deep blue JERSEY SWIRL salt, old, reproduced in different size, Lee calls it SWIRL, but it is much better known by the first name, maker unknown, circa 1890, 1" tall

427—Blue PRESSED DIAMOND salt by Central Glass, 1880's (see Reprint C), 3/4" tall

428—Fostoria FLEMISH pattern salt in color, possibly a novelty since the line was not generally made in color (see also Fig. 332), circa 1900-10, 1" tall

429—Blue TWO PANEL salt by Richards and Hartley, continued by U.S. Glass, 1880-1890's, oval shape, 1" tall

430—Plain rectangular salt with X's within squares (24) design in base, Duncan, circa 1890 (Reprint D), just under 1" tall

431—Tiny blue cut honeycomb design salt, maker unknown, circa 1910, 1/2" tall

432—This appears to be a salt with "Daisy" cut design on top, actually is a

lid to an ink well, shown to alert collectors, circa 1890, 3/4" tall

433—OCTAGON salt by Adams, Central, Duncan and McKee (plus others), circa 1890-1900, four feet on corners, 1" tall

434—Many-sided panelled low salt various colors, same as Fig. 394, maker and age unknown (may be recent), 3/4" tall, oval

435—Peterson calls this LEAF & RIB (Pet Sal, 32-E) one of the family of MAPLE LEAF designs (see Metz, page 72), American, circa 1885-90, 1" tall

436—McKee's "Tomato" table salt (see Reprint I), circa 1880-1905, scarce in color, well polished, 3/4" tall

437—Unusual pressed square salt with beaded rim, waffle design on base, maker unknown, circa 1890, about 3/4" tall

438—Westmoreland's ENGLISH HOBNAIL salt to toy cruet set, circa 1915 to recent years, the colored production may be recent, 3/4" tall

439—Cambridge No. 2933 shown in catalogue reprint (Welker 1, 110), probably lengthy production, early 1900's, almost 1" tall

440—Deep blue square shape with DIAMOND AND BUTTON design in base, plain sides, bevelled edges, maker unknown, circa 1890, 3/4" tall

441—Blue blending to clear (Bluina), mold-blown, three applied curled feet, English, circa 1890, 1 1/2" tall, quite rare

442—Tri-corner TRIANGLE (Pet Sal), sapphire blue, maker unknown, circa 1895, 1" diameter

443—Blown swirl design on clear top portion, low blue pedestal base, may be a mint cup or nut cup, circa 1925, probably American, 1 1/2" tall

444—Blue opalescent WREATH AND SHELL, Model Flint Glass Co., Albany, In., circa 1901-03, much sought after, three feet, 1 1/4" tall

445—Semi-rectangluar salt with pillared edges forming peg-like feet, star in base, maker unknown, circa 1885-1890, 1" tall

446—Blue cut honeycomb design, maker unknown, circa 1890, 1" tall

447-448—Two different shades of blue in Cambridge Glass Co.'s CAPRICE almond cups, four feet, orig. from 1920's with lengthy production, Fig. 447 is an Imperial Glass repro from 1970's

449—Rectangular salt in BAG WARE (Duncan's No. 800 line), electric blue, circa 1890, 1" tall

450—King Glass Co.'s FINE CUT AND BLOCK, circa 1890, continued by U.S. Glass, 1" tall

451—Rectangular pressed master salt with four peg feet, Many Diamonds pattern of unknown origin (may be foreign), circa 1895, 1 1/2" tall

ASSORTED COLORS

452—Amber VALENCIA WAFFLE

master salt by Adams & Co., also by U.S. Glass, circa 1885-1895, part of a complete service, rectangular shape, also known as "Block & Star" (Kamm)

453—Pressed, poor quality cobalt blue glass, pedestal shape almost 3" high, probably foreign from about 1920, lightly polished top with light flaking, 2¾" diam. at top

454—Marigold-flashed pressed salt, pedestal shape with panelling, possibly American circa 1925-30, maker unknown, pattern unknown, 3" diam.

455—Unusual amber nut cup, top rim "cupped" down, circa 1920-30, 2½" high, 3" diam., see Fig. 3550 for information

456—One of the more popular salts in early Sandwich glass, several different variations of this boat were made in several colors, detail of differences shown in Neal (this one is Neal #BT-40), dates from about 1830-40, shown here in powder blue opaque, signed inside boat "Sandwich"

457—Slightly different from Fig. 456, this is shown in Neal #BT-5 (also illustrated on cover of this book), signed "Sandwich" on the inside base, note that these are almost always found with some damage, deep blue opaque

458—"Bird & Berry" salt, originally made by McKee, circa 1880-1900, copied by Degenhart and possibly others in recent years, difficult to determine new from old (look for light flakes and age wear on flat base), almost 2" high

459—Scarce DAISY & BUTTON WITH THUMBPRINT master salt, square shape, made by Adams & Co., with production continued by U.S. Glass (1885-1895), 2⅝" square

460—Oval pressed master salt in early blue color, circa 1890, maker and pattern unknown, 3½" long

461—Blue pressed HONEYCOMB salt, a design used by many companies (orig. called "Cincinnati" or "Diamond" in catalogues, circa 1880-1895, see Reprints for detailed differences, 1⅝" diam.

462—Blue CABINET salt by Adams & Co., also U.S. Glass, circa 1880-1910 (see Reprint A & L) 1¾" diam.

463—Mold-blown with lightly cut top edge, 2¼" round shape, foreign, circa 1910

464—Square pressed salt with bevelled edges, Waffle design in base, maker unknown, circa 1890, 1½" square

465—OPAQUE FEATHER blue milk glass with goofus decoration, tiny "handle" at top edge indicates creamer top, pictured in S. T. Millard Book, plate 152, circa 1910, 3⅜" diam. at top, see Fig. 477 for more info

466-467—Heisey IPSWICH butter pats in Sahara and Cobalt colors, 1930's-40's, A.H. Heisey & Co., Newark, OH, frequently confused for salts, 2¼" square

468—Cobalt with clear base, French "Lacey Enamel" from early 1900's, 2⅝" diam.

469—Similar to Fig. 461, this one slightly shorter (1½" diam.), and this one is cut, not pressed, maker unknown, circa 1900

470—Odd color of amber BIRD & BERRY salt, hint of green color in base, damaged "berry" leads me to believe this is an old example, but beware—could be Degenhart

471—Clear with color-flashing, light iridescence, pattern and maker unknown, circa 1925-30, probably American, 4¼" wide handle to handle

472—Same as Fig. 2960, rare in color, pedestalled Colonial type pattern of unknown origin, six-sided, 2" high

473—Central Glass #822 figural STOVE salt, circa 1880-85, quite rare (see Reprint C), made in only one size and never reproduced, a real gem

474—Figural turtle Salt, similar to one made by Bellaire Goblet Co., Findlay, Ohio, (SM FIN, pg 51) probably French, circa 1930

475—Same as Fig. 369 except with single color, delicate mold-blown, reportedly a Steuben nut cup (Turkey Tracks?), dates circa 1920-30

ASSORTED OPAQUE COLORS

476—Low, round salt in opaque yellow, similar to "late" custard of the 1920's, this one is probably foreign, almost 1" high

477—Blue milk glass lid to OPAQUE FEATHER covered sugar (K1, 94), by Westmoreland, circa 1910, 3¼" diam.

478—Opaque blue of the French style, Diamond Point design in a pedestal shape, circa 1890, 2½" high

479—Another pedestal shape with Diamond Point design, blue milk glass, foreign, circa 1890, almost 2" tall

480—French blue milk, pedestalled in a swirl design, circa 1910, just over 1¾" tall

481—Green opaline oval low salt, possibly an insert, French, circa 1890, 1" high

482—Deeper green opaline, oval shape, either French or English, circa 1900, about 1" tall

483—Unusual shape blue milk, probably foreign, circa 1905, over 1½" tall

484—French blue milk, signed "Vallerystahl", rams' heads, 3-footed, circa 1910, almost 2" tall

485—French blue opaline with gold and enamel decoration, may be a small "shot" or brandy glass to a set, circa 1895, 2" tall, perfectly round shape

486—Green opaline pineapple shaped design, signed Baccarat, French, circa 1910, 1¾" tall

487—Green opaque, lightly fluted, round shape, similar to Akro Agate color, appears to date circa 1920's origin unknown, 1¼" tall

488—Identical to Fig. 476, except in swirled green opaque, origins uncertain, circa 1925, 7/8" tall

489—Custard glass souvenir of the early 20th Century ("Tacoma, Washington"), shaped like a chamber pot, maker unknown, American, 1½" tall

490—Unusual opaque color, probably from England, circa 1890, lightly crimped top, ornate pressed design, about 1½" tall, color appears to be by Edward Moore & Co.

491—Same as Fig. 490, except in a light green opaque

492—Blue opaque oval shape with Coralene decoration, English, circa 1895, 1¼" high

493—Very tiny blue-green opaque with floral design, rectangular shape, 1½" diam., origin unknown, circa 1920

494—Oval shaped blue opaline like Fig. 481

495—Slightly oval shaped basketweave pattern, probably Gillinder, circa 1905, 1¼" tall

496—Mold-blown black amethyst, possible nut cup, origin unknown, circa 1915-20, 1½" high

497—Hexagon shaped black amethyst, probably foreign, circa 1900, ½" high

498—Same as Fig. 421, this color made by Imperial in early 1970's, 2" tall, 1½" diam. at top

499—Cut and polished fluted six-sided salt, black amethyst with enamel decoration, probably English or French, circa 1895, about 1" high

500—Blue milk glass by Eagle Glass Co., circa 1900, scroll design at base, oval shape, 1½" high

501—Blue milk glass tub, appears to be American, circa 1900, 2½" high

502—English cased glass (blue inside white), tightly crimped top, quite scarce to find this hand-made glass in a salt, just under 1½" tall, circa 1885-90

503—Typical muddy blue milk from early English Sowerby production (circa 1878), with Peacock trademark and registration markings, square with four feet, 2⅛" square, 2¼" high

504—Low, round, flared shape in deep blue opaque, origin unknown, age unknown, ¾" high

AMBER SALTS

505—LEAF AND RIB (Pet Sal), maker unknown, circa 1885-95, may be part of a major set, 1" high

506—WILDFLOWER pattern salt with turtle base, Adams & Co., Pittsburgh, circa 1885-95, with production continued by U.S. Glass after 1891, see Figs. 898-899 for reproductions, 2⅛" high

507—FOSTORIA'S FLEMISH pattern, not usually known in color, thus salt must have been issued as a separate item in color, circa 1900-1920, 1" high

508—Nut cup in Fenton Glass Co.'s GEORGIAN pattern, scarce in amber, circa 1935, 2¼" high

509—Same as Fig. 397 except amber,

origin unknown, circa 1915 (?), almost 2½" high

510 — Square with bevelled rim, rectangular shape, Button & Diamond design in base, maker unknown, circa 1890, ¾" high

511 — Round with fancy pattern, probably European, circa 1900, about ¾" high

512 — FINE CUT & BLOCK by King Glass Co., circa 1885-95, later prod. by U.S. Glass, see also Fig. 450, 1⅛" high

513 — Round amber HOBNAIL ind. salt, different from Fig. 198, this one has four tight rows of hobs with a flat top, may be DEWDROP pattern by Columbia Glass, Findlay, Ohio, circa 1890, 1" high

514 — Hexagonal salt with impressed stars in each panel, made orig. by Cambridge Glass, circa 1910, production probably lengthy, see also Figs. 336 and 389, just under 1" high

515 — ENGLISH HOBNAIL pattern by Westmoreland, circa 1910 with lengthy production to recent years, difficult salt to date exactly, 1" high

516 — Amber "Octagon" salt made by several companies (see Reprints), impossible to determine exactly who made this one, circa 1890, 1" high

517 — This appears to be U.S. Glass' No. 18 novelty salt (see Reprint L), made in clear and color, circa 1891 to as late as 1910, 1⅛" high—part of a set only in clear

518 — Bryce Brothers No. 3 salt (see Reprint B), circa 1885-95, with production continued by U.S. Glass, about 1" high

519 — Round Hobnail salt, same as Fig. 198, probably part of OVER-ALL HOB pattern by Nickel Plate Glass, Fostoria, Ohio, circa 1891, 1" high

520 — Square shape with Waffle design in base, bevelled corners, maker unknown, 1890's, less than 1" high

521 — Pedestal swirled design, probably by Baccarat, marked "Portieux" (see also Fig. 480), circa 1900-10, 1½" high

522 — Westmoreland's LOTUS salt in amber, circa 1920-40, may have been reproduced or subject to lengthy production, see also Figs. 580, 607-608, 820, 1" high

523 — I believe this is also Westmoreland, fluted plain salt, found in known colors and decorations by this firm, circa 1920's with probably lengthy production, just under 1" high

524 — Triangular shape with bevelled edges, early 1900's, maker unknown, under 1" high

525 — Amber BAG WARE salt by Duncan, 1890's, rectangular shape, see Fig. 449 for base pattern, part of No. 800 line (see Reprint D), 1" high

526 — This multi-sided fluted low salt is found quite frequently, age unknown, origin unknown, about ¾" high, comes in several colors

527 — Pattern unknown, this appears to be a salt shaker base (top portion ground off), shown to alert collectors. To avoid, reflect light on top rim for signs of a smooth slick surface.

528-529 — Amber "Peking Glass", Chinese, age unknown (probably early 1900's), Fig. 528 has an interesting engraved design, both about 1½" high

530 — Fancy "lacy" pressed glass, probably foreign (French?), circa 1900, may be a butter pat (also made in a salt) or an underplate to a salt (unlikely), same pattern as #511, ½" high

531 — TWO PANEL pattern by Richards & Hartley, continued by U.S. Glass, 1885-1895, see also Fig. 328, never reproduced but relatively easy to find, 1" high

532 — Plain round salt with flanged base, partially frosted (no explanation), probably foreign, circa 1910, just under 1" high, polished top

533 — Reproduction of Cambridge nut cup, made by Imperial with decoration added by private decorator, 1¾" high, circa 1970-75

534 — CHIPPENDALE salt in rare amber color, pattern almost exclusively made in crystal, dates from 1907 to the late 1920's, made mostly by Jefferson Glass and Central Glass Companies (first made for a year by Ohio Flint Glass), 2¼" high

535 — Very similar to the TULIP WITH SAWTOOTH family (Metz 1, 32) of early patterns, some in flint, this is non-flint, possible French, circa 1885, rare, 2" high

536 — This is very similar to the "Prism" salt by King, Son & Co., 1880's (see Reprint K), but the shape is different, maker uncertain, 1½" high

AMBER AND CANARY YELLOW

537 — Low, polished amber glass, probably foreign, circa 1910, ¾" high

538 — Mold-blown pedestal salt, American, circa 1930, maker unknown, 1½" high

539 — Amber-flashed ENGLISH HOBNAIL pattern by Westmoreland, circa 1930's, 2" high

540-541 — Amber foot with crystal LOOP OPTIC mold-blown design bowl, made by Fostoria Glass Co., circa 1920's (Wea Fos, 118), Fig. 540 is an almond (1½" high), Fig. 541 a salt (1¼" High)

542 — Ind. salt in the same design as Fig. 460, maker unknown, American, circa 1890, 1" high

543-544 — Two different Honeycomb colored cut salts, with different base star designs, probably foreign, circa 1900-1910, both about ¼" high

545 — This appears to match U.S. Glass' No. 8 salt, shown in 1910 catalogue (Reprint L), probably made earlier by a member factory (circa 1890), Waffle design in base, 1" high

546 — Similar to a Fostoria salt, but not identical (Wea Fos, 22), this cut salt is probably foreign, circa 1900-1910, just under 1" high

547 — TRIANGLE, similar to "Stars & Bars", maker unknown, circa 1895, American, see also Fig. 442, just under 1" high

548 — Honey amber PRESSED DIAMOND salt by Central Glass, Wheeling (see Reprint C), circa 1880 to 1890, ¾" high

549 — "Late" salt from Depression era, oval shape with light optic, American circa 1930, ⅞" high, ¾" wide x 3" long, picture distorts shape, maker unknown

550 — Originally called a "Sailor Hat", this figural straw hat was made by Duncan in the 1890's, also U.S. Glass, hard to find, ¾" high

551 — Same as Fig. 542, except in "vaseline" (I prefer canary), maker unknown, 1" high

552 — Canary CABINET salt by Adams & Co., continued by U.S. Glass, 1890-1910, 1" high

553 — Canary BAG WARE, Duncan No. 800 (Heavy Panelled Finecut), circa 1890 (see Reprint D), made in several colors, 1¼" high

554 — Canary TWO PANEL salt, by Richards & Hartley (also U.S. Glass), circa 1885-1895, 1" high

555 — Canary cut Honeycomb salt, maker unknown, circa 1900, ¾" high

556 — Same as Fig. 432, this may be a salt or a lid to an ink well, circa 1890, maker unknown, only ½" high, plain sides, round shape, patterned bottom shown

557 — Canary WILDFLOWER salt by Adams & Co. (also U.S. Glass), circa 1890-1895, hard to find with a perfect turtle, 2" high

558 — Canary PRESSED DIAMOND salt, same maker and measurements as Fig. 548

559 — Canary BLOCK pattern or WAFFLE pattern salt, similar to one by McKee (Stout, 212), rectangular shape, probably English, 1" high

560 — U.S. Glass No. 18 salt (Reprint L), circa 1890-1910, not part of a set except in clear (PORTLAND), made in several colors, 1⅛" high

561 — Pressed rectangular salt with bevelled corners, Waffle type design in base, maker unknown, circa 1890-1895, 1" high

562 — Canary LEAF AND RIB salt, also known in salt shaker (Pet Sal, 32-E), circa 1890, about 1" high, maker unknown

563 — Same as Fig. 547, except in canary

564 — Master salt in canary TWO PANEL (see Fig. 554 for ind.), Richards & Hartley (also U.S. Glass), circa 1885-1895, 1¾" high, never reproduced

565 — DAISY & BUTTON WITH THUMBPRINT, Adams & Co. (also U.S. Glass), circa 1890-1895, square master salt, 1 1/4" high (see also Fig. 459)

566—Pressed oval master salt, maker unknown, circa 1885, combination of thumbprints and wide grooves at base, almost 2" high

ROSE PINK AND AMBER

The pale pink crystal known by many different names originally (Rose, Cheriglo, Flamingo) does not necessarily date from the Depression era as most people think. The color was made in England as early as 1890, based on registry marks, and was a popular color in machine made tableware during the 1930's. Note that some of the rose pieces shown here have a definite amber cast.

567—Same as Fig. 421, except in pale honey amber color, Cambridge Glass, fluted pedestal pattern, circa 1920, 2" high

568—Rose crystal WILLIAM & MARY pattern oval footed salt, same as Fig. 69, circa 1903, 2 3/4" long, English

569—Rose CHIPPENDALE salt, see notes and dimensions under Fig. 70

570—Same as Fig. 559, the color here leads me to believe both are English, circa 1900

571—Amber-pink Honeycomb pressed salt, popular design for early salts, circa 1895, maker unknown (signed BAYEL in base), probably foreign, 1 3/4" diam.

572—Unusual rose salt or pomade, origin unknown, circa 1925, 1 1/4" round

573—Rose cut honeycomb with grooved base, foreign, sometimes found in plated frame, circa 1900-1910, 2 1/2" diam.

574—Rose fancy cut Diamond and Fan motif, round shape, heavy, English, circa 1900, 1 1/4" diam.

575—Probably a butter pat, rose colored, unusual design, definitely foreign, circa 1900-1910, over 2 1/8" diam.

576—Rose crystal flared salt with optic design, origin unknown, circa 1915-20, 2 1/4" diam.

577—Six-sided cut low panelled salt, amber-pink, foreign, circa 1910, 1/2" high

578—Panelled pedestal shape salt with rayed bottom (similar to Fig. 2970) in rose pink, maker unknown, circa 1925, probably American, 1 1/4" high

579—Teutonic salt by McKee, 1900-05, similar to old Duncan pattern, reproduced by Guernsey in other colors, 1 1/8" high

580—Rose Westmoreland LOTUS pattern, circa 1930, with lengthy production, about 1" high

581—Appears to be identical to Fig. 489, this is probably made by Tarentum Glass Co., in the early 1900's (other patterns by this firm found in pink), 1 1/2" high

582—Pressed Honeycomb design in rose pink, possibly McKee, circa 1900-10, 1" high, round shape

583—Cut oval salt like Fig. 546, 2 1/2" long, probably foreign, circa 1910, 1" high

584—Same cut design as Fig. 583, except round, in plated holder shaped like leaf, English circa 1900-1910, 3 1/2" diam. to handle

585—Rose pink double salt, definitely European, circa 1900, 5" diam. end to end

586—Rectangular salt with fancy pattern in base (oblong rays with oval center), about 2 1/8" long, probably foreign, circa 1910

587—Amber NAUTILUS (No. 3450 line) insert with chrome Farber Bros. holder, glass made by Cambridge Glass Co., circa 1940's, 2 1/4" oval

588—Amber DIAMOND QUILTED salt by Bryce Bros. (also U.S. Glass), circa 1890-1895, see Reprint B, 2 1/4" long rectangular

589—Square low salt with bevelled corners, same as Fig. 520

590—Amber ENGLISH HOBNAIL oval pedestal salt by Westmoreland Glass, 1920's until recent years, 3 1/2" long oval

591-592—Two different amber "Octagon" salts, a footed rectangular salt made by several different companies (see Reprints), from about 1885-1910, both are 2" long

593—Pressed and cut salt similar to McKee's "Tomato" salt (Reprint I), six-sided, 1 5/8" diam., circa 1900

594—Not quite DAISY AND BUTTON, but a member of the family of variants, this rare rectangular salt is American, maker unknown, circa 1890, 2 1/8" long

595—Amber BAG WARE salt by Duncan, 1880's and early 1890's, continued by U.S. Glass, see Reprint D, 2" long

596—Same as Fig. 534, this is one of our duplications

597—This light yellow-amber color dates from the 1920-30 period and was called many names by different companies (Heisey called the color Sahara, quite descriptive), maker unknown on this one (may be Fostoria), but definitely American, and quite scarce, 1 1/2" high, similar to "Double Ring Panel"

598—Amber coach or buggie salt by Central Glass, 1880's (see Reprint C), hard to find, 2 3/4" long

ASSORTED COLORED GLASS

599—Cambridge MOUNT VERNON oval handled salt in Crown Tuscan color, gold decorated, the pattern also made in a small round salt (Welker 1, 83), circa 1920's-30's, 4 1/4" long

600—Deep amber pedestalled cut glass master salt, probably English, circa 1870 or possibly earlier, this shape is one of the earliest forms of salts in glass, almost 4" high

601—Dark emerald green salt, possibly early Waterford, Irish cut colored, circa 1870, this is 3 1/2" high

602—Another early colored cut salt, European, deep "vaseline" yellow color, also early, circa 1875, 3 1/4" high, seven sided top is about 2" diam.

603—Set of different colored salts or ind. ash trays, European, circa 1920, sectional sides with scalloped tops, base design a series of graduating diamonds toward center, these are cut, not pressed, 2 3/4" long

604—Opal glass hat salt with cranberry rim, French, circa 1895, too small to be a toothpick holder, only 1 5/8" high

605—Fostoria Grape Leaf salt, produced in the 40's in various colors and very hard to find, rare, 1" high, see notes under Fig. 415

606—Delicate blue colored cut salt, Foreign, circa 1920, 2 1/4" round crimped shape

607-608—Two different decorations in opal LOTUS pattern by Westmoreland Glass, circa 1925-35, also made in other colors, 1 1/2" diam.

609—Rare Italian early Millefiore salt, perfectly round, a much reproduced form of glass but not in salts, almost 2" round

610—Adorable French decorated crystal salt with applied feet, detailed enamelling, circa 1910

611—Duplication of Figure 128

612—Another pressed glass, low (1/2" high) example which may be an ind. ash, foreign, circa 1915-20, 2 1/2" diam.

613—Electric blue Intaglio salt which matches Fig. 217, except color different, 3 1/4" long

614-615—The same design in different colors, one attached to brass-plated frame with tiny rhinestones, foreign, circa 1920, slightly different sizes

616—Opaline glass with brass rim and base, sometimes found with lids, reportedly made in Italy, circa 1920, 2" round diam.

617—Polished amethyst colored salt, six-sided, foreign, circa 1915, 1 1/2" diam.

618—Amber-pink pedestalled salt, foreign, circa 1900-20, 2 1/8" diam.

619—Opaque green "slag" type salt, looks like Akro Agate to me, fluted design, age and origin unknown, most unusual, 1 3/4" diam.

620—Round clambroth opaque salt with gold-band, European, circa 1900, 2" diam.

621—Rose pink cut salt, European, circa 1920, 3 1/4" round

622—Rose pink cut boat-shaped salt, 3 1/2" long, oval, foreign, circa 1920

623—Smith Bros. master salt, un-

signed, American, circa 1890's, 2¾" round diam.
624—May not be a salt but an exceptional example of rich cranberry with applied rigaree and feet, English, circa 1890, 2¼" high, about 2½" round, three feet

COBALT BLUE/ COBALT WITH SILVER

625—Pressed pedestal shape with ornate "lacy" type pattern, probably French, prior to 1900, round shape, 2½" high
626—Another French lacy-type pressed salt in a pedestal shape, note the unfinished top rim with bits of glass protruding, age unknown, about 2" high
627—Small nut cup in cobalt, made by Cambridge Glass Co., 1930's, four-footed, 3" diam. at top
628—Pedestalled, round, mold-blown may be a nut cup, origin unknown, circa 1920-25
629—Early colored flint master salt, pedestal shape, six-sided top, American, circa 1860, 3⅛" high
630—Oval master salt, pressed, crudely finished, circa 1850-60, origin unknown, 1" high
631—Cobalt with silver deposit decoration, just under 1½" oval, silver well worn, polished bottom, ⅞" high, probably foreign, circa 1905
632—Another with silver deposit decoration (not an overlay), polished bottom, 1" high, foreign, circa 1900-1910
633—Oval shape, only ¾" high, cut-star bottom, may be a liner (insert for metal holder)
634—Oval with 12 panels, pressed, 1" high, Victorian, may be a liner
635—Oval-edge rectangular, 2" diam. by 1½" deep, mold-blown, possibly another liner
636—Fostoria's leaf-figured salt from the 1940's, original paper label still intact, made in many colors, 1" high, rare, see #605
637—Poor quality pressed glass probably dating from the 1940's, American, six sections with embrossed daisies, some have an extra cutting on the scallops, 1¼" high
638—Round liner with cut-star bottom, 1½" high, age undetermined
639—Round with polished and bevelled top, possible liner, circa 1900, ¾" high
640—Oval pressed liner, circa 1900, 1" high
641—Mold-blown oval liner, flared top, circa 1890, ¾" high
642—Sterling holder with cobalt liner, four feet, hallmarks identify this as German from about 1891, just over 1¾" high
643—Sterling frame, blown cobalt insert, European circa 1850, 1½" high, oval
644—Sterling, marked 800, ornate frame dates from mid-1800's, origin unknown, just over 1" high, oval
645—Sterling with blown and polished insert, German after 1891, 1¼" high, oval
646—Sterling, marked 800, larger version of Fig. 644, blown liner, European circa 1850, oval
647—Sterling frame marked Webster Co., hallmarks date this from about 1869, 1" high
648—Oval liner with Sterling frame, French from about 1884, just over 1" high
649—Marked Sterling with no hallmarks, American circa 1890, 1" high
650—Silver-plate over copper, probably English from about 1900, blown liner, just over 1" high
651—Sterling frame of unknown origin, unusual design, pressed liner, circa 1900-1905, ¾" high
652—Sterling frame with no hallmarks, origin unknown, pressed insert, circa 1890, ⅞" high
653—Silver-plated frame marked W&S, insert has cut-star bottom, American, circa 1890, ¾" high
654—Large cut and polished master in honeycomb design, probably American, circa 1880, round shape, 1¼" high
655—Cobalt "Mercury" lined blown glass, rare to find in color, origin uncertain, circa 1890, round shape, 1½" high
656—Enamel decorated cobalt, probably European circa 1900, 1⅝" high
657—Pedestalled, six-sided master, origin unknown, circa 1880-85, 2⅛" high

SILVER WITH COBALT LINERS

658—Plated, floral scroll with bead clusters in high relief, marked silver soldered, EP-Tiffany & Co. makers, circa 1891-1902, 1½" high
659—Plated, pierced forget-me-not border with forget-me-not medallion feet, American, no hallmarks, circa 1930, not original liner, 1½" high
660—Plated, Art Nouveau Knot & Swag pattern, signed L. Barth & Sons Inc., Mfg. for Ritz Carlton, circa 1900, just over 2" high, oval
661—Plated, wire loop design, beautiful molded liner, English EPNS hallmark, circa 1880, 2¼" high
662—Marked Sterling, removable frame fits over top, exceptional quality glass with thick bottom, pierced spearhead cuff, American or possibly Canadian, circa 1900, 1½" high
663—Plated, apple blossom & scroll design, unusual in that the pattern does not repeat itself, Derby Silver Co., circa 1900, just under 1½" high
664—Sterling, pierced scallop pattern, Frank M. Whiting Co. hallmark, after 1896, 1½" high oval
665—Marked Sterling, no additional hallmarks, lattice and wild rose pattern, American, circa 1925, 1" high
666—Sterling, beautiful cherubs and flower urn design, cut & beveled glass liner, French, circa 1838-1845, 1" high, oval
667—Marked Sterling, pierced circle design, American, no additional hallmarks, circa 1920, 1" high
668—Plated, psuedo-hallmarks, stylized Lion heads, medallion on other side, possibly new, just over 1½" high
669—Plated, marked "Made in England," half dome shape, circa 1950, 1½" high
670—Sterling, hallmarked 800, possibly Dutch or German, lattice and 10 panel design, circa 1900, just over 1" high, oval
671—Plated, marked "Made in England," gadroon top edge, circa 1930, 1¼" high
672—Sterling, hallmarked Black, Starr & Frost, embossed feather design, pressed glass liner, circa 1876-1929, 1¼" high
673—Sterling, marked "Fred Hirsch Co.," pressed glass liner, gadroon design on top edge, circa 1920-1945, 1½" high
674—Plated, has interesting 3 leaves in pattern bottom, no hallmarks, pressed glass liner, ribbed design with acanthus feet, approx. 1940, 1½" high
675—Plated, has same design on bottom as Fig. 674, mermaids & flower swag extend to form feet, liner identical to #674, circa 1940, 1¼" high
676—Sterling, marked 800, European origin, interesting heads "Three faces" at top rim portion of legs, molded liner, circa 1875, just under 2" high
677—Sterling, new, souvenir item from Panama Canal Zone, Llama, 1½" high
678—Plated over copper, marked "England," molded liner, lion heads and paw feet, heavy gadroon & shell border, circa 1890, 1½" high
679—Plated over copper, Old Sheffield, no hallmarks, modified claw feet, graduated rib design, circa 1820, 1¾" high, oval
680—Plated, psuedo-hallmarks, grape clusters in high relief, pressed glass liner, possibly new, just over 1¼" high
681—Plated over copper, "Made in England," registered 476140, pierced with simple gadroon top edge, excellent quality liner, circa 1920, just over 1¼" high on end, oval
682—Silver, marked 800 exquisite detail, cut glass liner, relief stylized lion heads with medallion & leaf swag, prior to 1894, just over 1½" high, oval
683—Plated, same leaf design on bottom and same liner as Fig. 674, lion faces and paw feet, rose swags, circa 1940, 1¼" high
684—Plated, marked "Made in England," not original liner, gadroon border

with acanthus handles on either end, circa 1920, 1¼" high

685—Sterling, Sheffield, English hallmarks, unusual flower & leaf design in high relief, beautiful craftsmanship in detail, circa 1852, 2" high

SILVER WITH COBALT LINERS

686—Gold over sterling, mythological character of the Norse God "Thor" forming full heads around bowl, molded glass liner, hallmarked German, early 1800's, 1" high

687—Plated, marked "Made in England," EP, circa 1920, 1½" high, 4" to top of handle, interesting spoon holder on side

688—Plated, German hallmarks, molded and polished liner, pattern of lattice and garlands, ball feet have flat bottoms, marked WMFN, circa 1890-1910, 2" high, oval

689—Sterling, blown liner, hallmarked Friedman Silver Co., picture looks like a seam on the salt but is only a shadow, after 1908, 2" high

690—Sterling, detail of ribbon garlands and streamers, cut glass liner, German marked 800 with import marks to France, circa 1893, 1⅓" high, oval

691—Sterling, hallmarked 800, European, interesting Art Nouveau style, other side has medallion for monograming, liner has cut starred bottom, circa 1900-1910, 1¼" high

692—Plated, marked EPNS, inlaid Jade stones on either side of salt, molded glass liner, registered 622524, circa 1909-1910, 1¾" high

693—Sterling, hallmarked Birmingham, England, cut glass liner, delicate and lovely detail, circa 1889-1890, 1¾" high, oval

694—Marked, Sterling, American, plain except for border trim, open at the bottom, liner may not be original, circa 1910, 1" high

695—Sterling, hallmarked London, England, molded glass liner, bottom closed, circa 1896, 1½" high

696—Sterling, Mappin & Webb, polished glass liner, no hallmarks (made for export), circa 1913, 1½" high

697—Marked "Made in England," molded glass liner, circa 1920, 1¼" high, oval

698—Sterling, Webster Co. hallmark, interesting detail of double thickness at top edge with inverted scallops, pressed glass liner, circa 1900-1910, 1" high, oval

699—Sterling, Genova Silver Co., American, Hallmark, circa 1950, 1½" high

700—Plated, poor detail, marked "Made in Japan," 1" high

701—Plated, mythological character "Thor" as seen on Fig. 686, detail crude circa 1900, just under 1½" high, bottom open, no marks

702—Sterling, W. B. Kerr hallmarks, exquisite Art Nouveau style and design, Kerr being one of the finest silver craftsman, molded glass liner circa 1880, 1¾" high

703—Sterling, very plain except for ribbing on base, Meuck Co.-Cary Co. hallmarks, circa 1940-1960, 2½" high

704—Sterling, cobalt bakelite liner, European origin, circa 1940, just over 1½" high

705—Sterling, Frank M. Whiting Co. hallmarks, very plain, pressed glass liner, circa 1900, 1" high

706—Plated over copper, E. G. Webster & Son hallmark design of pastoral scene on other side identical to Fig. 759, cut glass liner, typical of the Webster Co.'s manufacture of reproductions of German chased holloware, circa 1886-1928, 1½" high, oval

707—Marked Sterling, 12 beveled panels, pressed glass liner with starred bottom, circa 1925, just over 1" high

708—Sterling, part of a 6 piece set consisting of 2 each, pepper, salt and mustard, hallmarked from Birmingham, England, also marked Dobson, Picadilly, possibly a retailer, circa 1900-1910, salt just under 1"

709—Gold wash over Sterling, horse and parrot characters around bowl, heavy cut glass liner, no marks, European origin, circa 1900-1910, 2¼" high, oval

710—Plated, typical of very early European reproductions, flower and scroll motif, marked HI by each leg on the bottom, American, circa 1880, 1¼" high

711—Silver over copper, English, no marks, EP, cut glass liner, ball & claw feet motif of lattice and garland, with place for monogram, circa 1870, just over 1½" high

712—Sterling Gorham hallmark, no date letter, cut glass liner, starred bottom, circa 1920, 1¼" high

SILVER WITH COBALT LINERS

713—Sterling, Holland, 4-piece set consisting of 2 salts, pepper shaker & mustard, Cameo Medallions of Roman heads connected by garlands of flowers, different heads on mustard and slightly different pattern at top, hallmarked, cut and polished liners, circa 1921, salts are 1¼" high, oval

714—Sterling, German, hallmarked three flying swans holding bowl, before 1891, molded glass liner, 3¼" high

715—Marked EPNS, pierced geometric design, probably English, blown glass liner, circa 1920, 1¼" high

716—Sterling, Genova Co., American, Urn shape, very plain, circa 1950, 1½" high

717—Sterling, English, no hallmarks, Baroque & stippled pattern, circa 1890, 1½" high

718—Marked EPNS, pierced geo-

metric pattern, flower pot shape, American, circa 1920, 1" high

719—Sterling, plain vase shape, Sheffield, circa 1900, 1½" high

720—Sterling, French, pierced baroque with flying birds, hallmarked, circa 1838-1845, 1½" high

721—Marked Sheffield, England, CB&S Ltd., bell shape molded glass liner, circa 1920, 1½" high

722—Sterling, Austria, cloven hoof feet, three lamb's heads connected by floral garlands around top chrysanthemum base under liner circa 1885-1890, 1½" high

723—Sterling, Frank M. Whiting Co., goblet shape, very plain, circa 1896, just under 2" high

724—Sterling, German, fruit decorated swags with acanthus design on feet, cut & polished liner hallmarked, circa 1891, 1¾" high, oval

725—Plated over copper, probably German, flower garlands on pierced lattice with flower streamers, cut & polished insert, circa 1890, just under 1½" high, oval

726—Same as #724

727—Pewter, marked "Genuine by Quaker," cobalt enamel lining, tub shape with grooved design, matching spoon, American, circa 1920, 1" high

728—Sterling, beveled panels, amethyst liner with rayed bottom, circa 1920, 1" high

729—Sterling, pillar legs and engraved garlands, European hallmarks, early 1800's, 1¼" high, oval

730—Chromium, marked "Made in England," pierced, enamel crest reads "FRAE BONNIE SCOTLAND," circa 1940, just over 1" high

731—Plated, Victorian, sculptured dog heads with stylized feet, 1¾" high, oval

732—Plated, has music box in bottom, plays theme from Moulin Rouge, European origin, hallmarks, dolphins, cherubs & harp design, circa 1890, just under 5" high

733—Marked "Elkington Plate," England, bell shape, circa 1920, 1½" high

SILVER WITH COBALT LINERS

734—Plated, psuedo-hallmarks, English silver over copper, tureen shape on square pedestal, gadroon top edge, molded glass liner, circa 1900, 2½" high, oval

735—Plated, no hallmarks, pierced design around top edge with gadroon border, molded glass liner, purchased in Germany, dates about 1900, 2½" high, oval

736—Plated, no hallmarks, pressed glass liner, design of pressed floral and acanthus, note interesting spoon holder, circa 1920, 1½" high not including handle

737—Plated, marked "Victoria", lid folds down underneath, stylized 3-toe feet, knob on side controls position of lid, circa 1920, 3" high when covered

738 — Plated over copper, pierced scroll and leaf holder, molded glass liner, probably English, circa 1890, 2¼" high

739 — Sterling, English, lion heads with rings on either side, paw feet, cut glass liner, classic lattice design, circa 1880, 1¾" high

740 — Plated, acanthus leaves on sides with hallmarks partially obscured, thought to be pseudo-hallmarks, but have seen others marked the same way, pressed glass liner, Lion crest, beaded border, European, circa 1920, 1" high

741 — Sterling, R. W. Wallace & Sons, pierced circular pattern with beaded borders, cut glass liner, circa 1898, 1" high

742 — Silver over copper, no hallmarks, probably English, gadroon border, circa 1890, just over 1½" high, oblong shape

743 — Silver, marked 800, Germany, underplate has scroll medallion with cupids, not original liner, could also be a holder for tea strainer, circa 1891, just under 2" high with this liner

744 — Plated, marked "England", toed feet, gadroon top edge, molded glass liner, circa 1900, 1½" high

745 — Plated, floral and scroll piercing, molded glass lilner, no hallmarks, probably European, circa 1880, just under 2" high on ends

746 — Plated, probably English, lattice pattern with claw feet, cut glass liner, circa 1880, 2½" high, oval

747 — Plated, marked "Germany", floral garlands around, cut glass liner, circa 1880, just over 1½" high, oval

SILVER WITH COBALT LINERS

748 — Silver over copper, English, no hallmarks, pierced pattern, molded glass liner, circa 1880, 2½" high, oval

749 — Plated, marked "England EP", circa 1930, 2½" high, 4" to handle

750 — Plated, English, EPNS, pierced pattern with scallop top edge, molded and polished liner, circa 1930, just under 2" high

751 — Plated, an elegant double salt with pepper shaker in center, European, circa 1880, 6½" high

752 — Sterling, American reproduction of very early English style, molded glass liner, 3 hoof feet, circa 1930, 1½" high

753 — Sterling, oriental design around bowl, possibly American, circa 1880, 2" high

754 — Plated, marked "Italy", may not be original insert, circa 1950, 1¼" high

755 — Plated, no marks, possibly European, circa 1950, 1½" high

756 — Marked sterling, no hallmarks, American, pierced lattice design with acanthus feet, cut glass liner, circa 1890, 1½" high, oval

757 — Plated, Reed & Barton, EPNS,

molded glass liner, gadroon and pleated border, unusual round feet, circa 1933, just under 1½" high, oval

758 — Plated over copper, purchased in England, scallop pierced pattern with beaded edges, circa 1890, 2" high, oval

759 — Plated, pastoral scene with floral scrolls, E. G. Webster & Sons, circa 1886-1928, See Fig. 706 for detail on other side, 1½" high

ASSORTED COLORS IN SILVER HOLDERS

760 — Sterling, beautiful art glass Bohemian overlay cutback, Austrian or German, hallmarked circa 1850, just over 3" high

761 — Sterling, French, cut and bevelled glass, very early, circa 1845, 6" high to tip of handle

762 — Plated, no marks, probably American, circa 1920, 4½" high

763 — Plated, marked "Italy", not old, just over 3" high

764 — Marked sterling, no hallmarks, American, circa 1880, 1½" high, amethyst liner

765 — Plated frame, no hallmarks, possibly English, circa 1930's, 2" high

766 — Plated, American, no hallmarks, molded and polished liner, circa 1880, just under 1½" high, oval

767 — Plated, no marks, American, blown and polished liner, circa 1880, 1¾" high, oval

768 — Plated over pot metal, probably American, circa 1880, 1¾" high

769 — Worn plate, American, molded and polished liner, circa 1880, 1¾" high

770 — Sterling, American, hallmarked Wm. Gale, circa 1852, motif of grapes, leaves and medallions with scrolled feet, molded and polished liner, just under 2" high

771 — Plated, worn, old and brittle frame, Greek key design, American, molded liner, circa 1875, just over 1" high, oval

772 — Gold washed, European, probably dates from the 1920's, just over 4" high

INDIVIDUAL NUT CUPS

Not all tiny pedestalled receptacles are salt dips, even though the pedestal shape was one of the earliest forms of master salts. The items shown on this page are with little doubt individual nut cups, sometimes called mint dishes. However, their small size and charming shape have made them popular additions to collections of open salts.

774 — Yellow-green footed nut cup by Cambridge Glass Co., circa 1930-40's, 2½" diam., part of their No. 3400 line

775 — Amber flared nut cup, square stem, maker unknown, circa 1925, 2⅞" diam.

776 — Marigold carnival (clear base

glass) No. 923 flared nut cup, Made by Fenton Art Glass Co., circa 1925, see Fig. 780 for original form, 3¼" diam. at top

777 — Cambridge DECAGON pattern, also made in etched glass, pale blue color, 2½" diam., circa 1925-40

778 — Amber mold-blown nut cup, pattern and maker unknown, circa 1925, six-sided bowl, light optic effect in glass, 2" diam. at top

779 — Fenton's Jade Green color in their #923 mold, lightly flared top, deeper bowl, same as Fig. 776, 3" diam. at top, circa 1925-1932

780 — Fenton's same #923 nut cup, except in "Topaz" colored stretch, original form can be flared into shapes like Fig. 776 and 779, circa 1925, 2¼" diam. at top

781 — SPIRAL FLUTES, in a footed almond, made by Duncan & Miller, circa 1924, also known in crystal, amber and rose, 2½" diam. at top

782-783 — Fostoria's No. 2374 ind. nut cup, 1940's goes well with their LAFAYETTE pattern

784 — NORTHWOOD FLUTE electric blue nut cup with sterling deposit decoration, made in other colors, usually found with N-in-a-Circle trademark, circa 1924, 2¾" diam.

785-787 — Exactly the same as Fig. 775, the four different colors of amber, green, black and violet leads me to believe possible Cambridge Glass, circa 1925, 2⅞" round

788 — Pale rose-pink etched stemmed nut cup, shape matches one by Central Glass, but the etching is not known, circa 1926, 2½" diam.

789 — Similar to Fig. 784, the plain fluted pattern may be Imperial or Diamond Glass from the mid-20's, rose-pink, note difference in base, 2⅞" diam. at top

790 — Same as Fig. 782-783, in rose color

791 — Delicate rose colored mold-blown stemmed nut cup, decorated, frosted stem, may be European, circa 1920, 2½" diam. at top

COLORED GLASS DOUBLE SALTS

All of the salts shown on page 57 are probably European (French, German, English). Contrary to some opinions, the double or "twin" salt was not originally designed to hold pepper in the other half. The practical feature of this design is the handle in the center, making it easier to pass around the table. Rather than using a single master salt for two persons, the "twin" design makes it possible for two diners to dip their celery into their own half. Double salts were a very popular European table custom, and can still occasionally be found in finer restaurants on the Continent. Measured in height to top of handle.

792 – Sapphire blue pressed with "Twist" design, circa 1910-20, 3¾" high

793 – Aqua green with fan design, noticeable repairs, circa 1925, 2¾" high

794 – Clear with yellow cast, treebark and branch motif, most unusual, circa 1890, just over 3" high

795 – Pale green with twist design, diff. from Fig. 792, circa 1925, 3" high

796 – Teal blue with ornate pattern, circa 1900, just over 3" high

797 – Cobalt blue with plain flutes, circa 1930, 2½" high

798 – Amber with melon-ribbed design, circa 1920, 3" high

799 – Opaque green with panelled pattern, looks French, circa 1900, 2¾" high

800 – Blue opaque with small bird as handle, leaf design, French, circa 1895-1905, 3⅛" high

801 – Cobalt blue with shell-like pattern, circa 1925, 3½" high

802 – Blown-type salts, attached by stem, teal green, circa 1920, 1¼" high

803 – Pale green with ribbed pattern, circa 1930, 3⅛" high

804 – Apple green with fan design, same pattern as Fig. 793, circa 1900-10, 3" high

805 – Aquamarine color with melon-rib pattern, diff. from Fig. 798, circa 1930, 3¼" high

806 – Pale blue with zig-zag design, no handle, circa 1890, 1" high

807 – Periwinkle blue with similar pattern to Fig. 806, no handle, 1¼" high

ASSORTED COLORED GLASS

808 – Green pressed pedestalled master salt, plain fluted pattern, probably foreign, circa 1910-15, 3" high

809 – Pedestal Honeycomb design, foreign, circa 1900, non-flint, 2½" high

810 – Emerald green salt of unknown age and origin, I feel it is not very old (note glass still intact between scalloped top), still – a beautiful floral pattern, 2" high

811 – Blue AMAZON master salt (H5, 78) by Bryce Bros. (U.S. Glass), circa 1885-95, this pattern primarily in clear, scarce in color, 1½" high

812 – Green honeycomb master salt, origin unknown, circa 1885, 2½" diam.

813 – Amber DAISY & BUTTON tub salt by Duncan, 1885-95 (also U.S. Glass), just over 1" high

814 – Blue "Tomato" ind. salt by McKee (Reprint I), circa 1888-1905, non-pg, polished

815 – Pink cased (cranberry over white), mold-blown, polished top rim, probably English, circa 1890, just over 1" high

816 – Unusual opaque "slag" type salt, probably foreign, maker unknown, circa 1920, 1⅛" high

817 – Early vaseline glass salt, maker unknown, circa 1885, American, 1¼" high

818 – This appears to be U.S. RIB (H5, 38), circa 1899, a very rare pattern glass salt, just over 1" high, sometimes gold decorated on plain band

819 – Amber footed pressed salt, non pg, really quite common, American, circa 1900-1910, 1⅛" high, made in all colors, reproduced

820 – Westmoreland's LOTUS in clear with red painting, appears to be opaque, circa 1920's with lengthy production, possibly sold as a novelty set also, 1" high

821 – Ruby MT. VERNON salt by Cambridge, circa 1920's with lengthy production, made in all colors, this one is signed with C-in-a-Triangle, 2½" high, reproduced in crystal by Imperial

822 – Ruby-stained pressed salt, probably English or German, circa 1900, just over 1" high

823 – Hexagonal ruby salt with polished edges, 1" high, European, circa 1915-25

824 – Square with round center, small ash receiver or salt, teal green color, maker and country of origin unknown, circa 1930's (?), under 1" high, 2" square

825 – Emerald green liner to oval salt, 2" long, English, 1900-1910

826 – Six-sided honeycomb salt, pressed, 1½" diam., origin unknown

827 – "Octagon" salt, made by several companies, non-pg, shown here in emerald green, 2" diam.

828 – Multi-sided emerald green salt, age and origin unknown, 1⅝" oval shape

829 – Light green octagonal salt with tub shape handles tabbed to hold spoon, Cambridge Glass, circa 1920's-40's

830 – Pink crystal CHIPPENDALE salt by Davidson & Co., circa 1885-90, English, 6 tiny feet, 2½" round, see also Fig. 569

831 – Oval low plain salt in pink crystal, circa 1920-30, foreign (?), 2½" oval

832 – Pink crystal salt in same patterns as Fig. 829, made by Cambridge

833 – Pink crystal tub-shape salt, American, may be Heisey, circa 1925-35, 1¾" round

834 – Yellow-decorated LOTUS salt by Westmoreland, found in many different colors and decorations in this book, circa 1925 with lengthy production, about 1" high

835 – Westmoreland's ENGLISH HOBNAIL pattern in cranberry flashed color, originally made in 1920's with long production life, 2" high

836 – Ruby-stained early salt, pressed, large size of Fig. 822 salt, foreign, circa 1890's, may be English, 3½" diam.

837 – Amber-stained crystal FINE CUT AND BLOCK by King Glass (also U.S. Glass) circa 1885 to 1895, see late additions for ind. size, 3½" diam. round

838 – Apple green TWO PANEL by

Richards & Hartley (also U.S. Glass) circa 1885-1895, 3⅞" long, oval

ASSORTED NOVELTY SALTS OLD & NEW

839 – Clear lady's slipper, sun-turned amethyst, may not be a salt, but complements a collection of novelty salts, circa 1915-20, 4½" long

840 – Vaseline DAISY & BUTTON "Open" slipper, maker unknown, circa 1885-90, 4½" long

841 – Ruby DAISY & BUTTON slipper, repro by L. G. Wright, circa 1960-75, 3½" long

842 – Blue opalescent FENTON HOBNAIL hat, similar in size to early "hat salts", but this one is actually a cigarette holder (they were much shorter than today's cigarettes), circa 1940's, 1¾" high

843 – "Earl" ind. boat by Bryce Bros. (also U.S. Glass), probably meant for salt, circa 1890, amber color, 4½" long

844-845 – Amber and vaseline DAISY & BUTTON hats, these are definitely salts, as shown in orig. Duncan catalogue (see 1000 TPH, pg. 105), shorter than toothpick, 1¾" high

846 – Repro D&B hat, marked "Made in Taiwan", emerald green, note "buttons" are raised and rounded, unlike on old, 1¾" high, new

847 – Green D&B hat, recent, marked "Bottle made in France", may have been top to a liquor bottle or wine, 1¾" high

848 – Vaseline AETNA NO. 300 tub-shaped salt, deep color, Aetna Glass, Bellaire, Ohio, circa 1886, 2" diam., see Kamm 5

849 – Light blue round DAISY & BUTTON tub by Duncan, circa 1890, also U.S. Glass, 1¾" diam.

850 – Amber oval D&B salt, maker unknown, circa 1890, 2" long, dif. from Fig. 849

851 – Light blue repro D&B slipper, see Fig. 841

852 – Cobalt blue D&B canoe salt, not old, maker unknown, 5" long

853 – Reclining dog with Block pattern salt, Central Glass, circa 1880, vaseline color, 3¼" long

854 – Deep amber cradle salt, reproduction, diff. size from Fig. 855, 2⅛" high

855 – Lighter amber cradle salt, old, maker unknown, circa 1900, 1⅞" high

856 – Interesting vaseline figural canoe salt, origin unknown, circa 1900, 4⅝" long

857 – CANE pattern figural skate by Central Glass, circa 1880-85, back wheel is missing, 4" long

858 – Scarce blue buggy salt by Central Glass, circa 1880-1885, reproduction shown next to it, almost 3" diam., 1⅝" high

859 – Amber reproduction buggy salt by L. G. Wright, circa 1970, 3⅝" long, 1⅞" high

860—Apple green THOUSAND EYE cart salt, by Richards & Hartley (also U.S. Glass) circa 1885-1895, also other colors, 3½" long

861—Vaseline DAISY & BUTTON potty chair ink well with lid and pen holder, not a salt but frequently confused for one when lid is missing, circa 1880, very rare, 3¼" high

862—Amber band-master cap by Duncan, circa 1890, probably a toothpick but low enough to also be used as a salt, just under 2" tall

863—Blue FINE CUT purse, maker unknown, circa 1885, 2" tall, also used as a toothpick holder

REPRODUCTIONS AND CONTEMPORARY SALTS

864—Ruby rectangular WILDFLOWER salt, new mold, this shape never made old, L. G. Wright, circa 1970's, just over 3¼" hong

865—Westmoreland's ENGLISH HOBNAIL salt in green, recent, 3" diam.

866—Pedestal FLUTE pattern salt in blue carnival, marked "Anaheim 1969" on base. Made by Imperial Glass Co., Bellaire Ohio, just over 2" high

867—Cobalt with spun white rim Venetian style, 1⅞" high, 2¼" round, purchased new in Switzerland in 70's

868—Deep amethyst Anvil salt, maker unknown, but definitely new, 2" high

869—Green JERSEY SWIRL salt, new mold by L. G. Wright, never made before in this shape, circa 1970, 2¼" diam.

870—Emerald green MOON AND STAR salt, new, also Wright, this pattern never made originally in color, 2⅛" round

871—Olden End-o'-Day by Imperial Glass Co., Bellaire Ohio, new in 70's, repro of CAPRICE nut cup, 2" round

872—Pidgeon's blood ruby IVT salt with transfer decoration, not old, maker unknown, 2" diam.

873—Repro Wheelbarrow salt in cobalt blue, different from old Greentown salt, 3⅛" long, see #4668-70

874—Pressed ruby insert in cheap chrome frame, recent import, 2" diam.

875—Triangular D&B frosted blue, new, 2¼" diam.

876—Triangular D&B in amber, new, 2¼" diam., by L.G. Wright

877—Same as Fig. 872, emerald green with enamel decoration

878—Ice green carnival Swan salt by Smith Glass, 1970's, 2¼" high

879-880—Reproduction cobalt blue lacy pressed salts from 1920's, copied from original sandwich salt from 1840's. Fig. 879 is 1⅝" high, 2⅞" long. Fig. 880 is 2¼" high, 3⅛" long

881—This is another new mold by L. G. Wright simulating the early STIPPLED STAR pattern, never made before in this shape, from the 1970's, 2⅞" diam.

882—Lovely new salt with gold and enamel decoration, square base, round top, 3" diam., made by Imperial Glass Co., Bellaire Ohio, circa 1970

883—Light amethyst repro of old McKee pattern, made by Guernsey, 1970's, 1¾" diam.

884—Poor quality ruby glass pressed salt, new, maker unknown, 2¼" round

885—Cobalt blue round pressed salt, new from Mexico, 1970's, 1⅞" round

886—Repro of old Westmoreland No. 210 salt, unsigned, see Reprint W, just under 1½" diam.

887—Amber PANELLED THISTLE salt by Wright, original pattern never made in color, 2¼" round

888—Amethyst pressed six-sided salt by Imperial (?) from old Cambridge mold, 1½" diam.

889—Imported salt or nut cup, enamel on ruby, recent, 3⅛" round

890—Purple slag Degenhart signed salt (D-in-a-Heart), 1970's, 3⅛" round

891—Amber iridescent salt in same pattern, (#890) with crimped edge, probably by Hansen on Degenhart mold, refired to iridize and hand crimp top edge, circa 1960, 6 beaded stars on inside bottom

892—Cobalt blue Degenhart salt, unsigned, production continued by Boyd (Crystal Art Glass) late 1970's, Degenhart, early 1970's

REPRODUCTIONS AND CONTEMPORARY SALTS

893—Amber EYEWINKER salt, never made in orig. pattern, all of these are repro's by L. G. Wright, 1970's, 1¾" diam.

894—Considerable confusion over when and by whom these were made, the blue example here appears to be recent, 2¾" long. The market is currently flooded with these and the glass will also show bubbles.

895—Repro lacy glass salt in cobalt, signed M.M.A. (New York's Metropolitan Museum of Art), limited reproduction, 3" long, circa 1980

896—Ruby pressed ENGLISH HOBNAIL pattern by Westmoreland, circa 1978, 3" long, 2" high

897—New salt by L. G. Wright, circa 1970's, never made old, amethyst color, 3¼" long

898—Same as Fig. 864, except in amethyst, never made old in this shape

899—Amber boat-shaped WILDFLOWER salt, also by Wright, orig. examples have a turtle figural base, 1970's and possibly a little earlier, 3¾" long

900—Amberina PANELLED THISTLE salt, made by Wright and possibly also Viking, 1960's (?), 2¼" round diam.

901—Same as Fig. 900 except in amethyst—this pattern was made only in clear originally

902—Appears to be a ground off toothpick in BAD BUTTON ARCHES

(1000 TPH) by Guernsey Glass Co., 1970's, made in several colors, 1⅜" round

903—Same as Fig. 870, in light blue color

904—Cranberry-flashed crystal, recent import with paper label "Genuine lead Crystal—W. Germany", almost 2" diam. round

905—Blue D&B round salt, never made old, this is Degenhart, 1970's, 1¾" round

906—Same as Fig. 872 except undecorated

907-908—Same as Fig. 869, shown here in green and ruby pressed

909—The triangular shape is same as Fig. 876 repro, but this one is definitely old. Pattern known as TRIANGLE (PS, 42-0) 1" diam.

910—Blue iridized salt signed R. Wetzel, Ohio glassmaker, circa 1975, scarce, 1⅛" round

911—Ruby glass salt by Imperial Glass, Bellaire Ohio, circa 1970, 1½" diam. round

912-914—New Guernsey Glass salts in different colors and treatments, same as Fig. 883

915-921—Assortment of colors in contemporary salt by Guernsey, 1970's, 1⅜" round

922—Repro CAPRICE nut cup by Imperial in their "End o' Day" color, paper label, 2" round

923—Same as Fig. 881, except light blue with gold—never made old

924—Light cobalt repro of lacy pattern salt, oval shape, 3⅛" long, from Tiawan or Mexico

925—Vaseline color, same as Fig. 890-892, by both Degenhart & Boyd

SWANS, CHICKS AND OTHER BIRDS

926—The color on this tiny swan is flashed, very similar to Fig. 927, may be an early Smith Glass example (circa 1930) with slight mold changes in the more recent version, 2" high

927—Amber swan, paper label "Smith—Hand-Crafted", 1970's, made in many colors, 2¼" high

928—Poor quality green swan, appears to be an import, 2⅛" high, age unknown

929-930—Squirrel and stump salt by Guernsey, signed with B (Bennett), circa 1970's

931—BIRD AND BERRY salt, originally made by McKee, reproduced by Degenhart and Boyd, except for colors, and occasional trademarks, it is difficult to tell new from old, circa 1880-1900, 2" high, 3" diam.

932-933—The blue opaque example is signed Boyd (a B-in-a-Diamond), the deep amber is unsigned, but appears to be new (possibly unsigned Degenhart), same size as Fig. 931

934—Similar to, but not the same as, the "Bird" salt by Richards & Hartley

(Reprint E), the emerald green example here has a berry in its beak, age and origin unknown, 1⅝" high

935 —Light green Swan, probably Cambridge Glass, unsigned but definitely old, originally used as an ash tray, nut cup, open salt, novelty, etc., also made in a second mold shown next to it, 2⅝" high, 3⅝" diam.

936 —Second mold for Cambridge Swan in "Crown Tuscan" color, not signed (sometimes found with Cambridge "C-in-a-Triangle" trademark, circa 1940's, reproduced 1970, 2¼" high, 3¾" diam.

937 —One of the "reproduction" swans, this one signed M for Mosser (Cambridge, Ohio), circa late 1970's

938 —Amber Swan by L.G. Wright, circa 1960, also made in several other colors, 4" long

939 —BIRD AND NEST salt in clear glass with faded pink staining, age and maker unknown, reproduced by Mosser (see Fig. 940), 3½" long, 1" high

940 —Cobalt blue Mosser repro of BIRD AND NEST, signed with M-in-a-Circle, late 1970's, 3⅝" long

941 —SWAN AND SHELL, probably by St. Clair, 1970's, unmarked, cobalt carnival, 4¾" long, also available old in clear glass (LPG, 186)

942 —Signed Boyd (B-in-a-Diamond), made by Crystal Art Glass, circa 1980, deep amethyst, see others on page 63, 2⁹⁄₁₆" diam., 2" high

943 —Large master size covered hen in emerald green, age and maker unknown, no marks, 3½" diam.

944 —Poorly detailed chick salt, maker unknown, recent vintage, ruby color, 3½" diam.

945 —Similar to Fig. 942, this one signed WG (Westmoreland), 1970's, made from old mold (see WDG2, 368), 2½" diam., 2¼" high

946-947 —Master salt in BIRD & BERRY, Fig. 946 is new (L. G. Wright) and Fig. 947 is old (McKee, circa 1890-1900), note differences in mold detail and size of base. Fig. 946 is 1⅞" high, 4" long; Fig. 947 is just over 2" high and 3⅞" long

948 —CHICK IN EGG egg cup, often seen in salt collections, circa 1890, 2⅝" high, shown here in blue, also made in clear and amber

HENS AND CHICKS

949 —Milk glass, head turned, recent Westmoreland trademark, 2½" diam.

950 —Milk glass, head turned, early Westmoreland (1930's), 3½" diam.

951 —Ruby glass, head straight, recent origin, maker unknown, 3⅜" diam.

952 —Poor quality Mexican glass, unsigned, age unknown, 3⅜" diam.

953 —Green-stained clear glass, frosted, head straight, unsigned, circa 1930, 2⅜" diam.

954-955 —Frosted glass in blue and amber, probably early Westmoreland, unsigned, head turned, 2⅜" diam.

956 —Unmarked bisque, head turned slightly, probably German, circa 1900, 2½" diam.

957 —Unmarked bisque, European, head turned, 2¼" diam., circa 1900

958-960 —Three different colors marked "Vallerystahl", French from about 1930, head turned, made in several other colors, 2⅜" diam.

961-962 —New china in pink and blue glaze, unmarked, head straight, slightly different dimensions, pink example just over 2¼" diam., blue is 2¾" diam.

963-966 —Four milk glass examples, all with different decorations, all new with Westmoreland trademark, heads straight, 2⅞" diam.

967 —China, marked "Japan" circa 1950's, 2⅝" diam.

968-969 —Two different Degenhart examples, the amethyst signed with D-in-a-Heart, the opaque yellow unsigned, circa 1970-79, 2½" diam.

970 —Decorated milk glass, same as Figs. 963-966, except unsigned, old, 2½" diam.

971 —Blue milk glass, Westmoreland glass of undetermined age, unsigned

972 —Unmarked china decorated to look like pottery, unmarked, age unknown, 2¼" diam.

973 —China, marked "Made in Germany", circa 1920, 2½" diam.

974 —High-glaze pottery, unmarked, circa 1930, 3" diam.

975 —Unmarked china, circa 1920's, maker unknown, 3" diam.

976 —Cobalt blue glass, recent origin, 3⅛" diam.

977 —Delicate bisque, decorated, probably German, 1¾" high, circa 1900

BIRDS AND ANIMALS
(Glass & China)

The novelty items in the first four rows could be salts, pin trays, nut dishes or simple "what-nots", but are all favored by salt collectors.

978 —China, marked Bavaria, adorable elephant, circa 1930, 3¼" high

979 —China, marked "Made in Japan", circa 1930, 2½" high

980 —Another cute elephant, marked Japan, circa 1930's, 2¼" high

981 —China bunny, marked Germany, circa 1930, 2¼" high

982 —Pottery bunny, no marks, probably American, circa 1920, 1½" high

983 —China parrot, no marks, probably Japanese, circa 1930, just under 2" high

984 —China parrot, marked "Made in Japan" Gold Castle Mark, circa 1930, just over 2" high

985-986 —China, marked "Made in Japan", different decorations, approx. 2" high

987 —Carved stone or alabaster, birds

on birdbath, foreign, circa 1920's 1½" high

988 —Bisque, beautiful doves on edge of dish, incised mark indicates Germany, circa 1920, just over 2" high

989 —Elfinware, unmarked, German, circa 1900, 2" high

990 —Carved alabaster, circa 1925, just under 2" high

991 —China, marked "Made in Japan", matching spoon, circa 1930, 2" high

992 —China fish, incised marks indicate Germany, circa 1920, just under 1½" high

993 —Rare turtle figural salt dip by Bellaire Goblet Co., Findlay, Ohio, circa 1888, the example shown here in poor condition (portions of feet and tail missing), see Smith's Findlay Glass, pg. 51

994 —Very unusual amber satin glass ram, exquisite detail, probably English, circa 1920, 1¼" high

995 —China, crab, marked "Made in Japan", circa 1930, ¾" high

996 —China fish, no marks, incised numbers indicate German, has a cover, circa 1925, 1½" high

997-999 —"Bird & Berry" salt, first one in amber is old McKee version, the next two are recent by Degenhart (production continued by Boyd Glass), first made in 1880's

1000 —Horse pulling cart in deep amethyst, age unknown, probably recent, 1¾" high

1001 —Fostoria glass bird from 1930's (WFG, 235), scarce

1002 —Covered salt in cobalt with rabbit lid, age unknown, probably recent, 2½" high

1003 —Amber frog, probably foreign, age uncertain, 1920's?, 1½" high

1004 —Bird and nest in blue, recent, with M-in-circle trademark of Mosser Glass, 1970's, 1½" high

GLASS & CHINA
DUCKS, SWANS & CHICKENS

1005 —Covered/bisque Staffordshire turkey, circa 1880, 3" high, could also be something other than a salt

1006 —Bisque covered chicken, marked France in inside bottom, circa 1900, just over 3" high

1007 —Bisque covered duck, Staffordshire type, circa 1900, just over 3" high

1008 —Staffordshire duck, delicate detail, circa 1880, just under 2" high

1009 —Staffordshire turkey with broken beak, circa 1880, 2½" high

1010 —Staffordshire duck, fine detail, circa 1880, 2" high

1011 —Bisque duck, appears to be German, circa 1890, 2" high

1012 —Frosted glass duck, American, circa 1890, 2¼" high

1013 —Pottery duck, American, circa 1940, just over 2" high

1014 —Double pottery ducks with

matching spoons not shown, European origin, just over 2" high

1015 — Fine porcelain swan marked Belleek, green mark, circa 1906-1952, 2" high

1016 — Unglazed china swan, origin unknown, circa 1950, just over 2" high

1017-1018 — Duncan Miller glass swans, circa 1940, also known in clear and vaseline

1019 — Frosted amber duck, Westmoreland (WDG2,369), circa 1920's, just over 2" high, 5¼" long

1020 — Blue milk glass duck, French, old, just over 2" high, 5½" long

1021 — China swan, marked Limoges, new, 2¼" high

1022 — Pottery duck marked Japan, circa 1940, 2¾" high

1023 — Pottery chick, could be novelty item, no marks, probably Japan, circa 1940, just under 2½" high

1024 — China duck, no marks, fine detail, probably German, circa 1940, 2½" high

1025 — Pottery chick, probably Japan, not old, just over 2" high

1026 — Bisque chicken, good detail, no marks, circa 1920, 3½" high

1027 — Glass chick, see #948

1028-1029 — Staffordshire tops of excellent detail, probably to salts, child's dishes, pin trays etc.

CHINA SWANS

1030 — Bisque, Staffordshire goose, could be trinket box, circa 1880, 2¾" high

1031 — China swan, probably Japan, circa 1930, just under 3" high

1032 — Marked Germany, appears bottom to be part of child's tureen set, and perhaps married to top, circa 1880, 3" high

1033 — Swan, china, marked Dresden, circa 1875, 3½" high

1034 — China, marked Goebel, West Germany, circa 1950, 2" high

1035 — Bisque, no marks, could be German, circa 1890, 3" high

1036 — China, marked Tuscan China, England, circa 1890, 2½" high

1037 — China, marked Japan, circa 1950, just over 2" high

1038 — China, marked Made in Japan, circa 1920, just over 2" high

1039 — China, Elfinware, signed Germany, circa 1920, 2¼" high

1040 — China, signed Germany, Elfinware, circa 1920, 2¼" high

1041 — Elfinware type, pottery, could be Japan, circa 1920, 2¾" high

1042 — Bisque, elegant design, probably German, circa 1890, 2¾" high

1043 — China, marked Made in Japan, circa 1950, 2¼" high

1044 — Parian ware, no marks, age & origin unknown, just over 1½" high

1045 — China, marked Made in Japan, Noritake, circa 1930, 2" high

1046 — China, marked Japan, circa 1930, 2" high

1047 — China, signed Germany, circa 1890, just over 2" high

1048-1049 — China, signed Germany, circa 1890, 2¼" high

1050 — China, no marks, probably Japan, circa 1930, 1¾" high

1051 — China, signed Limoges, France, circa 1930, 2½" high

1052 — China, signed Lenox, Made in USA, relatively new, just over 2" high

1053 — China, signed Hand Painted Japan, circa 1950, 2" high

1054 — China, looks German, circa 1930, 2½" high

1055 — China, signed Limoges, France, new, just over 2" high

1056 — China, no marks, probably German, circa 1930, 2½" high

1057 — China, signed Noritake, Made in Japan, matching spoon, circa 1920, 2" high

1058 — China, Elfinware, looks German, circa 1890, 2½" high

FIGURAL CHINA

This page is almost all novelty items in salts, nut cups, trinkets, toothpicks, etc. but all favored by salt collectors.

1059 — China, signed Czecho-Slovakia, circa 1930, just over 3½" high

1060 — China, signed "Porcelaine", European origin, 1930, 3½" high

1061 — Bisque, signed Made in Germany, has springs for legs, circa 1930, 3½" high

1062 — China, Kewpie, probably Japan, circa 1930, 3½" high

1063 — Parianware Santa Claus, origin unknown, circa 1940, 2½" high

1064-1065 — Bisque, marked Germany, have seen these with applied lace, very delicate and beaded, circa 1920, 2" high

1066 — Bisque, marked Germany, circa 1900, 2¼" high

1067 — Bisque, marked Germany, circa 1900, 2¾" high

1068 — China, marked Germany, circa 1900, 2½" high

1069 — Bisque, signed "Hand Painted Japan," circa 1930, 3" high

1070 — China, signed "Porcelaine", probably German, just under 3" high, circa 1930

1071 — China, signed "Porcelaine", Fairling, England, circa 1900, 2½" high

1072 — China, marked Germany, circa 1920, 2¼" high

1073 — China, marked Made in Japan, circa 1940, 1¼" high

1074 — China, signed Germany, circa 1900, just over 2½" high

1075 — China, signed Germany, circa 1900, 2¾" high

1076 — China, marked "Foreign", circa 1920, 3" high

1077 — Bisque, signed Germany, circa 1920, 2¾" high

1078 — China, marked "Made in Japan," circa 1920, 3" high

1079 — China, marked Germany, circa 1920, 2¾" high

1080 — China, marked Germany, circa 1920, 2¾" high

1081 — China, appears to be German, circa 1920, 3¼" high

1082 — China, signed Germany, circa 1920, 2¾" high

1083 — China, signed Germany, circa 1920, 2¾" high

1084 — China, signed Germany, circa 1920, just over 3" high

FIGURAL CHINA

Another page almost all novelty items, of salts, nut cups, trinkets, toothpicks, etc., but all favored by salt collectors.

1085 — Pottery, signed Quimper, circa 1900, 3½" high

1086 — Bisque, signed Germany, circa 1900, just under 3" high

1087 — China, Kate Greenaway figure, signed "Possneck", circa 1900, almost 4" high

1088 — Bisque, probably German, circa 1900, 4" high

1089 — Pottery bear, no marks, American, circa 1930, just over 2½" high

1090 — China, marked Made in Japan, circa 1920, 2¼" high

1091 — Pottery, possibly German, circa 1920, just under 3" high

1092 — China, signed Germany, circa 1920, 2¼" high

1093 — China, marked Made in Japan, circa 1920, 2" high

1094 — China, marked Japan, circa 1930, 3½" high

1095 — China, marked Made in Japan, circa 1950, 3¾" high

1096 — Pottery, marked Japan, circa 1950, 2½" high

1097 — Bisque, marked Germany, circa 1910, 2¾" high

1098 — China, marked Japan, circa 1960, 1¾" high

1099 — China, marked Japan, circa 1930, 3¾" high

1100 — China, marked Made in Germany, circa 1920, 1¾" high

1101 — China, marked Made in Germany, circa 1920, 1¾" high

1102 — China, marked Germany, circa 1920, 2¾" high

1103 — Bisque, good detail on this cat and dog pulling hat in a circle, no marks, possibly German, circa 1920, 1½" high

1104 — China, marked Germany, circa 1920, 3" high

1105 — Bisque, marked Germany, circa 1920, 4" high

UNUSUAL CHINA

1106 — Fine porcelain, Royal Dux, unmarked, circa 1880, 5¼" high

1107 — Fine porcelain, signed KPM Berlin, circa 1820, 5" high

1108 — China, no marks, appears to be German, circa 1920, 3½" high

1109—Bisque, very interesting clown could also be match holder, no marks, appears to be German, circa 1920, 4½" high

1110—Porcelain, signed Heubach, circa 1850, 3¾" high

1111—China, Goss miniature, English, circa 1890, 2" high

1112—China, signed Made in Japan, Noritake, circa 1920, 2½" high

1113—China, signed Bavaria, and artist signed, China blank, circa 1900, pepper 3½" high

1114—China condiment set, appears to be German, circa 1930, just over 3" high

1115—China, no marks, German, circa 1900, just under 3" high, note spoon in upper section

1116—China, marked with incised numbers indicating Germany, circa 1920, 3½" high

CHINA SALT & PEPPER SETS

1117—China condiment set, salt, pepper & mustard, marked Germany, note matching spoon makes claw on lobster, circa 1910, 3½" high, similar to Royal Bayreuth

1118—China condiment set of salt, pepper & mustard, marked Germany, circa 1920, 2¾" high

1119—China condiment set consisting of salt and mustard with removable head for pepper shaker, underplate not shown, but signed Royal Bayreuth, circa 1920, 4½" high

1120—China, matching salt and pepper marked France, circa 1900, salt 1" high

1121—China, matching salt and pepper, Sterling rim hallmarked London 1908, salt 1¼" high

1122—Lustre china condiment set, double salt attached to mustard, no marks, German, circa 1930, 3" high

1123—China, Duck salt and pepper on tray, marked Germany-Pfeiffer, circa 1935, salt 1½" high

1124—China, interesting beehive, pepper sitting on top of salt, marked "Made in Japan," circa 1925, 2¾" high

1125—China, rabbit salt and pepper on tray, marked Germany-Pfeiffer, circa 1935, salt 1½" high

1126—China, matching salt and pepper, marked "Made in England," circa 1930, salt 1" high

1127—Semi-porcelain tomato pepper shaker sits on top of salt, probably Japan, circa 1940, salt 1" high

1128—China, marked Wedgewood Etruria, circa 1891, salt 1½" high

CHINA & POTTERY DOUBLE SALTS

1129—Pottery, signed Quimper, 19th Century, 3¾" high, another identical salt on other side

1130—China, no marks, probably English, 19th Century, 1¼" high

1131—Bisque, with glaze, marked Germany, circa 1920, 3½" high

1132—Pottery, signed Quimper, 19th Century, 2¼" high

1133—Pottery, signed Quimper, 19th Century, 2¾" high

1134—Pottery, signed France, 19th Century, 3" high, looks like Quimper

1135—Pottery, looks like Quimper, circa 1900, 3½" high

1136—China, looks German, "Skarlsbad" souvenir, 1¾" high, circa 1920

1137—China, no marks, appears to be German, circa 1920, 2½" high

1138—Pottery, marked France, 19th Century, 3¼" high

1139—China, no marks, possibly Japan, circa 1940, 2" high

1140—China, signed Quimper, 19th Century, 3½" high

CHINA & POTTERY DOUBLE SALTS

1141—Pottery, signed "Made in Occupied Japan," circa 1945-1952, just under 3" high

1142—China, KPM (Berlin), 20th Century mark, 2" high

1143—China, marked "Made in Portugal", circa 1930, 3¼" high

1144—China, no marks, possibly German, circa 1940, 2¼" high

1145—China, marked "Made in Poland, circa 1920, 3¾" high

1146—China, delicate flowers and bead work with matching spoon, incised numbers indicate German, 19th Century, just under 3" high

1147—Pottery, signed Quimper, 19th Century, just over 2" high

1148—China, no marks, possibly German, circa 1900, 1¾" high

1149—China, no marks, possibly German, circa 1900, 2¼" high

1150—China, hand painted flowers in one bowl, "With best Wishes" in other bowl, circa 1900, 2¼" high

1151—Tin Glaze, European, probably English, circa 1850, has marks similar to early Derby, 2½" high

1152—China, marked "Made in Germany," circa 1900, just over 2½" high

CHINA & POTTERY DOUBLE SALTS

1153—Pottery, no marks, possibly Czechoslovakia, circa 1920, just over 2½" high

1154—China, unidentified marks, German, pepper shaker is removable head, circa 1900, 5" high

1155—China, marked KPM, (Berlin), circa 1850, 5" high

1156—China, marked KPM (Berlin), circa 1850, 5" high

1157—Pottery, signed Quimper, 19th Century, 2¼" high

1158—Same as 1150

1159—China, signed KPM (Berlin), 20th Century mark, 2" high

1160—China, marked Germany, circa 1930, 2" high

1161—China, signed Bohemia, circa 1857, 3" high

1162—Pottery, signed Quimper, 19th Century, 2" high

1163—Pottery, signed Quimper, 19th Century, just over 2" high

1164—China, no marks, European origin, circa 1870, 2" high

1165—China, Teplitz type, no marks, circa 1920, 2" high

1166—China, no marks, European, circa 1920, just over 2" high

1167—China, signed Czechoslovakia, circa 1920, just over 2" high

1168—China, no marks, European, circa 1920, 2" high

1169—China, signed Meissen, unfortunately handle has been ground off, circa 1850, just over 1" high

1170—China, marked "Johann", European origin, circa 1880, just over 2" high

1171—China, no marks, possibly German, circa 1900, 2¼" high

1172—China, no marks, possibly German, circa 1900, 2¼" high

OPEN SALT & PEPPER SETS—CHINA & SILVER

1173—Plated holder with 3 piece condiment set, salt, pepper & mustard, no marks, probably English, circa 1900, salt 1¼" high

1174—Plated, 3 piece condiment set, salt, pepper & mustard, Thistle motif indicated Ireland, circa 1900, 4½" high

1175—China, matching open salt and pepper, marked Rosenthal (German) Sterling bases, hallmarked 1897

1176—China, open salt & pepper, EPNS rim, probably English, circa 1900, salt is 1½" high

1177—China, marked Czechoslavakia, hand painted, salt is ½" high, circa 1930

1178—China, marked Czechoslavakia, part of egg set with matching plate, circa 1930, salt is 1" high

1179—China, salt under pepper shaker, no marks, circa 1930, probably Japan, 2½" high

1180-1181—China, hand painted, pepper sitting on salt, circa 1920, 2" high, marked Japan

1182—Pottery, no marks, pepper sitting on top of salt, circa 1940, 3¼" high, American

1183—China, marked "Made in Japan", hand painted, circa 1925, 2" high

1184—Plated, EP, 1-piece condiment set, marked Roberts & Beek, Sheffield, London, circa 1900, 2¼" high

1185—Plated, Derby Silver Company, matching salt, pepper & spoon, circa 1900, salt is 1¼" high

1186—Plated, 1-piece condiment set, salt, pepper & mustard, marked Elkington Plate (English), engraved Gunard Steamship Crest, circa 1900, 3" high

MISCELLANEOUS CHINA SALTS

1187 — China, Kate Greenaway type figure with spoon "hole" at top of open salt, signed Possneck, late 19th Century, 3³⁄₄" high

1188 — China, matching salt & pepper, rim marked EPNC, probably English, circa 1900, salt, just under 1¹⁄₂" high

1189 — Bisque covered chicken, disc on inside of lid to absorb moisture, circa 1920, 2¹⁄₄" high

1190 — China, unusual swan, marked Volstedt, (Germany), circa 18th Century perhaps as early as 1760, 2¹⁄₂" high

1191 — Combination of wood, with EPNS rim, and porcelain lining, late 19th Century, 1³⁄₄" high, English

1192 — China, Limoges, circa 1940, just under 2" high

1193 — Bisque, no marks, incised numbers indicate Germany, circa 1900, just under 2" high

1194 — Bisque, no marks, incised numbers indicate Germany, delicate bead work, just over 1¹⁄₂" high

1195 — China, marked Albian China, (English) circa 1901, 1³⁄₄" high

1196 — China, Goss miniature type, circa 1900, 1¹⁄₄" high, English

1197 — China, Stoke-on-Trent, circa 1905-1924, 1¹⁄₂" high, English, 3 handles

1198 — China, signed Noritake Nippon, circa 1900, 1" high

1199 — China, Dresden Saxony mark, circa 1875, artist Potschappel, Carl Thieme, very delicate and lovely, 1" high

1200 — China, Royal Copenhagen, circa 1923, 1³⁄₄" high, oval

1201 — China, Royal Copenhagen, 19th Century, 1¹⁄₄" high, oval

1202 — China, no marks, appears to be Oriental, circa 1900, 1¹⁄₄" high

1203 — Enamel on Metal, could be child's toy dish, 1¹⁄₄" high

1204 — China, delicate baby buggy with matching spoon, incised numbers indicate Germany, circa 1890, 2¹⁄₄" high

1205 — China, marked Japan, frog is the pepper shaker, with salt on opposite end, just over 3" high to top of handle, circa 1920

1206 — China, marked Haviland, France, circa 1893, artist painted, just over ¹⁄₂" high

1207 — Stone, like petrified wood, has German lettering on side, 2" high

1208 — China, has many marks and identified 19th Century, 1¹⁄₂" high

1209 — Pottery, Sorreguemimes, French early 19th Century, 1¹⁄₂" high

1210 — China signed Worchester Royal Porcelain Co., for Richard Briggs, Boston, circa 1910, ³⁄₄" high

1211 — China, marked Maua Porcelain, circa 1920, 1³⁄₄" high

BASKETS AND SHELLS
(Glass, China and Pottery)

1212 — China, marked Czechoslovakia, circa 1920, 1³⁄₄" high

1213 — Glass basket, vaseline color, Tiffin Glass, circa 1930's, 3³⁄₄" high

1214 — Venetian glass double salt, delicate swan's-neck handle, circa 1890, 3³⁄₄" high, European

1215 — Pottery, probably German, 1930's, 2¹⁄₂" high

1216 — China, marked Occupied Japan, 1945-52, just under 2" high

1217 — China, marked "Made in Occupied Japan", 1945-52, just over 2" high

1218 — China, no marks, probably Japan, circa 1930, just over 2" high

1219 — Clay basket, no marks, American, age unknown, 1¹⁄₄" high

1220 — China, marked "Made in Japan," circa 1925-35, just under 2" high

1221 — China, marked Noritake/Made in Japan, matching spoon, just over 2" high

1222 — China, marked Japan, circa 1930, 1³⁄₄" high

1223 — China basket, marked Japan, circa 1930, just under 2" high

1224 — Pottery basket, marked Italy, 1920's, 2" high

1225 — Pottery basket, no marks, origin unknown, circa 1950's, 2" high

1226-1227 — China baskets, no marks, 1940's, just under 2¹⁄₂" high

1228-1229 — China baskets with slightly different shapes, marked Japan, circa 1930's, just over 2" high

1230 — Glass basket in amber, appears to be Mexican of recent origin, 2³⁄₄" high

1231 — China basket, marked "Made in Japan", 1930's, just under 2" high

1232 — China shell, with flower card holder, marked "Ardalt-Japan", rather new, 1¹⁄₄" high

1233 — Light blue glass shell, maker unknown, circa 1930's, American, 2¹⁄₄" wide

1234 — Marked "Genuine New Zealand Pula Shell, Ataahua Brand", matching spoon, bought in the 1970's, 2³⁄₄" diam.

1235 — Glass shell in Cambridge "Crown Tuscan" color, 1930's-40's, 1¹⁄₂" high, 2⁵⁄₈" diam.

1236 — Pottery shell, no marks, probably new, just under 1¹⁄₂" high

1237 — Same as Fig. 1235 except in light blue, with place card holder, Cambridge from the 1930's

1238 — Pottery conch shell, age and origin unknown, 2" high

1239 — China shell, conch type, Oriental marks incised into bottom, turn-of-the-century, 1³⁄₄" high

1240 — Decorated "Crown Tuscan" shell, Cambridge Glass Co. from 1930's-40's, 1¹⁄₂" high

ELFINWARE

1241 — Basket marked Made in Germany, 2" high

1242 — Wheelbarrow, marked Germany, 1¹⁄₂" high

1243 — Basket, marked Germany, just under 3" high

1244 — Wheelbarrow with movable wheel and registry marks, 2" high, English or French

1245-1253 — All marked Germany, #1250 has enamel medallion, all approx. 2" high

1254 — Egg on nest, has unidentified makers mark and matching spoon, 2¹⁄₄" high

1255 — Marked Made in Germany, just under 1" high

1256 — Egg, marked Germany, 1³⁄₄" high

1257-1259 — Baskets, all marked Germany, 2¹⁄₄", 1¹⁄₂" and just over 1" high

1260 — No marks, probably German, ³⁄₄" high

1261 — Basket, marked Germany, has birds for handles, 1¹⁄₄" high

1262-1264 — All marked Germany, 2", 1¹⁄₄", and 1" high

1265 — Wheelbarrow, marked Germany, 2¹⁄₄" high

1266 — Basket, marked Germany, 2¹⁄₄" high

1267 — Unmarked, probably German, 1¹⁄₂" high

1268 — Marked Made in Germany, just over 1" high

1269 — Marked Made in Germany, just under 1¹⁄₂" high

1270 — Marked Germany, just over 1" high

DECORATED CHINA

All china, all similar size and shape, these were painted during a period when china painting was popular for the ladies. The blanks were purchased from various companies. Sometimes the makers marks are painted over. The quality of the detail varies, some were artist signed. Many times they were painted to match a table setting of china. All circa 1890-1910.

1271 — No marks, ³⁄₄" high, circa 1900

1272 — Marked Royal Austria, probably factory painted, ³⁄₄" high, circa 1900

1273 — Marked Willets, Belleek, artist signed, ³⁄₄" high

1274 — No marks, ³⁄₄" high

1275 — Marked Limoges France, artist signed, P&P, ¹⁄₂" high

1276 — No marks, ³⁄₄" high

1277 — Marked Lennox, circa 1894-1896, ¹⁄₂" high

1278 — Marked Lennox, Belleek, circa 1897-1906, ¹⁄₂" high

1279 — Marked Willets, Belleek, circa 1897, ¹⁄₂" high

1280 — Marked Lennox, Belleek, circa 1894-1896, ¹⁄₂" high

1281 — Marked France, circa 1882-1898, ¹⁄₂" high

1282 — Marked Lennox, Belleek, circa 1897, ¹⁄₂" high

1283—Marked Royal Austria, circa 1890, $3/4$" high

1284—Marked B & Co., France, circa 1890, $3/4$" high

1285—Marked Lennox, circa 1894-1896, $1/2$" high

1286—Marked Lennox, Belleek, circa 1897-1906, $1/2$" high

1287—Marked Lennox, Belleek, circa 1897-1906, $1/2$" high

1288—Marked France, $1/2$" high, circa 1890

1289—Marked Vienna, Austria, circa 1890, $1/2$" high

1290—Marked Belleek, circa 1890, $1/2$" high

1291—Marked Lennox, Belleek, circa 1897-1906, $1/2$" high

1292—No marks, marked Made in Japan, circa 1920, $3/4$" high

1293—No marks, just under 1" high, circa 1900

1294—Marked Belleek, circa 1890, $1/2$" high

1295—Marked Royal Austria, circa 1890, $3/4$" high

1296—Marked Austria, circa 1890, $3/4$" high

1297—No marks, circa 1890, just under 1" high

1298—Marked France, circa 1890, $3/4$" high

1299—Marked T & V, France, circa 1890, just over $1/2$" high

1300—Marked Willets, Belleek, circa 1879, $1/2$" high

1301—Marked D & C, France, circa 1875, $3/4$" high

1302—Marked Vienna, Austria, circa 1890, $1/2$" high

1303—Marked Willets, Belleek, circa 1879, $1/2$" high

1304—No marks, circa 1890, $1/2$" high

1305—Marked Limoges, France, circa 1890, just over $1/2$" high

1306—Marked Dresden, circa 1900, 1" high

1307-1308—Marked Coxon, Belleek, rare mark, circa 1875, factory painted, $1/2$" high

1309—Marked Vienna, Austria, Leonard, circa 1890, $1/2$" high

1310—Marked Willets, Belleek, circa 1879, just over $1/2$" high

DECORATED CHINA
See heading on previous page

1311—Marked England, circa 1890, $1 1/2$" high

1312—Marked Meissen, circa 1880, 1" high

1313—No marks, appears to be Dresden, circa 1880, just over 1" high

1314—Marked Meissen, not old, 2" high

1315—Marked Czechoslavakia, circa 1920, 1" high

1316—Marked Bavaria, open underneath with shallow salt bowl, circa 1890, $1 1/2$" high

1317—No marks, Nippon type, circa 1900, 1" high

1318—Marked Austria, circa 1890, $3/4$" high, hand painted

1319—Marked Austria, circa 1890, $3/4$" high, hand painted

1320—Marked Limoges, circa 1890, $3/4$" high, hand painted

1321—Marked Limoges, circa 1890, hand painted, artist signed, $3/4$" high

1322—Marked Limoges, P & P France, hand painted, circa 1890, $3/4$" high

1323—No marks, pottery, probably new, $3/4$" high

1324—Marked Germany, circa 1890, just over $1/2$" high

1325—No marks, circa 1890, just under 1" high

1326—Signed Quimper, circa 1880, $3/4$" high

1327—Marked "Manufactured by the Worcester Royal Porcelain Co. for Richard Briggs, Boston", circa 1910, $3/4$" high

1328—Marked J. P. France, circa 1890, $1/2$" high

1329—No marks, circa 1890, $3/4$" high

1330—No marks, artist signed and dated 1919, $3/4$" high

1331—Signed with Nippon Green Wreath mark, circa 1900, just under 1" high

1332—Marked Royal Copenhagen, circa 1897, $3/4$" high

1333—Marked Dresden, circa 1910, $3/4$" high

1334—Marked Royal Copenhagen, circa 1894, $3/4$" high

1335—No marks, circa 1900, probably Nippon, $3/4$" high

1336-1337—Marked Royal Austria, circa 1920, 1" high

1338—Marked Royal Austria, circa 1900, $3/4$" high, hand painted

1339—No marks, small scalloped pedestal, circa 1900, 1" high

1340—Marked Vienna, Austria, artist signed, scalloped pedestal, circa 1900, $3/4$" high

1341—Marked Royal Austria, D & EG, scalloped pedestal, circa 1900, $3/4$" high

1342—Interesting oriental marks, could be English, circa 1875, just under 1" high

1343—Marked "Made in Japan," circa 1930, $3/4$" high

1344—Marked Vienna, Austria, circa 1930, 1" high

1345—Marked JP France, $1/2$" high

1346—French blank, hand painted & signed by Luker, reputed to be the best of the violet decorators, hollow underneath with shallow salt bowl, circa 1900-1914

DECORATED CHINA

1347—Unusual shape & design, no marks, European origin, circa 1880, 1" high

1348—Signed Delft, circa 1900, just under $1 1/2$" high

1349—No marks, circa 1920, just under 1" high

1350—Signed, hand painted Nippon, circa 1900, just over 1" high

1351—No marks, 3 tiny feet, probably German, circa 1900, $1 1/4$" high

1352—Signed Dresden with rare Lamb Mark, circa 1887, just over 1" high

1353—Signed Limoges, France, circa 1900, 1" high

1354—Signed Royal Austria, circa 1900, $3/4$" high

1355—Signed MZ Austria, circa 1900, just under 1" high

1356—Signed MZ Austria, circa 1900, just under 1" high

1357—Signed B & Co., France, circa 1900, $3/4$" high

1358—Signed Nippon, circa 1900, 1" high

1359—Unsigned Nippon, circa 1900, 1" high

1360-1365—Signed Nippon, circa 1900, 1" high

1366—Signed "Made in Japan", circa 1900, 1" high

1367—No marks, Nippon style, circa 1900, 1" high

1368—Signed MZ Austria, circa 1900, just under 1" high

1369—Signed Meissen, unusual, circa 1880, $1 1/4$" high

1370—Signed Nippon, circa 1900, 1" high

1371—Signed Nippon, circa 1900, 1" high

1372—No marks, probably Japan, circa 1920, 1" high

1373—Signed, hand painted Nippon, circa 1900, just over 1" high

1374-1376—Signed Limoges, France new, 1" high

1377—Signed Nippon, circa 1920, 1" high

1378—Signed Nippon, 3 feet, not shown, circa 1900, just under 1" high

1379—Signed "Made in Japan," circa 1900, 1" high

1380—No marks, unusual shape & design, circa 1880, oriental, high quality, $1 1/2$" high

1381—No marks, unusual shape & design, high quality oriental, circa 1880, $1 1/2$" high

CHINA—FOOTED & SCALLOP BASED

1382—Marked Belleek, dated 1889, just over 1" high

1383—Signed Dresden, factory painted, circa 1900, 1" high

1384—No marks, circa 1900, European origin, just over 1" high

1385—No marks, circa 1900, European origin, just over 1" high

1386—Marked Vienna, Austria, circa 1900, just over 1" high

1387—No marks, circa 1900, 1" high

1388—Signed Lennox Belleek, circa 1900, 1" high

1389—No marks, circa 1900, 1" high

1390—Signed Vienna Austria, circa 1900, 1" high

1391—Signed Vienna, Austria, circa 1900, 1" high

1392—No marks, circa 1900, European, 1" high

1393—No marks, matching spoon, circa 1900, 1" high

1394—Signed Haviland, France, Limoges, looks factory painted, circa 1915, just over ½" high

1395—Signed, hand painted Nippon Rising Sun mark, circa 1910, just over ½" high

1396-1397 — Signed, Haviland, France, pattern unknown, circa 1900, just over ½" high

1398—Signed Hand Painted Nippon, Rising Sun mark, circa 1900, just over ½" high

1399—Signed, Haviland, France, unknown pattern, circa 1900, just over ½" high

1400—Signed, Haviland, France, unknown pattern, circa 1900, just over ½" high

1401—Signed, Haviland, France, hand painted, circa 1900, just over ½" high

1402—No marks, stencil transfer portraits of Desiree, circa 1900, French, rare & unusual, just over ½" high

1403—No marks, stencil transfer portrait of Napoleon, rare & unusual, circa 1900, French, just over ½" high

1404—No marks, hand painted, circa 1900, European, just over ½" high

1405—No marks, European, circa 1900, just over ½" high

1406—No marks, European, circa 1900, just over ½" high

1407—No marks, circa 1900, 1" high

1408—Signed Hand Painted Nippon, TN mark, circa 1900, 1" high

1409—Signed Hand Painted Nippon, green leaf mark, circa 1900, 1" high

1410—No marks, circa 1900, European, 1" high

HAND PAINTED CHINA (FOOTED)

1411—Signed Lennox Belleek, unusual silver overlay, factory decorated, circa 1900, 1" high

1412—Signed Vienna, Austria, circa 1900, 1" high

1413—Signed Bavaria, circa 1900, just over 1" high

1414—Signed Haviland, France, circa 1893, just over 1" high

1415—Signed, Vienna, Austria, circa 1900, just over 1" high

1416—Signed, B & Co., France, artist signed, ¾" high

1417—Signed Victoria, Czeckoslovakia, circa 1900, 1" high

1418—Signed Royal Austria O & EG, circa 1900, just over ½" high

1419—Signed Royal Austria, circa 1900, just over ½" high

1420—Signed Royal Austria, circa 1900, just over ½" high

1421—No marks, circa 1900, just over ½" high

1422—Signed MZ Austria, circa 1900, just over ½" high

1423—Signed Nippon, Green Mark M-in-Wreath, circa 1900, 1" high

1424—Signed Hand Painted Nippon, circa 1900, 1" high

1425—Signed with Nippon Green M-in-Wreath Mark, circa 1900, 1" high

1426—Signed B & Co., France, circa 1900, ¾" high

1427—No mark, circa 1900, just under 1" high

1428—No marks, flower in bottom forming base of 7 petals, circa 1900, 1" high

1429—Signed "Made in Japan", circa 1930, 1" high

1430—Signed Japan, circa 1925, just under 1" high

1431—Signed Royal Austria O & EG, circa 1900, ¾" high

1432—Signed France, Swan crest on other side, circa 1900, 1" high

1433—Signed Japan, circa 1930, just over 1" high

1434—Signed Japan, circa 1900, just over 1" high

1435—No marks, circa 1920's, 1" high, probably German

1436—Signed Germany, circa 1920's, 1" high

1437—Signed Bavaria, artist signed, circa 1900, ¾" high

1438—Signed Limoges, France, circa 1900, 1" high

1439—Signed "Made in Japan", circa 1920, just over ½" high

1440—Signed Hand Painted Nippon, circa 1900, ¾" high

1441—No marks, Nippon type, circa 1900, 1" high

1442—Signed Nippon, circa 1920, probably a nut cup, circa 1920, 1" high

1443—Signed Nippon Green mark M-in-Wreath, could be nut cup, circa 1920, 1" high

1444—Signed "Made in Japan", could be nut cup, circa 1930, 1" high

1445—Signed "Made in Japan", could be nut cup, circa 1930, 1" high

HAND PAINTED CHINA WITH HANDLES

1446—Marked Noritake, Japan, circa 1930's, 1¼" high

1447—Marked Noritake, Made in Japan, circa 1900, 1¼" high

1448—Marked Nippon, RG mark, excellent quality hand painting, circa 1900, 1¼" high

1449—Marked Green M-in-Wreath, excellent quality of design, circa 1900, 1¼" high

1450—Marked Japan, circa 1920's 1¼" high

1451—No marks, European, circa 1920, 1½" high

1452—Marked with Blue M-on-Wreath, circa 1900, 1¼" high

1453—Marked with Blue M, Rising Sun Mark (Nippon), circa 1900, 1¼" high

1454—Marked Nippon with Blue Rising Sun, circa 1900, 1¼" high

1455—Marked Green M-in-Wreath, Nippon, circa 1900, 1" high

1456-1457—Marked Nippon, Blue Rising Sun Mark, circa 1900, 1" high

1458—Marked Nippon, Green M-in-Wreath, circa 1900, ¾" high

1459-1460 — Nippon, Red M-in-Wreath Mark, circa 1900, ¾" high

1461—Marked "Satsuma Nippon", excellent detail, circa 1900, ¾" high

1462—Marked Japan, circa 1910, ¾" high

1463—Marked "Royal Satsuma Nippon" with a plus mark in circle, excellent detail, circa 1900, ¾" high

1464-1465—Marked Nippon, Green M-in-Wreath Mark, circa 1920, ¾" high

1466—Marked Made in Japan, Noritake, circa 1930, ¾" high

1467—Marked Japan, circa 1930, 1½" high

1468-1470—Marked Nippon, Green M-in-Wreath Mark, circa 1900, 1½" high

1471—No marks, appears to be German, circa 1900, 1¼" high

1472—No marks, appears to be Nippon, circa 1900, ¾" high

1473—Marked Nippon, green leaf mark, circa 1900, just under 1½" high

1474—Marked Nippon, Green M-in-Wreath Mark, circa 1900, ¾" high

1475—Marked Nippon, Green M-in-Wreath Mark, interesting design in bottom of these two, ships, water and mountains, circa 1900, ¾" high

1476—Marked Noritake, Made in Japan, Red M-in-Wreath Mark, circa 1930, 1¼" high

1477—Marked RG Nippon, circa 1900, ¾" high

1478—Goss miniature marked "Model of Elizabethan Bushel Measure now in Appleby Moot Hall", circa 1910, English, 1⅜" high

HAND PAINTED CHINA— PEDESTAL BASED

1479—Marked Nippon, circa 1900, just over 1½" high

1480—Marked Nippon, circa 1900, just over 1¼" high

1481—Unsigned, circa 1890-1910, 1¾" high

1482—Signed Nippon, Green M-in-Wreath Mark, circa 1900, 1½" high

1483—No marks, Nippon type, circa 1900, 1½" high

1484-1485—Marked Nippon, circa 1900, 1½" high

1486—Nippon, Green M-in-Wreath Mark, 1½" high

1487-1488—Signed Nippon, Red M-in-Wreath Mark, 1½" high

1489—Marked Germany, circa 1920, just over 1" high

1490—Unmarked, circa 1900, probably Austrian, 1½" high

1491—No marks, circa 1900, 1¼" high, Austrian blank

1492—Marked Bavaria, circa 1900, 1¼" high

1493—Marked Royal Austria, circa 1900, 1¼" high

1494—No mark, artist signed, circa 1900, Austrian blank, 1¼" high

1495-1496—No marks, appears to be Nippon, circa 1900, just under 2" high

1497—Marked Limoges, new, 1¼" high

1498—Marked "Made in France, Limoges," circa 1900, 1" high

1499—Marked Austria, circa 1900, 1¼" high

1500-1501—Marked Limoges, France, B & H Co., circa 1900, just over 1" high

1502—Marked Royal Bayreuth (Blue Mark) circa 1905, interesting with one pattern inside and a floral pattern outside, 1¼" high

1503—No marks, probably Nippon, circa 1900, 1½" high

1504—Marked Limoges, France, new, stencil decor, 1¼" high

1505—No marks, probably Japan, circa 1930, 1½" high

1506—Marked Nippon, Green M-in-Wreath mark, circa 1900, 1¼" high

1507—Marked Nippon, circa 1900, 1¼" high

1508—Marked "Made in Japan," circa 1900, 1½" high

1509—Marked Nippon, circa 1900, just over 1¼" high

CHINA—PEDESTAL, FOOTED & PLAIN

1510—Goss miniature, "Model of Ancient Salt cellar in Glasstonbury Museum," English, circa 1900, 3¼" high

1511—Marked Japan, circa 1930's, 1½" high

1512—Marked "Made in Japan," circa 1920, 1½" high

1513—Marked "Made in Japan," green flower mark, circa 1930's, just over 1" high

1514—Marked "Made in Japan,"

green flower mark, circa 1930's, just over 1" high

1515—Marked "Made in Japan," green flower mark, circa 1930, 1½" high

1516-1518—Marked Vienna, Austria, circa 1900, 1¼" high

1519-1520—Marked Austria, circa 1900, 1¼" high

1521—Marked Germany, circa 1900, 1" high

1522—No marks, circa 1920, 1¼" high

1523—Marked "Made in Czeckoslavakia," circa 1920, 1¾" high

1524—No marks, appears to be Nippon, circa 1900, 1½" high

1525—No marks, probably Austrian, circa 1900, just over 1" high

1526—No marks, European, circa 1920, 1½" high

1527—No marks, probably Japan, circa 1920, just over 1¼" high

1528—Marked Germany, new, 1" high

1529—Marked Austria, circa 1900, 1¼" high

1530—Marked Nippon, Blue Rising Sun Mark, circa 1900, just under 1" high

1531—No marks, American, circa 1900, ¾" high

1532—No marks, looks Austrian, circa 1900, just over ½" high

1533—Marked Germany, six tiny feet, circa 1900, 1" high

1534—Marked "Good Friend Porcelain, Made In Spain, circa 1940, just under 2" high

1535—No marks, oval bowl, circa 1900, European, 1" high

1536—Marked Royal Austria, circa 1900, 1¼" high

1537—Marked Bavaria, circa 1900, 1¼" high

1538—Marked Germany, circa 1900, 1" high

1539—No marks, circa 1900, ¾" high

1540—Marked "Good Friend Porcelain, Made In Spain," matching spoon, circa 1940, 1¼" high

1541—No marks, European, circa 1900, just over 1" high

1542-1543—Marked Limoges, France, new, 1" high

1544—Marked Limoges, France, circa, 1950, just over 2" high

GOLD DECORATED CHINA

1545—Marked Pickard, Made in USA, circa 1930, 1¼" high

1546—Marked "Made in Japan", circa 1930's 1½" high

1547—Marked Noritake, circa 1925, 1¼" high

1548—No marks, probably American, circa 1900, ¾" high

1549—No marks, European shape, circa 1900, just over 1" high

1550—Marked Germany, circa 1900, just over ½" high

1551—No marks, Bavarian shape, circa 1900, 1" high

1552—No marks, European shape, 3 tiny feet, circa 1920, just over 1" high

1553—Marked Prussia, circa 1900, ¾" high

1554—Marked Limoges, France, circa 1900, ¾" high

1555—Marked Willets, Belleek, circa 1900, ½" high

1556—Marked "ARABIA, Made in Finland", circa 1930, ¼" high

1557—Marked Noritake, Nippon, circa 1920, 1" high

1558—Marked Noritake, Nippon, circa 1920, 1" high

1559—No marks, probably Nippon, circa 1900, just over 1¼" high

1560—Marked Limoges, France, circa 1900, ¾" high

1561—Marked California, circa 1950, 1½" high

1562—Marked Made in Germany, circa 1920, 1½" high

1563—Marked Bavaria, circa 1900, just over 1" high

1564—Marked France, probably new, 1¼" high

1565—Marked Czeckoslavakia, circa 1900, just over 1" high

1566—Marked "Stouffers-Encrusted Gold", Japanese blank, circa 1930, just over ½" high

1567—No marks, probably Japan, circa 1920, ¾" high

1568—No marks, circa 1930, 1½" high

1569—No marks, Pickard type, circa 1920, just over 1" high

1570—No marks, Belleek shape, very delicate, just over ½" high

1571—Marked Japan, circa 1920, 1½" high

1572—No marks, Bavarian shape, circa 1900, 1" high

1573—No marks, Pickard design, circa 1920, 1¼" high

1574—No marks, Japanese design, circa 1920, 2¼" high

1575—Marked "Stoke-on-Trent", England, circa 1911, 1¼" high

1576—Marked "Made in Japan-SHO-FU", circa 1930, 1" high

1577—No marks, European shape, circa 1900, 1" high

1578—Marked Bavaria, circa 1920, 1¼" high

CHINA—ASSORTED UNUSUAL SHAPES

1579-1580—Marked JP France, circa 1900, ¾" high

1581—No marks, appears to be Japan, circa 1930, just over ½" high

1582—Marked Nippon, Green M-in-Wreath Mark, circa 1920, ¾" high

1583—Marked Nippon, Blue Rising Sun Mark, circa 1920, ¾" high

1584—No marks, pottery, probably

European, circa 1950, just under 1" high

1585—Marked "Gemma," European, age unknown, ³/₄" high

1586—No marks, probably German, circa 1900, 1¼" high

1587—No marks, probably German, circa 1920, 1" high

1588—Marked Limoges, lovely heart shape, circa 1900, ½" high

1589—No marks, probably French, circa 1900, just over ½" high

1590—Marked Limoges, artist signed & dated 1910, just over ½" high

1591—Marked Limoges, circa 1900, just over ½" high

1592—No marks, shell thin transparent and delicate, interesting mold of square base, then a twist pattern to a square top, European origin, circa 1900, 1½" high

1593—Marked "Royal Stafford, Made in England," circa 1920, 1¼" high, salt is actually crooked and looks bent

1594—Marked with oriental type characters, probably new, just under 1" high

1595—Marked Meissen, circa 1884, just under 1" high

1596—Marked Carlsbad, Austria, just under 1" high, circa 1880

1597—Marked Bavaria, circa 1920, ³/₄" high

1598—No marks, circa 1920, 1" high

1599—No marks, European origin, circa 1930, ³/₄" high

1600—No marks, probably European, "Marie Antoinnette", circa 1890, just under 1" high, could be a butter pat or nut cup

1601—Marked Germany, circa 1920, 1" high

1602—Marked Limoges, France, circa 1920, just over ½" high

1603—Marked Royal Satsuma, Nippon with a plus mark in circle, just under 1" high

1604—No marks, unusual design, European origin, circa 1880, 1¼" high

1605—Marked Germany with 3 Crowns, unidentified mark, circa 1920, just under 1" high

1606-1607—Marked Germany, circa 1920, just under 1" high

1608-1609—Marked, "Noritake, Made in Japan," Green M-in-Wreath Mark, circa 1920, ³/₄" high

CHINA—ASSORTED UNUSUAL SHAPES

1610—Marked France, circa 1900, ³/₄" high

1611—No marks, probably French, circa 1900, ³/₄" high

1612-1613—Marked France, circa 1900, ³/₄" high

1614—No marks, probably French, circa 1900, ³/₄" high

1615—Marked Germany, circa 1920, ³/₄" high

1616—No marks, probably French, circa 1920, 1" high

1617—Marked Germany, 6 tiny feet, circa 1900, just over 1" high

1618—Marked Austria, circa 1900, 1" high

1619-1620—No marks, European shape, circa 1900, just over 1" high

1621—No marks, probably French, circa 1900, 1" high

1622—No marks, circa 1900, European shape, 1" high

1623—Marked Vienna, Austria, circa 1900, 1" high

1624—Marked Czechoslavakia, artist signed, circa 1900, 1" high

1625—Marked Czechoslavakia, circa 1900, just under 1" high

1626—Marked Limoges France, circa 1890, 1¼" high

1627—Marked Wheeling Pottery, circa 1920, 1" high

1628—No marks, probably European, circa 1920, 1" high

1629—No marks, probably Japan, circa 1930, just under 1" high

1630—Marked "Wittelsbach, Germany," circa 1900, just over 1" high

1631—No marks, American, circa 1930, ³/₄" high

1632—No marks, German shape, circa 1900, 1" high

1633—Marked "Porcelain, France" with paper label, new just over 1" high

1634—Marked with blue "Hour Glass" with H above it, very delicate, could be as early as 1850, 1" high

1635—Marked Limoges, circa 1940, 1" high

1636—Marked Royal Austria, circa 1930, 1" high

1637—Marked Wittelsbach, Germany, circa 1900, 1" high

1638—Marked "GDA France," circa 1920, just under 2" high

1639—No marks, has shape of Mt. Washington, but not Mt. Washington glass, circa 1920, 1¼" high

1640—Marked Limoges, France, possibly new, stenciled design, 1" high

1641—Marked Nippon, Red M-in-Wreath mark, circa 1920, 1" high

1642—No marks, European shape, circa 1890, ³/₄" high

1643—Signed with Japanese Kutani mark, circa 1890, 1" high

1644—Signed Lennox, Belleek, silver overlay, circa 1900, 1" high

CHINA—PEDESTAL, FOOTED & PLAIN

1645—Porcelain with metal rim, 3 lobster feet, matches salad bowl of same design attributed to Villeroy and Bock (German), early 19th Century, just over 1½" high

1646—China, probably Germany, could be miniature vase, circa 1930, 2" high

1647—Marked "Made in Germany," could also be miniature vase, circa 1930, 2" high

1648—Like design of 1645 green cauliflower leafs on bottom and forming 3 feet, with cauliflower buds for rest of design, metal rim at top edge, could be circa 1850 Villeroy and Bock, 1½" high

1649—Marked RS Germany, circa 1890, just under 1" high, has slits on sides

1650—Marked Bavaria, circa 1900, 1" high, has slits on side of bowl

1651—Marked Made in Germany, possibly new, stenciled pattern, just over 1" high, could be nut dish

1652—Marked Bavaria, circa 1900, 1" high

1653—Marked Bavaria, has slits on side of bowl, circa 1900, just over 1" high

1654—Bisque, no marks, probably German, circa 1930, just over 2" high

1655—Marked with a Wheel trademark, Germany on leaf base, circa 1930, just under 2" high

1656—Bisque, unmarked, probably German, circa 1870, unusual style, 1½" high

1657—Bisque, probably German, petal shape, circa 1870, just over 1¼" high

1658—Marked Germany, circa 1920, 1¼" high

1659—German Prussia griffin mark, circa 1891-1914, just over 1" high

1660—Marked Germany, artist signed, circa 1920, ³/₄" high, this shape is called "Celery Salt" usually sold in sets with long celery plates

1661—Bisque, probably German, circa 1880, 3" high

1662—No marks, German type, circa 1900, 1³/₄" high

1663—Marked, Made in Germany, celery salt, circa 1900, just under 1" high

1664—Unmarked Royal Bayreuth, circa 1905, 1½" high, unusual and rare

1665—No marks, German type, circa 1930, 1½" high

1666—Marked Bavaria, Royal Bayreuth Blue Mark, circa 1890, just over 1" high

1667—Unmarked Royal Bayreuth, circa 1910, ³/₄" high

1668—Signed Royal Bayreuth master, circa 1900, just over 1" high

1669—Unmarked Royal Bayreuth, part of a set of 6, all with turkeys grazing and mountains in the background, circa 1900, just under ½" high

1670—Signed Royal Bayreuth, part of the set of 6 small and master, turkeys grazing and farmer added to the pattern, circa 1900, just over 1" high

ASSORTED CHINA, ALL OVALS

1671—Danish mark, Bing and Grondahl, circa 1900, just over 1½" high, oval

1672—Royal Copenhagen, circa 1923, just over ½" high, oval

1673—Marked Meissen, circa 1880, 1" high, oval

1674—Marked C & G, Denmark, Bing & Grondahl, new, just over 1¼" high

1675—Marked Bavaria, artist signed Luker, (US), famous violet painter, circa 1900-1910, just over 1" high, see #1346

1676—Marked "Made in England," circa 1950, just over 1¼" high

1677—English, marked RHS Plant, circa 1898, 1¼" high

1678—French, marked Quimper, Stoneware, late 19th Century, just over 1" high

1679—Marked Germany, circa 1900, just over ½" high

1680—Marked Royal Copenhagen, circa 1923, just over 1" high

1681—Marked Meissen, circa 1870, 1" high

1682—English, RHSL Plant, circa 1898, 1½" high

1683—No marks, probably German, circa 1900, 1" high

1684—Marked Quimper, oval, circa late 19th Century, just over 1½" high

1685—Marked Nippon, Green M-in-Wreath Mark, circa 1900, just under 1" high

1686—No marks, probably European origin, circa 1920, 1" high

1687—Marked Nippon, purple mark, could be nut cup, circa 1900, 1¼" high

1688—Marked Japan, copy of German Elfinware, circa 1920, 1½" high

1689—Marked Germany, Dresden, circa 1920, 1½" high

1690—Marked "Made in Japan," Lefton, not old, just under 1" high

1691—English, marked Stoke-on-Trent, circa 1890, 1¼" high

1692—No marks, appears to be German, circa 1920, ¾" high

1693—Marked Limoges, France Elite, circa 1930, just under 1" high

1694—Marked Germany, Souvenir item from Des Moines, Iowa, circa 1920, 1½" high

1695—Marked Leuchlerburg, Germany, circa 1899, just under 1" high

1696—Marked Prussia, Royal Rudolstadt, circa 1900, just under 1" high

1697—Marked "Made in Germany," conch shell, delicate, circa 1880, 2" high

ASSORTED CHINA

1698—4-pc set consisting of salt, pepper, mustard and underplate, European origin, circa 1890, salt is 1¼" high

1699—Double salt with matching tray, European, circa 1920

1700—Pottery chick, the tail is the spoon handle, appears to be Japanese, circa 1930, 2¾" high, could also be mustard pot

1701—China, with Lenox Unicorn mark, silver overlay, unusual and rare, circa 1891, just over 1" high

1702—Same with different design in silver overlay

1703—Pottery duck, the tail is the spoon handle, appears to be Japanese, circa 1930, 2¾" high, could be mustard pot

1704—China celery salt, marked Nippon, Green M-in-Wreath Mark, circa 1920, ½" high

1705—China celery salt, signed Pickard, circa 1920, 1" high

1706—China celery salt, marked Ovington, TV, (England), circa 1920, ¾" high

1707—China, marked Meissen, circa 1884, ¾" high, popular pattern of Meissen

1708—Marked Nippon, red M-in-Wreath Mark, circa 1920, 1" high

1709—Marked Nippon, hand painted, blue flower mark, circa 1900, 1" high

1710—Heart shaped, probably Japan, circa 1930, 1" high

1711—Marked Nippon, Green M-in-Wreath Mark, circa 1920, 1" high

1712—Bavarian blank but probably decorated in U.S. sterling overlay including the garlands, part of a set of 4 with a 5" bowl, indicating perhaps nut dishes

1713—No marks, looks Nippon, circa 1900, just over ½" high

1714—Celery salt, marked Nippon, circa 1920, ¼" high

1715—Marked "Made in Japan," Noritake, Red M-in-Wreath Mark, circa 1920, 1¼" high

1716—China flower, no marks, circa 1940, ¾" high

1717—China lotus on leaf, one piece, probably Japan, circa 1930, 1" high

1718—Celery salt, no marks, probably Nippon, circa 1920, ½" high

1719—Marked "Made in Japan," this salt usually seen with birds on the side, circa 1920, 1½" high

1720—Celery salt, marked Nippon Cornation Ware, circa 1920, ¾" high

1721—Celery salt, marked Nippon, Red Wreath Mark, circa 1920, 1" high

1722—No marks, hollowed out bottom, European origin, circa 1900, 1" high

MISCELLANEOUS CHINA

1723—China, marked Nippon, circa 1920, just over 1" high, could also be butter pat

1724—China, marked "Victoria Czeckoslavakia," circa 1930, just over 1" high

1725—China, no marks, appears to be Japanese, circa 1920, 1¼" high

1726—China, no marks, probably American or Japanese, circa 1930, 1¼" high

1727—No marks, Bavarian mold design, circa 1900, 1" high

1728—China, no marks, European origin, circa 1950, 1½" high

1729—Pottery, signed Quimper, circa 1920, 1" high

1730—Pottery, Majolica type, circa 1930, just over 1½" high

1731—Pottery, same type, circa 1950, just over 1½" high

1732—Pottery, no marks, circa 1940, probably U.S., follows design of very early French lacey salts, 1½" high

1733—Stoneware, age and origin unknown, 1½" high

1734—Pottery, probably U.S., circa 1920, 2" high

1735—Pottery, signed Niloak Pottery, circa 1910-1946, also paper label, just over 1½" high

1736—China, marked Japan, copy of German Elfinware, circa 1920, 1½" high

1737—China, marked Japan, copy of German Elfinware, circa 1920, 1¾" high

1738—China, appears to be German, circa 1920, 1¼" high

1739—China, marked ARABIA, Made in Finland, circa 1930, ½" high

1740—China, marked "Made in Japan," shape of violin, circa 1930, 1" high

1741—China, marked "Made in Japan," green M-in-Wreath Mark, circa 1920, just under 1½" high, probably nut cup

1742—China, marked "Made in Japan," Green M-in-Wreath Mark, circa 1920, just under 1½" high, probably nut cup

1743—China, novelty Wheelbarrel marked Japan, circa 1930, just over 1¼" high

1744—China, novelty auto marked Japan, circa 1930, 1¼" high

1745—China, marked "Made in Japan," circa 1940, just over 1" high

1746—China, no marks, Japanese, circa 1940, 1½" high, could also be designed for nut cup

1747—China, marked "Hand Painted in Hong Kong," circa 1920, ¾" high

1748—China, no marks, circa 1920, 1" high

1749—China, no marks, circa 1920, just over 1" high

1750—China crude beading in scroll design around bowl, origin unknown, circa 1940, 1" high

1751—China, unusual shape and design, quality of Royal Worcester, signed Kutani, circa 1900, 1½" high

1752—China, signed "Made in Ireland," new, just over 1½" high

1753—China, signed "Made in Ireland," new, 1½" high

1754—China, very delicate and transparent, appears to be German, circa 1900, 1½" high

1755—China, artist signed MMD, marked Thomas, hollow bottom, circa 1920, European origin, just over 1" high

1756—China, marked Noritake Nippon, circa 1920, 1" high

MISCELLANEOUS CHINA

1757—Pottery marked Maling, England, circa 1924, just over 2" high

1758—China, marked Charlotte Royal Crown, Iron Stone England, circa 1925, just under 2" high

1759—No marks, china, European, just under 3" high

1760—China, no marks, English, EPNS Rim, circa 1900, salt is 1½" high

1761—Marked V. Foley China, England, circa 1892, 1½" high

1762—China, signed Moorcraft, rim is hallmarked London, England, circa 1920, 1½" high

1763—Signed Cresdent China, England, circa 1900, 1½" high

1764—Marked Made in England, PV, circa 1920, just over 1" high

1765—No marks, English, rim is hall-marked London, England 1900, 2" high

1766—Marked Rye England, Pottery, circa 1891, 1" high

1767—Pottery, marked Gray's Pottery, made in Stoke-on-Trent, England, circa 1912-1930, just over 1" high

1768—No marks, appears to be English, circa 1930, just over 1½" high

1769—Signed Stoke-on-Trent, England, circa after 1894, 1¼" high

1770—Signed Copeland China, England, circa 1891, 1½" high

1771—Signed Shelley China, "Model of bowl from Ancient British Lake Village near Glasstonbury," circa 1900, 1½" high

1772—Marked England, circa 1890, ¾" high

1773—No marks, appears to be English, circa 1920, just over 1" high

1774—Marked "Made in England," artist signed "Cobert," circa 1930, ¾" high

1775—Enamel over pottery, with oriental scenes, probably English, circa 1870, 1½" high

1776—Marked Czeckoslavakia, circa 1920, 1" high

1777—Marked Limoges, France, new, 1" high

1778—Pottery, appears to be English, circa 1930, 1" high

1779—No marks, appears to be hand made, probably U.S., circa 1950, ¾" high

1780—Pottery, no marks, could be English, circa 1940, just over 1" high

1781—Marked Victoria, Czeckoslavakia, circa 1940, just under 1" high, could be nut cup

1782—Marked "Made in Czeckoslavakia," circa 1930, just under 2" high

1783—No marks, Pottery, probably European, circa 1920, 1" high

1784—Signed Bloor Derby, circa 1811-1818, rare salt, just over 1½" high

MISCELLANEOUS CHINA & GLASS

1785—Unusual European porcelain, very delicate with blue enamel dots and pastel flowers, matching spoon, circa 1880, to top of handle 2½"

1786—French, signed Samson, reproduction of very early Chinese porcelain, Coat of Arms indicate Portugal, circa 1880-1890, just under 1½" oval

1787—China, decal type of decoration, signed in script Germany, circa 1940, 2½" high

1788—China, marked made in Germany, circa 1920, 3" to top of handle

1789—Very unusual, has incised numbers indicating Germany, delicate detail, ⅝" x 2" round

1790—Definitely Royal Bayreuth, unsigned, shown on cover, rare, very fine detail even to the beading at the center of the poppy, 1" high

1791—Unglazed china, European, circa 1890, just over 1" high

1792—China, marked Nippon, 3 feet not shown, 1" high, circa 1930

1793—Signed Stouffer, hollow underneath, circa 1920, identical to German mold, just over 1" high

1794—Hand painted, oriental artist signed, 1" high including bird

1795—Exceptional quality of European porcelain, typical of Royal Worcester, matching spoon, just over 1" high, circa 1890

1796—Hand painted, signed Leonard, Vienna, Austria, just over 1" high, circa 1900

1797—No marks, probably Bavarian, circa 1900, 1" high

1798—Transparent china with wrapped babies for legs, very unusual, circa 1910, just under 1½" high

1799—Hand Painted Nippon with gold beading bordering the flowers and center of beaded circles, circa 1900, 1" high

1800—English tin glaze, unidentified mark, circa 1850, 3" high to top of handle

1801—German, signed Bauer Pfeiffer Company, part of a 4 piece set consisting of 2 salts, mustard and tray, circa 1940, 1" high

1802—German, Signed RS Prussia, circa 1869, 1" high

1803—French, signed Quimper, circa 1900, to top of handle 3"

1804-1810—All salts from sets of doll dishes, #1810 has handle ground off

1811—Reproduction by Rockefeller Foundation entitled "Armorial Salt" Ch'ien Lung Period 1736-1795, Arms of family of Sir William Stanley, circa 1978

1812-1814—German, all signed Meissen with crossed swords, all 1½" high, oval, circa 1880-1900

MISCELLANEOUS CHINA

1815—Signed Lenox, with Silver overlay, circa 1920, just under 1" high

1816—Signed Nippon, green M-in-Wreath Mark, 1" high, circa 1920

1817—Signed Haviland, circa 1893, 1" high

1818—Signed GHR Bavaria, circa 1900, 1¼" high

1819—Signed Royal Bavarian, circa 1900, 1" high

1820—Signed O&EG Austria, ¾" high, circa 1900

1821—Signed Made in Western Germany, new just under 1½" high

1822—Signed France, very delicate, 1¼" high, circa 1890

1823—China, signed Crowned Staffordshire, circa 1889-1912, just over 1" high

1824—Signed Nehur Depose (French), just over 1" high, circa 1930

1825—No marks, Bavarian type mold, hollow bottom, just under 1¼" high, circa 1920

1826—No marks, oriental design, circa 1930, 1" high

1827—Unsigned, 3 pattern leafs on the bottom for short feet, circa 1910, 1" high

1828—No marks, coloring and mold identical to Japanese Kutani, circa 1920, 1½" high

1829—Signed GOA France, circa 1890, just over 1" high

1830—No marks, identical to Nippon molds, circa 1910, just over 1" high

1831—Heavy porcelain, signed France, probably new, just under 1¼" high

1832—Signed with Dresden mark of 20th Century, just over ½" high

1833—Signed Royal Kaga Nippon, circa 1920, just under 1¼" high

1834—Signed Limoges, circa 1910, ¾" high

1835—Unsigned Nippon, unusual decoration inside and out, circa 1900, 1" high

1836—Signed Germany, very delicate china, circa 1890, 1" high

1837—No marks, unglazed china, circa 1900, just under 1¼" high

1838—No marks, Nippon type mold, circa 1920, 1½" high

1839—No marks, identical to Bavarian molds, circa 1890, 1" high

1840—No marks, Nippon mold, circa 1920, just under 1½" high

1841—Signed Haviland, tableware pattern, circa 1880, ¾" high

1842—Unmarked, probably Bavarian, circa 1900, ¾" high

1843—No marks, Austrian mold, circa 1890, just over 1" high

1844—Signed Good Friend Spain, not old, just over 1½" high

ENGLISH POTTERY AND PORCELAIN

1845—Signed Wedgwood, Made in England, circa 1952, under 2" high

1846—Signed Wedgwood, Made in England, circa 1956, 1¾" high

1847—Signed Wedgwood, Made in England, called "Basalt", age uncertain 1¾" high

1848—Signed Doulton, Lambeth, combination of salt & toothpick (by turning over) Sterling rim hallmarked Birmingham 1891, just under 3" high

1849—Signed Tunstain, England, Adams, hallmarked 1902, 1½" high

1850—Signed Wedgwood, sterling rim, no date marks, circa 1900, 1½" high

1851—Signed Doulton, Lambeth England, hallmarked on sterling rim, Birmingham 1897, 1½" high

1852—Signed Doulton, Lambeth England, circa 1900 just over 1" high

1853—Signed Doulton Lambeth, hallmarked sterling rim, Birmingham 1896, 1¾" high

1854—Unsigned, appears to be mold of Tunnicliffe & Co Ltd, England, hallmarked London 1886, 1¼" high

1855—Unsigned, appears to be mold of Tunnicliffe & Co Ltd, England, hallmarked London 1886, 1¼" high

1856—Signed Taylor Tunnicliffe & Co Ltd, England, hallmarked London, circa 1889, unusual and rare, 1" high

1857—Signed Gresley, Made in England, heavy ironstone pottery, circa 1940, 1" high

1858—Signed Doulton Lambeth, hallmarked on sterling rim, Birmingham 1870, just over 1½" high

1859—Unmarked Royal Doulton, England, plated rim, circa 1890, 1½" high

1860—Signed Royal Doulton, plated rim, circa 1890, just over 1½" high

1861—Signed Worcester mark of circa after 1862, double wall, unusual and rare, 1¼" high

1862—Signed Gresley Pottery, Made in England, circa 1940, 1" high

1863—Signed Taylor Tunnicliffe & Co Ltd, England, unusual and rare, circa 1875-1898, 1½" high

1864—Signed Worcester, England, double wall, unusual and rare, circa after 1862, also signed with an entwined W & N, 1¼" high

1865—Signed Locke & Co., Worcester, England, plated rim, circa 1902, 2" high

1866—Signed Doulton Lambeth, England, circa 1870, 1½" high

1867—Unsigned Jasperware, plated rim, circa 1900, 1½" high

1868—Appears to be a imitation of above Wedgwoods, detail and coloring not of Wedgwood quality, could be German, circa 1900, 1¼" high

1869—Signed Doulton Lambeth, circa 1877, 1½" high

1870—Signed Royal Doulton, hallmarked sterling rim London 1873, just over 1" high

1871—Signed Wedgwood Etruria, circa 1900, plated rim, 1½" high

MISCELLANEOUS ORIENTAL SALTS & NOVELTY ITEMS

1872—Exceptionally beautiful, artist signed, 3 feet, not shown in picture, circa 1900, just over 1" high

1873—Unsigned, appears to be old, just over 1" high

1874-1875—Marked Hand Painted Japan, sometimes called Satsuma. Satsuma made both old and new in various shapes and sizes. Has crackle in glaze of pottery, circa 1920, 1" high, see #1903

1876—Chinese Rose Canton with butterflies, circa 1900, just under 1" high

1877—Japanese, artist signed, circa 1880, 1½" high

1878—Japanese, artist signed, crackle glaze, not old, see #1903, thousand birds, just under 1" high

1879—Signed China, incised floral pattern, enameled, circa 1900-1920, 1" high

1880—Chinese Peking glass, signed China, rare with lid included, circa 1890, just under 3" to top of lid

1881—No marks, probably Chinese, circa 1910, 1" high

1882—Korean Poo Ware, circa 1890, most generally seen in much larger pieces of many animals and people, very collectible and hard to find, could be brush washer, 1¾" high

1883-1888—Chinese, miniature lily pot made for the children of China, known in our country as "Chinese Export". They complement our salt collections and are hard to find, 1" high

1889—Japanese, crackle glaze, probably part of a set of four of various shapes, artist signed, 1¼" high

1890—Same type and similar to above row, but smaller in size, under 1" high

1891—Japanese, artist signed, typical of old Kutani ware, 3 tiny feet not shown in picture, circa 1900, 1½" high

1892—Japanese, artist signed, crackle glaze, circa 1920, 1" high, see #1903

1893—Japanese, artist signed, similar to #1874-1875 and probably part of a 4-piece set, see #1903

1894—Japanese, artist signed, circa 1900, just over 1" high

1895-1901—All of these have incised outlined patterns according to their designs. Questionable as to what they were, actually. My Chinese source indicates they were made for the children to play with. An American oriental dealer reports they were a novelty item made for export. Another dealer reports they were used for ink when signing with their character stamp. Circa 1900-1920, 1" high, round or square. #1899, appears to be much older.

1902—Korean Poo Ware, could be a sauce dish, circa 1890, just under 1" high

1903—Set of 4, new, purchased in Japan 1979, each is ½" high by approx. 1" across. Pamphlet included will clarify much of this crackle finish. "Satumayaki," the beautifully crackled pottery which has made the name Satsuma known to the whole artistic world, is produced at Kagoshima in Kyushu.

1904—Chinese, beautiful detail on the "1000 faces", just under ½" high, circa 1880

1905—Another "1000 Faces", circa 1880, ¾" high

1906—See #1878, #1903

MISCELLANEOUS ORIENTAL SALTS & NOVELTY ITEMS

1907-1924—All carved soapstone in interesting shapes, some were novelty items, age unknown, 2-3" high

1925—Chinese, see #1883-1888

1926—Porcelain, signed Kutani in the Japanese character, circa 1920, 1½" high

1927—Pottery, Chinese, age unknown, just over 1" high, could be sauce dish

1928-1929—Porcelain, signed China, incised patterns, could also be sauce dishes, circa 1900-1920, ¾" high

1930—Porcelain, round, appears to be bottom portion of like #'s 1895-1901, circa 1900-1920, ¾" high

1931-1933—See #1903 previous page

1934—Oriental artist signature on bottom, just under 1½" high, could also be sauce dish

1935—Carved Jade stone, engraved China, age unknown, 1½" high

1936—Porcelain, signed Kutani character, circa 1880, 1¼" high

1937—Porcelain, marked China, circa 1900, just over 1" high

1938—Incised pattern, could also be sauce dish, just over 1" high

1939—Porcelain, marked China, incised pattern design, circa 1920, could be egg cup, just over 2" high

1940—Enamel over brass, not cloisonne, hollow handle representing tree branch with leaves holding salt. "China" enameled into pattern on the bottom, circa 1890, 1½" high

1941—Marked China, could be sauce dish, circa 1920, 1" high

1942—Unmarked, probably Chinese, lots of gold trim with beading around edge, circa 1910, ¾" high

1943-1944—Cloisonne, unsigned Chinese, shown from the bottom side, circa 1920, ⅝" high

ORIENTAL CARVED, STONE & MISCELLANEOUS

1945—Carved quartz, probably Chinese, age unknown, 1½" high

1946—Carved nut shells, beading at top handle held together by wire. Center bead has magnifying glass and inside has map, picture and religious writing. This could be a ceremonial item. Liner not original, without handle 2" high

1947—Carved teakwood consisting of 5 sections all held together by a large ivory screw from the bottom, probably Chinese, just over 3" high, age unknown

1948 — Carved soapstone, could also be a novelty item 3½" high

1949 — Matching cloisonne salt & pepper, available currently as new

1950 — Carved Jadeite, one of a kind item, just under 1" high, purchased Switzerland 1975

1951 — Enamel over copper, Chinese, women on adjacent sides with a tree scene on the back side

1952 — Lacquer with pearl inlay for design, lined with sterling, circa 1870, 1½" high

1953 — Same 1¾" high

1954 — Carved stone with dragon on side, probably Chinese, age unknown, 1" high

1955-1956 — Rose quartz, purchased in Switzerland 1975, just under 1" high

1957 — Carved Jade on sterling base, probably Chinese, just over 1" high

1958 — Carved quartz on sterling ring, just under 1" high, age unknown

1959 — Enamel over metal, sterling base, double wall, Chinese, circa 1880, 1" high

1960 — Peking glass, one of set of 6, of different colors, matching spoons, ¾" high

1961 — Cloisonne, Chinese, unusual shape, 1" high, age unknown

1962 — Peking glass, Chinese, circa 1920, 1" high

1963 — Coral, part of a set of 4, all with carved bone spoons depicting totem poles, age unknown, 1½" high, from Alaska

1964 — Chinese cloisonne, dragon pattern, circa 1920, just over 1" high

1965 — Inlaid Israeli turquoise over copper, age unknown, just over 1" high

1966-1968 — Carved quartz with sterling trim, Chinese, approx. 1" high, #1968, ¾" high

1969 — Carved agate, age and origin unknown, 1" high

1970 — Mother of Pearl slats, held together by brass bands, bottom also Mother of Pearl, just under 1½" high, may have had handle

1971 — Chinese cloisonne, circa 1920, just over 1" high

1972 — Enamel over sterling base, no marks, European, age and origin unknown, just over 1" high

ALL CLOISONNE & ENAMELS

1973 — Cloisonne, signed China, circa 1910, could be sake cup, 1½" high

1974-1975 — Enamel over brass, delicate paintings on each side, circa 1920, Chinese, 1¼" high

1976 — Interesting enamel over copper with peacock legs, signed China, have seen this with matching pepper, Chinese, circa 1890, 1¼" high

1977 — See #1974

1978 — No marks, see #1973

1979-1984 — See #1973, all signed China except #1983, #1984

1985 — Very unusual cloisonne, no marks, Chinese, circa 1890, salt is 1" high

1986-1987 — Matching salt & peppers, Cloisonne, unsigned, circa 1920, salts are 1" high

1988 — Unsigned Cloisonne, circa 1920, 1" high

1989 — Cloisonne, signed China, circa 1910, 1" high

1990 — Enamel over sterling, Norway, circa 1880, opals individually set around top and bottom, just over 1" high

1991-1993 — Unmarked Chinese of the older types, 1" high circa 1910

1994-1996 — Matching salt & peppers of the newer types, circa 1970

1997 — Signed China, circa 1920, just over 1" high

1998 — Unsigned, Chinese, not old, just under 1" high

1999 — See row above, not old

2000 — Enamel over copper, signed China, scenic design, circa 1920, ½" high

2001 — See #1997, unsigned

ENAMEL & METALS

2002 — Enameled, gold wash over sterling, hallmarked Nórway 925 Sterling, age uncertain, 2" high, glass liner, also available new

2003 — Plique de jour. This is an ancient art of painting layers of enamel over a metal base, then the base removed leaving the enamel iridescent. Hallmarked Norway with the sterling base hallmarked Birmingham, England 1900, 3" high

2004 — Russian Enamel, gold wash bowl, hallmarked 1880, 1½" high

2005 — Identical to #2002 except for enamel coloring

2006 — Enamel over sterling with gold wash, blown and etched glass liner, matching spoon. Very fine detail, tiny opals individually set around bowl of salt and spoon. Hallmarked sterling 925, European origin, probably Norway, circa 1920, 1" high

2007 — Russian enamel hallmarked 875 sterling, purchased new in 1975, gold wash over sterling, matching spoon, just under 1½" high

2008 — Same, 1" high

2009 — Russian enamel, pressed glass liner, lesser quality, brass base, circa 1940, just over 1" high

2010 — Carved bone with enamel trim, age and origin unknown

2011 — Inlaid abalone shell over sterling base, matching spoon, new, 925 sterling, Mexico — 1" high

2012 — Enamel over sterling, gold wash, hallmarked Denmark 925S, age unknown, currently available new, salt is ¾" high. These are also now made in Mexico and marked accordingly

2013-2014 — Enamel over sterling, hallmarked Denmark 925S, age unknown, also available new, 1" high

2015 — Chinese cloisonne with underplate, note American flag with 12 stars, could be sake cup, circa 1880, 1½" high

2016-2020 — French enamel, not of the quality of either Norway or Russian, cut glass liners, matching spoons, circa 1920, 1" high. #2009 has a different shape on the underplate and enameling

2021 — Carved jade with gold wash over sterling lining and base, age and origin unknown, just under 2" high

2022 — Russian enamel over sterling, hallmarked and dated 1896, just under 2" high

2023 — Chinese pottery lined with sterling, incised enameling, age unknown but old, teak base. Base and salt just over 1½" high

2024 — Enamel over sterling, European, marked 935 Sterling, rare and very unusual, just over 1½" high

2025 — Sterling with jade rim, enameled flowers on rim and feet, very unusual, probably Chinese, age unknown, 1½" high

2026 — Russian enamel, not old, same type as #1999, circa 1940, 1½" high

2027 — English battersea, enamel over copper, has three different scenes around salt, rare and unusual, also seen in pink coloring, circa 1870, just over 1" high

2028 — Bronze and brass with enameling around waist, enameling design identical to #2019. this comes apart in four sections plus glass insert all held together by a permanently soldered screw on the top side of the bottom plate. European origin, probably French, late 19th Century.

LATE ADDITIONS (Glass & China)

2029 — W. H. Goss porcelain, Model of Ancient Salt Cellar, reg. #605731, circa 1920, just over 3" high

2030 — French porcelain, probably a small mustard pot, pattern matches Fig. 2044, circa 1900, just over 2" high

2031 — GEORGIAN pattern nut cup by Fenton, deep ruby color, from the 1930's, this pattern also made by several others in slightly different shapes, see also Fig. 508

2032 — English purple slag, rare pedestal Hobnail salt, no trademarks, circa 1880, 2½" high

2033 — Plated silver with no hallmarks, ruby colored salt holder, ornate Victorian, circa 1880, 2½" high

2034-2035 — Sterling with glass inlay, Frank. M. Whiting Co., also signed with Gorham "G", glass is blown into silver frame and protrudes through the framework, circa 1900, just under 1" high with opal and cobalt inlay

2036 — French blue bristol with enamel decoration, circa 1890, rectangular, 1¼" high

2037 — Unsigned Tiffany-type salt, iridescent blown art glass, maker unknown, circa 1900, 1" high

2038 — Amethyst, signed Hawkes, with etching, very unusual in color, circa 1920, 1½" high

2039 — Black Amethyst, oval shape, cut starred base, six flutes, after 1900, just under 1" high

2040 — Reproduction of Victorian novelty from recent years, possibly Mexican

2041 — Unsigned Steuben jade nut cup, same shape as on page 56, opal stem, 1¾" high

2042 — English yellow cased glass, EPNS rim, no marks, circa 1910, 1¾" high

2043 — Canary or "vaseline" D & B canoe salt, made by Hobbs, circa 1890, under 1" high

2044 — Sterling with cobalt liner (not orig.), marked Germany 800, after 1891, just under 1" high

2045 — Sterling with cobalt, Holland hallmarks, circa 1910, 1½" high

2046 — Sterling with cobalt, h.m. Germany 800, after 1891, not orig. liner, 1¾" high

2047 — Cut black amethyst in honeycomb design, cut star base, European circa 1900, just under 1" high

2048 — Sterling frame with replaced liner, h.m. 800, origin unknown but definitely European, turn-of-the-Century, 1½" high

2049 — China, signed Austria, circa 1890, just over 1" high

2050 — China, signed Lenox, circa 1900, ⅝" high

2051 — China, very delicate, no marks, circa 1890, just over 1" high

2052 — China, no marks, circa 1920, 1" high

2053 — China, no marks, Austrian mold, circa 1920, 1¼" high

2054 — French porcelain matches mustard pot (Fig. 2020), same crest design on back, circa 1900, 1" high

2055 — China, French blank (HR France), hand painted by noted American china decorater "Luker" (violets a specialty), circa 1910, 1" high

2056 — Plated holder with replaced liner, no marks, age unknown, 1¾" high

2057 — Ruby-stained Florene pattern base to small covered dish, New Martinsville Glass, circa 1915, frequently sold as a master salt, tops usually souvenired, 1¾" high

2058 — Plated frame with Bohemian ruby cut insert, Toronto Silver Plate Co., matching spoon with same trademark, circa 1895, 1¾" high not including handle

LATE ADDITIONS IN COLORED GLASS

2059 — Sterling with no hallmarks, European, cobalt liners, circa 1880, 1¾" high not including handle

2060 — Amber-stained with cut-back, definitely European circa 1880, 3½" high, rare

2061 — European Sterling, double salt with delicate cranberry holders, circa 1850, 2¾" high not including handle

2062 — Sterling 800, Continental Silver, fox figural at top of handle with orig. spoons with fox-tails for handles, just under 4" high to head of fox, cobalt liners

2063 — Sterling, hallmarks from Holland, circa 1811 with import marks to Italy, molded liner in cobalt was apparently inserted while still cooling as it shows detail of holder's open design, 3¾" high to top of handle, oval

2064 — English double salt, emerald green inserts, unmarked plated over copper, circa 1880, 1½" high not including handle

2065 — French bristol with delicate enamel decor, brass trim, circa 1890, 1½" high

2066 — English cranberry glass in frame with handle, plated over brass, circa 1870, 2" high not including handle

2067 — Green cased glass with ornate handled frame and lid, marked "Made in Austria", circa 1920, 3½" high to top of handle

2068 — Ruby-stained molded liner in plated frame, marked "Schiffers", American, circa 1895, 1½" high not including handle

2069 — Same as Fig. 460

2070 — D&B oval tub-shaped salt with wire handle, maker unknown, circa 1895, 3" long

2071 — Rare chocolate glass salt in Honeycomb, this is actually the THOUSAND EYE BAND pattern (Metz 2, 130) also made in very rare individual salt, circa 1903, just over 3" diam.

2072 — Green blown salt with applied clear rigaree, scarce in ind. size, polished top rim, circa 1890, 1½" high

2073 — Bohemian etched pedestal salt, German, circa 1890, 2¼" high

2074 — Emerald green MT. VERNON pattern by Cambridge, signed, circa 1920, 2¼" high

2075 — Cranberry polished liner in a hand-made gold plated ornate frame, very early, European, circa 1850-60, oval shape, 1½" high

2076 — Deep cranberry insert, plated over copper, oval, American, no marks, just under 1½" high

2077 — Rose colored salt in EPNS frame, circa 1920, English, just over 1" high

2078 — English cranberry glass with applied rigaree and feet, circa 1890, 1¾" high

2079 — Czechoslovakian Intaglio-type salt (see pgs. 34-35), design of Victorian couple holding hands, brass holder orig. had jewelled ornamentation, circa 1920, 1¼" high

2080 — English rubina art glass, EPNS holder, circa 1890, just under 2" high (see pg. 28)

2081 — Westmoreland blue frosted glass duck, circa 1920's, 2" to top of head, 5¼" long

2082 — Sterling 800 with cobalt inserts, 4 horses pulling salt, European origin of recent vintage, blown liners seem new, under 1½" high

2083 — Blue reproduction of Greentown glass wheelbarrow, signed St. Clair, 2" high

2084 — Amber novelty wagon or cart, maker unknown, American, circa 1895, 2" high

2085 — Blue STARS & BARS figural flat-car, Findlay glass, circa 1890, 2" high

2086 — Apple green D&B canoe by Hobbs, rare in amberina, circa 1890, 1" high

2087 — See Fig. 794 for information

2088 — Another European double salt, probably French, bird handle, circa 1900, 3" high to head

2089 — French blue opaline pressed double, circa 1920, 1¼" high

LATE ADDITIONS IN COLORED GLASS

2090 — Green opalescent unusual rectangular salt, ornate pattern, signed Sowerby, England, registry mark dates from Sept. 18, 1879, 2" high

2091 — Rose colored pressed salt, English, circa 1900-1910, maker unknown

2092 — Rose colored salt, double with spoon rests, unusual, circa 1940, Cambridge #339 "Twin"

2093 — Rose colored FANCY COLONIAL salt by Imperial Glass Co. (WDG2, 156), circa 1920's, part of a complete set, 2" high

2094 — Triangular shape, rose color, pressed with polished edges, cut star base, circa 1920, less than an inch high

2095 — Six-sided, rose colored, Cambridge #2933 salt, cut star each side and bottom, circa 1915-25, under 1" high

2096 — Amethyst DIAMOND QUILTED pattern, scarce color, see notes Fig. 430, circa 1890

2097 — See Notes. Fig. 518 for this scarce color

2098 — Vaseline colored "Octagon" salt, made by many companies, see notes Fig. 327

2099 — Reproduction D&B salt by L.G. Wright, never made old in this shape, 1½" high

2100 — Amber-stained FINECUT & BLOCK pattern by King Glass (also U.S.), just over 1" high

2101 — See notes Fig. 552 on this amber example

2102—Amber Block pattern salt with attached reclining dog, Central Glass 1880's, 1" high

2103—See notes Fig. 197 on this rare amber salt

2104—Amber pedestalled salt in Cambridge Glass' DECAGON pattern salt, rare in amber or any color, circa 1925-30, just under 2" high

2105—Emerald green six-sided cut & bevelled salt, cut star base, maker unknown, circa 1900, ³⁄₄" high

2106—Cranberry threaded glass over crystal, sterling rim hallmarked Birmingham 1901, made In England, about 1" high

2107—YUTEC pattern salt in rare blue color, possibly a novelty in this color, made by McKee in the early 1900's, design does not match "mother" pattern, ³⁄₄" high

2108—Waffle design on base of polished square cobalt salt, rare color, maker uncertain, circa 1890, just under 1" high

2109—Blue AETNA NO. 300 (KS,SS) tub-shape salt, Aetna Glass, circa 1887, 1¹⁄₂" high

2110—Periwinkle blue colored cut and bevelled rectangular salt, Czechoslovakian, circa 1920, 1¹⁄₂" high, scarce

2111—Footed nut cup in Topaz color with original Cambridge paper label, circa 1930's, 2¹⁄₂" diam.

2112—Honey amber salt in Central's PRESSED DIAMOND pattern, circa 1880, 1" high

2113-2116—Four marigold-flashed iridescent salts by Westmoreland Glass (Reprint W), also known to have been made earlier (circa 1890) by Dalzell at Findlay (SM FIN, pg. 63). The Westmoreland production dates from circa 1915-25. See also Figs. 3017-3027

2117—Amber French lacy salt, reproduction of Neal #OP 15, see Fig. 390

2118—Another amber lacy pressed glass salt, probably French, circa 1900, 1¹⁄₂" high

2119—Smith Bros. decorated, melon rib salt, see others on page 26, 1¹⁄₄" high

2120—Shiny opal with hint of gold decoration, Same as Fig. 46, 4 tiny feet, 1¹⁄₄" high

2121—Emerald green blown salt with unusual silver decoration, English or French, circa 1915, just over 1" high

ROUND SHAPES—FLAT TOP—PRESSED

2500 2501 2502 2503 2504 2505

2506 2507 2508 2509 2510 2511

2512 2513 2514 2415 2516

2517 2518 2519 2520 2521

2522 2523 2524 2525 2526 2527

2528 2529 2530 2531

Please see pages 152, 159, 160, 161, 162, 163 & 165 for additional examples of round shapes, flat tops, pressed.

ROUND SHAPES—FLAT TOP—PRESSED

2532	2533	2534	2535	2536	2537
2538	2539	2540	2541	2542	2543
2544	2545	2546	2547	2548	2549
2550	2551	2552	2553	2554	
2555	2556	2557	2558	2559	
2560	2561	2562	2563	2564	

ROUND SHAPES—FLAT TOP—PRESSED

2565

2566

2567

2568

2569

2570

2571

2572

2573

2574

2575

2576

2577

2578

2579

2580

2581

2582

2583

2584

2585

2586

2587

2588

2589

2590

2591

2592

2593

NOTES:

ROUND SHAPES—FLAT TOP—PRESSED

2594 2595 2596 2597 2598

2599 2600 2601 2602 2603

2604 2605 2606 2607 2608 2609

2610 2611 2612 2613 2614

2615 2616 2617 2618 2619

2620 2621 2622 2623

ROUND SHAPES—UNEVEN TOPS—PRESSED

2624 2625 2626 2627 2628

2629 2630 2631 2632 2633 2634

2635 2636 2637 2638 2639 2640

2641 2642 2643 2644 2645

2646 2647 2648 2649 2650

2651 2652 2653 2654

Please see pages 152, 160, 161, 162, 163 & 165 for additional examples of Round Shapes, uneven tops, pressed.

ROUND SHAPES—UNEVEN TOPS—PRESSED

2655	2656	2657	2658	2659	2660
2661	2662	2663	2664	2665	
2666	2667	2668	2669	2670	2671
2672	2673	2674	2675	2676	
2677	2678	2679	2680	2681	2682
2683	2684	2685	2686	2687	

NOTES:

OVAL SHAPES—PRESSED

2688

2689

2690

2691

2692

2693

2694

2695

2696

2697

2698

2699

2700

2701

2702

2703

2704

2705

2706

2707

2708

2709

2710

2711

2712

2713

2714

Please see pages 160, 161, 162, 163 & 165 for additional examples of pressed glass ovals.

OVAL SHAPES—PRESSED

2715   2716   2717   2718

2719   2720   2721   2722

2723   2724   2725   2726

2727   2728   2729   2730

2731   2732   2733   2734

2735   2736   2737   2738

SQUARE SHAPES—PRESSED

2739 2740 2741 2742 2743 2744

2745 2746 2747 2748 2749 2750

2751 2752 2753 2754 2755

2756 2757 2758 2759 2760 2761

2762 2763 2764 2765 2766 2767

2768 2769 2770 2771 2772 2773

Please see pages 144,158,160,161,162,163 & 165
for additional examples of square shapes, pressed.

RECTANGULAR SHAPES—PRESSED

2774   2775   2776   2777   2778

2779   2780   2781   2782   2783

2784   2785   2786   2787   2788

2789   2790   2791   2792   2793

2794   2795   2796   2797   2798

2799   2800   2801   2802   2803

ASSORTED SHAPES—PRESSED

2804   2805   2806   2807   2808

2809   2810   2811   2812   2813   2814

2815   2816   2817   2818   2819   2820

2821   2822   2823   2824   2825   2826

2827   2828   2829   2830   2831   2832

2833   2834   2835   2836

2837   2838   2839   2840   2841

2842   2843   2844   2845   2846

2847   2848   2849   2850   2851

2852   2853   2854   2855   2856

2857   2858   2859   2860

2861   2862   2863   2864   2865

MULTI–SIDED SHAPES—PRESSED

2866 2867 2868 2869 2870

2871 2872 2873 2874 2875

2876 2877 2878 2879 2880

2881 2882 2883 2884 2885

2886 2887 2888 2889 2890

2891 2892 2893 2894 2895

Please see pages 151, 152, 160, 162 & 165 for additional examples of Multi-sided shapes—pressed.

FACETED & HONEYCOMB MOTIFS—CUT & PRESSED

FOOTED SALTS

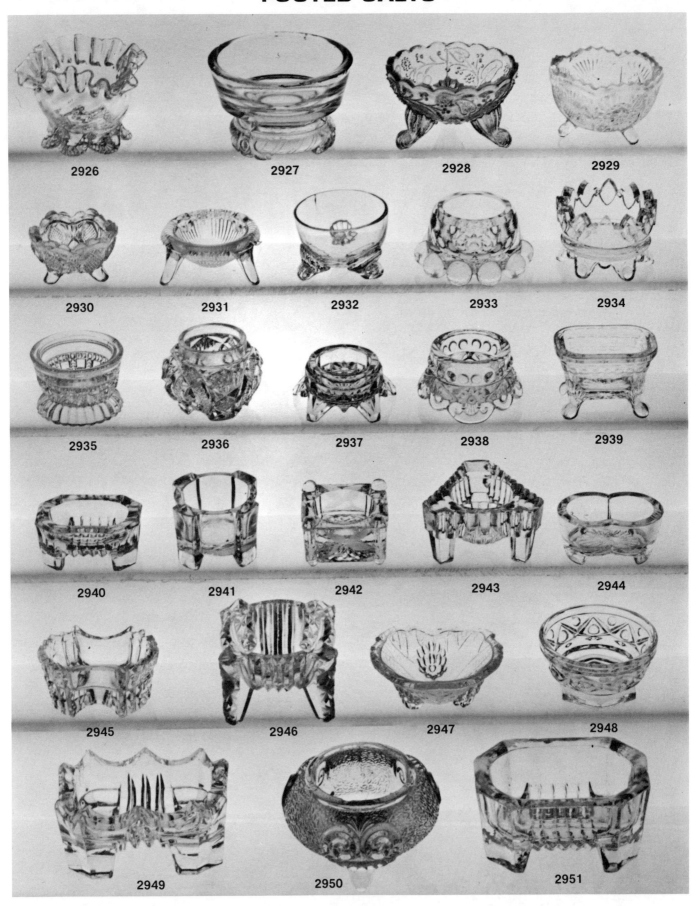

2926

2927

2928

2929

2930

2931

2932

2933

2934

2935

2936

2937

2938

2939

2940

2941

2942

2943

2944

2945

2946

2947

2948

2949

2950

2951

See pages 152, 159, 160 & 163 for additional examples
of footed salts—pressed.

PEDESTAL-BASED SALTS

2952   2953   2954   2955   2956

2957   2958   2959   2960   2961   2962

2963   2964   2965   2966   2967   2968

2969   2970   2971   2972   2973

2974   2975   2976   2977   2978   2979

2980   2981   2982   2983

149

PEDESTAL-BASED SALTS

2984   2985   2986   2987

2988   2989   2990   2991   2992

2993   2994   2995   2996   2997

2998   2999   3000   3001   3002

3003   3004   3005   3006

3007   3008   3009   3010   3011

**See pages 152, 159, 161, 162 & 163 for additional examples
of pedestal-based pressed salts.**

UNUSUAL SHAPES—PRESSED & CUT

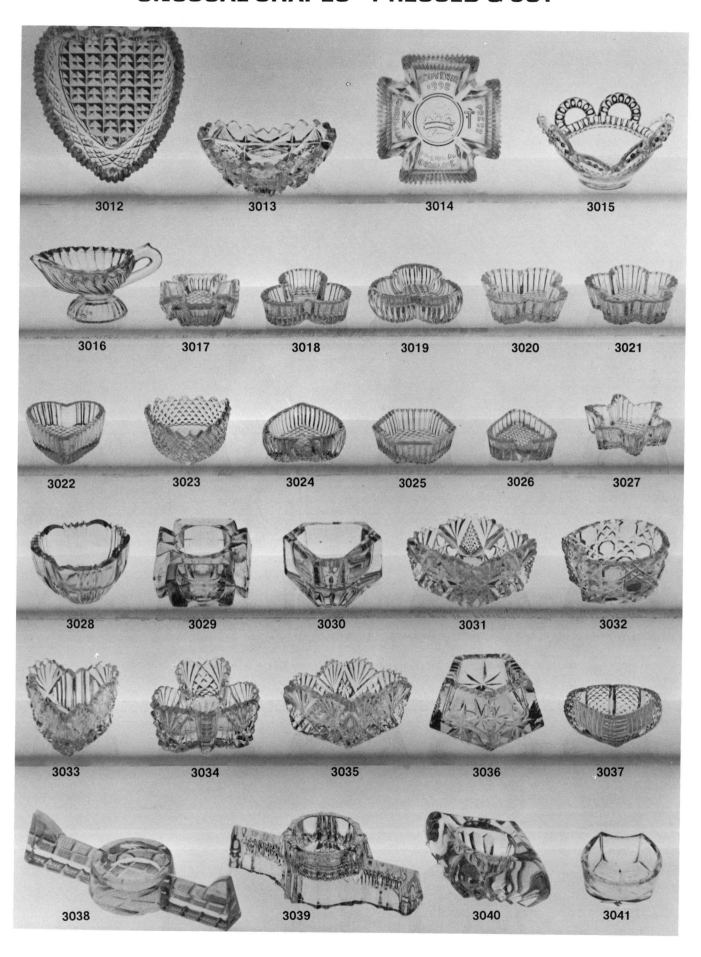

3012

3013

3014

3015

3016

3017

3018

3019

3020

3021

3022

3023

3024

3025

3026

3027

3028

3029

3030

3031

3032

3033

3034

3035

3036

3037

3038

3039

3040

3041

PATTERN GLASS & CUT GLASS—VARIOUS SHAPES

3042 3043 3044 3045 3046 3047

3048 3049 3050 3051 3052 3053

3054 3055 3056 3057 3058

3059 3060 3062 3063

3061

3064 3065 3066 3067 3068

3069 3070 3071 3072 3073

NOTES:

CUT GLASS—ROUND SHAPES—FLAT TOPS

3074 3075 3076 3077 3078 3079

3080 3081 3082 3083 3084 3085

3086 3087 3088 3089 3090 3091

3092 3093 3094 3095 3096 3097

3098 3099 3100 3101 3102 3103

3104 3105 3106 3107 3108

NOTES:

CUT GLASS—ROUND SHAPES—FLAT TOPS

3109 3110 3111 3112 3113

3114 3115 3116 3117 3118

3119 3120 3121 3122 3123

3124 3125 3126 3127 3128

3129 3130 3131 3132 3133

3134 3135 3136 3137

NOTES:

CUT GLASS—ROUND—UNEVEN TOPS

3138 3139 3140 3141 3142
3143 3144 3145 3146 3147
3148 3149 3150 3151 3152
3153 3154 3155 3156 3157
3158 3159 3160 3161 3162
3163 3164 3165 3166 3167

155

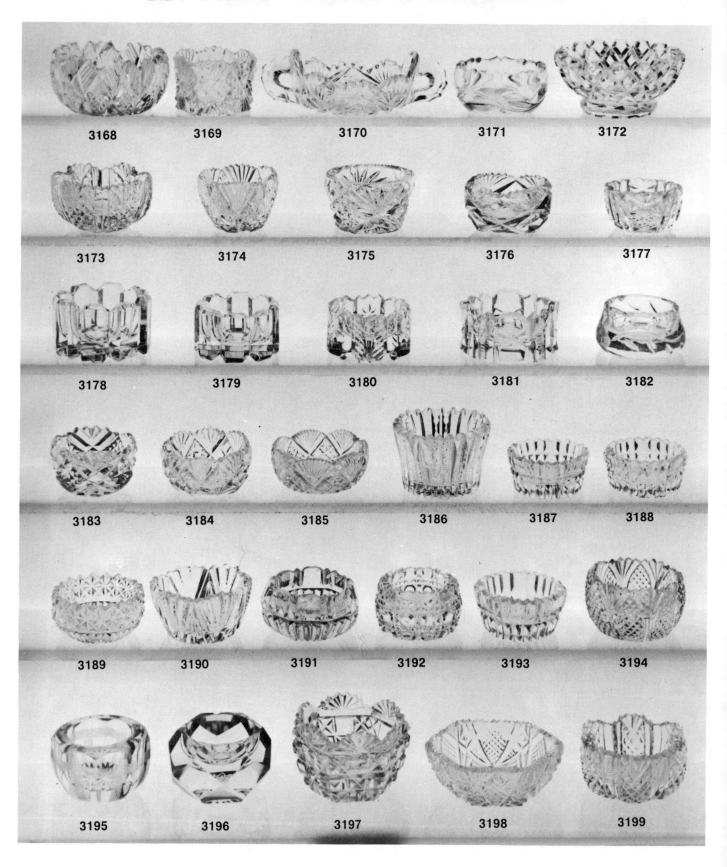

3168	3169	3170	3171	3172
3173	3174	3175	3176	3177
3178	3179	3180	3181	3182
3183	3184	3185	3186	3187	3188
3189	3190	3191	3192	3193	3194
3195	3196	3197	3198	3199

NOTES:

CUT GLASS—OVAL SHAPES

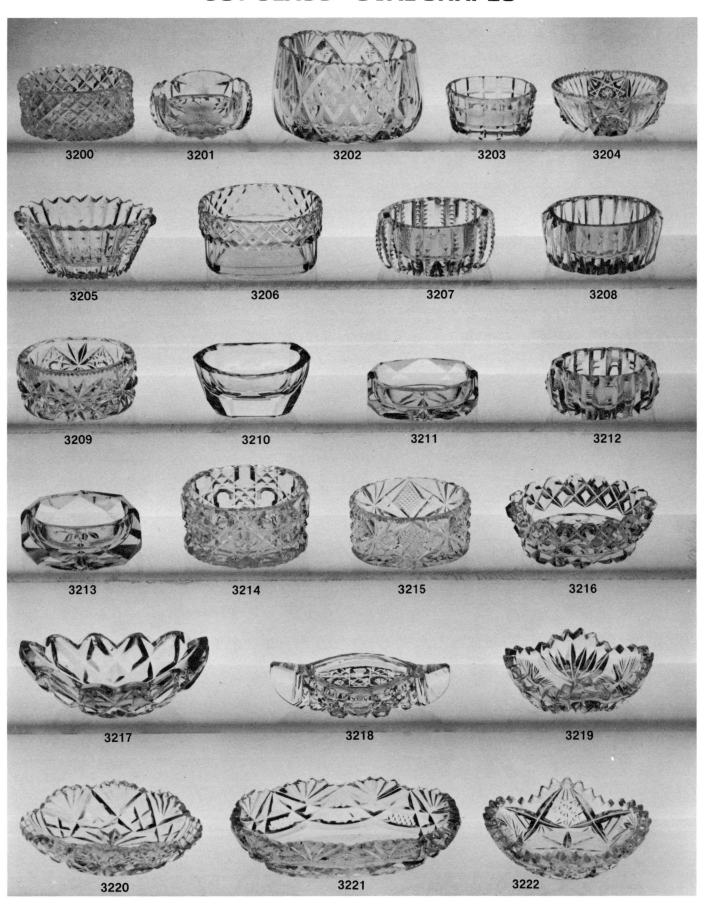

3200 3201 3202 3203 3204

3205 3206 3207 3208

3209 3210 3211 3212

3213 3214 3215 3216

3217 3218 3219

3220 3221 3222

CUT GLASS—SQUARE SHAPES

3223   3224   3225   3226   3227   3228

3229   3230   3231   3232   3233   3234

3235   3236   3237   3238   3239   3240

3241   3242   3243   3244   3245   3246   3247

3248   3249   3250   3251   3252   3253

3254   3255   3256   3257   3258   3259

MISCELLANEOUS SALTS—PRESSED & CUT

3260   3261   3262   3263

3264   3265   3266   3267

3268   3269   3270   3271   3272   3273

3274   3275   3276   3277   3278

3279   3280   3281   3282   3283

3284   3285   3286   3287

MISCELLANEOUS SALTS—PRESSED & CUT

3288   3289   3290   3291   3292   3293

3294   3295   3296   3297   3298   3299

3300   3301   3302   3303   3304

3305   3306   3307   3308   3309

3310   3311   3312   3313   3314

3315   3316   3317   3318

NOTES:

MISCELLANEOUS SALTS—PRESSED & CUT

3319	3320	3321	3322	3323
3324	3325	3326	3327	3328	3329
3330	3331	3332	3333	3334
3335	3336	3337	3338	3339	3340
3341	3342	3343	3344	3345
3346	3347	3348	3349	3350

NOTES:

MISCELLANEOUS SALTS—PRESSED & CUT

3351 3352 3353 3354

3355 3356 3357 3358 3359

3360 3361 3362 3363 3364 3365

3366 3367 3368 3369 3370

3371 3372 3373 3374 3375

3376 3377 3378 3379

NOTES:

MISCELLANEOUS SALTS—PRESSED & CUT

3380

3381

3382

3383

3384

3385

3386

3387

3388

3389

3390

3391

3392

3393

3394

3395

3396

3397

3398

3399

3400

3401

3402

3403

3404

3405

3406

3407

3408

3409

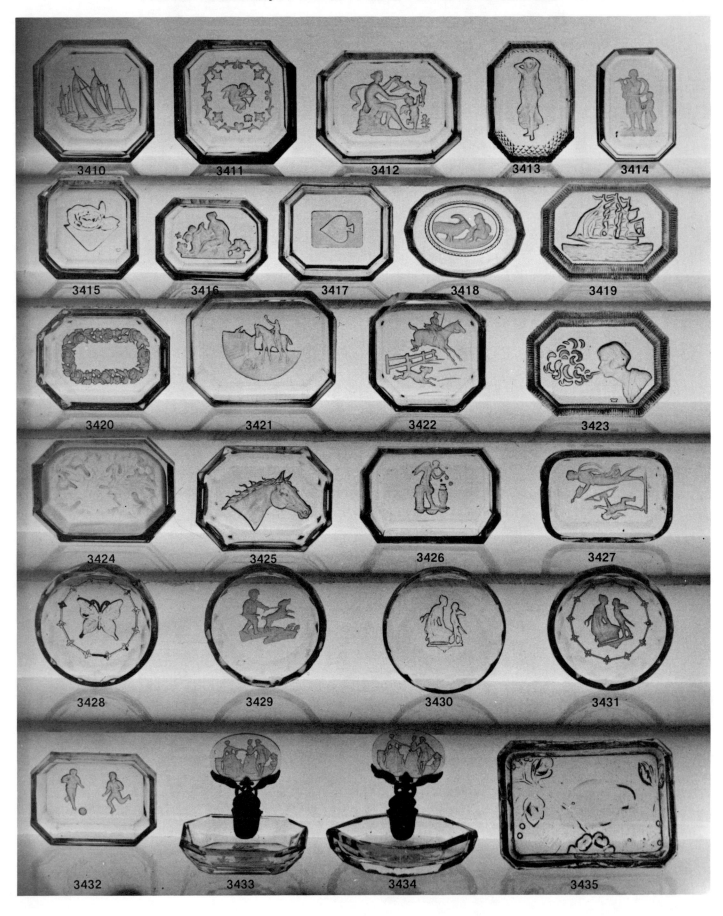

NEW SALTS IN CRYSTAL—INDIVIDUAL SIZE

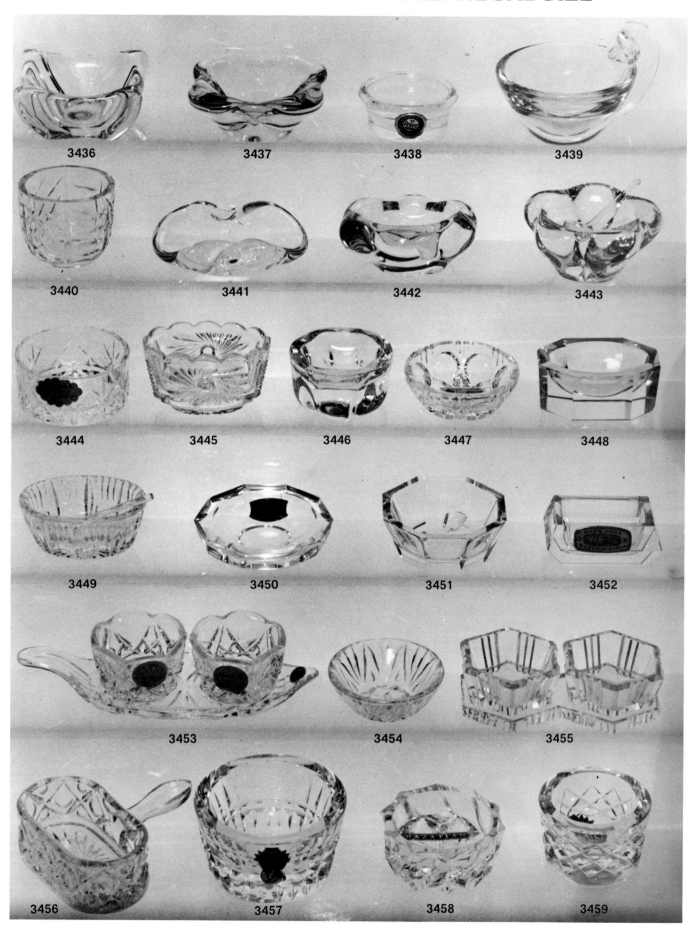

3436

3437

3438

3439

3440

3441

3442

3443

3444

3445

3446

3447

3448

3449

3450

3451

3452

3453

3454

3455

3456

3457

3458

3459

PRESSED GLASS SALTS OF THE LACY PERIOD

3460

3461

3462

3463

3464

3465

3466

3467

3468

3469

3470

3471

3472

3473

3474

3475

3476

3477

PRESSED GLASS SALTS OF THE LACY PERIOD

3478

3479

3480

3481

3482

3483

3484

3485

3486

3487

3488

3489

NOTES:

PRESSED GLASS SALTS OF THE LACY PERIOD

3490   3491   3492   3493

3494   3495   3496

3497   3498   3499

3500   3501   3502

NOTES:

LACY SALTS—OLD—NEW—QUESTIONABLE

3503

3504

3505

3506

3507

3508

3509

NOTES:

PATTERN GLASS—OVAL MASTERS—PRESSED

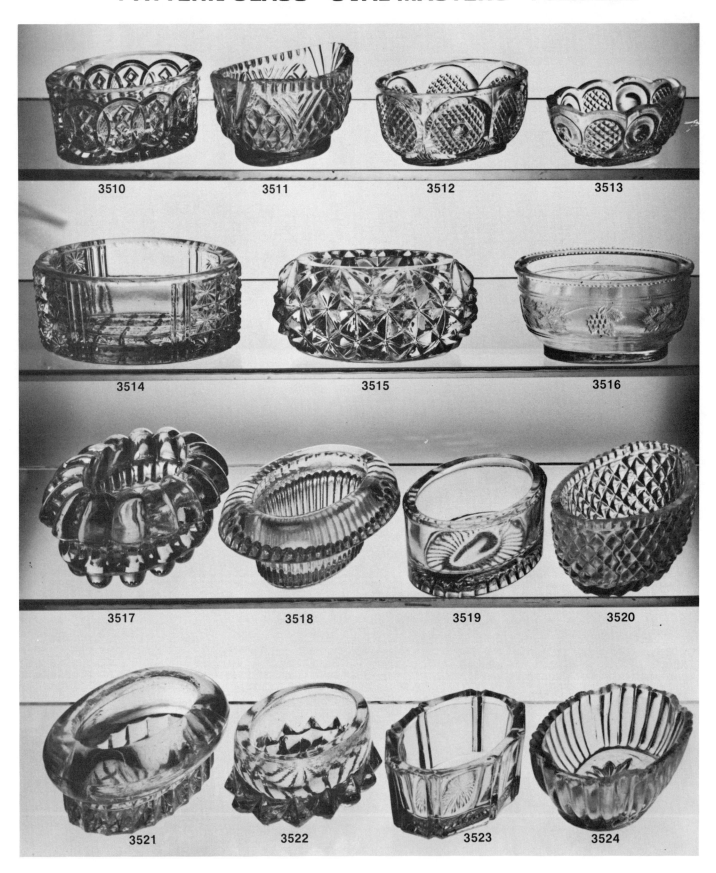

3510   3511   3512   3513

3514   3515   3516

3517   3518   3519   3520

3521   3522   3523   3524

NOTES:

3525 3526 3527 3528

3529 3530 3531 3532

3533 3534 3535 3536

3537 3538 3539 3540

PATTERN GLASS—STEMS OR PEDESTALS
PRESSED—MASTERS

3541
3542
3543
3544
3545
3546
3547
3548
3549
3550
3551
3552
3553
3554
3555

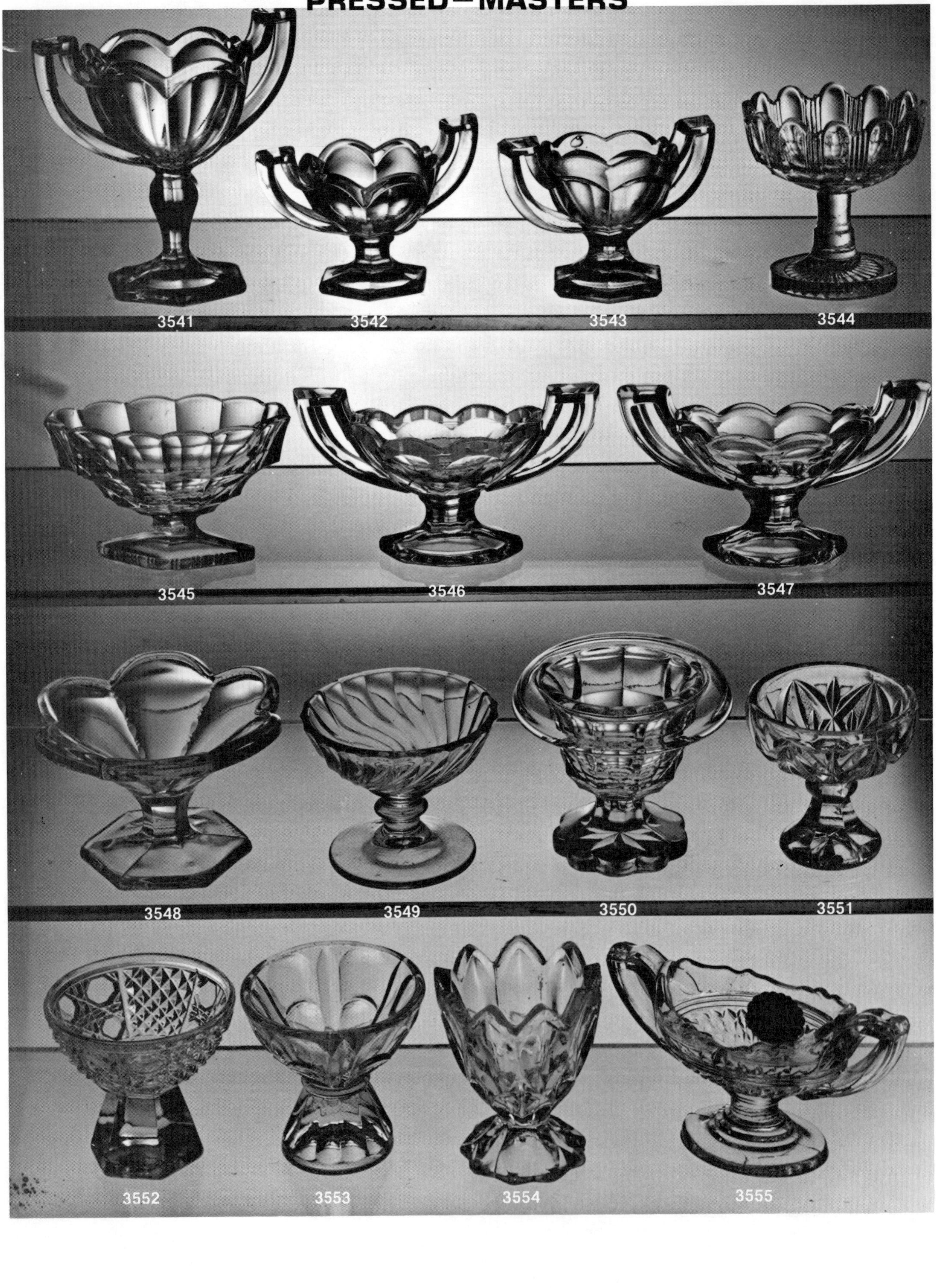

PATTERN GLASS—PRESSED—MASTERS

3556   3557   3558   3559

3560   3561   3562   3563

3564   3565   3566   3567

3568 3569 3570 3571

3572 3573 3574 3575

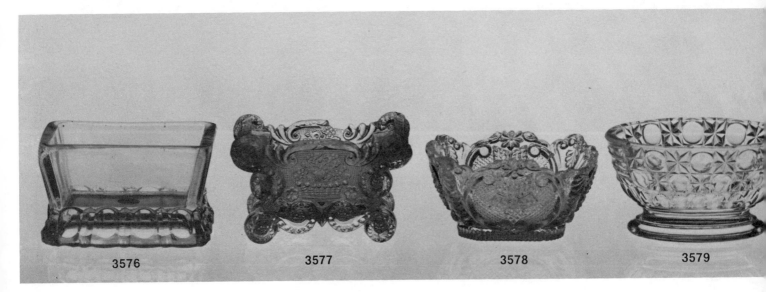

3576 3577 3578 3579

3580 3581 3582 3583
3584 3585 3586 3587
3588 3589 3590 3591
3592 3593 3594 3595

3596 3597 3598 3599
3600 3601 3602 3603
3604 3605 3606 3607
3608 3609 3610 3611

NOTES:

3612

3613

3614

3615

3616

3617

3618

3619

3620

3621

3622

3623

3624

3625

3626

PATTERN GLASS—PRESSED—MASTERS

3627

3628

3629

3630

3631

3632

3633

3634

3635

3636

3637

3638

3639

RECTANGULAR MASTERS—PRESSED

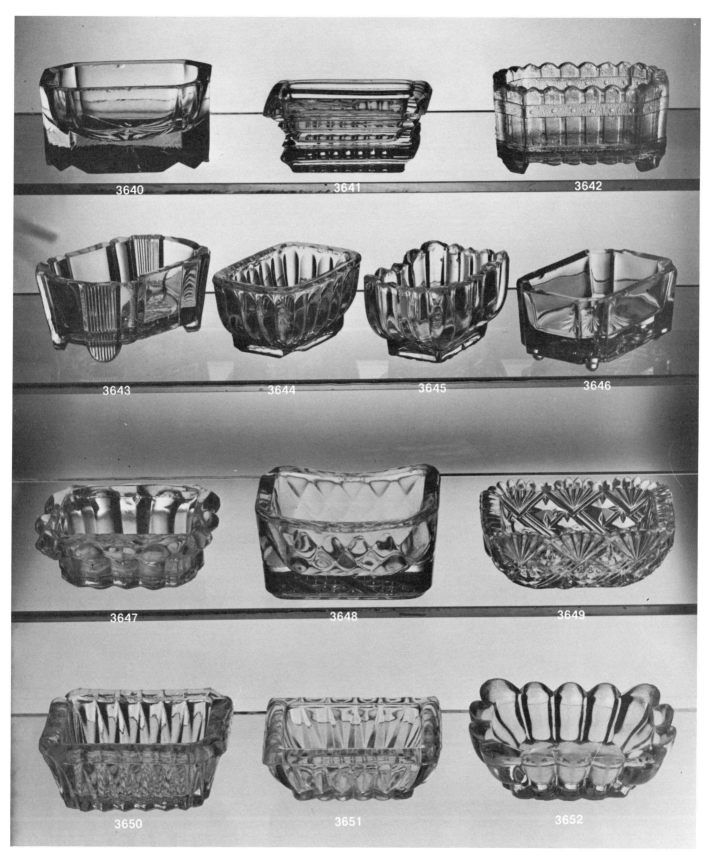

3640 3641 3642

3643 3644 3645 3646

3647 3648 3649

3650 3651 3652

NOTES:

PRESSED GLASS MASTERS

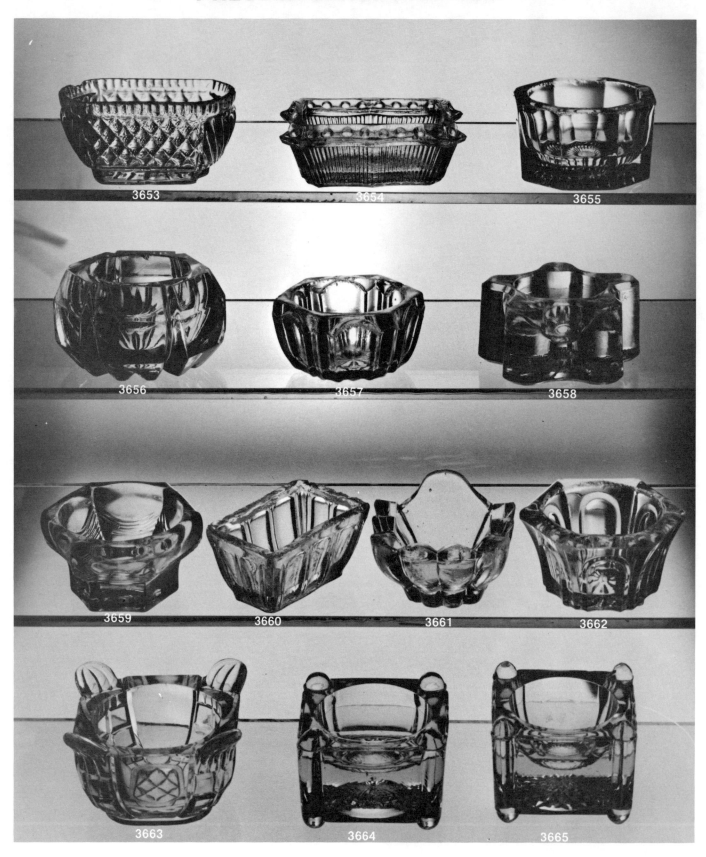

3653   3654   3655

3656   3657   3658

3659   3660   3661   3662

3663   3664   3665

NOTES:

PRESSED GLASS MASTERS

3666
3667
3668
3669
3670
3671
3672
3673
3674
3675
3676
3677

NOTES:

CUT GLASS MASTERS

3692 3693 3694

3695 3696 3697

3698 3699 3700

3701 3702 3703 3704

CUT GLASS MASTERS

3705

3706

3707

3708

3709

3710

3711

3712

3713

3714

3715

3716

CUT GLASS MASTERS

3717   3718   3719

3720   3721   3722

3723   3724   3725

3726   3727   3728

VICTORIAN NOVELTIES

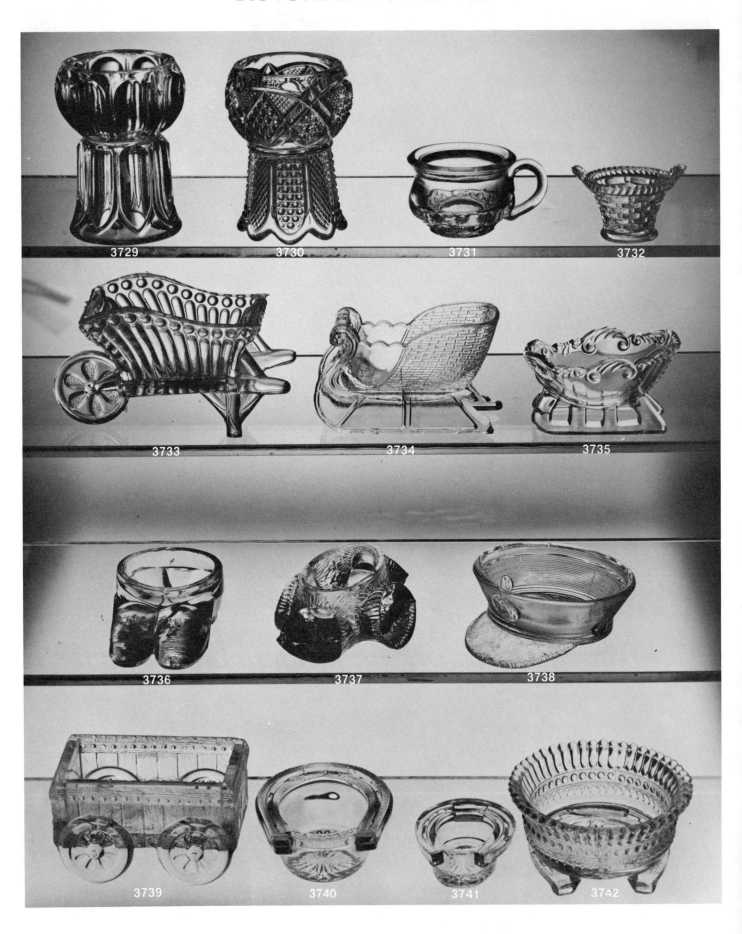

3729   3730   3731   3732

3733   3734   3735

3736   3737   3738

3739   3740   3741   3742

ANIMALS—PRESSED GLASS

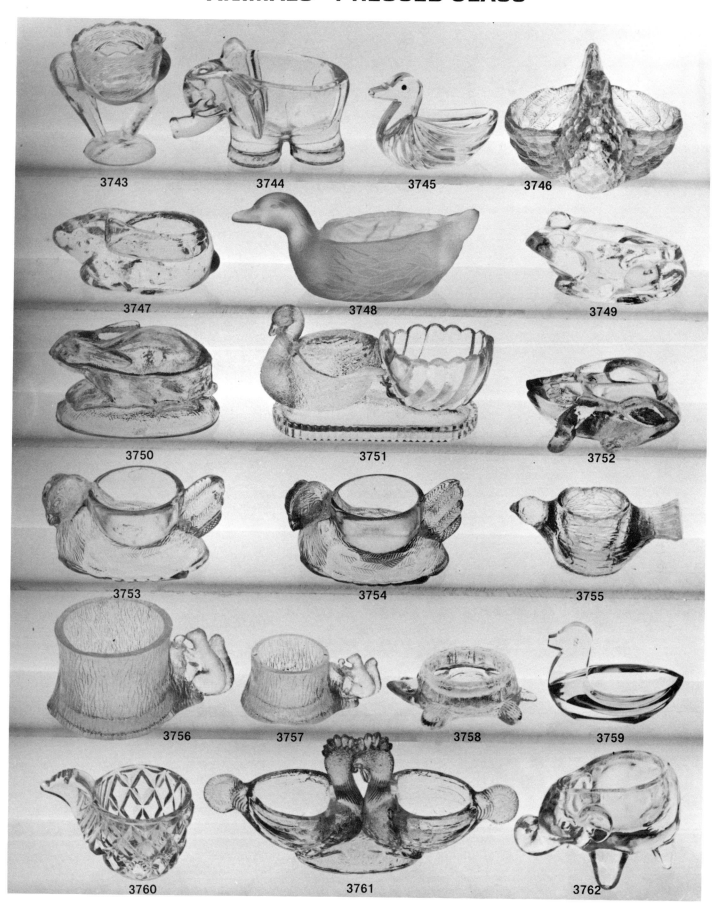

3743

3744

3745

3746

3747

3748

3749

3750

3751

3752

3753

3754

3755

3756

3757

3758

3759

3760

3761

3762

DOUBLES—PRESSED GLASS

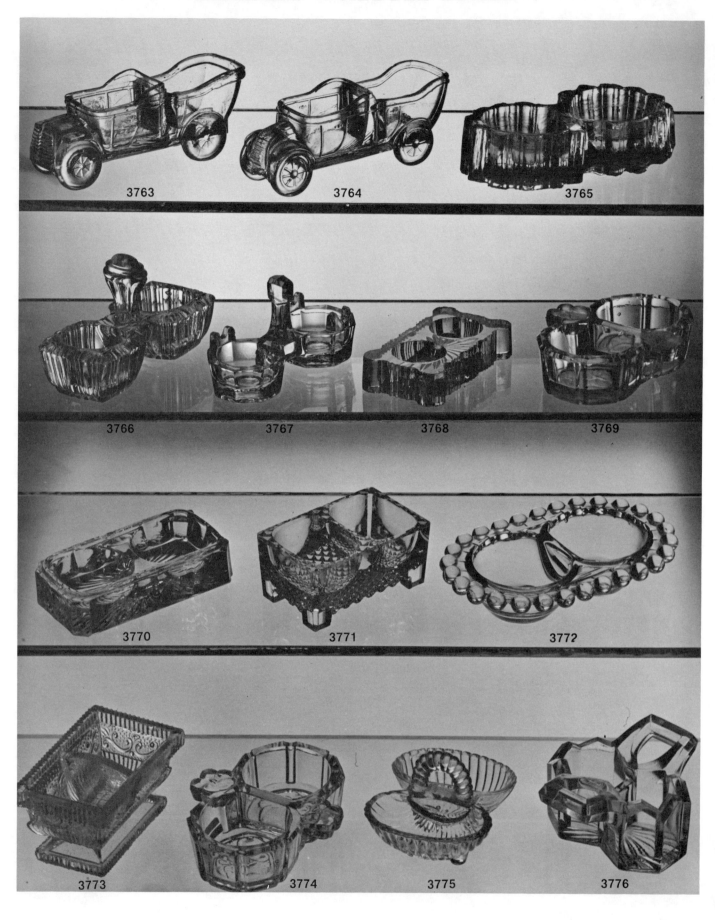

3763

3764

3765

3766

3767

3768

3769

3770

3771

3772

3773

3774

3775

3776

EUROPEAN DOUBLES—PRESSED GLASS

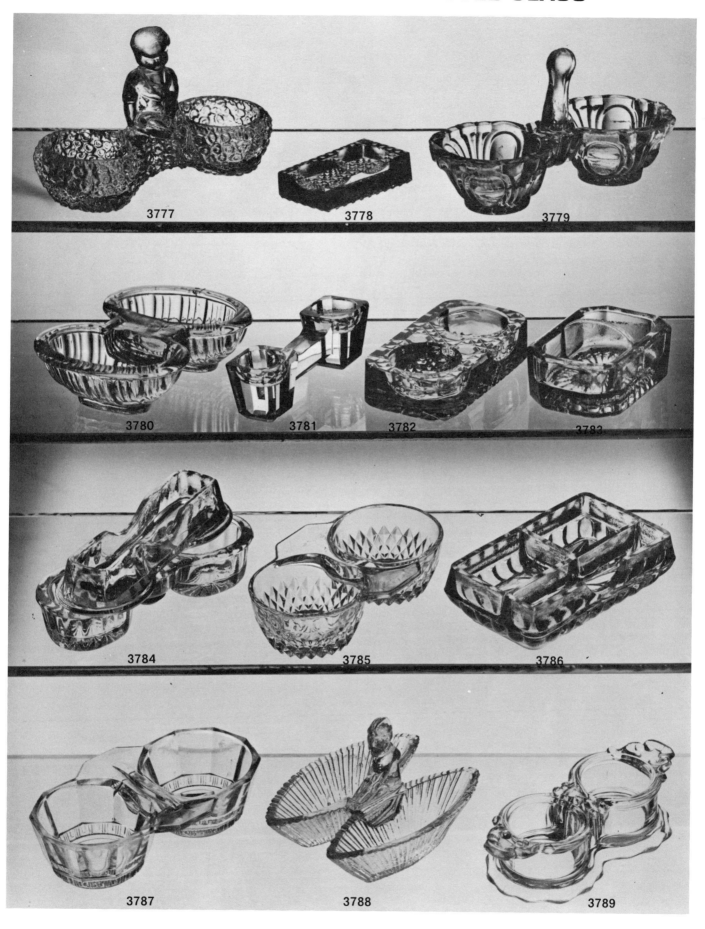

3777

3778

3779

3780

3781

3782

3783

3784

3785

3786

3787

3788

3789

3790

3791

3792

3793

3794

3795

3796

3797

3798

3799

3800

3801

EUROPEAN DOUBLES—PRESSED GLASS

3802   3803   3804

3805   3806   3807

3808   3809   3810

3811   3812

EUROPEAN DOUBLES – PRESSED GLASS

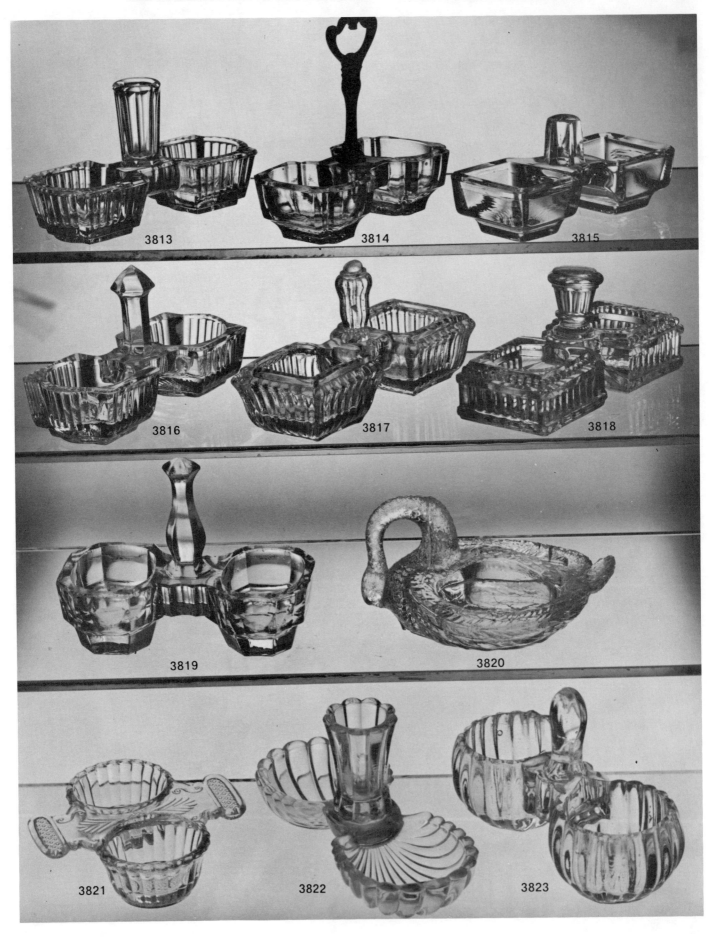

3813

3814

3815

3816

3817

3818

3819

3820

3821

3822

3823

MISCELLANEOUS SILVER & GLASS—PRESSED & CUT

3824

3825

3826

3827

3828

3829

3830

3831

3832

3833

3834

3835

3836

3837

3838

3839

3840

3841

3842

3843

3844

3845

3846

3847

3848

3849

3850

3851

3852

3853

3854

3855

3856

3857

3858

3859

GLASS WITH SILVER TRIM

3860   3861   3862   3863   3864

3865   3866   3867   3868   3869

3870   3871   3872   3873   3874

3875   3876   3877   3878   3879

3880   3881   3882   3883   3884

3885   3886   3887   3888   3889

GLASS WITH SILVER TRIM

3890

3891

3892

3893

3894

3895

3896

3897

3898

3899

3900

3901

3902

3903

3904

3905

3906

3907

3908

3909

3910

3911

3912

3913

3914

3915

3916

STERLING & PLATED WITH GLASS INSERTS

3917 3918 3919 3920 3921
3922 3923 3924 3925 3926 3927
3928 3929 3930 3931 3932
3933 3934 3935 3936 3937
3938 3939 3940 3941 3942
3943 3944 3945 3946

STERLING & PLATED—MISCELLANEOUS SHAPES

3947   3948   3949   3950   3951

3952   3953   3954   3955   3956

3957   3958   3959   3960   3961   3962

3963   3964   3965   3966   3967   3968

3969   3970   3971   3972   3973   3974   3975

3976   3977   3978   3979

STERLING & PLATED—ALL FLAT BASES

3980   3981   3982   3983   3984   3985

3986   3987   3988   3989   3990   3991

3992   3993   3994   3995   3996   3997

3998   3999   4000   4001   4002   4003   4004

4006   4007   4003   4009   4010   4011   4012

4013   4014   4015   4016   4017

NOTES:

STERLING & PLATED—PEDESTAL & FLAT BASES

4018 4019 4020 4021 4022

4023 4024 4025 4026 4027

4028 4029 4030 4031 4032 4033

4034 4035 4036 4037 4038

4039 4040 4041 4042 4043 4044

4045 4046 4047 4048

STERLING & PLATED—ALL FOOTED

4049　4050　4051　4052

4053　4054　4055　4056

4057　4058　4059　4060　4061

4062　4063　4064　4065　4066

4067　4068　4069　4070

4071　4072　4073　4074

STERLING & PLATED—MISCELLANEOUS SHAPES

4075   4076   4077   4078

4079   4080   4081   4082   4083

4084   4085   4086   4087

4088   4089   4090   4091   4092

4093   4094   4095   4096

4097   4098   4099   4100

NOTES:

STERLING & PLATED—FOOTED & PEDESTAL

4101   4102   4103   4104

4105   4106   4107   4108   4109   4110   4111

4112   4113   4114   4115   4116

4117   4118   4119   4120   4121   4122   4123

4124   4125   4126   4127   4128   4129

4130   4131   4132   4133

4134

4135

4136

4137

4138

4139

4140

4141

4142

4143

4144

4145

4146

4147

4148

4149

4150

4151

4152

4153

4154

4155

4156

4157

4158

4159

4160

4161

4162

STERLING & PLATED—FOOTED

4163   4164   4165   4166   4167

4168   4169   4170   4171   4172

4173   4174   4175   4176   4177

4178   4179   4180   4181   4182

4183   4184   4185   4186   4187

4188   4189   4190   4191

4192

4193

4194

4195

4196

4197

4198

4199

4200

4201

4202

4203

4204

4205

4206

4207

4208

4209

4210

4211

4212

4213

4214

4215

4216

4217

4218

4219

4220

4221

4222

4223

4224

4225

4226

4227

4228

4229

4230

4231

4232

MISCELLANEOUS STERLING & PLATED

4233

4234

4235

4236

4237

4238

4239

4240

4241

4242

4243

4244

4245

4246

4247

4248

4249

4250

4251

4252

4253

4254

4255

NOTES:

STERLING & PLATED FIGURALS

4256   4257   4258   4259

4260   4261   4262   4263   4264

4265   4266   4267   4268   4269   4270

4271   4272   4273   4274   4275   4276   4277

4278   4279   4280   4281   4282

4283   4284   4285   4286

4287

4288

4289

4290

4291

4292

4293

4294

4295

4296

4297

4298

4299

4300

4301

4302

4303

4304

4305

4306

4307

4308

4309

4310

4311

4312

4313

4314

4315

4316

4317

4318

4319

4320

4321

4322

4323

4324

4325

4326

4327

4328

4329

4330

4331

4332

4333

4334

4335

4336

4337

4338

4339

4340

4341

4342

4343

4344

4345

4346

4347

4348

4349

4350

4351

4352

4353

4354

4355

4356

4357

4358

4359

STERLING & PLATED ORIENTAL

4360

4361

4362

4363

4364

4365

4366

4367

4368

4369

4370

4371

4372

4373

4374

4375

4376

4377

4378

4379

4380

4381

4382

4383

4384

4385

4386

4387

4388

STERLING, PLATED, PEWTER & POTTERY

4389   4390   4391   4392   4393

4394   4395   4396   4397

4398   4399   4400   4401   4402

4403   4404   4405   4406   4407   4408

4409   4410   4411   4412   4413

4414   4415   4416   4417   4418

NOTES:

FROSTED, MERCURY & MILK GLASS

4419 4420 4421 4422

4423 4424 4425 4426 4427

4428 4429 4430 4431 4432 4433

4434 4435 4436 4437

4438 4439 4440 4441 4442

4443 4444 4445 4446

NOTES:

OPAQUE WHITE & MILK GLASS

4447

4448

4449

4450

4451

4452

4453

4454

4455

4456

4457

4458

4459

4460

4461

4462

4463

ASSORTED MILK GLASS

4464

4465

4466

4467

4468

4469

4470

4471

4472

4473

4474

4475

4476

4477

4478

4479

4480

4481

4482

4483

4484

4485

4486

4487

4488

4489

4490

MISCELLANEOUS WHITE CHINA

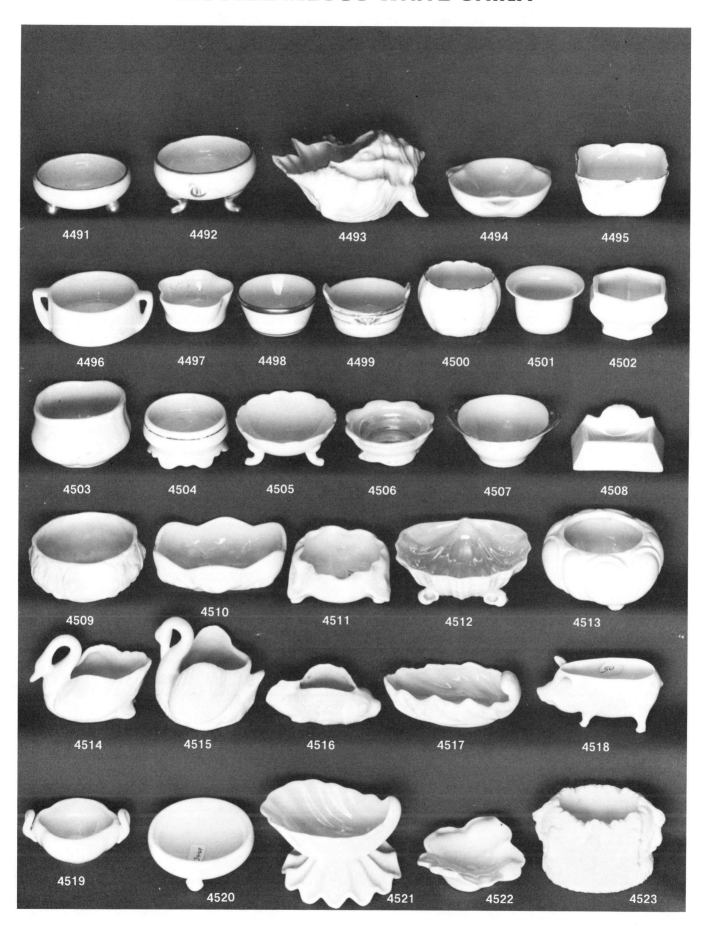

4491 4492 4493 4494 4495

4496 4497 4498 4499 4500 4501 4502

4503 4504 4505 4506 4507 4508

4509 4510 4511 4512 4513

4514 4515 4516 4517 4518

4519 4520 4521 4522 4523

MISCELLANEOUS VARIETIES

4524

4525

4526

4527

4528

4529

4530

4531

4532

4533

4534

4535

4536

4537

4538

4539

4540

4541

4542

4543

4544

4545

4546

CHINA & POTTERY

4547

4548

4549

4550

4551

4552

4553

4554

4555

4556

4557

4558

4559

4560

4561

4562

4563

4564

4565

4566

4567

4568

4569

4570

4571

4572

221

4573

4574

4575

SALT

4576

4577

4578

4579

4580

4581

4582

Go aisy wi' the salt

4583

4584

4586

4587

4588

4589

4590

MISTAKEN IDENTITIES

4591
4592
4593
4594
4595
4596
4597
4598
4599
4600
4601
4602
4603
4604
4605
4606
4607
4608
4609
4610
4611
4612
4613
4614
4615
4616
4617

NOTES:

MISCELLANEOUS
LATE ADDITIONS & CLOSE-UPS

On the next several pages are pictured a number of salts which were photographed as spotted in antique shows and private collections. Most of the English examples were from the outstanding collection of Mr. Cyril Manley of England. Many more of his salts are shown in Book 4 of the Lagerberg series on **Collectible Glass** (out-of-print) and in Mr. Manley's own recently published book **Decorative Victorian Glass.** Some of the photographs were taken to illustrate close-up detail of reproduc-

tions. Others were purchased after the major photography was discontinued, but were considered too unique to wait for any future editions of this book. Unfortunately, because many of these were photographed "on the run" at shows, I occasionally failed to note the name of the dealer displaying the salt. My apologies for this oversight, and my sincerest appreciation for your permission to capture your treasure on film. Measurements are unknown on many examples. Most are individual size. A few are table size.

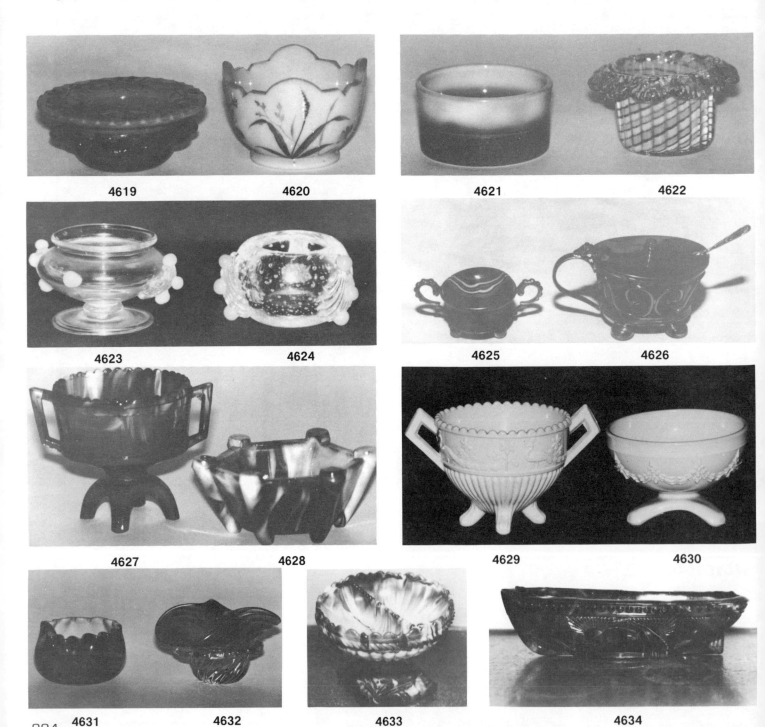

4619   4620   4621   4622

4623   4624   4625   4626

4627   4628   4629   4630

4631   4632   4633   4634

MISCELLANEOUS LATE ADDITIONS

4635

4636

4637

4638

4639

4640

4641

4642

4643

4644

4645

4646

4647

4648

4649

4650

4651

4652

MISCELLANEOUS LATE ADDITIONS

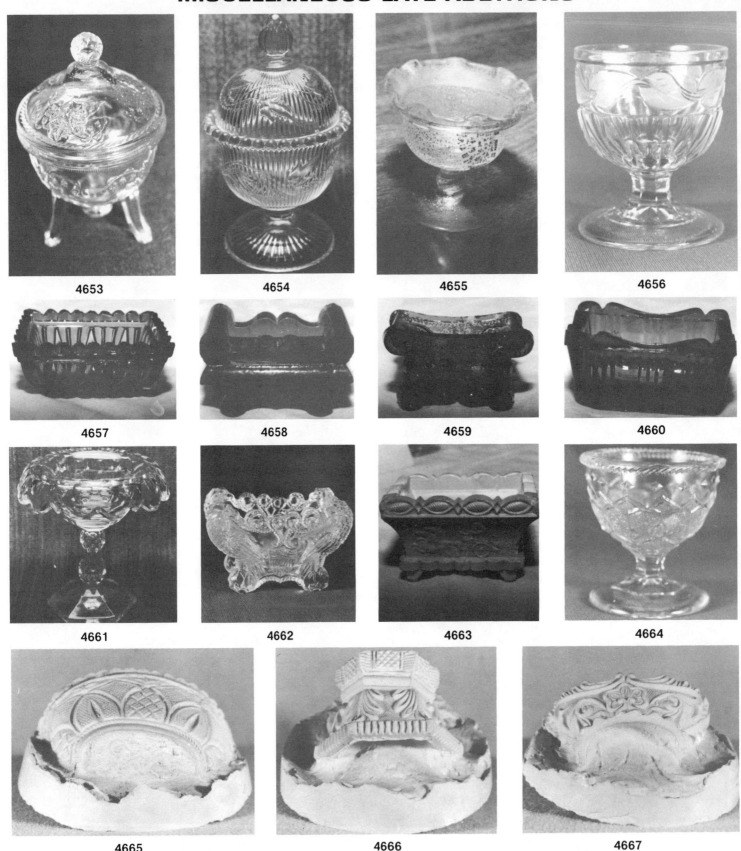

4653

4654

4655

4656

4657

4658

4659

4660

4661

4662

4663

4664

4665

4666

4667

It was originally believed these were part of the original molds used in the manufacture of the lacy salts. However in a recent conversation with Mrs. Dorothy Neal she stated plaster of paris was never used in any of the original molds. (see McKearin's book "American Glass" chapter V11 early pressed glass). Mrs. Neal further states these are probably the molds she and her husband made during the time they were doing the research for their book "Pressed Glass Salt Dishes of the Lacy Period 1825-1850". In addition to their own collection, they traveled extensively to museums and to private collections for additional examples, sometimes doing 50-60 at a time. They first made a mold from a dental material called hydrocolloid, then later at home made the above molds from the hydrocolloid ones. This process enabled them to insure all detail for their drawings. Photos could not be used as the glass reflects the light and distorts the detail.

MISCELLANEOUS LATE ADDITIONS

4668

4669

4670

4671

4672

4673

4674

4675

4676

4677

4678

4679

4680

4681   4682   4683

4684

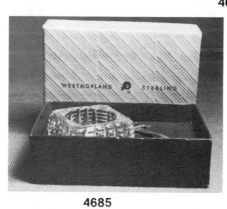

4685

4686

MISCELLANEOUS LATE ADDITIONS

4687

4688

4689

4690

4691

4692

4693

4694

4695

4696

4697

4698

4699

4700

4701

4702

4703

4704

4705

4706

4707

4708

4709

4710

MISCELLANEOUS LATE ADDITIONS

4711

4712

4713

4714

4715

4716

4717

4718

4719

4720

4721

4722

4723

4724

4725

4726

4727

4728

4729

4730

4731

4732

4733

4734

229

MISCELLANEOUS LATE ADDITIONS

4735

4736

4737

4738

4739

4740

4741

4742

4743

4744

4745   4746

4747

4748

4749

4750

MISCELLANEOUS LATE ADDITIONS

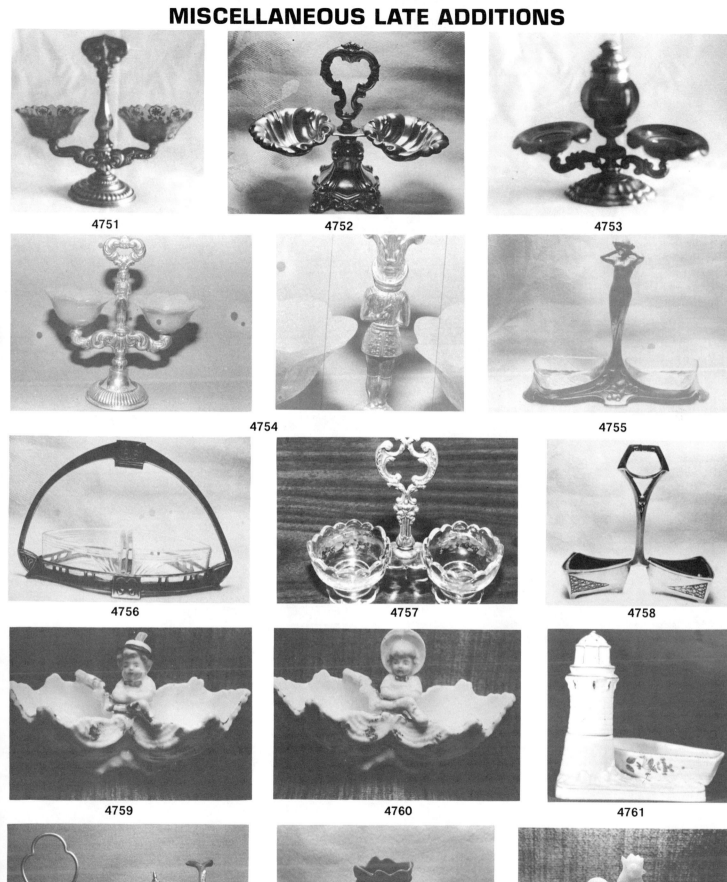

4751

4752

4753

4754

4755

4756

4757

4758

4759

4760

4761

4762

4763

4764

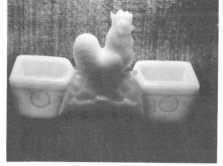

4765

BOXED PRESENTATION SETS

4766

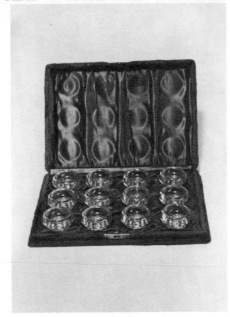

4767

4768

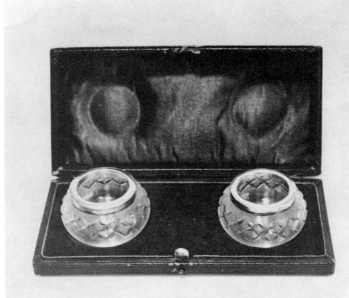

4769

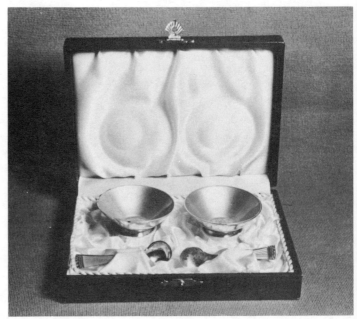

4770

4771

4772

BOXED PRESENTATION SETS

4773

4774

4775

4776

4777

4778

4779

233

BOXED PRESENTATION SETS

4780

4781

4782

4783

4784

4785

4786

234

BOXED PRESENTATION SETS

4787

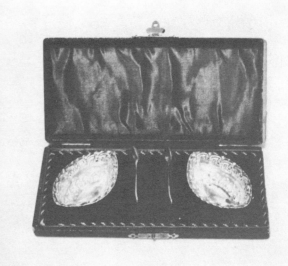

4788

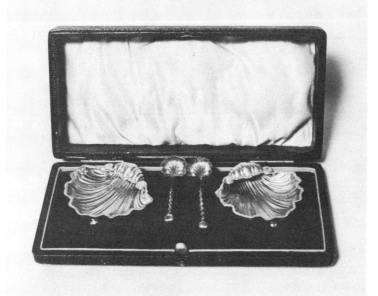

4789

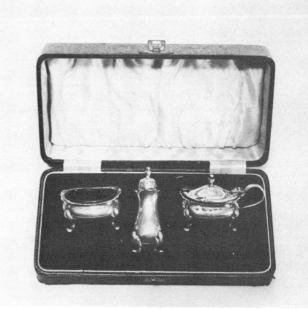

4790

4791

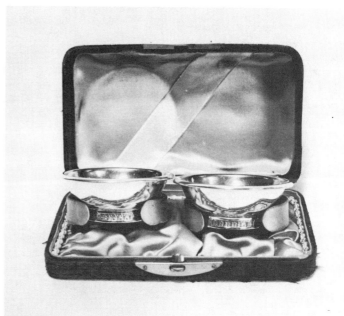

4792

235

BOXED PRESENTATION SETS

4793

4794

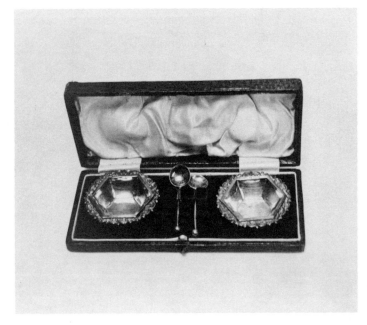

4795

4796

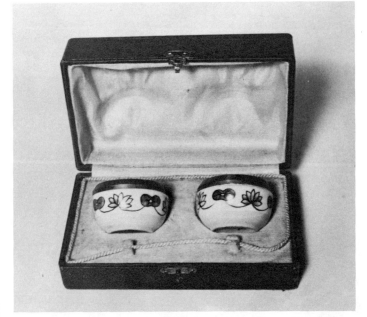

4797

4798

4800

**GEORGE C. SHREVE & CO., SAN FRANCISCO
CIRCA 1892**

237

4800A
Salt—5 Francs, France, 1827
Saucer—5 Francs, France, 1869
Pepper—Napoleon Head—France date worn off. Eagle, Mexico date worn off.
Bottom—50 centavos, Republic Bolivia, 1855

4800B
Salt:—One yen, Japan, 18th century dynasty
Saucer—5 Francs, France, 1826Q
Pepper—Head, Ferdinand VII, Spain, 1821. Shield, Uruguay, year mark worn
Bottom—Bolivia, 1858

4800C
Salt—5 Francs, France, 1852
Saucer—5 Francs, France, 1873
Pepper—Scales—un peso, Mexico, age mark worn. Shield, Uruguay 1867
Bottom—Columbia, 1881

4800D
Salt—Un sol, Republic Peruana, 1865
Saucer—Hawaiian, 1883
Pepper—Head to right, Germany Saxony, 1836-1838. Head to left Napoleon, France, 1861-1870
Bottom—50 centavos, Mexico, 1885

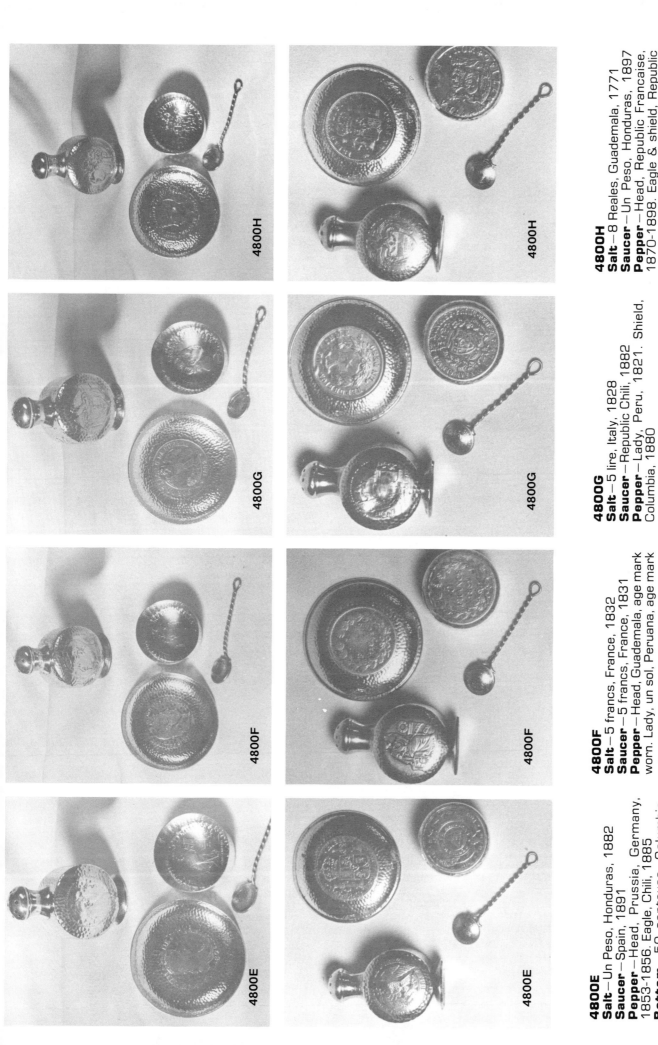

4800E
Salt—Un Peso, Honduras, 1882
Saucer—Spain, 1891
Pepper—Head, Prussia, Germany, 1853-1856. Eagle, Chili, 1885
Bottom—50 centavos, Columbia, 1882

4800F
Salt—5 francs, France, 1832
Saucer—5 francs, France, 1831
Pepper—Head, Guademala, age mark worn. Lady, un sol, Peruana, age mark worn
Bottom—Hawaiian, 1883

4800G
Salt—5 lire, Italy, 1828
Saucer—Republic Chili, 1882
Pepper—Lady, Peru, 1821. Shield, Columbia, 1880

4800H
Salt—8 Reales, Guademala, 1771
Saucer—Un Peso, Honduras, 1897
Pepper—Head, Republic Francaise, 1870-1898. Eagle & shield, Republic Nueva Granda (Bogota), 1858
Bottom—British India, ¹/₂ anna, after 1877

239

4800L

4800L

4800K

4800K

4800J

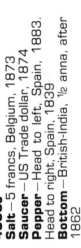

4800J

4800I

4800I

OPEN SALTS IN BLACK AND WHITE

ROUND SHAPE—FLAT TOP—PRESSED

2500—Two rows of ellipses with cable band between, sim. to Fig. 2505, maker unknown, circa 1885, 1⅞" diam.

2501—Row of thumbprints at top, ribbing at bottom, maker unknown, circa 1885-90, 1⅞" diam.

2502—Plain, round with mold line around center, maker unknown, circa 1890, 1¾" diam.

2503—Parallel rows of large thumbprints, similar to "St. Louis" salt by Bryce (Reprint B), maker unknown, circa 1880, just under 2" diam.

2504—WASHINGTON pattern by New England Glass, 1860's, see Revi, 252, 1⅞" diam.

2505—"Ellipse" salt by Bryce Bros. (also U.S. Glass), 1880's-90's, see Reprint B, 2⅛" diam.

2506—Plain top half, swirled bottom half, maker unknown, circa 1885, 1⅞" diam.

2507—A member of the ICICLE family of similar early patterns (Metz 1, 52), circa 1870's, 2" diam.

2508—Interesting example with rows of rings, maker unknown, circa 1880, 2" diam.

2509—Plain round, may be Central (Reprint C), circa 1880, 1¾" diam.

2510—Plain round with criss-cross design in base, maker unknown, 1880's, 1¾" diam.

2511—Plain round with impressed sunburst design in base, maker unknown, 1880's, 1⅝" diam.

2512—Plain round with collar base, made by Duncan (Reprint D), 1880's-90's, 1¾" diam.

2513—Plain round with another base design, maker unknown, circa 1880's, 1¾" diam.

2514—Plain round with no design in base, may be Central (Reprint C), possible sponge cup, just over 2" diam.

2515—Plain round with base design shown, maker undetermined, 1880's, 1¾" diam.

2516—Another plain round with base design reflecting in glass, maker unknown, also from the 1880's, 2⅛" diam.

2517—Central's No. 439 (Reprint C), circa 1880, similar to one by Bryce (Reprint B), also known in color (rare), 2½" diam.

2518—WASHINGTON "state" pattern by U.S. Glass, circa 1903, 2" diam.

2519—Pattern unknown, appears to be p.g., circa 1900-05, maker unknown, 1¼" diam.

2520—Known as CABLE, this would go with any of the members of that pattern family, circa 1890, maker unknown, just under 2" diam.

2521—Parallel rows of ribbing, maker unknown, 1890's, 2" diam.

2522—BEADED GRAPE MEDALLION, Boston Silver-Glass Co., 1869-71 (Revi, 76), 1⅛" diam.

2523—SILVER QUEEN pattern by Ripley (also U.S. Glass), 1890's, 1¾" diam.

2524—McKee's #410 or #98, Stout pg. 166, similar to Cambridge #4060 (Welker 1, 119), circa 1905-10, 1½" diam.

2525—Central's No 178 (Reprint C), circa 1880, 1⅞" diam.

2526—PANEL WITH DIAMOND POINT ind. salt, see also Fig. 2517, Central, 1880's, Reprint C, also known in color, 1¾" diam.

2527—Plain top with panelled bottom half, called PRISM by Richards & Hartley (Reprint E), also made by U.S. Glass, 1890's, just over 1½" diam.

2528—Plain melon-ribbed pattern, maker unknown, circa 1900, 2⅛" diam.

2529—Early thumbprint design, maker unknown, circa 1880, 2¼" diam.

2530—Imitation cut salt of early 1900's, maker unknown, circa 1905-15, 1¾" diam.

2531—Plain round with extended flange at top rim, possibly to hold lid, maker unknown, circa 1900-10, 2½" diam.

ROUND SHAPE—FLAT TOP—PRESSED

2532—JOSEPHINE'S FAN by Robinson Glass, also Cambridge Glass, circa 1900-1903, 1½" diam.

2533—BUTTON & STAR PANEL by Higbee, circa 1900-05, 1 1/4" diam.
2534—MARDIS GRAS (D&M #42), Duncan and Miller, circa 1900 with lengthy production, 1 1/2" diam., also in oval
2535—SERRATED RIB & FINECUT, maker unknown, circa 1901, 1 5/8" diam.
2536—ZIPPERED SWIRL & DIAMOND, U.S. Glass, circa 1895, 1 3/8" diam.
2537—SUNK HONEYCOMB by McKee Glass, circa 1901, 1 1/2" diam.
2538—HARVARD pattern by Tarentum Glass, circa 1900, 1 3/4" diam.
2539—TEPEE pattern by Duncan, circa 1897, 1 1/4" diam.
2540—SCALLOPED SIX-POINT by Duncan & Miller, circa 1900, 1 1/2" diam.
2541—TEUTONIC salt by McKee, circa 1900, reproduced in colors, 1 1/4" diam.
2542—PALM LEAF FAN by Higbee, circa 1900-05, 1 3/8" diam.
2543—MEDALLION SUNBURST by Higbee, circa 1900-05, 1 1/4" diam.
2544—Part of a celery set by John B Higbee Glass Co, circa 1900-1910, sold with a Euclid Celery vase and called celery salts, 1 1/4" diam.
2545—WESTMORELAND pattern by Gillinder, also U.S. Glass, circa 1890's 1 1/2" diam.
2546—DIAMOND POINT design made by several companies, maker unknown on this one, circa 1890, 1 3/8" diam.
2547—Pressed design in npg pomade, maker unknown, rim for metal lid, circa 1900, 1 1/4" diam.
2548—BOW-TIE pattern by Thompson Glass, circa 1890, 1 3/8" diam.
2549—TORPEDO pattern also by Thompson Glass, circa 1889, 1 1/2" diam.
2550—This swirled pattern appears to be pg, maker unknown, circa 1895, 1 3/8" diam.
2551—Paden City No. 12 (Barnett, 75), circa 1920, same mold as No. 2553, 1 3/8" diam.
2552—TILE pattern by Thompson Glass, circa 1890's 1 1/2" diam.
2553—Paden City No. 12 with light cutting, same as #2551, circa 1920, 1 1/4" diam.
2554—King Glass Co.'s "Jewel" salt (Revi, 222), 1870's, aka PITCAIRN, 1 1/2" diam.
2555—WASHINGTON early pattern by New England Glass, see Fig. 2504, 1 1/2" diam.
2556—Fostoria's No. 585 (Reprint N) with light cutting on panels, circa 1900, 2" diam.
2557—Imitation cut PRISM & BROKEN COLUMN, maker unknown, (Metz 2, 160), circa 1905-10, 1 1/2" diam.
2558—Another zippered design similar to PRIZE, but not same, maker unknown, circa 1900-10, 1 3/8" diam.
2559—HONEYCOMB salt, a design made by (see Figs. 2906-2911) many companies, this one is an early example, circa 1880, maker unknown 1 1/2" diam.
2560—PLAIN BAND salt by Heisey, circa 1900-05, 1 7/8" diam.
2561—VIGILANT pattern by Fostoria Glass Co., circa 1900-05, 1 3/4" diam.
2562—Block pattern from about 1900, another design made by many companies, 1 3/4" diam.
2563—STRIGIL pattern by Tarentum Glass, circa 1900, similar to McKee's NELLY, 1 1/2" diam.
2564—The polished base to a salt shaker or mustard, shown to alert readers to avoid these misrepresentations, pattern and maker undetermined, 1 3/4" diam.

ROUND SHAPE—FLAT TOP—PRESSED

2565—See notes Fig. 2538
2566—STAR GALAXY pattern by Central Glass, circa 1880, 1 7/8" diam.
2567—ELECTRIC pattern by U.S. Glass, circa 1891, 1 1/2" diam.
2568—AMAZON pattern by Bryce Bros., circa 1880's-90's, 1 7/8" diam.
2569—ROMONA pattern by McKee, circa 1900-05, 2 1/2" diam.
2570—Possibly pattern glass but not recognized, circa 1885, 2" diam.
2571—Duncan's LATE BLOCK pattern this salt known in ruby-stained, circa 1890's, also by U.S. Glass, 1 3/4" diam.
2572—BRAZILLIAN pattern by Fostoria, circa 1900, rare in green, 1 3/4" diam.
2573—LONG BUTTRESS pattern by Fostoria, circa 1900-05, 2" diam.
2574—AMERICAN pattern by Fostoria, early 1900's with lengthy production, salt made only during the earliest years, circa 1910, 2" diam.
2575—Plain ribbed salt, maker unknown, npg, circa 1900, 1 3/4" diam.
2576—SEELY pattern by Nickel Plate Glass, Fostoria, OH., circa 1890, also U.S. Glass 1 5/8" diam., aka FOSTORIA
2577—HAWAIIAN LEI by Higbee, circa 1910, 1" diameter
2578—Round hat-shaped salt with light cutting on brim, maker unknown, circa 1910, 1 5/8" diam.
2579—Bryce Bros. No. 3 salt (Reprint B), also U.S. Glass, circa 1890's rare in color, 8 panels, 1 3/4" diam.
2580—Finely ribbed pressed salt, pattern unknown, circa 1905, 2" diam.
2581—Plain round salt with button design in base, maker unknown, circa 1890, 1 3/4" diam.
2582—MASCOTTE pattern by Ripley & Co., also U.S. Glass, 1890's, 1 3/4" diam.
2583—Appears to be Hobbs' No. 53 (Reprint H) ind. salt, plain with starred base, also by U.S. Glass, circa 1890's, 1 7/8" diam.
2584—Plain round salt with no base pattern, maker unknown, circa 1900, 1 7/8" diam.
2585—Advertising salt with "ULLMAN MFG CO.—NEW YORK" in base shown, circa 1900, 2" diam.
2586—Plain round salt with rayed base, straight sides, maker unknown, circa 1890, just over 1 1/2" diam.
2587—Same as Fig. 2586 except with light cutting
2588—Small plain round salt, maker unknown, circa 1900, just over 1 1/4" diam.
2589—Ribbed npg salt by Richards & Hartley (Reprint E), circa 1890's, also U.S. Glass, just over 1 1/2" diam.
2590—Finely ribbed pressed salt, late period, circa 1920's or later, almost 2" round
2591—NOONDAY SUN pattern by King Glass, late 1880's, rare, just over 2" diam.
2592—Foreign pressed salt with frosted design around rim, circa 1900, 2 1/8" diam.
2593—Another foreign salt with cherub design embossed all around, circa 1890, 2 5/8" diam.

ROUND SHAPE—FLAT TOPS—PRESSED

2594—Plain round with "Durelex-Made in France" stamped in base, may not be a salt, but most unusual, 2 1/4" diam.
2595—VINCENNES ind. salt by McKee (Stout, 212), circa 1900, 1 1/2" diam.
2596—Engraved & sand-blast etched crystal salt or ash tray signed D. T., California glass engraver Dorothy Thorpe, circa 1940's, 2 1/2" diam.
2597—Foreign pressed salt in imitation cut design, circa 1910, 2 1/4" diam.
2598—WHIRLPOOL pattern by Heisey, circa 1940's, 2 3/4" diam.
2599—Foreign mold-blown glass with frosted design at top, possibly base to pomade, early 1900's, 2" diam.
2600—Swirled pattern from France, signed "Portieux", circa 1900-10, possibly Baccarat, 2" diam.
2601—A later version of the early "Tulip" pattern family, circa 1910, maker unknown, 2 3/4" diameter
2602—Tiny panelled rib salt with light notching, maker unknown, circa 1910, 1 1/2" diam.
2603—RIB & PANEL pattern by Heisey (signed), circa 1930's, 2 1/4" diam.
2604—YUTEC pattern by McKee (Stout, 329), does not match "mother" line, rare in color, 1 3/4" diam.
2605—Possibly "Saxon" ind. salt by Bakewell, Pears (Reprint G), circa 1870, 2" diam.
2606—A similar ribbed design to Fig. 2605, maker unknown, circa 1880, 2" diam.
2607—Plain top with ribbed base, maker unknown, circa 1890, 1 3/4" diam.
2608—"Prism" ind. salt by Bakewell (Reprint G), also made by Greensburg Glass (K8, pl. 65), circa 1870-90's, 2" diam.

2609 — The plain fluted salt is probably Westmoreland, circa 1920's with lengthy production, 1¾" diam.

2610 — Plain, round, patternless salt, maker unknown, circa 1910, 2" diam.

2611 — Oval thumbprint design around top, maker unknown, circa 1890, 1¾" diam.

2612 — Either Bakewell (Reprint G) or "Argus" salt by Duncan (Reprint D), dating from 1870's through the 1890's, 2" diam., also made by King (Reprint K)

2613 — Similar to Fig. 2612, this appears to be Hobbs' #200 (Reprint H), 1⅞" diam.

2614 — FINE PRISM by Heisey, circa 1910, 2" diam.

2615 — A delicate interior diamond optic is almost unnoticeable on this old salt, circa 1890, maker unknown, 1¾" diam.

2616 — Either foreign or late pressed, circa 1915, maker unknown, 2¼" diam. at top

2617 — Another round salt with interesting diamond pattern, circa 1890, maker unknown, 1⅞" diam.

2618 — The diamond pattern on this early salt matches KALBACH (Metz 1, 166), maker unknown, from the 1870's, 2¼" diam.

2619 — Plain round foreign salt with unusual mushroom shaped trademark inside base, circa 1920's or later, 2¼" diam.

2620 — PATTEE CROSS pattern by U.S. Glass, part of toy berry set (Revi, 317), leaf-like design found either plain or with lines, circa 1910, 2" diam.

2621 — LATE PANELLED DIAMOND POINT by Higbee, circa 1900, different from early version (Fig. 2712), 2½" diam.

2622 — Round salt with impressed rose design in base, probably foreign, circa 1900, 2⅜" diam., identical to 2616, except for bottom

2623 — This must be CAMBRIDGE FEATHER (pattern No. 2660) salt or toy berry dish, circa 1905-10, 2⅛" diam., ref. K7, 176

ROUND SHAPE—UNEVEN TOPS—PRESSED

2624 — NEVADA state pattern by U.S. Glass, circa 1902, 2¼" diam., also made in master size

2625 — ENGLISH HOBNAIL by Westmoreland, circa 1920, production continued in some forms until recent years, salt made in other sizes, this one probably a master, 2⅜" diam.

2626 — FINE DIAMOND POINT by Heisey from the 1930's, listed as a "jelly dish", with trademark, just over 2½" diam.

2627 — POINTED OVAL IN DIAMOND POINT by Heisey, circa 1900, just over 2½" diam.

2628 — Patternless mold-blown salt

with crimped top, circa 1915, maker unknown, 1⅝" diam.

2629 — PLAIN SCALLOPED PANEL by U.S. Glass, circa 1900-1910, 2" diam.

2630 — Highly polished panelled salt with delicate floral cutting, maker unknown, circa 1905, 1¾" diam.

2631 — ALEXIS pattern by Fostoria, circa 1900-1905, just over 1½" diam.

2632 — HIGBEE COLONIAL by Higbee with molds reissued by Paden City Glass after 1918, with "bee" trademark on Higbee version, 1⅝" diam.

2633 — CAMBRIDGE COLONIAL, No. 2570 pattern, by Cambridge Glass, circa 1905-1910, Wekler 1, 96, 1⅞" diam.

2634 — FOSTORIA REGAL by Fostoria Glass, circa 1900-1910, just over 2" diam.

2635 — Round DEWDROP or HOBNAIL salt, probably by Columbia Glass, circa 1890, just under 2" diam.

2636 — Same as Fig. 2637, tilted to show "bee" trademark and base design

2637 — STYLE pattern by Higbee, sometimes signed, circa 1910-1915, 1¾" diam.

2638 — DEEP FILE by Dalzell, and later by Cambridge Glass, circa 1900-1905, 1¾" diam.

2639 — This appears to be Fostoria's DIANA pattern (WFG, 16), circa 1900-1910, but it is difficult to be certain on these plain salts, 2" diam.

2640 — LOTUS pattern by Westmoreland, pattern No. 1921 (WDG2, 378), circa 1920's with lengthy production, also made in colors, just over 1" diam.

2641 — CANDLEWICK by Imperial, 1940's until recently, a popular line which has several "look-alikes", almost 2½" diam.

2642 — Smaller size in CANDLEWICK by Imperial, about 2" diam.

2643 — CANNON BALL from the early 1900's, frequently confused for "Atlas" by Bryce, maker unknown, 2¾" diam.

2644 — Interesting salt with rings on the outside and rings on the inside, maker unknown, possibly foreign, circa 1910, 2½" diam.

2645 — A similar pattern of rings and ribbing, also looks foreign, circa 1910-1915, circular rings in base, 2¼" diam.

2646 — Paden City's No. 11 cut and pressed salt, circa 1918, 1¾" diam.

2647 — INVERTED STRAWBERRY by Cambridge, small dish to toy berry set, circa 1910-1920, just over 2⅛" diam.

2648 — LACY DAISY by Westmoreland, small dish to toy berry set, circa 1920, name from Kamm 2 for diff. pattern, this design copied by other companies, 2½" diam.

2649 — NURSERY TALES dish to toy berry set, by U.S. Glass, circa 1910, just under 2½" diam.

2650 — Fluted and ribbed design with 16-ray star base, maker unknown, circa 1900, 1¾" diam.

2651 — ALL-OVER DIAMOND type pattern, made by several companies in

different forms, this one is master size, almost 3" diam., maker unknown, circa 1895

2652 — Plain fluted pattern by Paden City Glass, circa 1918, just over 2" diam.

2653 — Pressed glass foreign design with panels in unusual watery effect, circa 1915-20, 2¾" diam.

2654 — Inverted Thumbprint design with tiny fans at top rim, probably foreign, circa 1910, just over 2½" diam.

ROUND SHAPE— UNEVEN TOPS—PRESSED

2655 — LADDER WITH DIAMOND by Duncan & Miller, circa 1903, almost 2" diam.

2656 — SNAIL pattern by George Duncan Sons & Co., circa 1890, 1¾" diam.

2657 — DUNCAN'S CLOVER, also by Duncan & Miller, circa 1903, 1½" diam.

2658 — BUTTON PANEL, also by Duncan & Miller, circa 1903, 1½" diam.

2659 — TWO-PLY SWIRL, Duncan & Miller, circa 1902, 1⅞" diam.

2660 — McKEE'S RAINBOW by McKee Glass, circa 1902, 2" diam.

2661 — SCALLOPED SIX-POINT, Duncan's No. 30, circa 1896, over 2½" diam.

2662 — SUNBEAM by McKee, circa 1900-05, just under 2½" diam.

2663 — ADA pattern by Ohio Flint Glass and later Cambridge Glass, circa 1898-1903, very similar to Fig. 2538 HARVARD salt, just over 2" diam.

2664 — A foreign "diamond and fan" with frosted base and 12-rayed star, 2¼" diam., circa 1900

2665 — SUNRAY ind. ash tray by Fostoria Glass, circa 1935-40, also made in a salt and a nut cup, 2¼" diam.

2666 — SHOSHONE by U.S. Glass, circa 1896-1900, 18-ray base, just under 2" diam.

2667 — HICKMAN by McKee Glass, circa 1900-05, just under 2" diam.

2668 — See notes Fig. 2600

2669 — NPG design of Ellipses, maker unknown, circa 1890, 1¾" diam.

2670 — PINEAPPLE & FAN by U.S. Glass (No. 15041), aka CUBE WITH FAN, 18-rayed base, 2" diam.

2671 — PRISMATIC pattern by Pittsburgh Lamp, Brass & Glass Co., circa 1905, 18-ray base, 1¾" diam.

2672 — BEADED PANEL & SUNBURST by Heisey, circa 1900, 2" diam.

2673 — FANDANGO by Heisey, aka DIAMOND SWAG, circa 1896, 16-ray base, 2" diam.

2674 — FANCY LOOP by Heisey, rare in green, circa 1900, just under 2" diam.

2675 — Unknown pattern, possibly Canadian, circa 1900, 2¼" diam.

2676 — MARJORIE early pressed pattern by Cambridge, circa 1905-10, similar to Fostoria's ROSBY pattern, just under 2" diam.

2677—INDIANA NO. 300 tiny dish to toy berry set (Bond, 62), circa 1908, similar to McKee's "Carltec", 2¼" diam.

2678—PAVONIA by Ripley & Co., circa 1890 (also U.S. Glass), just under 2" diam.

2679—See notes Fig. 2623 for this Cambridge salt

2680—ENGLISH HOBNAIL salt to toy condiment set by Westmoreland, (WDG, 380), circa 1920 with lengthy production, this example just under 1" high and 1¾" diam.

2681—Same as one next to it but this example is a full 1" high and 1⅝" diam., apparently a different mold from earlier or later production, possibly a copy from competitor

2682—ENGLISH HOBNAIL without the fans at top, probably the ind. salt to the full-size table line by Westmoreland (not the toy set), circa 1920, 1¾" diam.

2683—Ribbed design with 18-ray star on base, maker unknown, age unknown, just over 2" diam.

2684—Diamond pattern with ribbed design at base, 16-ray star underneath, maker unknown, circa 1900, 2½" diam.

2685—Similar to Fig. 2683, this ribbed design also has a 16-rayed star on the base, 1⅞" diam.

2686—Bryce Bros. No. 150 pattern (H5, 82), not previously listed as tableware, circa 1890, (also by U.S. Glass), just over 2" diam.

2687—EARLY AMERICAN SANDWICH by Duncan & Miller, circa 1925 with lengthy production, this "salted almond" dish was only part of this large service, salted almond is 2½" diam., underplate is 3¼" diam.

OVAL SHAPE—PRESSED
(Widest Dimensions Given)

2688—Plain oval salt with rayed oval design in base, Bryce Bros. (also U.S. Glass), circa 1890 (Reprint B), 2¼" long

2689—LIBERTY BELL salt by Gillinder, circa 1876, two examples have different inner depth due to pressure on plunger. Fig. 2689 is ⁹⁄₁₆" deep. Fig. 2690 is ½" deep, both are 2¼" long

2690—No. 99 salt by U.S. Glass, circa 1910 and earlier, long production, similar to Fig. 2688, 2¼" long

2691—Another similar salt, plain sides with rayed base, maker unknown, circa 1900, 1⅞" long

2692—Clear pressed salt, not pattern glass, rare in color, circa 1880-90, 10-rayed base, almost 3" long

2693—"Prism" salt by King Glass Co., Innes 336, much copied by others, 1870's and later, 12-rayed base, 2½" long, rare in color

2694-2695—Two almost identical salts, a popular design made by several companies including Heisey. Fig. 2694

is 2¼" long, ½" deep inside to thick base. Fig. 2695 has fine notches on design, 2⅜" long and ⅜" deep inside. Both date circa 1890-1905, rare in color

2696—A member of the "Finecut" family of patterns, this appears to be English, circa 1880-90, finecut design in base, no marks, 2¼" long

2697—HEISEY PILLOWS pattern, Heisey Glass Co., circa 1900-1910, 18-ray base, 2½" long

2698—MARDIS GRAS in oval shape (also made round), Duncan & Miller No. 42 pattern, circa 1896-1910, 16-ray base, 2¼" long

2699—DIAMOND RIDGE pattern by Duncan, 1890's, 2¼" diam.

2700—GREENSBURG'S #130 pattern (K5, 49), circa 1889, similar to Fostoria's No. 551, 2" long

2701—PANTAGRAPH BAND (Metz 2,138), orig. the "Brilliant" pattern by King Glass (Reprint K), circa 1870's-80's, 2½" long

2702—Zippered panels with hexagonal blocks, probably English, circa 1880, 20-rayed base, 2½" long

2703—Oval with light thumbprint interior, maker unknown, circa 1890, 2½" long

2704—Almost identical to Fig. 2703 except with light inside Optic design, maker unknown, circa 1890, 2½" long

2705—Squatty honeycomb cut salt, oval shape, 8-point star in base, circa 1900, 2" long

2706—BEDFORD pattern by Fostoria (WFG, 24), after 1900, just over 2½" long

2707—Foreign pressed salt bought in Denmark, imitation cut pressed design, circa 1900-10, 8-point star in base, 2⅛" long

2708—HOMESTEAD pattern salt by Bryce, Higbee & Co., 1880's, also made square, 14-rayed star base, 2" long

2709—Similar in shape to Fig. 2694-95, fewer ribs, thick base, 20-ray star in base, circa 1890, 2¼" long, oval

2710—Panelled outside, smooth inside, 12-rayed base, serrated top rim, 2⅝" long

2711—English patterned salt with Lion trademark (Greener), circa 1890, beaded top, 12-rayed base, 2⅜" long

2712—EARLY PANELLED DIAMOND POINT (LPG, 104), non-flint, design copied by other firms, this version with fans, 3⅝" long

2713—Pointed button feet on base, plain oval top, circa 1880's, maker unknown, 2⅞" long

2714—KENNETH pattern marked Krys-tol, made by Ohio Flint and Jefferson Glass, 1908-1918, imitation cut pressed pattern, 2¾" oval

OVAL SHAPES—PRESSED

(Widest dimensions given)

2715—Early flint glass with "icicle" type pattern, maker unknown, circa 1870, 16-ray base, 3⅝" long

2716—Another early swirled design, pattern unknown, circa 1880, 3⅝" long

2717—McKee's "Block" pattern salt, novelty (Stout, 212), 20-ray base, 1900, 2¼" long

2718—Double salt with block design in base, maker unknown, circa 1890, 2¾" long

2719—RIDGELEIGH oval salt, signed Heisey, 3⅛" long, see also Fig. 2741, circa 1920's

2720—Thick, heavy glass, highly polished, plain base, 1920's, 2⅝" long

2721—Melon ribbed bottom half with tiny "icicles" below plain top half, maker unknown, circa 1890, 2¾" long

2722—Imitation cut, probably European from the 1920's, 8-point star in base, 3¼" long

2723—Honeycomb design with oval cable impressed in base, very thick solid glass, 1880's, 2" long

2724—Cut Honeycomb, polished with eight-point star in base, 1890's, 2⅝" long, oval

2725—OAK WREATH pattern by Central (Reprint C), circa 1880, rare, 3¼" long

2726—Foreign salt with embossed design of vines and tiny frog at front, circa 1900, 3" long

2727—"Boston" salt by Adams (Reprint A), circa 1890, plain oval side with horizontal rows of tiny squares in base, 2⅛" long

2728—No. 6 salt by Bryce (Reprint B), circa 1890, tiny squares in base in diagonal rows, ind. size, also made in table size, just under 1⅞" long

2729—Early HEAVY DRAPE pattern salt (not Fostoria), flint glass, 1860's, 3¼" long

2730—STIPPLED BAND (LPG, 107) with rope-like rim, 36-ray base, 1870's, 3¼" long

2731—This appears to match U.S. LACY DAISY (H5, 162), an imitation cut design copied by many companies in different shapes, circa 1915-20, 30-ray base, 2⅜" long

2732—Similar to McKee's PLUTEC, may be same, circa 1910, 16-ray base, just under 2½" long

2733—Oval, multi-sided salt, 20-ray base, after 1900, made in several colors, 1¾" long

2734—Late unusual example, circa 1920, maker unknown, quality pressed crystal, 3¼" long

2735—Oval shaped salt to Cambridge's "Round" line, circle in base, circa 1910-20, 2¼" diam.

2736—Mold-blown crystal, may be insert, circa 1900, 1⅞" long

2737—Mold-blown with light cut leaf spray, circa 1920, 3⅞" long

2738—Mold-blown with 16-ray cut star in base, possible insert, circa 1900, 2½" long

SQUARE SHAPE—PRESSED

2739—Panelled design of groves and loops, 24-rayed base, maker unknown, circa 1910, 1⁹⁄₁₆" square

2740—Ribbed design with waffled button base, maker unknown, circa 1890, 1¾" square

2741—RIDGELEIGH square salt by Heisey, also made oval, H in base, 1920's-30's, 1¼" square

2742—No. 572 salt by Central (Reprint C), 12-ray star base, circa 1880, 1⅞" square

2743—Cambridge glass salt with paper label, circa 1910 with lengthy production, 1½" square

2744—Member of the "waffle" or "Block" family of patterns, maker unknown, 1890's, 2" square

2745—Pressed "Block" pattern with polished finish for brilliance, circa 1900, plain base is 1⅝" square

2746—SQUARE WAFFLE salt (Metz 1,166), circa 1890's, maker unknown, 1½" square

2747—Another block pattern, maker unknown, circa 1890, star in base, 1⅝" square

2748—No. 112 salt by Fostoria (WFG, 22), circa 1900, 20-ray star base, 1½" square

2749—Another member of LACY DAISY family, imitation cut pattern made by many, 1905-1920's, pattern continued on base, 1⅝" square

2750—DOUBLE-EYE HOBNAIL, square shape, Columbia Glass, circa 1890, just under 1¾" square hob to hob, rare in color

2751—Diamond pattern with 16-ray star in base, bought in New Zealand, so probably foreign, appears to date from 1930's, 2⅝" square

2752—Sawtooth type design of later vintage, circa 1910-20's, maker unknown, 2" square

2753—New, highly polished geometric design with 8-point star impressed in base, 1⅞" square

2754—"Cabinet" salt by Adams (Reprint A) circa 1890, also U.S. Glass, just under 1" high, 1¾" circular opening

2755—Similar to Fig. 2754 except just over 1" high, just over 1⅛" opening, this example is lightly etched, may also be Adams, circa 1890

2756—Panelled pattern with deeply impressed 10-point star in base, maker unknown, circa 1900, 1½" square

2757—Same as Fig. 2756 except the star on the base is lightly impressed

2758—ATLANTA or LATE LION pattern by Fostoria, circa 1900, just under 1⅞" square

2759—PLANET pattern by Model Flint Glass, circa 1900, part of tiny toy condiment set (Bond, 20) 1⅛" square

2760—ILLINOIS state pattern by U.S. Glass, circa 1900-10, 1⅝" square, rare in color

2761—Pillar on three sides, plain on

one, foreign example of poor quality, circa 1920's, 1⅞" square

2762—Plain sides with waffle design in base, ⅞" high x 1½" square, deep center, bevelled top, U.S. Glass from about 1900-1910

2763—Plain sides with waffle design in base, ⅝" high x 1½" square, shallow center, polished top and sides

2764—Plain sides with waffle design in base, ⅞" high x 1⅝" square, smaller but deeper opening in center, bevelled top, possibly Hobbs (Reprint H)

2765—Similar to Fig. 2764 except higher, bevelled at top, 1" high x 1½" square

2766—Plain sides with waffle design in base, very deep center, 1" high x 1¾" high square, circa 1890

2767—Plain sides with diamond-point design in base, shallow center, slightly bevelled top, ¾" high, just over 1½" square, Fostoria's No. 93 (WFG, 22)

2768—Plain sides with waffle design in base, just over 1" tall x 1⅝" square, deep center, lightly bev. top and bevelled corners, circa 1890, maker unknown

2769—Plain with bevelled corners and circle of tiny hobnails in base, thick base, ¾" high x 1½" square

2770—Same as Fig. 2769 except thinner base, due to plunger pressure

2771—Plain with button and diamond base, bevelled corner and top, 1890's, 1" high x 1½" square

2772—Plain with lightly impressed diamond waffle design on base, bevelled corner and base, just under 1" high x 1½" square

2773—Plain with diamond optic base, poor quality glass, bevelled edges, ⅞" high x 1½" square

RECTANGULAR SHAPES— PRESSED

(Measurements given are length)

2774—LITTLE BAND pattern (K2, 40) with plain sides and a thin row of fans along base, pictured to show Star of David base design, maker unknown, circa 1880, almost 2" long

2775—English version of our FINECUT pattern, registered with RD 194638, dating it from 1892, most unusual and scarce, 2½" long

2776—KING'S CROWN by Adams, also U.S. Glass, rare salt in ruby-stain (called RUBY THUMBPRINT), circa 1890's, 2½" long

2777—Ribbed pattern of unknown origin, circa 1900, 2" long

2778—PANEL, RIB & SHELL pattern by Central (Kamm 3, 53), not quite rectangular (six-sided), circa 1880, ornate design in base, 2¼" long

2779—No. 594 salt by Fostoria Glass (Reprint N), circa 1900, 2" long

2780—MELROSE pattern by Brilliant

(also Greensburg), circa 1890, pattern in base, almost 2" long

2781—See notes Figure 2798 for this duplicate

2782—BEVELLED BUTTONS pattern by Duncan (also U.S. Glass), see H5, 99, circa 1890, 2⅛" long

2783—This looks like pattern glass, but name undetermined, circa 1880, 2½" long

2784—Similar to several others on this page, plain sides with 14-rayed star in base, 4 tiny knob feet on corners, seen with a Higbee mark, circa 1910-15, 2" long

2785—"Rope" salt by McKee (Stout, 75), similar to Fig. 2797, circa 1880's with long production, 2⅛" long

2786—Could be salt to MASONIC by McKee, plain flat panels with diamond design at base, 2¼" long

2787—Plain bevelled band at top, convex ribbing at bottom half, 26-rayed star base, 1⅞" long

2788—Rectangular plain sides with rows of tiny squares in base, similar to Fig. 2796, except larger, 1¼" wide, 1½" long, maker unknown, circa 1895

2789—Plain sides with ribbed button feet at base, 1¼" wide, 2½" long, maker unknown, circa 1890

2790—Identical to Fig. 2789 except larger in size, 1⅞" wide, 2⅜" long

2791—Convex ribs around sides, base design like Fig. 2797, 1½" long, circa 1900

2792—PICKET pattern by King Glass Co., circa 1880's, rare in color, 1⅞" long

2793—Plain top with ribbed base, maker unknown, circa 1900, 1¼" wide, 2" long

2794—DAISY ROSETTE salt, probably Duncan, 1890's, 2⅛" long

2795—BAG WARE salt by Duncan, aka HEAVY PANELLED FINECUT, circa 1890, plain sides, 2¼" long

2796—Early Cambridge pressed salt, plain sides with rows of tiny squares at base, 2" long

2797—No. 4 ind. salt by Bryce Bros., circa 1890, Reprint B, just under 2" long, similar to Fig. 2785

2798—No. 5 ind. salt by Bryce Bros., circa 1890, curved sides, same design in base as Fig. 2797, just under 2" long at widest

2799—Another salt similar to four others on this page, this example has a swan figure embossed in the center base circa 1890, may be foreign, 2¼" long

2800—No. 900 salt by Bryce, Reprint B, also in color, circa 1890's, just under 2" long

2801—Six-sided, plain sides with waffle design in base, just under 2" long, circa 1890

2802—Same as Fig. 2801 except much thinner base, due to plunger pressure or amount of glass in mold, has unusual flaw on left side

2803—"Cobb" salt by Richards & Hartley, Reprint E, circa 1890, 2" long at widest

ASSORTED SHAPES—PRESSED

2804—This appears to be the PURITAN pattern by Fostoria (WFG, 43), circa 1905, 1½" diam.

2805—GALLOWAY pattern by U.S. Glass, circa 1901-10, this salt or honey dish previously unlisted, 3½" diam.

2806—Oval salt with parallel rows of tiny cubes, maker unknown, circa 1900, 1¾" long, oval

2807—Round salt with arched beads separating a lobed top from a flat ribbed bottom half, 22 beads in a circle, 1¼" diam.

2808—The flanged top indicates this is the base to a covered piece, pattern design matched MT. VERNON by Cambridge glass, dates from about 1910-20, 2¼" diam.

2809—Oval shaped tub salt in DAISY & BUTTON, maker unknown, circa 1890, 2⅛" long, oval

2810—Hexagonal salt with six-point star in base and sides, Cambridge Glass Co., circa 1910, just under 2¼" diam.

2811—FLORICUT pattern salt, round shape, by U.S. Glass, circa 1916 (H5, 161), pressed leaves with cut flowers, 1¾" diam.

2812—No. 1191 pressed round salt by Cambridge Glass, circa 1910-20, (Welker 1, 110), 1¾" diam.

2813—No. 1201 hexagonal pressed & cut salt by Cambridge Glass, circa 1910-20, (Welker 1, 110), 2⅛" diam.

2814—Round salt, combination pressed/cut, maker unknown, circa 1910-15, 2" diam.

2815—Notched rib design of imitation cut glass, maker unknown, circa 1910, 2" diam., six-sided

2816-17—Two different sizes in same salt pattern, probably by Bryce Bros. (Reprint B), circa 1890, larger example is 2¼" long, smaller is 1⅝" long

2818—Square pressed salt with engraved floral design in base, maker unknown, circa 1905, 1⅝" square

2819—This square salt matches McKee's example shown in Stout, 212, but could be a similar copy, circa 1900-10, 1½" square

2820—Square pressed with light parallel ribbing, just under 1½" square

2821—Highly polished with impressed flower & leaf design on flat polished base, almost 1¾" square

2822—Nine diagonal raised ribs surrounding an impressed square in base, 1¾" square, circa 1880

2823—Square shape with bevelled corners, light waffle design in base, 1½" square, circa 1895

2824—Square with bevelled top and base, cable impressed in base, circa 1890, 1½" square

2825—Square with criss-cross in base, circa 1890, 1¾" square

2826—Square with 8-point star in base, bevelled corners, almost 1½" square

2827—Square with snowflake design in base, made by Duncan, circa 1890 (Reprint D), very similar to Fig. 2828, 1½" square

2828—Sim. to Fig. 2827, square with bevelled top and bottom edge, snowflake recessed in base, just under 1½" square

2829—Square with bev. edges, deeply impressed 17-ray star in base, ribbed edges creating a most unusual view from the side, circa 1890, maker unknown, 1½" square

2830—Plain sides with bev. top, 15 rays, circa 1890, 1⅞" square

2831—Duplication of Fig. 2826

2832—Square with bev. top and base, 14-spoke wheel in base, circa 1890, 1⅝" square

2833—Hexagonal table size salt with crossed rib design, maker unknown, circa 1900, 2¾" square

2834—Round, unusual pressed diamond optic design, possibly foreign, circa 1900, 2⅜" diam.

2835—MASON salt by McKee (Stout, 75) circa 1880, 2⅜" square at widest point, almost 1" high, named after Mason's symbol

2836—Round table salt with button design in base, maker unknown, circa 1890, 2½" diam.

TUB SHAPED (Pressed and Cut)

2837—TUB pressed ind. salt by McKee, circa 1900 (Stout, 212), round, 1⅞" diam.

2838—Another natural looking pressed tub with stippled background, may be foreign, circa 1895, 1⅞" round diam.

2839—Tub-shaped pressed, AETNA NO 300, Bellaire, Ohio, circa 1886-1887, rare in color

2840—No. 515 salt by Fostoria Glass, circa 1900 (WFG, 22), in clear only, 2" round

2841—Plain fluted pattern by U.S. Glass (trademarked U.S.), circa 1910, 2½" round

2842-2844—Fluted pattern in plain and cut versions, maker unknown, circa 1930, 8-sided, 1¾" diam.

2845—Panelled sides with flared handles, probably Heisey, 1920's-30's, 12-flutes, 1⅞" diam.

2846—Similar to #2845, with 12 panels, also from 20's, 1⅝" diam. round

2847—Round panelled tub with spoon-rest handles, 8-rayed star base, Cambridge's #400 "Round" pattern, circa 1915, 8-sided, 1¾" diam.

2848—Similar to #2847 with 16-rayed star in base, no spoon rests, D&M #54, 1¾" diam., circa 1920

2849—Same as Fig. 2847, except with light cutting

2850-2851—Plain and cut versions of same salt, 12-rayed star base, possibly Heisey, circa 1930's, 2" diam.

2852—PERSIAN pattern salt by Fostoria Glass (Reprint N), circa 1900, pressed, 2" diam.

2853—Round cut glass in "Cane" motif, 1¾" diam., circa 1900

2854—Round cut glass in "Diamond & Fan" motif, flared handles, 2" diam.

2855—Round cut in diamond motif, 1⅞" diam.

2856—Duplication of Fig. 2853

2857—Oval cut salt in "English Strawberry & Diamond" motif, 2⅛" long

2858—Oval cut in "Cane" design (Fig. 2853), also 2⅛" long

2859—Duplicate of Fig. 2857

2860—Oval cut salt in diamond motif (compare to Fig. 2855), 2⅛" long

2861—Almost square cut salt in diamond & fan motif, about 1¾" sq.

2862—Square cut salt in a different cane motif, 1½" square

2863—Similar to #2862, except smaller, 1¼" square

2864—Tiny round cut salt in block design, 1¼" diam.

2865—Table size salt in cut cane design, round shape, 2¾" diam.

MULTI-SIDED—PRESSED
Check also Miscellaneous and Round shapes for additional examples

2866—No. 205 salt by Hobbs, Brockunier, circa 1890, 1⅞" diam., see Reprint H

2867—Six-sided panelled salt, maker unknown, circa 1905, 2" diam.

2868—Six-sided fluted pattern, similar to Figs. 2634 & 2652, maker unknown, circa 1915, 2¼" diam.

2869—8-sided panelled salt, rayed base, maker unknown, circa 1900, 1¾" diam.

2870—Six-sided cut panelled salt, rayed base, 2¼" diam., circa 1910

2871—Plain many-panelled salt, maker unknown, after 1900, 2⅜" diam.

2872—This is a Duncan copy of Heisey's URN pattern, previously undocumented, rayed base, circa 1915-20, 2½" diam.

2873—Unusual pressed salt or candleholder in shape resembling an iceberg, maker and age unknown, 2½" diam.

2874—No. 2933 salt of Cambridge Glass (Welker 1, 110), circa 1910, also in color, 1¾" diam.

2875—No. 54 pattern of Duncan & Miller, also matches one by Paden City, another by Cambridge, circa 1905-1920, 1¾" diam.

2876—VULCAN pattern by Fostoria Glass, circa 1900, 1⅝" diam.

2877—PORTLAND pattern salt by U.S. Glass (Reprint L), pictured in assortment of this pattern in wholesale catalogue, made in color as a novelty, 1⅛" high, 1¾" diam.

2878—Same as Fig. 2877 except about 1¼" high

2879—PURITAN pattern by Fostoria Glass, circa 1905, six-sided, light cutting, 2¼" diam.

2880—Same as Fig. 2874, except with light cutting, Cambridge Glass, 1¾" diam.

2881—Round fluted salt of quality pressed crystal, maker unknown, circa 1910, 1¾" diam.

2882—Multi-sided panel pattern, maker unknown, circa 1915, almost 2" diam.

2883—Similar to Fig. 2879, this is Cambirdge #2800-19 "Community" hexagon salt

2884—Six-sided panelled salt with acid cutting, maker unknown, circa 1920, 2" diam.

2885—BLOCK pattern salt, known in ruby-stained, probably Duncan, circa 1890's 1¾" diam.

2886—Another six-sided panelled salt, rayed base, maker unknown, circa 1910, 1½" diam.

2887—No. 72 pattern of Duncan & Miller, with cutting, Kamm calls the pattern FLAWLESS, circa 1905-10, slightly oval shaped, 2" diam. at widest point

2888—Eight panels atop plain base, maker unknown, circa 1910, 2" diam. round

2889—Round top flange with six flat panels, pattern unknown, circa 1890, 2" diam.

2890—Another six-sided panelled salt with waffle design in base, circa 1895-1900, 1¾" diam.

2891—Five rounded points on this star-shaped salt, maker unknown, circa 1890, 1¾" diam.

2892—Multi-sided panels with cut ribbing at center, maker unknown, circa 1910, 1⅞" diam.

2893—Virtually identical to Fig. 2890, this one is almost 2" diam.

2894—A table salt in this same shape is shown in the Bakewell, Pears & co. catalogue (Reprint G), perhaps this smaller 2" diam. ind. size is also Bakewell, circa 1870

2895—Similar to #2884 except eight-sided, made by Fostoria (paper label inside), circa 1940, 1¾" diam.

FACETED & HONEYCOMBS (Cut & Pressed)

2896—Unusual shape in pressed glass, maker unknown, circa 1900, 1¾" diam. at top

2897—Square pressed salt with faceted pattern, circa 1910, 1" high, 2¼" square

2898—Round faceted cut salt with large cut star in base, circa 1905, 1¼" high, 3¼" diam.

2899—Square faceted cut glass salt, old, ¾" high, 2½" square

2900—Triangular cut salt, circa 1910, ¾" high, 1¾" across side

2901—Pressed "Honeycomb" salt, 1" high, 2¼" diam., this type salt was made by MANY different companies, originally called "Diamond" or "New York"—see Reprint C, D, G, H, I, L

2902—Pressed six-sided salt, maker unknown, circa 1900, 2¾" diam.

2903—Unusual cut glass salt with geometric cutting, circa 1910, 1¾" across

2904—Pressed octagonal salt, maker unknown, circa 1915, 1⅞" diam.

2905—Charming cut glass salt with faceted cutting, circa 1910, 2" diam.

2906—Honeycomb salt (see notes Fig. 2901), 1¼" high, 2" diam., pressed glass, 1870-1910

2907—Same design, different size, 1" high, 2½" diam.

2908—Same design, different size, 1" high 2" diam.

2909—Same design, different size, 1¼" high, 2" diam.

2910—Same design, different size, ¾" high, 2" diam.

2911—Same dimensions as #2910, but different, less polished

2912-2914—Three different sizes of same design, known made by Fostoria, circa 1910 (WFG, 22), probably made by others, including English. Faceted top with ribbed round base, #2912 is 2¼", #2913 is 2" diam., #2914 is 1¾" diam.

2915—Same design in large oval shape, maker unknown, circa 1900, 2¾" long

2916—Cut honeycomb tiny salt, old, 1½" diam.

2917—See notes Fig. 2901, 1⅛" high, almost 2" diam.

2918—Cut honeycomb salt of exceptional brilliance, 1⅝" high, 2¼" diam.

2919—See notes Fig. 2901 for this Honeycomb pressed salt, just under 1" high, 2¼" diam.

2920—Another Honeycomb pressed salt, ¾" high, 2" diam., similar to Fig. 2910

2921—Cut Honeycomb salt with star in base, ⅝" high, 1¾" diam.

2922—Pressed glass faceted salt with flanged ribbed round base, 2¾" diam. at base, maker unknown, circa 1900

2923—Cut Honeycomb table salt, circa 1900, 2¾" diam.

2924—Ind. cut Honeycomb salt, old, 1" high, 2¼" diam.

2925—Somewhat different faceted design, cut glass, 1¾" high, 2½" diam.

FOOTED SALTS— PRESSED UNLESS NOTED

2926—Free-blown English salt with applied feet, all crystal, crimped top, almost 3" diam., circa 1895

2927—FROSTED EAGLE pattern by Crystal Glass Co., circa 1880, name

based on covered pieces which have eagle finial, also in rare ind. size (Fig. 2967), 2⅞" diam.

2928—Crude pressed glass salt, foreign, age uncertain, reportedly Mexican, 2⅝" diam.

2929—Unsigned PANELLED THISTLE by Higbee, circa 1915, coloring has slight tinge of yellow compared to Fig. 3409, 1⅜" high and 2¼" diam.

2930—DIAMOND POINT DISCS by Higbee, circa 1905-10, 1¾" diam.

2931—Ribbed design with three tri-pod feet, English, circa 1890, 2" diam.

2932—Round blown salt with applied reeded feet, probably English, 1900, 1⅞" diam.

2933—ATLAS pattern by Bryce (also U.S. Glass), circa 1890, also made in table size (Fig. 3686), 1½" high, 2¼" diam. at base

2934—APPLIED BANDS pattern (Metz 2, 128), maker unknown, circa 1890, 2" diam.

2935—Bryce, Higbee & Co.'s PERSIAN pattern (aka PRISM & BLOCK BAND), circa 1880's 1¾" diam.

2936—Imitation cut pressed salt or pomade, no pattern name known, circa 1900-10, 2" diam.

2937—Five-footed salt with 10-point star in base, may be English, circa 1885-90, 2" diam. at top

2938—EMPRESS pattern by Riverside, circa 1899, rare in green, 2" diam. at top

2939—BANDED STAR by King, Son & Co., 1880, name by Lee (VG), very rare, 2" long rectangular

2940—"Octagon" footed salt, made by many different companies, circa 1880-1900, 2" long rectangular

2941—Unusual round footed salt, maker unknown, circa 1890, 2" diam.

2942—"Cabinet" salt by Adams, ind. size, circa 1890 (Reprint A), about 2" square

2943—Triangular shaped footed salt, seen in Scottish catalogue, circa 1880, 2" across side

2944—Unusual "figure eight" salt, rayed base, maker unknown, circa 1890, 2" long, 1" high

2945—Another unique cut shape, ribs and arched panels, 2¼" long, circa 1895, maker unknown

2946—Four-footed geometric pressed salt, foreign, circa 1885, 2¾" diam.

2947—Fostoria's No. 2513 "individual almond" in GRAPE-LEAF pattern, circa 1935-42, 2½" diam.

2948—This has all the pattern character of Imperial's CAPE COD (WDG2, 173), lacking the diamond-point band at the top, circa 1930, 2¼" diam. round

2949—Rectangular footed table salt with scalloped top, 3¼" long, maker unknown, circa 1890

2950—Unusual foreign pressed salt, circa 1895, 3" diam. at widest point, round shape

2951—Table size "Octagon" salt (see

Fig. 2940), may be Adams or McKee, 3¼" long rectangular, circa 1890-1900

PEDESTAL-BASED SALTS
PRESSED UNLESS NOTED

2952—TREE OF LIFE pattern by Portland Glass, circa 1860's, 1⅞" high, just over 2" diam.

2953—TUXEDO pattern by Fostoria Glass, circa 1900-10, 2¼" high, 2" diam.

2954—LADY HAMILTON by Richards & Hartley, aka PEERLESS (OMN), circa 1880, 1¾" diam.

2955—LOOP & DART by Portland Glass, patented 1869, flint glass, 2⅜" diam.

2956—PANELLED ACORN BAND, non-flint pattern of 1870's, maker unknown, just over 2¼" diam.

2957—D & M #54 by Duncan & Miller, circa 1905-10 (H6, 83), just over 1½" diam., 1⅝" high

2958—Same except with light cutting around center

2959—FLAT PANEL by Heisey, trade-marked, 1⅞" diam. at top, circa 1905

2960—Uncertain, but this may be HEISEY COLONIAL, not signed, 1¾" diam., circa 1900

2961—Most confusing of all, this matches D&M #61 and D&M #65, McKee's No. 20 COLONIAL (Stout, 249), and Cambridge #2800-21 "Community" footed salt, all date circa 1900-1920, example here is 2" high, 1¾" diam.

2962—Cambridge No. 2630 COLONIAL (Welker 2, 96), circa 1910, 1¾" high, 1⅞" diam.

2963—LUCERE pattern by Fostoria, circa 1900-1910, 2" high, 1¾" diam.

2964—Cannot match to mother pattern, double-step stem is unique, another "Colonial" type pattern from the 1900-1910 period, 1½" diam., almost 1⅞" high

2965—Almost identical to Fig. 2957, slight diff. in size, cut with sprig and geometric design, may be Duncan, circa 1910, 1¾" diam., 1¾" high

2966—SPRIG IN SNOW pattern (PS, 40), maker unknown, circa 1890, rare in blue, 1⅜" square

2967—See notes Fig. 2927 on this FROSTED EAGLE ind. salt, 1½" high, 2" diam.

2968—Pressed glass pedestal salt with light IVT, circa 1915, maker unknown, 2" diam.

2969—URN pattern by Heisey, circa 1905-15, 2" diam.

2970—BEADED TRIANGLE or DIAMOND PYRAMIDS rare salt, advertised by Fostoria in 1902, the salt shaker is known in chocolate, 1¾" diam. at six-sided top

2971—Unusual salt marked "Patent Applied For", maker unknown, circa 1900, 1¾" high 1½" diam.

2972—HARTFORD pattern by Fostoria, circa 1900-10, 1¾" square

2973—Most unusual design, probably foreign, circa 1910, 2⅜" long at widest

2974—Light mold-blown stemmed salt of the 1920-40 period, lightly etched, 1⅝" high, 1½" diam.

2975—Same type as #2974, low stem, 1¼" high, 1½" diam.

2976—Identical to Fig. 2974, different etching

2977—This appears to be No. 355 salt by Cambridge (Welker 1, 108), circa 1920's, 1½" diam.

2978—Another etched mold-blown salt of this same period, maker unknown, circa 1920's, 1½" high, 2" diam. at top

2979—Low-stem etched salt, maker unknown, circa 1920's, 1½" high, 1⅝" diam. at top

2980—This appears to be FOSTORIA SWIRL (K5, 20) oval salt, circa 1905, 2¾" long

2981—Same as Fig. 521 except unsigned, probably French, circa 1900-10, 2¼" diam. at top

2982—Similar to Fig. 781 but not same, maker unknown, circa 1920, may be an almond dish, just over 2½" diam.

2983—Unusual foreign pressed glass example, circa 1900-10, 1¾" high, 2¾" diam.

MORE PEDESTAL-BASED SALTS
PRESSED UNLESS NOTED

2984—Either Mexican or other foreign origin, pressed floral pattern, circa 1920, 2½" diam.

2985—Late pressed pattern with thin band of diamond-point over fluted panels, maker unknown, pattern unknown, circa 1920-30, 2½" diam.

2986—POWDER & SHOT pattern from the 1870 period, attributed to Sandwich based on shards, 2¾" diam.

2987—BEADED GRAPE MEDALLION, by Boston-Silver Glass Co., patented 1869, see also Fig. 2522, 2¾" diam.

2988—Mold-blown, etched salt or nut cup, 1920's vintage, maker unknown, 2¼" diam.

2989—The iridescent acidized finish on this salt is typically Fostoria, circa 1930's, 2" diam. at top

2990—Same shape, slightly larger than #2989, cut design, may be Fostoria, circa 1930's or 40's, 2⅛" diam. at top

2991—SUNRAY pattern by Fostoria, circa 1935-45, almond cup, 2¼" diam. at top

2992—No. 2374 salt by Fostoria, goes well with LAFAYETTE pattern (WFG, 227), 2¼" diam. at top, made in several colors

2993-2994—Same design, different sizes, in crimped mold-blown salt and "almond", possibly by Cambridge, circa 1920. Fig. 2993 is 1¾" high, 2" diam., Fig. 2994 is 2" high, 2¼" diam.

2995—Duplicate of Fig. 2975 with slightly different etching

2996—Mold-blown with light cutting, probably an almond dish, circa 1920's, 2⅜" diam. at top

2997—Small enough to be a salt, etched mold-blown, maker unknown, 1⅞" diam.

2998—A pressed diamond band pattern on fluted pedestal, maker unknown, circa 1900, 1⅝" diam.

2999—Cut diamond band on fluted base, circa 1900, 2" diam. at top

3000—Pressed diamond and fan design of unknown origin, circa 1910, 1½" diam.

3001—Unusual cut geometric design, circa 1910, 1¾" diam.

3002—Tiny diamond-point cutting, early 1900's, 1⅜" diam.

3003-3005—The first one is cut, the next two are etched, 3003 & 3005 are same mold, all three are 2½" diam. at top, maker uncertain

3006—Low pedestal cut salt or almond, appears to be signed but unrecognizable, circa 1920, 2⅜" diam., maker unknown

3007—Intricate geometric cut salt, quite choice, 2" diam., circa 1890

3008—Duplicate of Fig. 2999

3009—Late cut salt signed "Clark", circa 1915-25, 1⅝" diam.

3010—Another intricate cut salt, delicate cutting, 1¾" diam. at top, old

3011—Cut diamond & fan family salt, similar design to Fig. 3000, 2" diam. at top

UNUSUAL SHAPES—
PRESSED & CUT

3012—Almost heart-shaped cut glass salt or small nappy, 3½" from top to bottom, circa 1900, 1" high

3013—Tri-cornered ornate cut glass salt, 2¾" each side

3014—Probably an ash tray, this 1898 souvenir for a lodge convention is probably by U.S. Glass, who made most known Pittsburgh souvenirs, 2½" across, ¾" high

3015—Tri-corner shape, most unusual open-work edge, maker unknown, circa 1930, 2-¾" diam.

3016—Small swirled design pedestal salt with handle, shaped like toy gravy boat, maker unknown, circa 1905, NMT, also reproduced

3017-3027—A wide variety of salts from a No. 200 set by Westmoreland Glass, circa 1915-20's, also made by Dalzell at Findlay (SM FIN, 63) called EUCHRE SALTS. Note there is some duplication in shapes, except one is straight-sided, the other slightly rounded on the sides. The Westmoreland catalogue shows straight-sided shapes (Figs. 3018, 3020, 3021,

3022, 3025, 3027). Fig. 3023 is cut, not part of these confusing copies.

3028 — SUNRAY salt by Fostoria, circa 1935-45, see also Fig. 2991, 1¾" each side, #2991 almond cup in same pattern

3029 — Maltese Cross shaped salt by Hobbs, Brockunier, circa 1890 (Reprint H), 1¾" across

3030 — Triangular shape in polished crystal, maker unknown, 1¾" each side

3031 — Diamond shape in cut glass, brilliant period, 2¾" diam. at widest point

3032 — Horse-shoe shape cut salt with paper label "Made in Czechoslavakia", recent import, 2" diam. at widest point

3033-3035 — Heart, Club & Diamond shape in cut glass, probably a bridge set, circa 1915, exceptional detail, all three are 1" high, 4th to set is Spade shape

3036 — Another cut glass example with five-sides with cut-star, circa 1910, 1¼" high

3037 — Heart-shaped cut glass salt, panels of diamond-point, ¾" high

3038 — A rarity in open salts — a combination knife rest/salt in cut glass, highly polished mirrored crystal, may be foreign, circa 1900, 4½" long

3039 — Pressed glass knife rest/salt by George Duncan & Sons, marked "Pat'd Feb 27, 1872", appeared in Duncan catalogue for 1880's, 4" long

3040 — Diamond-shaped pressed glass salt, most unusual, maker unknown, 1⅛" high

3041 — Another horse-shoe shape, light mold-blown crystal, may be foreign, ¾" high

PATTERN GLASS & CUT GLASS

3042 — CLEAR & DIAMOND PANELS (Metz 1, 199), maker unknown, toy table set known in color, dates from about 1900, 1¼" high

3043 — CHAMPION pattern by McKee, circa 1900-1910, 1¼" high

3044 — MOON & STAR salt by Adams (U.S. Glass), hard to find an old example as shown here, much reproduced in color (never made originally), 1½" high, see Fig. 4672-4673

3045 — AZTEC pomade jar by McKee, circa 1900-05, 1¼" high

3046 — PRISM COLUMN by U.S. Glass, pomade jar, circa 1892, one of many zippered panel patterns

3047 — PRIZE pattern by McKee, pomade jar, circa 1900-10, 1¼" high

3048 — URN pattern by Heisey, duplication of Fig. 2969

3049 — WESTON pattern by Robinson Glass Co., circa 1899, rare, 1¼" high

3050 — OLD PANELLED THISTLE salt, smaller than reproduction, made by Higbee, circa 1915, under 1" high

3051 — HEISEY'S PINEAPPLE & FAN pattern, circa 1900, salt rare in green, NMT

3052 — Early LENOX pattern by McKee, circa 1900, this same name used on a later McKee pattern, salt is rare, also made in a pomade, NMT

3053 — VIGILANT pattern by Fostoria, circa 1900, larger pieces have a dividing line on the bulge at base, NMT

3054 — ALEXIS pattern by Fostoria, circa 1900-05, scarce in color, see notes Fig. 332

3055 — Sim. to Fig. 3021 except larger, possibly Westmoreland, circa 1920, just under 1" high

3056 — Bird figural salt or other novelty by Fostoria (WFG, 235), circa 1940, just under 1½" high

3057 — CORDOVA pattern salt by O'Hara (also U.S.) circa 1890's, rare in green, 1" high

3058 — FANCY ARCH by McKee Glass, circa 1900-05, 1¼" high

3059 — ALLOVER DIAMOND by Duncan, circa 1890, also U.S. Glass (H5, 103), NMT

3060 — Rectangular salt with plain sides, buttoned waffle design in base, maker unknown, circa 1890, 1" high

3061 — SHELL & TASSEL ind. butter pat by Duncan, circa 1881-1890, Reprint D, could also be used as a salt, scarce in color, 3¼" diam. Some documentation will indicate this was originally made at Portland Glass Co. in 1869

3062 — Plain square salt with impressed 8-point star in base, circa 1890, stars on each base corner, 1" high

3063 — WINONA pattern by Greensburgh Glass, circa 1890's, (K3, 135), NMT

3064 — Exceptionally brilliant cut salt, round shape, choice and old, under 1" high

3065 — Cut glass with cane design on base, polished panels on sides, 1" high

3066 — Cut glass in popular "diamond & fan" motif, good detail, 1" high

3067 — Another old cut glass salt of special detail, diamond ellipses with fans, oval shape, 1" high

3068 — Square-shaped, variation of diamond & fan with plain panels, star-cut base is different from most, just over 1" high

3069 — Square shape, tapered style, diamond & fan cutting, old, 1¼" high

3070 — Triangluar rounded shape with strawberry-diamond & fan cutting, very nice, 1¼" high

3071 — Cut oval shape in pinwheel & star cutting, some grinding on center rim, 1" high

3072 — Round with unique geometric cutting extending from base to sides, 1" high

3073 — Square shape with two rows of horizontal star borders, cut, serrated corners, 1¼" high

CUT GLASS INDIVIDUALS

Anyone familiar with researching cut glass is very much aware that there are literally thousands of different variations in design. Even a popular singular motif can be found in dozens of slightly different forms. Cut glass is the creation of an artist, a glass cutter working with a cutting wheel and his imagination. Many of the designs were copied in pressed glass, and some of the examples shown here could easily be confused for pressed. However, each one was carefully examined to separate the two categories. We considered describing the cutting on each of the examples shown on the next six pages, but decided that the photographs could do a much better job than words. It is virtually impossible to name makers, except for the few examples which are marked or signed, nor is it possible to determine which examples are American and which are European. By far the most difficult job is telling you which are from 1880 and which from 1920. We ask that you bear with us on these limitations. Only a brief discription is provided. Most of the salts are turn-of-the century.

ROUND SHAPE — FLAT TOP

3074 — Thick, heavy, brilliant cutting, 1⅞" diam.

3075 — Star in diamond cut, 1¾" diam.

3076 — Unusual combination of two cut motifs, 1⅞" diam.

3077 — Feather and fan cut, 1⅞" diam.

3078 — Ornate diamond cut, 1⅞" diam.

3079 — Outstanding "Russian" cut with fan, heavy, 1⅞" diam.

3080 — Unusual design, almost 2" diam.

3081 — Cut diamond and flute, 1¾" diam.

3082 — Unique diamond cutting, 1¾" diam.

3083 — Etched laurel spray around top, diamond cut at bottom, 1⅞" diam.

3084 — Panels of prisms and star cut, just under 2" diam.

3085 — Strawberry diamond cutting, 1¾" diam.

3086 — Rows of double prisms, 1¾" diam.

3087 — Prism cut in high relief, 1¾" diam.

3088 — Tapered shape in prism cut, 1⅜" diam.

3089 — Another round prism cut, 1⅞" diam.

3090 — Low round prism cut, 1½" diam.

3091 — Straight-sided prism cut with 10-point sides, 1¾" diam.

3092 — Geometric cut of many motifs, 1⅞" diam.

3093 — Similar to Fig. 3082, 1¾" diam.

3094—Prism cut with open star 1⅝" diam.

3095—Prism cut with bulging plain panels between, just under 1½" diam.

3096—Ornate brilliant cut, exceptionally nice, 1⅞" diam.

3097—Interesting combination of cuttings, 1⅞" diam.

3098—Panels of diamonds and star cut, 2" diam.

3099—Lined star cut, different, 1½" diam.

3100—Another variation of the popular diamond and fan motif, 1⅛" diam.

3101—Diamond point cutting, just over 1¼" diam.

3102—Another diamond point cutting, 1½" diam.

3103—Unique block cutting, 1" high, 1½" diam.

3104—Variation of the notched prism cutting, similar to Fig. 3089, 1¾" diam.

3105—Combination of double and triple rows of prisms, 1½" diam.

3106—Double rows of prisms with cut stars, 1¾" diam.

3107—Cut cane motif, 1¾" diam.

3108—Combination of several cut motifs, zippers, panels, prism, etc. almost 2" diam.

CUT GLASS, ROUND SHAPE, MOSTLY FLAT TOPS

3109—Prism cutting similar cutting to smaller Fig. 3120, 2¼" diam.

3110—Diamond point cut with fluting at base, 1⅞" diam.

3111—An interesting punty type cut, unusual 2½" diam.

3112—Panels of diamond point and pillar, 1⅞" diam.

3113—An unusual double flute cutting, just over 2" diam.

3114—Very pretty geometric cut of varying motifs, 2¼" diam.

3115—All-over diamond cut, 2⅛" diam.

3116—Combination of ellipses and notched prism cutting, just over 2" diam.

3117—Alternating panels of zippered blocks and prism cut, 2" diam.

3118—Very delicately cut diamond pattern on a heavy, thick salt, 2" diam.

3119—Another variation of prism cutting, a common motif, 1¾" diam.

3120—Compare to Fig. 3109, virtually identical except in size, 1¾" diam.

3121—Delicate cut design, most attractive, 2⅛" diam.

3122—Unusual criss-cross cutting to create a honeycomb effect, 2" diam.

3123—Oval sections of diamond cutting with double fan, 2" diam.

3124—Pinwheel cutting, possibly Cambridge, circa 1920, 1¾" diam.

3125—Combination of acid cut flower on honeycomb background, 1½" diam.

3126—Tiny diamond-point cut, just over 1" diam.

3127—Another variation of pinwheel cutting, 1⅝" diam.

3128—Combined floral and geometric cut from later period (1915), 2" diam.

3129—Cut fluting, scalloped top, highly polished, 2½" diam.

3130—Unusual protruding star and prism cut at bottom, plain flange top, possibly a patch box or pomade, 2⅛" diam.

3131—Attractive and unusual grooved cutting, 2" diam.

3132—Combination of prism and honeycomb cut panels, 1⅞" diam.

3133—Plain round mold-blown with band of tiny punty cutting, 2" diam.

3134—Deep ball-shaped with fringe motif cut, 2" diam.

3135—Unusual geometric diamond cut, sharp and angular, 2¾" diam. point to point

3136—Large size with lovely "picket" style cutting, 2½" diam.

3137—Variation of geometric cuttings, very nice, 2¼" diam.

CUT GLASS, ROUND SHAPE, UNEVEN TOPS

3138—Outstanding star and prism cutting, 2¾" diam.

3139—Same as Fig. 3130 except with scalloped top, 2" diam.

3140—Lovely example of cane and prism motifs with cutting extending into base, 2⅞" diam.

3141—Exceptional example with star in diamond cutting, 2" round

3142—Interesting notched step cut with serrated top rim, just over 2½" diam.

3143—Similar cut to Fig. 3141, with a fan motif, very nice, 2¼" diam.

3144—One of many diamond and fan (pineapple & fan) cuttings, 2" diam.

3145—Outstanding fan cut motif, unusual shape, choice, 2¼" diam.

3146-3147—Two examples of popular diamond and fan cutting, slight difference in size represents the unique nature of cut glass—no two pieces are exactly the same. Fig. 3146 is just over 1" high, 2¼" diam., Fig. 3147 is 1" high, 2¼" diam., same exact cutting

3148—Unusual diagonal groove cutting, 2" diam.

3149—A reversed variation of diamond and fan cut with fans open downward, choice, 2½" diam.

3150—A combination of stars, diamonds and fans in this brilliant period example, 2" diam.

3151—Attractive shape in another variation of diamond and fan cut, 2" diam.

3152—Rows of parallel prisms, 2¼" diam.

3153—Stars cut inside diamonds with fan border, very pretty, just under 2" diam.

3154—Most unusual shape and geometric cut, 1¾" diam.

3155—Another example of common all-over diamond cutting (see 3115, 3158, 3217, 3244) 1⅞" diam.

3156—Alternating diamond cut with double fans, 2" diam.

3157—Cut panels with ornate diamond border along base, notched scallops, 1⅞" diam.

3158—Diamond point cut similar to several pressed glass patterns, 1¾" diam.

3159—Ornate star and prism cutting, 1⅞" diam.

3160—Another star and prism panel cutting, 1¾" diam.

3161—Similar to Fig. 3156, slightly different size and shape, 1⅞" diam.

3162—Geometric fan design with prism panels, 2" diam.

3163—Another diamond and fan cutting, different shape from #3144, 3146-47, 3151, 1⅞" diam.

3164—Ornate diamond cutting, unusual notched base design, 2" diam.

3165—Another ornate geometric design of diamonds and cross-cut panels, 1¾" diam.

3166—Ornate star and prism panel cut, finely serrated top, 1⅞" diam.

3167—Most unusual fluted cutting with bands of cane cutting underneath, choice, 1¾" diam.

CUT GLASS, ROUND SHAPE

3168—Combination of diamond and feather cutting, most attractive, 2¼" diam.

3169—Another variation of diamond and fan cutting, 1¾" diam.

3170—Unusual handled cut salt with star and fan motif, 2½" diam. plus handles

3171—Combination of pressed and cut, floral spray, 1¾" diam.

3172—All-over diamond cutting on small collared base, 2¾" diam.

3173—Panelled variation of diamond and fan cut motif, 1⅞" diam.

3174—A tiny example of popular diamond and fan cutting, 1⅝" diam.

3175—Choice example of star and double fan cutting, 1¾" diam.

3176—Large size cut diamonds with fan border, 1¾" diam.

3177—Tiny geometric combination of varying motifs, similar to others (3108, 3162) but as stated before, they are all hand cut, 1½" diam.

3178—Cut sectional block motif, 1⅞" diam.

3179—Similar to Fig. 3178, except slightly smaller, 1⅝" diam.

3180—Westmoreland's No. 210 cut salt (Reprint W), circa 1920, 1⅝" diam.

3181—Prism cutting with double-fan panels, 2" diam.

3182—Combination of pressed & cut, Cambridge Glass Co., 1¾" diam.

3183—Another diamond and fan variation with cross-bars between, 1⅝" diam.

3184—Star and diamond cut with fan borders, 1¾" diam.

3185—Delicate fine-cut diamond and fan, choice, just under 2" diam.

3186—One of many variations of prism cutting, 1⅞" diam.

3187-88—The same cutting in prism motif, subtle differences in shape, both 1½" diam.

3189—Exceptional band of "finecut" at top, serration at bottom, very nice, 1⅝" diam.

3190—Reversed sections of prism cut fans, 1¾" diam.

3191—Varying geometric linear cuttings, 1¾" diam.

3192—All-over cane motif of exceptional brilliance, 1½" diam.

3193—Another pleated cut with grooved waist, 1¾" diam.

3194—Diamond point cut pointed ellipses with fans between, 1¾" diam.

3195—Pressed and cut salt, see notes Fig. 2875, Cambridge/Duncan/Paden City, 1⅝" diam.

3196—Cut faceted honeycomb motif, other examples on next page, 1⅞" diam.

3197—Exceptional example from brilliant period, six-sided, just over 2" diam.

3198—Ornate geometric cut motif, six-sided, 2¼" diam.

3199—Unusual alternating panels of clear and diamond/fan motifs, 2" diam.

CUT GLASS, OVAL SHAPE

3200—Popular "strawberry-diamond" cutting, 2⅛" long

3201—Combination of acid floral and geometric cut, very nice, 2" long

3202—Large table size salt in variation of diamond and fan cutting, 2⅝" long

3203—Block pattern cutting, found in several shapes and variations, almost 2" long

3204—Very choice star and fan motif, serrated top, 2½" long

3205—Tapered shape in a prism cutting, serrated top, 2⅝" long

3206—Diamond cut at the top, plain at the base, 2½" long

3207—Oval variation of the popular prism cut, 2½" long

3208—Interesting elongated diamond cut, 1⅝" long

3209—Another variation of star and double fan cutting, very pretty, 2¼" long

3210—Multisided with faceted cutting, 2¼" long

3211—Another low salt with faceted cutting, 2⅛" long

3212—Another beautiful prism cut oval salt, 2¼" long

3213—Faceted cutting, highly polished crystal, 2⅛" long

3214—Cane pattern cutting, similar to pressed pattern, 2⅜" long

3215—Variation of diamond and double fan cutting, 2¼" long

3216—All-over diamond cutting along top and on base, plain band between, almost 3" long

3217—Large all-over diamond cutting, 3½" long

3218—Canoe shaped salt with cane cutting on base, extremely choice, 3¼" long

3219—Choice star and fan design, serrated top, just over 3¼" long

3220—Crossed diamond and fan cutting, just over 3¼" long

3221—Low, elongated swag and fan cutting, 4⅛" long

3222—Combination of diamond borders stars and hobstars, nice shape, exceptional, 3" long

CUT GLASS—SQUARE AND RECTANGULAR SHAPES

3223—Interesting geometric design, unusual top, choice, 1⅜" square

3224—Westmoreland's No. 209 cut salt, circa 1920, see Reprint W, 1⅝" square

3225—Low square salt with combination of pressed and cut designs, 1⅝" square

3226—Rectangular table salt with diamond and fan motif, 3" long

3227—Four-sided but rounded ind. salt with outstanding cutting, 1⅝" square

3228—Another exceptional square example with intricate cutting, 1⅝" square

3229—Pillar and star combination, 1¾" square

3230—Plain and prism cut panels, serrated top, 1¾" square

3231—Sectional block cutting, 1⅞" square

3232—Nailhead diamond cut, unusual, 1¾" square

3233—Squared version of popular "strawberry-diamond" cutting, 1⅞" square

3234—Assorted geometric motifs in an appealing combination, 1½" square

3235—Pillar cut square salt with rounded interior bowl, 1½" square

3236—Single star motif bordered by sawtooth cutting, nice, 1⅝" square

3237—Possibly an ind. ashtray or pin dish, tilted to show base, 2½" long rectangular, ½" high

3238—Plain cut square with bevelled corners, 1½" square

3239—Diamond with double fan cutting, prism cut corners, 1¾" long rectangular

3240—Another variation of prism cutting, 1⅝" long rectangular

3241—Small all-over diamond cut, 1⅛" square

3242—Artistically cut geometric shape, unique stepped base, 1⅜" square

3243—Single star with prism cut borders, very nice, 1½" square

3244—All-over diamond cut with collared base, similar to Fig. 3172, 1½" square, import from 1970's as small candle holder

3245—Geometric fan type cut, 1¼" square

3246—All-over diamond point cutting, unusual, 1⅛" square

3247—Rectangular with light criss-cross cutting, just over 2" long, 1⅞" wide, almost square

3248—Square with bevelled corners, 1½" square

3249—Fostoria No. 2593 salt (WFG, pg. 246), circa 1940's, 1½" square

3250—Tapered polished cut crystal, recent vintage, 1¾" square

3251—Slightly tapered sides, octagonal interior opening, wide bevelled corners, 1½" square at top, 1⅝" square at base

3252—Cut and polished with bevelled top edge, round interior bowl, 1½" square

3253—Cut faceted salt with fluted cutting, 1¾" square

3254—Recent cut salt with original paper label, Czechoslovakian, 1⅞" square

3255—Recent import, pedestal based, 1⅝" square at top

3256-3257—Look identical in photograph but both have subtle differences in size and cutting, both are 1¾" square

3258—Another highly polished plain cut salt, 1⅝" square at widest

3259—Cut and engraved with leaf design intaglio cut, 1½" square

MISCELLANEOUS PRESSED AND CUT

3260 — Pedestal-based non-flint pressed salt, pattern appears to match RIBBED LOOP (Metz 2, 12), circa 1870, maker unknown, 2¾" diam.

3261—As stated before, it is difficult to match fluted or colonial salts to "mother" line, this example is flint, circa 1865, 2¾" diam.

3262—Lacy period salt, non-flint, Neal RP-25, Sandwich Glass, circa 1850's, 2¾" diam.

3263—Early blown three-mold salt from early 1800's, probably American, 2½" diam.

3264—Four-footed oval pressed salt with frosted background, floral unfrosted design in slight relief, 3⅜" long, appears to be foreign, circa 1920

3265—Probably by same maker, frosted and clear floral design, paper label on base looks like a trademark from Europe, circa 1920's

3266—Non-flint small lacy pressed salt, origin unknown, possibly French, circa 1840's, 2" diam. round

3267—Another round lacy salt with French characteristics, non-flint, circa 1840's, 2½" diam.

3268-3269—Signed Hawkes ind. salts with light cut wreath around waist, same salt in slightly different sizes, about 1" high, 1½" diam., circa 1920's

3270—Square geometric cut salt, probably foreign, age unknown, just over 1¼" square

3271—Delicately frosted and cut salt or pomade, Verre de Soi type iridescence, circa 1920, 1⅝" diam.

3272—Pressed round blank with lightly cut leaf spray, circa 1915, 1⅝" diam.

3273—Signed Hawkes pedestal-based salt with delicate cut floral spray, circa 1920's, just under 2" diam.

3274—Pedestal-based cut with diamond-star motif, oval shape, 2¼" long

3275—Round pedestal-based example with cut diamond point band, fluted base, just over 2" diam.

3276—Small size with ornate geometric cutting, 1¼" diam.

3277—Fine variation of cut strawberry-diamond with fan border motif, 2⅛" diam., choice

3278—Pressed round salt with delicate crosshatch cutting, 1¾" diam.

3279—The stark linear cutting dates this post-1920, probably foreign, 1⅞" diam.

3280—Cut panels of diamond point and zippered motifs, very nice, 2" diam.

3281—Round all-over diamond of superior quality, 2⅛" diam.

3282—Signed Hawkes ornately cut salt, circa 1900-10, 1⅞" diam.

3283—Smocking type cut motif, round shape, good quality, 2⅛" diam.

3284—Pedestal based hobstar cut salt or almond dish, 2¼" high. 2½" diam.

3285—Very nice example using cane and prism cutting, 2⅜" diam.

3286—Delicate mold-blown with threading motif, scalloped top, 2½" diam.

3287—Round cut punty design, 2⅜" diam.

ASSORTED SHAPES— PRESSED & CUT

3288—Another variation of popular diamond and fan cut motif, 1⅞" diam. round

3289—Very choice combination of geometric cuttings, round shape, 2" diam.

3290—Duplication of Fig. 3223

3291—Brilliant cut salt with panels of prism and star motifs, very nice, 2" diam. round

3292—Another fancy cut ind. with variety motifs, 1¾" diam. round

3293—Duplication of Fig. 3156, apparently a common salt

3294—Oval variation of cane type cutting, 2" long

3295—Square tab-handled ind., cut with cane motif, 1¼" square

3296—Plain cut salt with eight sides, new from Czechoslovakia, 1¾" diam.

3297—Six-sided plain panel cut salt, new from Czechoslovakia, 1⅝" diam.

3298—Plain block cut salt, six sections, 1¾" diam.

3299—Low eight-sided cut salt, signed Val St. Lambert, Belgium, just under 2" diam.

3300—Oval pressed salt with light wreath cut spray, 2" long

3301—Delicately engraved floral motif, may be a pomade, foreign, 1½" diam.

3302—Large oval salt with paper label from Tiffany & Co., made in West Germany, recent vintage, 2⅞" long

3303—Oval hat-shaped salt with extending "brim", light cutting almost invisible in photo, 2⅝" long

3304—Etched Greek Key motif, frosted and clear, foreign, circa 1910, 1⅞" diam. round

3305—Pressed oval salt with etched floral spray, notched upper rim, 2⅞" long.

3306—Pressed hexagonal star by Cambridge, also in colors, 1⅝" diam.

3307—May be accidental, but this leaning, panelled six-sided salt is unique, 1¾" diam.

3308—Plain sides with pressed stars impressed in base, 1½" square

3309—8-sided rectangular salt with plain panels, 1½" by 2¼" long

3310—Cut pleated salt, six-sided, 1¾" diam.

3311—Plain cut six-sided salt with impressed cut star in base, 1½" diam. at top, tapered

3312—Round top with six-sided panels, pressed, almost 2" diam. at top

3313—Round "intaglio" salt with cupid design, 1⅞" diam.

3314—Rectangular "intaglio" salt or ash receiver with Oriental scene, 1½" by 1¾" long

3315—Pressed three-footed salt or ash tray, probably European, circa 1920, cut design, 2¾" diam. round

3316—Round pressed table salt with ribbed "button" feet on base, American, circa 1890, 2½" diam.

3317—Another round three-footed salt with light engraving, foreign, circa 1920, 2½" diam.

3318—Tub-shaped table salt with tab handles, light engraving, 2½" diam., circa 1920

MISCELLANEOUS, PRESSED, CUT & BLOWN

3319—Lovely blown crystal salt with lightly crimped top, delicate hand engraving, probably foreign, circa 1885, 2½" diam.

3320—Pedestal-based salt with cane cutting at top, fluted stem, plain frosted top rim, 2¼" high, 1⅝" diam.

3321—HERRINGBONE BAND table salt, maker unknown, listed Kamm 3, 20, similar to RIPPLE pattern, scarce, 2½" high, 2½" diam.

3322—Unusual cut glass round salt, unique geometric cutting, 1¾" high, 1¾" diam.

3323—Flat round salt or butter pat, signed Lalique in script, bought in France, 3" diam.

3324—Cut glass ind., round shape, prism and double star cutting, 2¼" diam.

3325—Unusual pedestal ind. salt with diamond point cutting and tab handles, 1¼" diam.

3326—Cut glass, square, diamond and fan cut motif, choice, 2" square

3327—Four-footed cut glass, round, notched top rim, unusual shape, 2" square

3328—Plain square salt with acid cut intaglio decoration, possibly Heisey blank, just under 2" square

3329—Square ind. salt with frosted intaglio floral decoration, very nice, 1½" square

3330—Round cut salt with ellipses, serrated top, rayed base, 2⅛" diam.

3331—Another square variation of diamond and fan cutting, 2" square

3332—Plain round salt in heavy crystal, age unknown, 1½" diam.

3333—Another version of diamond and fan cutting, fluted pedestal base, round shape, 2" diam.

3334—Choice little ind. salt with a star and diamond cutting, notched rim, 1⅞" diam.

3335—Cut glass ind. with a finecut and panel motif, serrated top, round shape, 1⅞" diam.

3336-Alternating panels of ribbed and diamond point cuttings, round shape, 1½" diam.

3337—Oval pressed salt with hand-painted tulips in red & green, age unknown, 1⅞" long, Czechoslovakian

3338—Low five-sided salt or ind. ash, diagonal cut ribs, foreign, circa 1920's, 2" long each side

3339—Low triangular salt with tulip etched in base, circa 1920's, also in colors, 2" long each side

3340—Unusual shell-shaped cut salt with notched ribs, scalloped top, 2" diam.

3341—Hexagonal low salt or ind. ash tray, maker unknown, 2½" diam.

3342—Boat-shaped cut salt with diagonal ribbing, 4" long

3343—Boat-shaped cut salt in diamond & fan motif, 3⅛" long

3344—Pedestal-based oval salt with diamond point cutting, 2⅝" long

3345—Rectangular cut salt with bands of diamond cutting at top and base, choice, 2⅛" long

3346—CAPRICE double salt dish by Cambridge, circa 1930's, oval shape, just over 4" long

3347—Round block cut ind. salt, 1⅝" diam.

3348—Round tub-shaped salt with diamond-point cutting, tab handles, 1½" diam.

3349—Low oval cut faceted salt with faded floral decoration, oval shape, 1¾" long, Czechoslovakian

3350—Very choice oval salt with geometric diamond in oval cutting, 2" long

MISCELLANEOUS PRESSED, CUT & BLOWN

3351—GRAPE LEAF salt by Fostoria, circa 1940's, 2½" diam.

3352—SCROLL WITH FLOWERS open table salt, maker unknown, circa 1880, also made in color (salt would be rare), do not confuse for similar egg cup and mustard pot base, 3½" wide including handles

3353—Pedestal based crystal cut salt with etched floral design, foreign shape, early 1900's, just under 2½" high, 2⅜" diam. at top

3354—Matching pressed "prism" open salt and pepper by Cambridge, sterling spoon, circa 1940's, salt is 1⅜" square, given as party gift for Westmoreland Sterling Company sales promotion

3355—DUNCAN'S NO. 54 salt with silver deposit decoration, circa 1920, 1⅝" diam.

3356—Plain tub-shaped pressed salt by Cambridge Glass, circa 1920's, 1¾" diam.

3357—Same salt as Fig. 3355 except with light engraving

3358—Cut pedestal-based oval salt with typical European cutting, 2¼" long

3359—Tree-trunk figural salt, possibly part of LOG CABIN set, if not it does go well with the design, Central Glass (?), circa 1880, 2½" diam. at bottom

3360—Round faceted cut salt with painted decoration unfired, 1¾" diam.

3361—Round panelled salt, pressed, 1⅜" diam.

3362—Unique advertising salt, marked "Lawson Valetine Co., New York", 2" diam. round

3363—Similar to Fig. 2503, this example has a scalloped uneven top, maker unknown, circa 1880, 2¼" diam. round

3364—Pressed round pleated design, seems to match FINE PRISM pattern (Metzl, 48), maker unknown, circa 1870, 2" diam. round

3365—Interesting shell-shaped salt, pressed, maker unknown, circa 1920, 2⅝" long

3366—Rectangular plain-sided salt with rosette design pressed into base, circa 1890, 2⅛" long

3367—Low rectangular salt with waffle design in base, pressed, circa 1885-90, 1⅞" long

3368—Square-shaped low salt tilted to show pressed base design, circa 1890, 1½" square

3369—The pressed star design here matches the same on O'Hara's BARTHOLDI (aka "Daisy & Button Band"), see Innes, pg. 377, circa 1885, also known in color, 1⅝" square

3370—Heisey's RIDGELEIGH salt, circa 1920's and later, 1¾" square

3371—Oval hat-shaped low salt with light engraving, 2⅞" long

3372—Plain oval pressed salt, no pattern, no decoration, 2" long

3373—Oval pressed salt with diamond-point band at the center, crude glass appears to be early or possibly foreign, circa 1870's, 2¾" long

3374—Signed Heisey plain pressed panelled salt, good crystal, 2¾" diam.

3375—Oval shaped pressed and cut salt, probably foreign, circa 1920's, 2⅜" long

3376—"Mason" salt, made by McKee as early as 1860's, lengthy production, 1½" high, 2¾" diam.

3377-3378—Two different diamond and fan type pressed designs, probably European, with matching underplates, possibly individual jelly or honey dishes, circa 1915-20, Fig. 3377 has a 2" diam. round saucer, Fig. 3378 has a 2¾" diam. saucer

3379—Early flint round salt, Neal #RD-9A, French, circa 1850, 2⅝" diam.

MISCELLANEOUS SALTS (Pressed & Cut)

3380—Early cut table-size salt, possibly foreign, circa 1880-90, six-sided base on stem, 3¼" long oval

3381—LINCOLN DRAPE pattern from late 1860's, reportedly a Sandwich pattern (see also Fig. 3619), flint glass, 2¾" diam.

3382—HARP pattern by Bryce, Richards & Co., 1850's, flint glass, see also Fig. 3601

3383—GROOVED THUMBPRINTS (Name by Authors) made by Gillinder (Revi, 164), flint, circa 1875-90, round, 2½" diam.

3384—PAVONIA pattern by Ripley (also U.S. Glass), circa 1890's, NMT

3385—MORNING GLORY pattern by Boston & Sandwich Glass, 1860's, very rare, 2" diam.

3386—D&M No. 40 pattern, never named, by Duncan & Miller, circa 1900-05, 1¾" diam. at top

3387—JERSEY SWIRL by Windsor Glass, circa 1880-90's, scarce in color, 1¾" diam. round

3388—BUTTON ARCHES by Duncan & Miller, also U.S. Glass, circa 1895-1910, salt is scarce, 2" diam. round

3389—Pressed, part of a celery set by John B. Higbee Glass Co, circa 1900-1910, sold with a Euclid Celery vase and called celery salts

3390—Round cut salt in "strawberry-diamond" motif, serrated top, 1⅞" diam.

3391—Brilliant period cut salt, round shape with fancy cutting, signed Hawkes, circa 1905, 2" diam.

3392—Unusual geometric cut salt with scalloped top, circa 1910, 1¾" diam. round

3393—Duplicate of Fig. 3068

3394—Round cut ind. salt in pinwheel and star motif, 2" diam.

3395—Another variation of the popular diamond and fan cut motif, 1½" diam.

3396—Round cut salt with plain and star-cut diamonds, flat top, 8-point star base, 2" diam.

3397—Fancy cut heavy ind. salt, may be English, 2" diam.

3398—Interesting tiny geometric cut salt, unusual cutting, 1½" diam.

3399—Lovely combination of diamond-point cutting with sterling applied rim, probably English, circa 1900-05, 8-point cut star in base, 2" diam.

3400—"Gem" salt by King, Son & Co., circa 1875, (Reprint K) 2½" diam. oval shape

3401—Cut glass tub-shaped salt, circa 1910-20, round, 1½" diam.

3402—Ind. pedestal-base salt with leaf spray engraving, circa 1920's, possibly Cambridge, 1¾" high, 1½" diam.

3403—European "intaglio" salt with decorated rose, bevelled edges, 2½" long

3404—Foreign pressed glass square salt, sunburst design with wreathed borders, four feet, 1¾" square

3405—Clear glass Block salt with reclining dog, Central Glass, circa 1880 (Reprint C), also shown in this book in two colors, salt is 1½" square plus dog

3406—HOMESTEAD pattern by Duncan & Miller, circa 1900-1905, 1¾" round

3407—DIAMOND ROSETTES pattern (Metz 1, 114), maker unknown, frequently confused for BUCKLE pattern, circles are round on this version, circa 1875, 2¼" diam.

3408—Foreign pressed glass "Tree of Life" type pattern, may be salt or base of covered piece, circa 1890-1900, 4" long

3409—PANELLED THISTLE, signed with the Higbee "bee" but not the letters HIG, age uncertain, repros were made in this size in the 1960's by Viking and LG Wright, see Fig. 2929 and Fig. 3050, 1⅜" high, 2¼" diam.

INTAGLIO SALTS

See notes page 108 concerning origins of these salts/ash trays

3410—Square shaped with sailboat scene, 2½" square

3411—Square shape with cupid in center, 2½" square, butterfly "signature"

3412—Rectangular shaped with mythological figures, 3" long

3413—Rectangular shape with classic figure of woman, 1⅞" wide, 2¾" long

3414—Rectangular shape with classical music-players, 1⅛" wide, just over 2¼" long

3415—Square shape with a rose in center, butterfly mark, 2" square

3416—Rectangular shape with same mythological scene as Fig. 217, smaller size, 2¼" long, butterfly signature.

3417—Rectangular shape with ace of spades figure, part of a bridge set, 2⅛" long

3418—Oval shape with boy and goat in oval framed center, 2½" long

3419—Rectangular shape with one of Columbus' ships Santa Maria, by Consolidated Lamp & Glass, circa 1938, 2¾" long, see also No. 240, copied in Japan, also found with "butterfly" mark

3420—Rectangular, almost oval shape with wreath of roses in center, 2⅝" long, unsigned Libbey (see Fig. 259)

3421—Rectangular with man on horseback, 3" long

3422—Square shaped with fox-hunt scene, approx. 2¼" square

3423—Rectangular shaped with "liberated" female smoker of the 1920's, butterfly mark, see also Fig. 236, 2⅞" long

3424—Rectangular shape with maple leaf naturalistic design, frosted, diff. from "intaglio" types, 2¾" long, butterfly signature

3425—Rectangular shape with horse head design diff. from Fig. 218, 2⅝" long, unsigned Libbey (see Fig. 259)

3426—Rectangular shape with same design as Fig. 234, same size, 2¾" long

3427—Rectangular shape with oval corners, same as Fig. 242, 2½" long

3428—Round shape with butterfly design, 2¼" diam.

3429—Round shape with same boy & dog design as Fig. 231, 2¼" diam.

3430—Round shape with same "Cupid & Venus" design as on Fig. 249, 2¼" diam.

3431—Same as Fig. 3430 except for ornate framed circle, 2¼" diam.

3432—Rectangular shape with diff. soccer (rugby) players than Fig. 228, 2¼" long

3433-34—Combination salt and card holder with early 18th Century characters in small frame at top, rectangular and canoe-shaped bases, #3433 is 2½" long, #3434 is 2⅝" long, signed "Made in Czechoslovakia" in metal portion

3435—Not of the "intaglio" family, the design on the base is embossed, rectangular shape, 3⅛" long

NEW SALTS IN CRYSTAL
(No measurements taken)

3436—Modern salt or ind. ash tray marked Daum, France, recent

3437—Another modern crystal piece, signed Daum, France in acidized signature

3438—Recent import with paper label, Made in Japan

3439—Foreign crystal with a possibly fake needle etched Steuben signature, BEWARE!

3440—Cut crystal, recent Waterford from Ireland

3441—Modern shape, but interesting, foreign crystal

3442-3443—Both of these fine crystal examples are marked with Daum, France acid signatures

3444—Round shape with "Vitra Hand Cut Lead Crystal" Label, foreign

3445—Believe these are recent German imports, still available in gift shops

3446—Another modern crystal example, foreign of good quality

3447—Paper label identifies this as West Germany, also recent

3448—Fine polished cut crystal, probably foreign from recent years

3449—Pressed crystal salt with glass spoon, both new, and foreign

3450—Paper label attached identifies this as from Belgium

3451—Octagonal shape in fine cut crystal, glass spoon, probably foreign

3452—Paper label clearly attributes this to Czechoslovakia, marked Weil

3453—Pair of pressed salts on original handled tray, from West Germany

3454—Pressed salt in crystal, also made in color (Fig. 884), foreign

3455—Another double set on original tray, European from recent years

3456—Called a handled mint in 1970's Imperial catalogue, also held salt & pepper shakers

3457—Label identifies this as Waterford fine cut crystal, recent

3458—Pressed crystal clearly identified from Mazatlan

3459—Another fine Waterford cut crystal example, paper label inside, shape similar to Fig. 3440

EARLY LACY PRESSED SALTS

We are referencing to Neal in identifying and attributing the examples on Figures 3460 to 3509. Some are not found in his books, possibly because the Neals did not consider them "lacy", or perhaps because they are very rare. Anyone familiar with the Neal book, or lacy salts in general, will realize that what appears to be a single pattern can be found in many different variations. Salts were a very popular form of early pressed glass, and the earliest molds were very crude (some were even made out of wood), and frequently had to be replaced with new molds. Very slight differences appeared in the replacement molds. The Neal books are outstanding additions to any reference library, but unfortunately are presently out-of-print. But great books never die; and certainly some enterprising publisher will see that this book is again put on the market in the near future for new generations of salt collectors. All of these salts date circa 1825-1850. Few are pattern glass, and thus mainly found only in these salt forms.

3460—Neal #DI-8, page 60, Sandwich, divided double salt, listed as rare, almost 3" long. rectangular, just over 1½" high

3461—Neal #SC-14, pg. 399, French, listed as very rare, just over 3" long rectangular, 1¾" high

3462—Neal #BF-1c, Sandwich, listed as very rare, 2⅞" long rectangular, just over 2" high

3463—Neal #OO-2, pg. 166, Sandwich, listed as plentiful, 1½" high, 3" long, diff. size from Fig. 3464, 2¼" wide compared to just over 2½" wide

3464—Similar to Neal #OO-2, except 3⅛" long, over 2½" wide, 1½" high

3465—Neal #MV-1, pg. 303, Boston & Sandwich Glass, 1⅝" high, just over 2" wide, 2¾" long, listed as plentiful

3466—Neal #OL-16, pg. 220, Sandwich, listed as scarce, very rare in color, 1" high, 3¼" long oval shape

3467—Neal #OL-14, pg. 218, Sandwich, plentiful in clear, extremely rare in color, 3½" long oval shape

3468—Neal #SN-ld, pg. 431, Sandwich, listed only in amber in Neal, example here is clear, design under base can differ based on plunger used, rare, 2⅞" long rectangular

3469—Neal #OL-22, pg. 230, Sandwich, listed scarce in clear, very rare in color, just under 3½" long, oval

3470—Neal #GA-2, pg. 90, Sandwich, plentiful in clear, scarce to extremely rare in several colors, 2⅞" long rectangular

3471—Neal #BS-2, pg. 9, Sandwich, plentiful in clear, also made in colors (Scarce to extremely rare), just under 3¼" long rectangular

3472—Duplicate of Figure 3468

3473—Duplicate of Figure 3465

3474—Not shown in Neal, this very rare example is probably French (Innes, pg. 299), circa 1840, 3⅜" long at top, rectangular

3475—Also not shown in Neal, this is not quite "lacy" period, dating instead from about 1875, pattern seems to match BULLS EYE VARIATION (LVG, 47), reissued by U.S. Glass after 1890, 3⅛" long rectangular

3476—Neal #OP-21, pg. 271, listed as very rare, clear only, French, 5⅛" long, 1¾" high

3477—Neal #SC-7, pg. 392, by Providence Flint Glass, scarce in clear, rare in pale green, almost 3" long rectangular, just over 1½" high

PRESSED GLASS SALTS OF LACY PERIOD
Circa 1825-1860

3478—Unusual and rare fiery opal salt from Pittsburgh, layered geometric design and color matches example shown in Innes, plate 399, circa 1850, 1¾" high, 3" long

3479—Neal #BF-1b, pg. 3, Sandwich, opalescent, scarce in clear, rare to extremely rare in color, 2⅛" high, 3" long rectangular

3480—Neal #NE-4, pg. 139, signed N.E. Glass Company, Boston (New England), listed as plentiful in clear, no colors known, 2" high, 2¾" long

3481—Neal #BH-1, pg. 16, very rare in clear, unique in color, has a beehive on one side, New England Glass, 2" high, 3" long

3482—Neal #EE-1a, pg. 75, Sandwich, listed as plentiful, in clear only, 2" high, 2⅞" long

3483—Neal #OG-2, pg. 147, in clear (rare) and purple-blue (unique), New England Glass, 2⅛" high, 3" long

3484—Neal #DD-1, pg. 50, made in Pittsburgh area, extremely rare, diamond-shaped, 1⅞" high, 3¼" across end to end

3485—Neal #SL-14b, pg. 420, Sandwich, in clear only (rare), similar to Fig. 3503, 1¾" high, 3⅛" long

3486—A member of the Neal #SD-4 family of six almost identical salts, except this one has a scalloped rim unlike any listed, atop an unusual added band of glass, very crude finish work, compare to Fig. 3500-3502, Sandwich, 2¼" high, 3" long

3487—Neal #OL-12A, pg. 215, Sandwich, scarce in clear, very rare in color, 1½" high, 3¼" long oval

3488—Neal #RD-31, pg. 342, French, listed in clear only 3" diam. round, very rare

3489—Neal #CN-1, pg. 46, Sandwich, clear only, listed as very rare, 2¼" high, 3" long

PRESSED SALTS OF THE LACY PERIOD

3490-3492—Not listed in Neal, these all have the distinctive shape and pattern characteristics of lacy French, circa 1840 (ref. Innes, pg. 300), all three about 3" diam. at round top

3493—Neal #RP-10, pg. 358, Sandwich, rare in clear, extremely rare in amethyst, 2¾" diam. round

3494—Not lacy glass, this appears to be DIAMOND SHIELD (Metz, 196), maker unknown, circa 1880-85, just under 3" diam. at top

3495—Neal #HN-18, pg. 114, listed in clear and amber-stained, clear is plentiful, six-sided top, French, 1¾" diam. opening

3496—Neal #OP-3, pg. 253, Sandwich, scarce in clear, ext. rare in opaque violet, 3¼" long oval top, rectangular base has one foot missing, see Fig. 3506 for Avon repro, also reproduced in Taiwan in blue & clear in oval shape

3497—Neal #NE-1 type, signed New England Glass, Neal lists only white

opaque, shown here in clear, apparently very rare, similar to one next to it, 2⅞" long rectangular

3498—Neal #NE-2, pg. 139, New England glass (signed), 2⅞" long, similar to Fig. 3497

3499—Neal #GA-5, pg. 94, Sandwich, scarce in clear, rare in amethyst, 2¾" long rectangular

3500—Neal #SD-4d, pg. 444, Sandwich, scarce, in clear only, compare wavy mold to Fig. 3501 curved mold and Fig. 3502 straight mold, 3⅛" long rectangular

3501—Neal #SD-15a, pg. 459, note finer differences in pattern detail, Sandwich, Neal lists this only in colors, thus clear must be very rare, 2¾" long rectangular

3502—Neal SD-5 family, pg. 446, except pegged feet seem smaller, attributed to New England area, about 3" long rectangular

THE NEW, THE OLD & THE QUESTIONABLE

3503—Neal #SL-11, pg. 415, Sandwich salt reproduced later by Metropolitan Museum of Art (NY), Fig. 3504, Neal lists old version in clear and color, all very rare, 3¼" long rectangular

3504—MMA sponsored reproduction, clearly marked, made in 1970's, same dimensions as old Sandwich version, also made in cobalt

3505—Neal #SD-2, pg. 437, careful study of this example revealed "questionable" age in the glass, old version listed in clear, opalescent and cobalt, 3" long rectangular

3506—This reproduction is clearly marked AVON, copy of Neal #OP 2 & 3, made in 1970's, no dimensions taken

3507—Questionable age wear on base (none anywhere) and quality of glass leads me to conclude this may be another reproduction, possibly from the 1930's, a copy of Neal #BF1 (a-f), feet are different, 2" high, 3" long rectangular

3508—Obvious poor quality reproduction of Neal #SC-9, badly (and apparently deliberately) broken feet, no age wear, 3¼" long rectangular

3509—Age is difficult to authenticate on this example, Neal #SL pgs. 403-409, family, Sandwich, also made in double salt, detail extremely poor, may be authentic but I see no signs of age or flint in the glass, 3" long rectangular

OVAL MASTER SALTS (Table Size)

3510—WASHINGTON CENTENNIAL, made by Gillinder & Sons, circa 1876, 3½" long oval

3511—SMALL FLOWERED TULIP (Metz 1, 32), maker unknown, circa 1870, 3½" diam. boat shaped

3512—BUCKLE (LPG, 102) or possibly DIAMOND ROSETTES (Metz 1, 122), two sister patterns, probably

New England Glass, circa 1860's and 70's, 3¼" long oval

3513—HORN OF PLENTY salt by McKee Brothers, circa 1860-75, 3⅛" long oval

3514—TWO PANEL master salt by Richards & Hartley, also U.S. Glass, circa 1890, also made in color and ind. size, 3" long oval

3515—SANDWICH STAR (LPG, 14), Boston & Sandwich Glass, circa 1850's-60's, rare in color, 3¾" long oval

3516—PANELLED GRAPE BAND (LVG, 32), maker unknown, listed in Lee in only 3 shapes but many others exist, incorrectly attributed to King in Revi, 211 ("Maple" is HOPS BAND), 2⅜" long, oval

3517—Probably a novelty salt, npg, maker unknown, circa 1870, 3⅞" long, oval

3518—Plain top half with pleated bottom half, npg, maker unknown, circa 1880, 3⅞" long

3519—Oval plain salt by Bryce/USG, circa 1890 (see Reprint B), 3¼" long

3520—An early SAWTOOTH oval salt, possibly New England Glass, Cambridge, Mass., circa 1860, 3⅛" long, oval design copied by many others (see Figs. 3527, 3600, 3603 & 3653)

3521—Plain top half with ribbed base, made by Central Glass, circa 1880 (Reprint C), 3⅞" long oval

3522—AMAZON table salt, aka SAWTOOTH BAND, Bryce Bros./USG, circa 1880-1895, see H5, 78, 3" long, oval, possibly exists in color

3523—Oval shape with panelled squared sections, pattern unknown, may be a novelty, circa 1880-90, maker unknown, 3¼" long

3524—The pattern matches (PRISM Metz 1, 49), maker unknown of the 1860's, 3⅝" long

ROUND MASTER SALTS
(Footed or Pedestalled)

3525—LEAF & DART covered salt or "horseradish", Richards & Hartley/USG, circa 1880-90's, 4" high, 2⅜" diam.

3526—AMAZON by Bryce Bros./USG, toy sugar bowl to child's table set, identifiable only by the creamer to this toy set which matches the "mother" pattern (H5, 78), finial has been ground on example shown here, should be 5" high, 2½" diam.

3527—SAWTOOTH pattern covered sugar to toy table set, this pattern was made in several variations by many factories, including New England Glass, Sandwich, Bryce Bros., Gillinder, Ripley, who made this version is unknown, circa 1860-90's, 5" high, about 3" diam.

3528—LILY-OF-THE-VALLEY (LPG, 126), maker unknown, this is a base to a covered horse-radish, circa 1870's, 2½" high without lid, 2⅞" diam.

3529—CABBAGE ROSE by Central Glass, circa 1880, see Reprint C, similar to OPEN ROSE (Fig. 3556), just over 2½" diam.

3530—ARCHED LEAF (Metz 1, 100), maker unknown, circa 1870's, 1⅞" diam.

3531—This appears to be OVOID PANELS (Metz 1, 10), circa 1870, but may be a similar pattern, maker unknown, 2½" diam.

3532—Early HONEYCOMB pattern, another design made in many variations by several firms, made by McKee, New England Glass, O'Hara, Bakewell, and others, example shown here has a delicate cut spray of flowers, circa 1875-80, see also Figs. 3597-99, 2⅝" diam., 2½" high

3533—BEADED ACORN MEDALLION table salt (see Fig. 2522 for ind. size), Boston Silver-Glass Co., E. Cambridge, Mass., 1869-71, 3¼" high, 2½" diam.

3534—GRAPE BAND by Bryce, Walker & Co., circa 1869 (patented that year), 2½" high, just over 2½" diam. round

3535—RIBBED PALM, early McKee pattern from 1860's, 2¾" high, 2½" diam.

3536—THUMBPRINT & HOBNAIL (Metz 1, 44), circa 1860's, 2½" high, just under 2¾" diam., maker unknown at this time

3537—PALMETTE, an early popular pattern whose maker is unknown, circa 1870's, probably Pittsburgh area, 2½" high, 2⅝" diam.

3538—STIPPLED SCROLL (K7, 70), by Geo. Duncan & Sons, circa 1880-85, also known as SCROLL (LPG, 140), 2⅜" high, 2½" diam.

3539—BUTTERFLY & CATTAILS salt, shown but unnamed in LPG, pl. 190, name by authors, maker undetermined, circa 1880, 2¼" high, 2⅝" diam.

3540—SAWTOOTH CIRCLE (Metz 2, 56), maker unknown, circa 1860's, flint, see also Fig. 3592, 2⅛" high, 2½" diam.

SALTS WITH STEMS OR PEDESTALS

3541—CHIPPENDALE "salted almond" (see Reprint W), first made in 1907 by Ohio Flint Glass, production continued by Jefferson and later Central Glass until late 1920's, 4" high

3542—CHIPPENDALE salt, see notes Fig. 3541, almost identical to Fig. 3543, circa 1907-1927, signed Krystol, 2½" high

3543—Possibly No. 253 pattern salt by Indiana Glass Co., circa 1910, a deliberate copy of Chippendale, note wider band, also similar to Fig. 534, just over 2½" high

3544—PANELLED FINETOOTH (Metz 2, 48) seems to match this pattern salt, circa 1865-70, maker unknown, 2¾" high

3545—SECTIONAL BLOCK (Md 2, 109) seems to match this salt. a design at parallel graduating blocks, possibly by Imperial (their No. 711 line) or USG, (their "Jacobean" line) circa 1920's, 2¼" high, 3¼" long

3546-3547—Same CHIPPENDALE pattern in an oval shape, with and without cutting, see notes Fig. 3541, 2½" high, 4¼" handle to handle

3548—Flared panelled salt or almond, light cutting on panels, maker unknown, circa 1920, 2¼" high, 3½" diam.

3549—SPIRAL FLUTES by Duncan & Miller (No. 40), circa 1924-30, shown here in almond dish, see Fig. 781 for colored example, 2¼" high, 2½" diam.

3550—Similar design to Fig. 3545, this rounded-shape is also known in amber (Fig. 455), possibly Imperial or U.S. Glass, circa 1920, may be a nut cup, 2¾" high

3551—Pattern, shape and glass composition convince me this is Foreign, circa 1920's to recent, 2½" high, 2¼" diam.

3552—Another foreign pressed salt, circa 1920, 2¼" high, 2¼" diam.

3553—Similar shape to previous two, this is also foreign, circa 1920, 2½" high, 2½" diam.

3554—This appears to be the same as ENGLISH POINTED THUMBPRINT (K2, 3), from the 1850's, tiny hole in glass where it separated, very crude flint, 2½" high, 2" diam.

3555—Reproduction MT. VERNON salt with original Imperial Glass paper label made from original Cambridge mold, circa 1970's, 2½" tall, 4¼" handle to handle, some escaped factory with C-in-a-Diamond trademark still intact

MASTER SALTS

3556—OPEN ROSE (LPG, 122), reportedly Sandwich, circa 1870's, very similar to "Cabbage Rose", just over 2½" high

3557—BLACKBERRY (LPG, 151) by Hobbs, Brockunier & Co., circa 1870 (patented that year), also made in milk glass, 2¾" high

3558-3559—GRAPE & FESTOON, reportedly made at Sandwich, and also proven made by Doyle as their "Wreath" pattern, which possibly explains the two different sized salts, Fig. 3558 is 2¾" high, Fig. 3559 is 3" high, also made in "low" unstemmed salt, circa 1870

3560—Obviously pattern glass, but unable to determine which one, possibly unlisted, dates from about 1875, maker undetermined, definitely American, 2½" high

3561—BIRCH LEAF (Metz 2, 72), maker unknown, circa 1875, frequently confused for McKee's "Pressed Leaf", which has bigger leaves and the band just above the leaves (shown in Stout, pg. 37), also in milk glass, flint, 2¾" high

3562—STAR IN HONEYCOMB by Bryce Bros., circa 1875-80, aka LE-VERNE, 2¾" high

3563—STIPPLED PEPPERS made at Sandwich, circa 1870's, 3" high

3564—Early pressed round table salt, pattern unknown, circa 1880, 1½" high

3565—GIANT THUMBPRINT (Metz 1, 8), an early flint pattern, circa 1860, similar to Bakewell's "Argus" pattern except circles are round here, oval on Argus, 1¾" high

3566—DIAMOND MIRROR pattern, an early Fostoria line made while still in Ohio, circa 1888, attribution based on local residents of Fostoria, Ohio, date confirmed by trade catalogues, 1½" high at ends, slightly oval shape

3567—OPEN PLAID, by Central Glass, circa 1885-90, attribution by Revi, some later production by U.S. Glass, circa 1891, just over 1½" high

MASTER SALTS

3568—STIPPLED SCROLL (K7, 70) by Geo. Duncan & Sons, circa 1880-85, previously unattributed, aka "Scroll" (LPG, 140), 2¾" high

3569—HOLLY, attributed to Sandwich based on shards, circa 1860-70, one of several early patterns using Holly as a pattern motif, about 2¾" high

3570—STAR & PILLAR (K8, 14), orig. the "Paris" pattern by McKee, circa 1880 (Stout), 2" high

3571—This may be Bakewell's ARGUS pattern, or a copy of same, which some collectors call GIANT BABY THUMBPRINT (Metz 2, 38), circa 1870, shown again as Fig. 3591, 2¼" high

3572—French lacy salt, Neal #RD-23, scarce, in clear only, circa 1840, 1½" high

3573—GRASSHOPPER pattern, named after the insect appearing on some pieces, maker unknown, circa 1885, round shape, 1½" high, very rare in color, pattern reproduced in some shapes, but not the salt

3574—GRAPE & FESTOON (LPG, 63), patented by Doyle in 1870, made with clear or stippled leaves, reportedly also made at Sandwich, round shape, 1½" high

3575—A member of the Finecut family of patterns, the pattern and peg-feet is similar to FLATTENED FINECUT (K1, 86), maker unknown, circa 1885, also seems to match HOURGLASS (LVG, 56), 1¾" high, round shape

3576—APOLLO pattern by Adams/USG, circa 1885-1895, rectangular shaped salt, 3¼" long

3577—Lacy pattern salt, Neal #BS-1, pg. 8, clear only listed, rare, Sandwich, 3¼" long

3578—Another lacy pressed salt, Neal #OL-19, pg. 226, listed clear only, rare, Sandwich, 3¼" long. oval shape

3579—CURRIER & IVES pattern, Bellaire Goblet Co., Findlay, OH, circa 1887-1892, salt is rare, 3½" long. oval shape

MASTER SALTS

3580—JACOB'S LADDER by Bryce/USG, circa 1885-1895, sometimes called by original name MALTESE, also made in color (very rare), 2⅞" high, 2⅞" diam., round

3581—TREE OF LIFE salt made by Portland Glass, circa 1869, most sought after, just over 3" high, 2¼" diam. at top, round

3582—ROMAN KEY pattern, flint glass from 1860's, attributed to Sandwich factory based on shard diggings, 2⅞" high, 2½" diam. round

3583—EXCELSIOR pattern by McKee & Brothers, Pittsburgh, circa 1860's, 2¼" diam. round

3584—BARBERRY pattern, made by McKee, circa 1880 (Stout, 64) with production continued into 1890's, in clear only, 2½" high, 2¼" diam.

3585—GRAPE BAND by Bryce, Walker & Co., circa 1869 (patented that year), 2½" high, just over 2½" diam. at top

3586—Commonly known as SANDWICH LOOP (LVG, 31), Metz calls this HAIRPIN (M1, 24), attributed to Boston & Sandwich Glass, 1840-50's, the quality of the glass seems later (1860's), the pattern was copied by O'Hara (Innes, pg. 309, and Bakewell (LPG, pl. 17), 2¼" high, 2½" diam. round

3587—HOPS BAND by King Glass Co., patented in 1871, 2⅝" high, just over 2¾" diam.

3588—BULL'S EYE (LPG, 49) with the pattern reversed on the salt from what is found on larger table pieces, pattern attributed to New England Glass, also Sandwich, probably others, circa 1850-60's, almost 3" high

3589—STIPPLED BOWL (Metz 1, 182), maker unknown, circa 1870's, just over 2¾" high, 2⅛" diam. round

3590—There are several FLUTE patterns, of which this is just one, maker uncertain, dating from about 1870, 2¾" high, 2¼" diam.

3591—See notes Fig. 3571 for this duplication

3592—See notes Fig. 3540 for this duplication

3593—STIPPLED IVY (LPG, pl. 119), maker unknown, from the 1870's, 2⅞" high

3594—PLAIN OCTAGON (Metz 1, 179), circa 1850's, maker unknown, just under 2" high, 2⅝" diam.

3595—PANELLED ACORN BAND, maker unknown, from the 1870's, just under 2" high, 2⅜" diam.

MASTER SALTS (Pedestalled)

3596—PETAL & LOOP (LPG, 4),

made at Sandwich, also by O'Hara, circa 1850-60's, 2½" high, 3" diam.

3597—One of the large family of HONEYCOMB patterns, a source of confusion to many collectors, as the design was made in dozens of forms by dozens of companies. Metz 1, 42 shows a large selection of different goblets in EAPG. Certainly the Honeycomb design can be found in as many different forms of salts. We make no attempt here to identify makers on these examples. All date circa 1840-70. This example is engraved with a wreathed design at the plain upper portion, 3" high, 2¼" diam.

3598—See notes Fig. 3532 on this salt, example here is not etched

3599—This example seems to match the one in LPG, pl. 60, 2½" high, 2¼" diam.

3600—See Fig. 3494, the example here appears to have a distortion in the glass, a flaw. The diamond-point design and the ribbed panel between convinces me this is the same as DIAMOND SHIELD (Metz 1, 196), even though the goblet seems so different, from the 1880's.

3601—HARP pattern by Bryce, Richards & Co. (see Revi, 81), circa 1860's with continued production, sometimes attributed to Sandwich, almost 2" high, 3¼" diam.

3602—Another BULL'S EYE salt, probably from a different company (see also Fig. 3588), probably Sandwich, circa 1850-60, 2" high, 3⅛" diam.

3603—Member of the DIAMOND POINT family of patterns, maker unknown, circa 1870, note the distinctive band of diamonds at the top, 2½" high, 2¾" diam.

3604—PRESSED LEAF (LPG, 125), reportedly made at Sandwich, but also McKee (Stout, 37) design dates from the 1870's to early 80's. 2¾" high, 2½" diam.

3605—SCALLOPED TAPE pattern, maker unknown, circa 1880, rare in color, 2¾" high, 2⅞" diam.

3606—Obviously an early salt, circa 1865-75, but I cannot find the pattern name, possibly unlisted, about 2½" high, 2⅝" diam.

3607—This matches YUMA LOOP, probably by Bakewell (their "Pillar" pattern), similar to the BULL'S EYE family, circa 1860's, just over 2½" high, 2¼" diam.

3608—BUCKLE salt, has fine ribbing underneath main pattern, Lee reports Gillinder as maker, pattern copied by others (Banded Buckle, Diamond Rosettes), 1870's, 2¼" round

3609—The framed oval on this unlisted pattern matches the one on "Beaded Acorn with Leaf Band" (Metz 2, 72), but everything else is different, maker unknown, circa 1875, just under 2½" diam.

3610—DIAMOND & SUNBURST by Bryce, Walker & Co., patented in

1874, design copied later by several factories, 2¾" high, 2½" diam. round

3611—An early ribbed pattern from the 1870's whose name is undetermined, could be EUGENIE by McKee (Stout, 38) or their EUREKA (Stout, 39), no salt shown in catalogue reprints to help authenticate, from the 1860's, 2¾" high, 2¾" diam.

PRESSED GLASS MASTERS— PEDESTAL-BASED

3612—Pressed fluted pattern of unknown origin, circa 1870, six-sided, 3⅛" high

3613—PRISMS WITH DIAMOND POINT by Bryce/USG, circa 1885-90's, see also Fig. 3616, 3¼" high

3614—Similar to Fig. 3627, this early salt has a bulge of connecting bulls-eyes, pattern undetermined, 3¼" high, circa 1865-70's

3615—LARGE DROP (Metz 1, 28) made by both Bakewell, Pears & Co., and McKee, circa 1850's-60's, originally called "Lotus" salt, 3¾" high

3616—PRISMS WITH DIAMOND POINT by Bryce/USG, circa 1885-91, probably a base to covered horseradish, 3¼" high

3617—Another EARLY FLUTE pattern (Metz 1, 40), one of more than a dozen similar plain panelled patterns (see also Fig. 3590), maker unknown, circa 1870's, 2⅝" high

3618—Six panels of horizontal steps, probably not pattern glass, maker unknown, circa 1870, 2½" high

3619—LINCOLN DRAPE pattern, made at Sandwich and probably other locations, circa 1860's and later, 2¾" high

3620—Not positive, but appears to be BIGLER (LPG, 10), made at Sandwich, or possibly BARRELLED EXCELSIOR by McKee, with dates from 1860's, 3¼" high

3621—TULIP WITH SAWTOOTH by Bryce, Richards & Co., circa 1850's (Revi, 80), 3⅜" high

3622—LATE BUCKLE pattern (LPG, 72) by Bryce/USG, originally called "Jasper", circa 1880-90's, just over 3" high

3623—HORIZONTAL FRAMED OVALS (Metz 2, 12), maker unknown, circa 1870, 3" high

3624—"Berlin" salt by McKee (Stout, 75), circa 1860's-70's, 2½" high, 2¾" diam.

3625—WAFFLE & THUMBPRINT, made by several companies, Lyon, Fort Pitt, Sandwich, circa 1860's, see Innes, 306, almost 2" high

3626—Plain vertically ribbed design on stemmed base, round shape, just over 2" high, 2⅞" diam.

MASTER SALTS—PRESSED GLASS, Footed or Pedestal-based

3627—Plain fluted pattern with pedestal base and bulge at middle, 3" high, 3¾" diam.

3628—Tall pedestal-based "diamond" pattern, fluted base, may be foreign, circa 1895, 3¾" high, just over 3¼" diam.

3629—Fluted design in stem and lower bowl, plain upper bowl and lower base, maker unknown, circa 1890, just under 3" high, 2¾" diam. round

3630—ICICLE & LOOPS pattern (Metz 2, 34), maker unknown, popular design used by more than one firm in different variants, circa 1880, 2⅞" high, 2⅝" diam. round

3631—"Imperial" salt by Bakewell, Pears & Co., Pittsburgh (Reprint G), circa 1860, 2¼" high, 3⅝" diam. round

3632—Similar to Figs. 3631 and 3633, maker unknown, circa 1860-75, 2" high, 3¾" diam.

3633—"Imperial" salt by McKee (OMN), similar copy to salt of same name by Bakewell (Fig. 3631), this example is 2⅝" high, 3⅛" diam., rare in color, circa 1860-70

3634—Fascinating embossed floral pattern of unknown origin, may be foreign, circa 1880's, 2¾" high, 2¾" diam. round

3635—BUTTERFLY HANDLES pattern, probably by Aetna Glass Co., based on trade journal quotes, circa 1881, (LVG, pl. 27 calls this "Butterfly"), 2¼" high, 2¾" diam. round

3636—VIKING (LVG) or BEARDED HEAD (K7, 64) by Hobbs, Brockunier, circa 1876, almost 2" high, 2⅞" diam. round

3637—This pressed glass salt may be pattern glass, but cannot match to any specific pattern, horizontal bands of diamond point, blocks and pleating, circa 1880-85, almost 2" high, 3" diam. round

3638—Blown salt with three applied reeded glass feet, origin unknown, circa 1880, 2¼" high, just over 2¾" diam.

3639—Another plain fluted pattern salt, origin unknown, circa 1880, 2¼" high, 2½" diam., six-sided

PRESSED GLASS MASTERS—RECTANGULAR SHAPES

3640—Plain rectangular salt with angled corners extending somewhat into a footed effect, maker unknown, circa 1880, 3¼" long, 1⅝" high

3641—The design matches STEPPED HEXAGONS (Metz 2, 50), maker unknown, circa 1870, 1⅜" high, 3¼" long

3642—PICKET pattern master salt by King Glass Co., circa 1880, also made in ind. size, very rare salt in color, 1⅞" high, almost 3½" long

3643—CLEAR RIBBON pattern (LPG, pl. 70), circa 1880-85, maker unknown, 1½" high, 3¼" long

3644—Pleated rib pattern, probably not pattern glass, maker unknown, circa 1890, just over 1½" high, 2⅞" long

3645—Similar to Fig. 3644, except top is fluted, maker unknown, circa 1885-90, 1½" high, 2⅞" long

3646—Plain HOMESTEAD pattern salt, by Bryce, Higbee & Co., Pittsburgh, circa 1880's, part of a pattern service (see Kamm 8, pl. 19), just over 1½" high, 3½" long, also made in oval and ind. sizes

3647—Another plain ribbed salt, maker unknown, circa 1880, 1¼" high, 3⅝" long

3648—DIAMOND QUILTED pattern salt by O'Hara/USG, circa 1890, also made in ind. size and in several colors, 1⅝" high, 3⅜" long

3649—SUNBURST AND BAR (LVG, 58) by Hobbs, Brockunier, Wheeling, circa 1890, the salt is missing the distinctive shell design at the side (see H6, 61), 1¼" high, 3⅜" long

3650—Interesting inverted elongated triangle pressed pattern, similar to one next to it, maker unknown, circa 1880, 1¼" high, 3¾" long

3651—PEGGED FLUTE pattern (Metz 1,8), maker unknown, circa 1870, 1⅛" high, 3⅛" long

3652—Another bulging ribbed pattern, similar to three others on same page, fluted top rim, maker unknown, circa 1870's, 1¼" high, just over 3¼" long

PRESSED GLASS MASTERS—ASSORTED SHAPES

3653—Early pressed salt in a diamond fan pattern, very old, circa 1819, American, somewhat oval with rectangular base, 1¾" high, 3½" long

3654—Pleated pattern with beaded design at top rim, odd shape, maker unknown, circa 1875, 1¼" high, 2¾" long

3655—Octagonal plain panelled salt, maker unknown, circa 1870's, 1⅝" high, 2¾" diam.

3656—McKee's "Tomato" table salt, lengthy production, circa 1860-1900, also in ind. size, six-sided, 2⅛" high, 3" diam.

3657—Another six-sided salt with arched design inside panelled sections, maker unknown, circa 1870, 1½" high, 2⅞" diam.

3658—Five-lobed star-shaped salt with plain round interior bowl, maker unknown, circa 1880, 1¾" high, 2⅞" diam.

3659—SCALLOPED LINES pattern (LVG, 21) by Sweeney, McCluney & Co., Wheeling (Revi, 300), circa 1874, rare salt, six-sided, 1½" high, 2⅝" diam.

3660—Rectangular salt with panelled sections, maker unknown, circa 1875-80, 1½" high, 2⅞" long

3661—Interesting lobed salt with large plain panel at back, possibly a finger grip, probably foreign, circa 1880, just under 2½" high at back, over 2½" long

3662—Bakewell, Pears & Co. "Leaf" salt (Reprint G), circa 1860, similar design to Fig. 3657, just over 2" high, 2⅝" diam., six-sided

3663—HIDALGO pattern table salt by Adams/USG, circa 1885-91, 1⅞" high plus "tabs", 2⅞" wide square

3664-3665—Two different size salts in SQUARE PANES or POST pattern (Metz 1, 6), circa 1880's, maker unknown, Fig. 3664 is 2" high, 2⅝" square, Fig. 3665 is just over 2" high, just over 2½" square

PRESSED GLASS MASTERS—ASSORTED SHAPES

3666—Plain round four-footed salt with an unusual 8-point star design impressed in base, maker unknown, circa 1880's, 1¼" high, 2½" diam.

3667—Triangular ribbed salt with three feet, made by a glass firm in Scotland, circa 1870, 1½" high, 3" wide

3668—Figure-8 shape with feet at sides, plain sides, maker unknown, circa 1880, 1¾" high, 3¼" long

3669—Tub-shaped master with tab handles, fine diamond point design in natural wooden tub effect, maker unknown, may be foreign, circa 1890, 2" high, 3¼" diam. round

3670—Plain rectangular salt with ribbed pegs on base, maker unknown, circa 1890, 1¼" high, 2⅞" long

3671—Rectangular pleated pattern with horizontal pleats at corners, early, circa 1860-70, almost 1½" high, almost 3" long

3672—Round master with horizontal ladder pattern, vertical ribbing at base, maker unknown, circa 1870's, 1½" high, 3⅜" diam. round

3673—This salt, also made in ind. size, was made by more than one company—this appears to be Fostoria, but could be foreign, circa 1890-1900, 1½" high, just over 3" diam.

3674—FOOTED PANELLED RIB pattern (Metz 1, 170), maker unknown, circa 1880's, 1⅞" high, 3¾" diam.

3675—GIANT SAWTOOTH (Metz 2, 40), made by more than one firm, circa 1860's and possibly earlier, just over 1½" high, 3½" diam.

3676—Gear shaped salt with six "cogs", maker unknown, circa 1880, 1⅞" high, 3⅜" diam.

3677—Same pattern as Fig. 3674 except different size, 2" high, 3½" diam.

PRESSED GLASS MASTERS—ROUND SHAPES

3678—PINWHEEL pattern salt (LPG,

44), maker unknown, circa 1880-90, 3" diam. round
3679—FOSTORIA'S NO. 112 (WFG, 32) also known as SHORT SWIRL, circa 1900, 2 1/8" diam.
3680—Early mold-blown type salt in diamond-point design, circa 1825, 2 3/8" diam.
3681—Plain round with notched design at bottom half, may be "Prism" by King Glass Co., circa 1880, 3" diam.
3682—Another plain top with pleated design at base, maker unknown, circa 1900, just under 2 1/2" diam.
3683—LAMINATED PETALS pattern (Metz 1, 10) from the 1860's, 2 3/4" diam. round
3684—Honeycomb pressed salt with waffle design in base, maker unknown, circa 1880-1900, 1 7/8" diam.
3685—Basketweave design, maker unknown, circa 1900, 3" diam. round
3686—ATLAS by Bryce Bros./USG, circa 1880-95, also made in ind. size, 3 1/2" diam. round
3687—No. 194 salt by Central Glass Co., Wheeling, circa 1880, also in ind. size, 2 7/8" diam.
3688—GRATED DIAMOND & SUNBURST by Duncan, circa 1895-1900, 3 1/4" diam. round
3689—Round melon-ribbed salt with 16 ribs, maker unknown, circa 1880, 3" diam. round
3690—Plain round salt with faceted design at base, maker unknown, circa 1870-80, 3" diam.
3691—Bulging bulls-eye design appears to be foreign, circa 1880, 3 5/8" diam.

CUT GLASS MASTERS—PEDESTAL-BASED

3692—Lovely hobstar design cutting, very intricate, appears to be American, circa 1885-90, 3 1/4" high, 2 1/2" diam. at top
3693—Early French cut salt, oval shaped bowl on pedestal, band of diamond cutting with interesting scalloped top, circa 1870-80, 3 1/4" high, 3" long
3694—Another early French cut master with octagonal diamond cut bowl on fluted stem, exceptional, 3 3/4" high, 2 7/8" diam.
3695—Round all-over diamond cut bowl on stem, foreign origin, circa 1960-1970, 2 1/2" high, almost 3" diam. round
3696—Boat-shaped linear cut bowl on fluted stem, 3 1/4" high, 3 5/8" long, appears to be English, circa 1900
3697—Beautiful diamond and star cutting on boat-shaped bowl, origin unknown, circa 1900, 2 5/8" high, just under 3 1/2" long
3698—Very nice boat-shaped salt with delicate cutting, signed Waterford, recent, 2 1/2" high, 3 1/4" long
3699—Early Waterford cut salt, boat-shaped bowl has a division in center, making this an unusual double, 2 3/4" high, 3 3/4" long, circa 1800-50
3700—Another nice boat-shaped pedestal-based salt, serrated top, fluted stem, also of European origin, circa 1900-10, 2 7/8" high, 3 5/8" long
3701—Triangular shaped salt on stem with all-over diamond cutting, European, relatively new, 2 1/2" high, 1 3/4" wide
3702—Delicate stemmed salt with round bowl, fine diamond-point cutting, squared base, fine crystal from post 1900 period, probably foreign, 2 1/4" high, 1 3/4" diam. round
3703—Boat-shaped salt with band of fine diamond-point cutting, serrated top, diamond base, European, circa 1900-20, 2 1/4" high, 3" long
3704—Another European diamond cut salt with fluted stem, square base, post-1900's, 2 1/2" high, 1 7/8" diam. round

CUT GLASS MASTERS—ASSORTED SHAPES

3705—Rectangular with diamond cutting, probably English, circa 1900, 2 1/2" high, 3 1/8" long
3706—Round shape on pedestal base, diamond cut with prisms along top, 2 3/4" high, 3" diam. circa 1895, probably American
3707—Boat-shaped bowl on pedestal, hexagonal base, 3 1/2" high, 4 1/8" long, European origin, circa 1890-1900
3708—Beautifully all-over "Russian" cut round master, very heavy, American, circa 1900, 2 1/4" high, 3 3/8" diam.
3709—Popular English-strawberry & Diamond/Fan cut motif, round shape, heavy brilliant cutting, 2" high, 3 1/8" diam.
3710—Cane cutting on round shape, American, circa 1905, 1 3/4" high, 3 1/4" diam.
3711—Exceptional round master with cuttings of diamonds, stars and fans, serrated top, American, circa 1900, 1 1/2" high, 3 1/4" diam.
3712—Strawberry-diamond cutting round salt, American or English, circa 1895, 1 5/8" high, 2 3/4" diam.
3713—European round diamond cut, notched design around top, cut starred bottom, 1 7/8" high, 3 1/2" diam.
3714—Lovely oval cut salt with diamond and fan motif, serrated top, 1 1/2" high, 3 5/8" long, probably American
3715—Rectangular diamond and fan cut, appears to be early, circa 1880, origin unknown, just over 1 1/2" high, just over 3 1/4" long
3716—Oval shape with band of diamond point, notched top rim, English, circa 1890, just under 2" high, 3 1/4" long

CUT GLASS MASTERS—ASSORTED SHAPES

3717—Lovely French stemmed salt with shell-shaped bowl, circa 1920, delicate cutting, 4 7/8" high
3718—Stemmed salt with boat shaped bowl, band of fine diamond point cutting, probably English/Irish, circa 1900, 4 1/8" high
3719—Fluted cut stemmed salt, highly polished quality crystal, origin unknown, circa 1900, 3 7/8" high
3720—Very nice stemmed salt with rectangular bowl, band of diamond cutting, stepped stem with square base, notched rim, 2 7/8" high, just over 3" long
3721—Interesting rectangular diamond cut with exceptional brilliance, probably American, circa 1890, 1 5/8" high, 3 1/8" long
3722—Waterford salt from Ireland, new, round bowl with square-based stem, delicate cutting, 2 3/4" high, 1 5/8" diam. round
3723—Rectangular block cut master, age and origin unknown, 1 3/4" high, just over 3 1/8" long
3724—Plain rectangular cut and polished salt, probably foreign, after 1900, 2 1/8" high, 3 1/4" long
3725—Low cut salt with fluted cut sections, origin unknown, 1 3/8" high, 3 1/4" long
3726—Another rectangular block cut master, oval interior bowl, 2" high, 3 1/2" long
3727—Master salt in popular notched prism cutting, frequently found in ind. size, 3 7/8" diam. round
3728—Mold-blown plain salt with notched cutting at top rim, rayed star cut base, 2 1/4" diam. round

NOVELTIES

3729—CHURCH WINDOWS match safe by U.S. Glass Co., circa 1903, aka U.S. COLUMBIA (OMN), this and Fig. 3730 are frequently collected as reversible combination "toothpick holder-salt dips", orig. catalogues call these match safes, 3 1/2" high, 2 3/8" diam.
3730—MASSACHUSETTS state pattern by USG, circa 1898-1910, also a match safe, but sometimes bought as toothpick-salt, hollow base at top, 3 1/2" high, 2 3/8" diam.
3731—Tiny pressed glass potty or chamber-pot with scroll design at base, maker unknown, early 1900's, 2 1/4" diam. at top, see also Fig. 489
3732—Tiny basketweave novelty salt marked Germany on inside bottom, circa 1920, just under 1 1/2" diam.
3733—Figural wheelbarrow salt, may be foreign, circa 1893, 4 1/2" long
3734—Santa sleigh, Victorian novelty from about 1900-10, maker unknown, 3 5/8" long
3735—Small Fostoria sleigh, made in several sizes, circa 1940, just under 3" long

3736—Unusual double "pilgrim style" slipper salt with single receptacle, maker unknown, circa 1900, bowl is 2" diam. round

3737—Figural stump or log salt, reportedly Portland Glass, circa 1860's-70's (attribution questionable), definitely old, 3" long

3738—Officer's Cap ash tray by Paden City Glass Mfg. Co., circa 1940's, also made in a covered powder jar with mirrored top, rare in colors, bowl is 3" diam.

3739—Figural wagon salt, maker unknown, circa 1890, also in color, 3¼" long

3740-41—Horseshoe table and ind. size salts by O'Hara Glass, circa 1890, frequently purchased as part of GOOD LUCK setting, with which it goes well, Fig. 3740 is 3" long, Fig. 3741 is 2" long

3742—Unusual master salt with horseshoe design at base, a goblet is also known with this design (Metz 1, 93), this appears to be the previously undocumented salt to the GOOD LUCK pattern (design around bowl matches), no owl is found on other pieces to the setting, made by Adams & Co., circa 1880's (K1, 66 attribution), 3½" diam. round

ANIMALS AND BIRDS

3743—Stork salt, appears to be new, unusual, 2½" high

3744—Elephant in crystal, probably foreign, new, 2⅛" high, circa 1940

3745—Duck with paper label "Made in West Germany", recent, 2" high, 3" long

3746—Hen double salt, old, marked S.V. (France), 2½" high, 3¾" long

3747—Rabbit, new, maker unknown, 1½" high, 3½" long, current import

3748—Westmoreland frosted duck, circa 1920's, also in colors, 2" high, 5" long

3749—Frog, new import, origin unknown, 1½" high, 3⅓" long

3750—Covered rabbit dish, marked Vallerystahl, France, age unknown, 1¾" high, 3¼" long

3751—New swan and shell salt by St. Clair, unmarked, also in colors, 4⅛" long

3752—Frog, recent production, 1½" high, 3¼" long

3753-54—The same salt with differences in size and detail, may be egg cups, Fig. 3753, recent import, has poor mold detail and extra glass on beak, 1⅞" high, bowl is 2" diam., Fig. 3754 is just over 1¾" high, 2⅛" diam. bowl, probably old

3755—Bird salt by Richards & Hartley/USG, circa 1890's (Reprint E), scarce, 1½" high, 3½" long

3756-57—Table and ind. size in Squirrel and Stump salt, Portland Glass Co., circa 1870, usually found with light damage, Fig. 3756 is 2¼" diam. bowl; Fig. 3757 is just over 1" diam. on round bowl

3758—Old figural turtle salt, maker unknown, choice, 3⅛" long

3759—English duck salt, paper label Watford Crystal, duck's bill has been slightly ground, 2" high, 2¾" long

3760—Recent import in shape of duck with patterned bowl in all-over diamonds, 1⅞" high, 3" long

3761—Two roosters double salt, marked S.V. (France), exact age unknown, 2¾" high, 6" long

3762—Cute elephant, may be pin cushion holder (as are some of the others with deep hollow rounded bowls), 2" high, 3½" long, current import

PRESSED GLASS DOUBLE SALTS

Referred to as "Twin" salts in most American catalogues, the vast majority of "doubles" are European in origin, primarily from France and Germany. Few can be considered pattern glass, most falling into the novelty category. For further notes concerning doubles, see the info. under Figures 792-807, in the colored glass section.

3763—Unusual double in the shape of an early convertible automobile, circa 1915-20, 5" long

3764—Almost identical, but mold work and hood are different, also 5" long, signed "Portieux"

3765—Ribbed spokes with round center bowls, 5" long

3766—Square shaped salts with fine ribbing, fancy handle, 3" long

3767—Plain panelled salts with spoon rest tabs, may be American, circa 1920's, 3" long

3768—Low, flat ribbed design with round bowls, protruding corners, 2½" long

3769—Panelled design with tiny finger grips at center, 3" long

3770—Low flat double with fluted design on side, rayed base, 3½" long

3771—Footed plain salt with diamond-point design under base, 2½" long

3772—CANDLEWICK pattern by Imperial Glass, holder for salt & pepper, circa 1950, 4½" long

3773—Repro of early lacy pressed salt, age unknown, probably American, 2½" long, Neal #OG14, pg. 160

3774—Same as Figure 3769, 3" long, note design in base

3775—Footed shell-shaped double with rope-loop handle, made in Japan, circa 1950's, 2" long

3776—Plain blocked design with finger-grip handles, may be holder for salt & pepper, 3" long

PRESSED GLASS DOUBLES

3777—Unusual ornate double with child figure for handle, choice, 5" long

3778—Low flat double with ribbing around side, 2¼" long

3779—Looped fan design with plain handle at center, 5" long

3780—Oval shaped double with swirled rib design, 2½" long

3781—Polished crystal with tiny salts at end of open center, age unknown, 2½" long

3782—Cut glass double with cane motif in base, round bowls, 2½" long

3783—Plain panelled pattern with rayed base, arched divider in center, 1½" long

3784—Unusual covered double with a toothpick holder as cover, rotates to open and close, panelled design, 4½" long

3785—Pressed diamond salt with finger grips at side, 4" long, new from 1970's. Purchased in France.

3786—Another combination salt and toothpick holder, very unusual, 3" long

3787—Panelled design with finger grips, 4½" long

3788—Boat-shaped doubles with figural handle, fine rib design, 3" long

3789—Plain handled double with flanged base, 4½" long

PRESSED GLASS DOUBLES

3790—Fancy pressed design, high ribbed handle at center, 4½" long

3791—Honeycomb design, 4½" long

3792—Plain panelled double with center handle, 4½" long

3793—Ribbed design with center handle, 4½" long

3794—Footed shell-shaped salts with fancy handle at center, about 4" long

3795—Another plain panelled salt similar in style to one above it, 4½" long

3796—Pressed geometric grooves and angles, handle at center, 5½" long

3797—Plain panelled salt with sharp teardrop handle at center, 4½" long

3798—Unusual geometric design with a tiny toothpick holder at center as handle, 5¼" long

3799—Very ornate pressed double with fancy handle at center, 5½" long

3800—Another combination double and toothpick holder handle, 5" long

3801—Fascinating leaf design on salts with perching owl handle at center, 5½" long

PRESSED GLASS DOUBLES

3802—Swirled diamond panel design with ribbed handle, 5½" long

3803—Unusual ribbed double with covered mustard at center, choice, 5½" long

3804—Ribbed design with fancy handle at center, 5" long

3805 — Swirled salts with ribbed handle at center, 5½" long

3806 — Lovely diamond-cane with fan design, handle at center, 5½" long

3807 — Footed ribbed salts with open ring handle at center, 4" long

3808 — Basket shaped double with open handle, 4" long

3809 — Similar to Fig. 3807, also open-ring handled, footed, 4½" long

3810 — Very fancy pressed design with bud-like handle at center, 5¼" long

3811 — Appears to be the same as Figure 3791

3812 — Scarce covered double with openings for salt spoons, panelled design, 5" long

PRESSED GLASS DOUBLES

3813 — Appears to be duplication of Figure 3800

3814 — Plain panelled double with metal handle at center, 4½" long

3815 — Plain square non-pattern double with short stem handle at center, 4½" long

3816 — Similar in design to Fig. 3813, without toothpick, 5¼" long

3817 — Square ribbed pattern with ribbed handle at center, 5½" long

3818 — Vertical ribs with beaded border, attractive ribbed handle, 5" long

3819 — Panelled design double with high handle at center, 4½" long

3820 — Unique swan figural salt with double receptacles, very nice, 5" long

3821 — Very nice ribbed double with ornate finger grips, 4" long

3822 — Shell-shaped double with ribbed toothpick holder as handle, 6" long

3823 — Melon-ribbed double with handle at center, 5½" long

MISCELLANEOUS LATE ADDITIONS

3824 — Unusual salt set with cut master at bottom with sterling rim and loop handle, six ind. sterling salts on middle ring, HM Frank M. Whiting Co., circa 1910, just under 6" high

3825 — Oval cut table salt, diamond shaped base, geometric cutting from about 1910-20, 3½" high, 5⅝" across including handles

3826 — A second variant of the BARBERRY pattern (see also Fig. 3584), this one has oval shaped berries (LPG, pl. 139), the earlier variant has round berries (Metz 1, 90) reportedly made in 1860's at Sandwich, this one is McKee (Stout, 64) circa 1880's, 2⅜" diam. round

3827 — Pressed honeycomb double salt with wooden moose handle, European from the 1920's, just over 4" high, 4" long

3828 — Open salt and pepper shaker set, with handle, circa 1930's origin unknown, unusual, 2½" high, 4¾" long

3829 — Reproduction salt in Lion pattern frequently confused for old, made in clear only, circa 1975, 3" diam. NEVER MADE OLD

3830 — Pressed oval salt with waffle design in bottom, 3¼" long

3831 — Oval cut salt with pointed ends, European from about 1890, 3½" long

3832 — Lacy pressed salt similar to Neal #RD-23 and 24, circa 1840, Sandwich, 2¾" diam.

3833 — Early unsigned FANCY LOOP crimped salt by Heisey, circa 1898, may be a small honey dish or nut dish, 3" diam.

3834 — Cambridge CAPRICE salt or ash tray, circa 1930's with lengthy production, triangular shape, 2⅝" across side

3835 — Pressed repro of old candy container, this one marked "Taiwan" circa 1970, 3½" long

3836 — Unusual triangular handled plated holder with cut and polished crystal liner, American, circa 1910, three ball feet, 3" across

3837 — Pressed "crackle" glass in chrome holder, not old, oval shape, 1¾" long

3838 — Figural leaf plated frame with pressed insert, probably English, circa 1900, 3" across

3839 — Early flint pressed salt, also made in color and opalescent, circa 1830-50, 3½" long

3840 — Pressed double with figural dog handle, circa 1890-1900, European, 4½" long

3841 — Oblong cut salt with spoon rests at each end, may be ash tray, circa 1920's, 3" long

3842 — Heavy pressed oval table salt, maker unknown, circa 1880, 4" long

3843 — Plated frame with pressed block salt, not old, Made in Italy, 3" across

3844 — Cut glass round ind. salt with sterling rim, HM Frank M. Whiting Co., circa 1920, starred bottom, 2" diam.

3845 — STIPPLED SWAG salt (Metz 1, 134) by Central Glass, 1880's (Reprint C), Metz reports a spooner in this pattern, but it could be just a novelty salt not produced in other shapes, 3" diam. round

MISCELLANEOUS PLATED & STERLING

3846 — Plated, very unusual handles, American, circa 1880, 3¼" x 3½"

3847 — Rare plated medallion double salt, men on either side at top of handle, women on the four legs, 5¼" high x 2¾" wide x 5" long

3848 — Sterling handles & rim, leather covered over wood base, lion heads at top rim, circa early 1800's, European 3½" high x 2¾" round

3849 — Sterling double with toothpick holder, not old, hallmarked Argentina, 3½" high x 4" long

3850 — Plated handles over cut glass, European, circa 1890, 2¾" high x 5½" long, oval

3851 — Victorian Kate Greenaway, signed James W. Tuft, Boston, not original insert, could also be toothpick, circa 1890, 3½" high x 3½" long

3852 — Sterling lattice holder with Limoges insert, circa 1890, 1" x just over 2" long, oval

3853 — Matching salt, pepper & spoon, Shreve & Co., circa 1897-1906, sterling, salt is 1" x 1⅜" round

3854 — Sterling, hallmarked Shreve & Co., circa 1904, Lenox insert, 1" x 1⅝" round

3855 — Marked sterling, Limoges insert, 1" x 1½" round, circa 1890

3856 — Sterling, Shreve & Co., Lenox insert, circa 1890, ¾" high x 1¼" round

3857 — Sterling, hallmarked London, 1794-1795, Ann & Peter Bateman, 2¾" high x 3" long, oval

3858 — Silver over copper on wooden base, early 1800's, European, 3¾" high x 2⅞" wide at top

3859 — Sterling, three lion heads & paw feet, circa 1880, American, just under 2" high x 3" round

GLASS & SILVER

3860 — Sterling base, cut glass top, European origin, circa 1790, 2¾" high, 2⅝" round at top

3861 — Pressed glass with silver deposit decoration, just under 2" high, 1½" round, circa 1920

3862 — Sterling base, fine cut glass upper, Austria-Hungary, circa 1850, 2¾" high, just over 3" round

3863 — Pressed, silver deposit, 1¾" high, just under 2" round, American, circa 1915

3864 — Sterling base, cut glass upper, hallmarked London 1904, 2" high, 2½" round

3865-3874 — All pressed with silver deposit decoration, various sizes from ¾" high to 2½" round or long, circa 1915-20, Fostoria, Duncan & others

3875 — Sterling rim on cut glass, hallmarked London, circa 1830, 1" high, 2¼" round

3876 — Cut with sterling rim, no marks, 1¼" high, 1¾" round

3877 — Cut cane pattern with sterling rim, no marks, 1¼" high, 2¼" round

3878 — Cut cane pattern with sterling rim, hallmarked London, circa 1928, just over 1¼" high, under 2" round

3879 — Cut diamond point with sterling rim, no marks, 1" x 1¾" round

3880 — Cut, sterling rim, no marks, 1" high, 1¾" round

3881 — Cut, sterling rim hallmarked Birmingham, England, circa 1896, just over 1" high, 2" diam. plus handles

3882 — Cut with sterling rim, European style cut, no marks, 1½" high, 2" round

3883—Cut with short pedestal & sterling rim, hallmarked London 1906, 1 3/8" high, 2" round

3884—European cut with sterling rim, no marks, 1 1/4" high, 2 1/4" round

3885—Cut with sterling overlay, no marks, 1 1/4" high, 2" round

3886—Cut with sterling rim just over 1" high, 2" round

3887—Cut cane pattern with sterling rim, hallmarked London 1928, 1 1/4" high, 1 3/4" round

3888—Cut with sterling rim, hallmarked Birmingham, circa 1910, 1" high x just under 2" round

3889—Cut with sterling rim, no marks, gadroon top edge, 1" high x 2" round

GLASS & SILVER

3890—Frosted glass in plated holder, origin unknown, just under 4" high, shell shape

3891—Cut glass top with sterling base, new from Spain, paper label, just under 2" high

3892—Sterling, pedestal base, marked 800, hallmarked Germany, very delicate etched glass, circa 1870-1880, 2 1/4" high

3893—Pressed with silver deposit, no marks, just over 1/2" high, 1" round

3894—Crystal with sterling overlay, scroll feet, 1 1/4" high

3895—Cut with sterling rim, hallmarked London 1917, just over 1" high

3896—Pressed with sterling rim, hallmarked London 1919, just over 1 1/2" high

3897—Cut with sterling overlay on top edge, origin unknown, 3/4" high

3898—Cut with sterling rim, European, circa 1910, just over 1" high

3899—Sterling with blown glass liner, hallmarked Sheffield, Mappin & Webb, circa 1880, just over 1" high

3900—Pressed with sterling rim, no marks, just over 1 1/2" high, circa 1910

3901—Pressed with sterling rim, hallmarked Frank M. Whiting Co., circa 1920, just over 1 1/4" high

3902—Pressed with sterling rim, no marks, lamp of knowledge signature on bottom, circa 1920, 1 1/4" high

3903—Cut with sterling gadroon trim on top edge, no marks, just over 1" high

3904—Blown with silver deposit, American, circa 1910, 1 1/4" high

3905—Cut diamond point with brass rim, origin unknown, 1 1/4" high

3906—Sterling lattice holder with pressed glass liner, no marks, 1 1/4" high, American

3907—Sterling lattice holder with pressed glass liner, American, circa 1920, just under 1" high

3908—Cut & etched with sterling rim, origin unknown, circa 1920, 1" high

3909—Cut with sterling gadroon border, origin unknown, under 1" high

3910—Mold-blown, threaded and etched with sterling rim, European, circa 1890, just over 1 1/4" high

3911—Pressed with silver deposit, American, circa 1920, 1 1/4" high

3912—Pressed with silver deposit, American, circa 1920, 2" round

3913—Pressed with silver deposit, CAPITOL pattern by Westmoreland, circa 1910, also seen with gold overlay & in carnival glass, 2" high

3914—Pressed with silver deposit, could be nut cup, American, circa 1920, just over 1 1/2" high, sometimes found signed Northwood

3915—Same as #3914

3916—Pressed with sterling rim, hallmarked London 1904, just over 1" high

STERLING & PLATED WITH GLASS INSERTS

3917—Ornate sterling with blown glass liner & matching spoon, French, circa 1870, 1" high, 2" long, oval, 4 feet

3918—Victorian plated, hallmarked Meriden circa 1877, polished glass, appears to be serrated in picture but is chipped, unusual scene on holder with people and palm trees, 4" high, 3 3/4" long

3919—Sterling lattice holder, hallmarked Webster Co., circa 1940, just under 1" high, under 2" round

3920—Sterling with blown glass liner, European, circa 1910, 2" round

3921—Sterling with cut and polished liner, matching spoon, French circa 1870, 1 3/4" high, 3 3/4" long, oval

3922—Sterling, blown liner, French circa 1880, just over 1 1/2" high, 2 1/2" long, oval

3923—Plated, marked Made in Japan, circa 1930, 1" high, under 2" round

3924—Sterling with pressed glass liner, Wagner Co., circa 1940, just under 1" high, 1 1/2" round

3925—Sterling, hallmarked Fred Bucker & Son, circa 1877-1879, 1" high, 1 3/4" round

3926—Sterling with blown glass liner, French, circa 1845, 1 1/2" high, 2 1/4" long, oval

3927—Sterling, marked 830S, no other marks, European circa 1880, just over 1" high, 2" oblong

3928—Sterling double, delicately etched glass, twig design, hallmarked Germany, circa 1880, 2" high, 2 1/2" long, oval

3929—Brass with frosted liner, "Made in Italy", new, 1 3/4" high, 4" long, oval

3930—Sterling, no other marks, American circa 1900, 1 5/8" high & same round

3931—Plated, no marks, American pressed glass, 3" across

3932—Sterling, no other marks, American circa 1880, 1 3/4" high, 2" round

3933—Sterling, blown glass liner, Hungary-Austria, circa 1866-1922, oblong with rounded corners 1 1/4" high, 2" long

3934—Sterling marked 1000, type made in Japan for export, some age, oblong, 1 3/4" high, just over 2 1/2" long

3935—Sterling with blown glass liner, matching spoon, French circa 1845, just under 1 1/4" high x 1 1/2" round

3936—Russian of recent date, low grade of silver, 1 1/4" high, just over 2" round

3937—Sterling with molded and polished liner, matching spoon, French circa 1845, 1 1/2" high, 2 1/2" long, oval

3938—Sterling, hallmarked Germany, signed Hesselberg, before 1894, 1" high, just over 1 1/2" round

3939—Plated over brass, French circa 1850, 1 3/8" high x 2 3/8" long, oval

3940—Plated with molded frosted liner, engraved Gunard Steamship Co., circa 1900, 1 1/2" high, 2 1/4" oblong

3941—Sterling marked 800 Germany, before 1891, 1 1/2" high, 2 1/4" long, oval

3942—Sterling, molded glass liner, French circa 1870, gold wash inside and outside, 2" high, 2 1/2" long, oval

3943—Sterling, molded glass liner, French circa 1880, just over 1 1/4" high by 2 3/4" long, oval

3944—Sterling, hallmarked Germany-Austria, circa 1880, 1" high, 2 3/4" across, matching spoon, delicate cupids on top corners of salt & spoon

3945—Plated over copper, hallmarked Sheffield, James Dixon & Sons, molded liner, just over 2" high, 3 1/4" long, oval

3946—Sterling, unusual square shape, molded glass liner, matching spoon, French circa 1838-1845, just over 1" high, 2" square

STERLING & PLATED

3947—Sterling, hallmarked Wallace circa 1940, matching spoon, just over 2 1/2" high

3948—Plated hallmarked Meriden Co, circa 1890, 1 3/4" high

3949—Sterling, unusual applied design, alternating panels of falling leaves and scrolls, hallmarked London 1898, 1 3/4" high

3950—Sterling, hallmarked Gorham circa 1876, baby heads on either tab end with garlands of flowers between, just over 2" high

3951—Sterling, American circa 1880, engraved design underneath band of beads, just over 1 1/2" high

3952—Sterling, hallmarked Maltby Stevens & Curtiss, circa 1894, 1 1/4" high

3953—Sterling, French or Austrian, circa 1890, 1 1/4" high, oval with pointed ends

3954—Sterling marked "Foreign", glass liner, sea horses for legs, palm leaves, just over 1" high, age unknown

3955—Sterling, hallmarked Birmingham, circa 1906-1907, 1 3/4" high

3956—Sterling oblong base & bowl, gold wash, purchased new in Austria 1970's, 1¼" high

3957—Sterling, not old, Mexican, just under 1" high

3958—Sterling, hallmarked Birmingham, circa 1897, weighted base to prevent tipping, just under 1" high, 3" long, oval

3959—Sterling, Mexican, not very old, short pedestal, 1½" high

3960—Sterling, Mexican, not very old, just under 1" high

3961—Plated, no marks, American circa 1890, just under 1" high

3962—Sterling highly chased, hollow/double wall indicating Chinese, 1½" high

3963—Sterling, not original insert, no marks, just under 1¼" high

3964—Sterling, no marks, pastoral scenes around, almost 1" high, circa 1920

3965—Sterling, unusual bathtub shape, hallmarked Dixon & Sons, Sheffield, England, highly chased, circa 1894, just over 1" high

3966—Sterling, no marks, probably Mexican, not very old, ¾" high

3967—Sterling, hallmarked Birmingham, circa 1914, ⅝" high oval

3968—Sterling, hallmarked Birmingham, circa 1899, just over ½" high

3969-3970—Sterling, American Indian, age unknown, matching spoons, just under 1" high

3971—Plated, no marks, gold wash bowl, circa 1920, just under 1" high

3972—Sterling, purchased in Germany, no marks, circa 1940, just under 1" high

3973—Sterling, Tiffany & Co., circa 1900, ¾" high

3974—Sterling, no marks, appears to have had liner, circa 1890, just under 1" high

3975—Plated, trademarked Meriden, circa 1869, 1" high

3976—Sterling, trademarked Gorham, undated, medallion tabs, circa 1870, just over 2" high

3977—Plated, flower on leaf figural, circa 1880, no marks, just over 1½" high

3978—Sterling, hallmarked Kirk & Sons, circa 1885, 1" high

3979—Sterling, blown glass liner, French circa 1880, just over 1¼" high, 2¾" long, oval

**STERLING & PLATED—
ALL FLAT BASED**

3980—Sterling, hallmarked London, circa 1900, 1" high

3981—Sterling, heavy embossing, hallmarked Wallace & Sons, circa 1908, 1" high

3982—Sterling, hallmarked Gorham, circa 1899, 1" high

3983—Sterling, hallmarked export marks from Belgium or France, after 1920, 1⅞" high

3984—Plated, marked Roger & Bros., circa 1890, round with square top, just over 1" high

3985—Plated, no marks, circa 1890, just under 1" high

3986—Sterling, etched pattern around bowl, hallmarked Gorham, circa 1922-1926, just under 1" high

3987—Sterling, hallmarked Birmingham, circa 1890, 1" high

3988—Plated, marked Pairpoint, Sheffield reproduction, circa 1890, 1" high

3989—Plated, marked Reed & Barton circa 1890, just under 1" high

3990—Sterling, hallmarked Gorham, circa 1887, just under 1" high

3991—Sterling, hallmarked Ortega 900, Mexico—Hand made, age unknown, 1" high

3992—Sterling, hallmarked Gorham, circa 1930, ¾" high

3993—Sterling, marked "Century of Progress 1934 Chicago Worlds Fair", ¾" high

3994—Sterling, hallmarked Cheapside, London, Fink & Co., circa 1920, just under 1" high

3995—Sterling, hallmarked Wilcox Wagoner, prior to 1905, 1" high

3996—Sterling, no marks, not original liner, American circa 1900, 1" high

3997—Sterling, hallmarked G. H. French & Co, circa 1935-1943, ¾" high

3998—Sterling, hallmarked Alvin Co., circa 1930, just under 1" high

3999—Sterling, no marks, American circa 1940, ½" high

4000—Silver soldered, hallmarked Pairpoint Mfg Co, prior to 1900, ¾" high

4001—Plated—has liner, no marks, American circa 1910, ¾" high

4002—Sterling, no hallmarks, American, circa 1920, ¾" high

4003—Sterling, no hallmarks, American, circa 1940, ½" high

4004—Plated, marked Roger Bros., circa 1890, just under 1" high

4006—Plated, no marks, band of decoration around top, circa 1910, just under 1" high

4007—Sterling, no hallmarks, American, circa 1920, ½" high

4008—Sterling, no hallmarks, rosette border, American circa 1920, ½" high

4009—Sterling, hallmarks worn off, American, circa 1910, ⅝" high

4010—Sterling, hallmarked Gorham with no date mark, circa 1910, ¾" high

4011—Sterling, hallmarked Newburyport Silver Co., circa 1905-1914, just under 1" high

4012—Sterling—has busy embossed pattern, looks like it could have been part of a condiment set (marks on bottom), circa 1880, ¾" high

4013—Plated, hallmarked James Tuft, Boston, prior to 1895, ¾" high

4014—Sterling, gadroon top border, hallmarked Wallace, circa 1900, gold wash interior, ½" high

4015—Sterling, hallmarked Birks, scalloped & decorated top edge, circa 1940, ¾" high

4016—Sterling, hallmarked Gorham, circa 1891, just under 1" high

4017—Plated, marked Meriden Co., circa 1900, 1" high

**STERLING & PLATED—
PEDESTAL & FLAT-BASED TYPES**

4018—Sterling, European origin, no hallmarks, circa 1870, just over 2½" high, comes apart in 3 sections

4019—Coin silver, hallmarked Gorham, circa 1860, just over 1½" high

4020—Sterling, hallmarked Frank Whiting Co., circa 1896-1920, 1¾" high

4021—Sterling, hallmarked Austria circa 1867-1890, just over 1½" high

4022—Plated, gold wash bowl, no marks, circa 1880, European, 1¾" high

4023—Sterling, hallmarks - Near East circa 1920, 1½" high

4024—Sterling, hallmarked Gorham, circa 1868, just over 1½" high

4025—Sterling, very ornate, hallmarked Birmingham, circa 1897, 1¾" high

4026—Sterling, hallmarked Webster Co., circa 1920, 1¼" high

4027—Sterling, hallmarked Austria 800, after 1921, glass liner does not belong in this salt, 1¾" high

4028—Plated, no marks, American circa 1920, just under 1½" high

4029—Sterling, hallmarked Germany, circa 1888-1914, 1" high, blown glass liner

4030—Sterling, hallmarked Hungary-Austria circa 1866-1926, blown glass liner, just over 1" high

4031—Sterling, hallmarked Germany, circa 1884, just over 1" high

4032—Sterling, hallmarked Wilson, circa 1883, just over 1½" high

4033—Sterling, hallmarked Gorham, no date marks, circa 1920, just under 1" high

4034—Sterling, no hallmarks, circa 1930 American, just under 1½" high

4035—Sterling, hallmarked Genova Silver Co., circa 1950, 1½" high

4036—Sterling, weighted in the bottom, no hallmarks, circa 1940, just over 1½" high

4037—Coin silver, hallmarked Middletown Coin, circa 1866-1899, 2" high

4038—Sterling, hallmarked Fred Hirsch circa 1920-1945, just over 1½" high

4039—Plated, no hallmarks, American circa 1920 hollow underneath, ½" high

4040—Sterling, hallmarked Denmark, circa 1939, matching spoon, 1" high

4041—Sterling, no hallmarks, American circa 1940, just under 1" high

4042—Plated no hallmarks, American circa 1940, 1" high

4043—Sterling, Mexican—not old, ½" high

4044—Sterling, hallmarked Napier, American, circa 1930, 1" high

4045—Plated, hollow underneath English EP, dated Mar. 24, 1874, 1¼" high

4046—Sterling, hallmarked Reed & Barton, circa 1890, just under 1" high, could be nut cup

4047—Plated, no marks, original box indicates James Tuft Co, circa 1900, ¾" high, could also be nut cup

4048—Sterling, hallmarked Finland, circa 1890, gold wash bowl, 1½" high

STERLING—ALL FOOTED

4049—Sterling, hallmarked Walker & Hall, England circa 1900, just over 1" high

4050—Plated, hallmarked Meridan Co circa 1852-1898, just under 1" high

4051—Sterling, hallmarked South American or India, peacock handles circa 1940, just over 2" high

4052—Sterling, Mexico 900, not old, just over 1" high, sea lion legs

4053—Sterling, hallmarked Russian circa 1893, just over 1½" high

4054—Sterling, hallmarked Towle, circa 1920, just under 1½" high

4055—Sterling, hallmarked Gorham circa 1915, just over 1" high

4056—Plated, no hallmarks, pearls set in the top of each leg, could be novelty of some kind, circa 1940, just over 1½" high

4057—Sterling, no hallmarks, circa 1940, 1¾" high

4058—Sterling, European origin, circa 1880, just over 1" high

4059—Coin silver, South America, circa 1940, 1" high

4060—Plated, hallmarked Roger Bros., prior to 1908, 1" high

4061—Sterling, hallmarked, M. Eisenstadt Jewelry Co., circa 1866-1904, 1½" high

4062—Plated, no marks, American, circa 1920, 1" high, 3 ball feet

4063—Sterling, hallmarked R. Suiza— no information available, ¾" high

4064—Plated, no marks, origin unknown, circa 1880, 1½" high

4065—Sterling, hallmarked Russia, circa 1908-1917, 1" high

4066—Sterling, exceptional detail on lion head feet, no hallmarks, European circa 1880, 1½" high

4067—Plated, marked Wilcox Co., prior to 1898, ¾" high

4068—Sterling, hallmarked Denmark, Kopenhagen, ¾" high, circa 1920

4069—Sterling, hallmarked Sheffield, circa 1907, 1½" high, oval

4070—Sterling, made from Equador Coin, 1890, just under 1" high, 3 llamas for feet

4071—Sterling, hallmarked London, circa 1910, just under 1½" high

4072—Coin silver, hallmarked Creswick & Co, circa 1850-1860, Mandarin characters at top of each leg, roman key design around the top is very unusual, just under 2" high

4073—Sterling, probably reproduction of very early English Sheffield, circa 1890, 1½" high, note hoof feet as on #4071

4074—Sterling, hallmarked Haller & Methanau, Berlin, Germany, circa 1900, 1½" high, delicate etching and monogramming around bowl

STERLING & PLATED

4075—Sterling, hallmarked Gorham, circa 1874, just over 2½" high

4076—Sterling, hallmarked Barber Silver co., circa 1898, just under 2" high

4077—Sterling, Chinese — hollow bottom & double wall on bowl of salt, exceptional quality and very ornate embossing, just over 1½" high

4078—Sterling, hallmarked Udall & Ballow, circa 1875-1890, very unusual detail, just over 2½" high

4079—Sterling, hallmarked Birmingham, circa 1911, 1¼" high

4080—Sterling, hallmarked International Sterling Co., circa 1900

4081—Sterling, hallmarked Marcus & Co., New York, circa 1918-1927, 1½" high, oval

4082—Sterling, no hallmarks, circa 1940, just over 1½" high

4083—Sterling, hallmarked 830, dated 25 April, 1914, monogram/on building reads "AKURSHUS", 1½" high

4084—Sterling, hallmarked Gorham, circa 1871, just over 1½" high

4085—Sterling, Registry mark 27830, circa 1885-1886, English, 1¾" high

4086—Sterling, hallmarked MSC circa 1896, 1¼" high

4087—Sterling, hallmarked Dominick & Haff, hand made hammered design, circa 1892, 1¼" high

4088—Plated, marked Meriden Co., circa 1900, 1⅜" high

4089—Plated, no marks, American, circa 1890, 1¾" high

4090—Sterling, hallmarked Wm. B. Kerr, circa 1855-1906, 1½" high

4091—Sterling, no hallmarks, American, circa 1880, 2" high

4092—Sterling, hallmarked France, circa 1838-1845, 1½" high

4093—Plated, no marks, could be egg cup or toothpick, engraving reads "Just Out" 2" high

4094—Plated, no marks, circa 1890, could also be toothpick or egg cup, 1¾" high

4095—Sterling, hallmarked France, circa 1819-1838, 1¾" high oval

4096—Sterling overlay on oyster shells, matching spoon, dated 1886, handmade, 1¾" high

4097—Sterling, hallmarked Russia, dated 1869, 1½" high

4098—Plated, unidentified marks, American, circa 1920, just under 2" high

4099—Sterling, hallmarked France, circa 1838-1845, 1¼" high, oval

4100—Sterling, hallmarked Juarez, TL & Co., Mexico, not old, just under 1" high

STERLING & PLATED

4101—Sterling, no hallmarks, American circa 1920, just over 1½" high

4102-4103—Tray & two salts with matching spoons, Mexico, not old, trays are 5" long, salts 1" high

4104—Sterling, hallmarked Locklin & Sons, circa 1920, just under 1½" high

4105—Sterling, no hallmarks, circa 1880, just over 1" high

4106—Sterling, hallmarked Mexico, not old, just over 1" high

4107—Sterling, no hallmarks, circa 1920, 1¼" high

4108—Sterling, hallmarked Birmingham, circa 1909, 1" high

4109—Sterling, hallmarked Gorham, no date mark, circa 1920, 1" high

4110—Sterling, no hallmarks, circa 1940, just over 1½" high

4111—Sterling, hallmarked Webster Co., circa 1900, just over 1" high

4112—Sterling, hallmarked Austria, circa 1866, just over 1" high

4113—Sterling, hallmarked Frank W. Smith, circa 1886-1910, just under 1½" high

4114—Sterling, purchased new in Vienna 1970, gold wash bowl, just over 1" high

4115—Sterling, hallmarked Webster & Co., circa 1950, just under 1½" high

4116—Sterling, hallmarked Tiffany circa 1875-1891, just under 1" high

4117—Sterling, marked 800, no other hallmarks, circa 1890, 1" high

4118—Sterling, no hallmarks, circa 1920, just under 1" high

4119—Sterling, hallmarked JH, origin unknown, circa 1920, just under 1½" high

4120—Sterling, no marks, origin unknown, circa 1920, just under 1½" high

4121—Plated, no hallmarks, 1¼" high

4122—Sterling, hallmarked Mexico, not old, just over 1¼" high

4123—Plated, no hallmarks, fits Victorian condiment set, just over 1" high

4124—Sterling, dated 1904, has trophy presentation engraved, just under 2" high

4125—Sterling, hallmarked Mexico, not old, 1" high

4126—Sterling, hallmarked Tiffany, matching spoon, circa 1875-1891, ¾" high

4127—Sterling, no hallmarks, American, circa 1920, just over 1" high

4128—Sterling, hallmarked Le Bolt & Co, circa 1915-1922, 1" high

4129—Sterling, hallmarked Wallace, circa 1910, just under 1" high

4130—Sterling, hallmarked Fisher, circa 1936, 1¼" high

4131 — Plated, no marks, foreign, circa 1930, 1¾" high

4132 — Plated, marked Reed & Barton, roman key design around bowl, circa 1928, 1¾" high

4133 — Sterling, hallmarked Mexico 900, not old, 1¼" high

STERLING & PLATED

4134 — Plated, matching salt & pepper, English design, no marks, circa 1890, salt is 1¾" high

4135 — Sterling, marked Gorham-Georgian Reproduction, circa 1929, very elegant design, just under 2" high

4136 — Sterling no hallmarks, English design, circa 1890, just under 2" high

4137 — Sterling, no hallmarks, American, circa 1890, monogrammed "Lizzie", 2" high

4138 — Sterling, no hallmarks, American, circa 1900, 2" high

4139 — Sterling, hallmarked Webster Co., weighted base, circa 1920, this salt has cover with slot for card holder (not pictured), 2" with lid

4140 — Plated, marked Rockford Silver Co., circa 1900, just over 1" high

4141 — Sterling, hallmarked Towle, prior to 1909, 1" high

4142 — Sterling, hallmarked James Tuft, Boston, prior to 1915, 1¼" high

4143 — Sterling, hallmarked Barbour Silver Co., circa 1892, 1¼" high

4144 — Coin silver, no other marks, American, circa 1880-1890, ⅜" high

4145 — Plated, marked Sheffield, circa 1902, registered, 1½" high

4146 — Sterling, hallmarked Germany 800, circa 1894, ¼" high

4147 — Sterling, hallmarked London, circa 1868, just over 1½" high

4148 — Sterling, European, handmade, circa 1900, 1" high

4149 — Sterling, hallmarked B&F, American, circa 1890, gold wash all over, just over ¼" high

4150 — Sterling, hallmarked Birmingham 1897, embossed design, 1½" high

4151 — Sterling, hallmarked Roden Bros. Ltd., Canadian, circa 1891-1904, just over ½" high, matching spoon

4152 — Plated, marked Meriden Co., circa 1896, just over 1" high

4153 — Sterling, matching salt & pepper, hallmarked Weidlich, circa 1915-1952, tiny garlands of grapes around, salt is 1½" high

4154 — Sterling, no hallmarks, American, circa 1920, salt is 1¾" high

4155 — Plated, no hallmarks, American, circa 1890, 1½" high

4156 — Sterling, hallmarked Meriden B & Co., circa 1890, ¾" high

4157 — Sterling, hallmarked Gorham, circa 1920, ½" high

4158 — Plated, no hallmarks, American, circa 1910, 1" high

4159 — Sterling no hallmarks, Ameri-

can, circa 1860-1870, blown glass liner, 1¼" high

4160 — Sterling, hallmarked Wood & Hughes (American), circa 1865, rare medallion salt with warrior heads on either side, 1½" high

4161 — Sterling, hallmarked London, circa 1892, this style called "Trencher type", 1¼" high, oval bowl

4162 — Sterling, hallmarked Whiting Mfg. Co., prior to 1926, just over 1½" high

STERLING & PLATED – ALL FOOTED

4163 — Sterling, no hallmarks, embossed cupids around bowl, probably European, circa 1880, 1¾" high

4164 — Sterling, hallmarked Reed & Barton, prior to 1928, 1¼" high

4165 — Sterling, hallmarked London, circa 1899, very heavy baroque design, 2" high, oval

4166 — Sterling, handmade from Thailand, circa 1940, 1¼" high

4167 — Sterling, hallmarked Tiffany & Co., circa 1879, pattern of all over beads, also seen on spoon handle, 1" high

4168 — Sterling, no hallmarks, American, circa 1920, just over 1" high

4169 — Sterling, no hallmarks, American, circa 1910, just over 1" high

4170 — Plated, marked Sheffield EP, circa 1885, 1" high

4171 — Sterling, hallmarked "Stieff – Hand Chased", has matching pepper, circa 1900, just over 1" high

4172 — Sterling, hallmarked Dominick & Haff, before 1928, 1¼" high

4173 — Sterling, no hallmarks, Near East origin, embossed design with 3 different animals in their habitat around bowl, age unknown, just over 1" high

4174 — Sterling, hallmarked with Austria import mark, circa 1866-1922, acanthus leafs for legs, 1¼" high

4175 — Sterling, hallmarked Walker & Hall (English) circa 1900, 1¼" high

4176 — Plated, marked Sheffield – dated 1889, 1¼" high

4177 — Sterling, hallmarked Sheffield circa 1859, just over 1" high

4178 — Sterling, hallmarked Gorham, circa 1900, 1" high

4179 — Sterling, hallmarked Germany, circa 1910, 1¼" high

4180 — Sterling, no hallmarks, gadroon border, American, circa 1920, 1" high

4181 — Sterling, hallmarked Birmingham, circa 1898, just over 1" high

4182 — Sterling, heart shaped, hallmarked Dominick & Haff, prior to 1928, 1" high

4183 — Sterling, hallmarked Birmingham, circa 1907, 1½" high, oval

4184 — Sterling, hallmarks of European country, age unknown, 1" high

4185 — Sterling, handmade, Near East origin, carved scrolls and leaves, 1" high

4186 — Sterling, hallmarked Birmingham, circa 1936, 1¼" high

4187 — Sterling, no hallmarks, South American, circa 1940, 1" high

4188 — Silver over Brass, could be old Sheffield, no hallmarks, 1½" high, circa 1880

4189 — Plated, no hallmarks, could have had liner, American, circa 1940, 1¾" high

4190 — Plated, marked Adelphi, before 1915, 1¾" high

4191 — Sterling, hallmarked Birmingham, circa 1899, very unusual design, matching spoon, 1¾" high

STERLING AND PLATED

4192 — Plated, hallmarked James Tuft, circa 1885, hat shaped liner, unusual style in handles, just over 3" high

4193 — Crystal on sterling weighted base, thumbprint design on bowl, no hallmarks, just over 2½" high

4194 — Sterling double, no hallmarks, European origin, circa 1880, blown and polished glass liners, 3¾" long

4195 — Sterling holder, hallmarked Hungary – Austria, circa 1820, excellent design of dolphins and horses, handles at top open to accommodate a 4" wide dish. Goss portion dates London 1905. With proper dish, it would measure 4" high

4196 — Coin silver with medallion heads of Greek god Mercury, American, circa 1870, 2" high

4197 — Sterling, no hallmarks, embossed in high relief of flowers and scrolls, American, circa 1890, just over 2" high

4198 — Sterling, hallmarked Wood & Hughes, circa 1856, medallion heads of Greek goddess, just under 2½" high

4199 — Sterling, hallmarked Black, Starr & Frost, circa 1896, 1¾" high

4200 — Sterling, English hallmarks, circa 1890, just over 1½" high

4201 — Sterling, no hallmarks, embossed swirls around bowl, just over 1½" high, oval

4202 — Sterling, hallmarked Barbour Silver Co., after 1898, octagon with blown glass liner, just under 1½" high

4203 — Sterling, hallmarked Mexico 900, not old, 3½" high

4204 — Sterling, no hallmarks, American circa 1890, matching spoon, 2 patterns around bowl, toe feet, 1¼" high

4205 — Sterling, no hallmarks, Foreign, handmade, leaf designs on branch base with butterfly on cover, just under 2" high

4206 — Sterling, hallmarked Gorham, circa 1890, butterfly handles, 2" high

4207 — Sterling viking boat, glass liner hallmarked 830S Norge and town marks of Norway. These are made in Norway dating quite old and also new. Mostly sold with matching spoons

4208 — Sterling, hallmarked Albert

Cole, American, circa 1836-1876, Medallion heads of Greek god, hollow underneath, 2¼" high

4209—Sterling, hallmarked Gorham, circa 1874, 1¾" high

4210—Sterling 800, Germany, before 1891, hallmarked Berlin, just over 1½" high, very unusual wheelbarrow with moving wheel

4211-4212—Sterling, no hallmarks, dolphins holding shells, each different, origin unknown, circa 1920, 2¼" high

4213—Plated over copper, unidentified European mark, blown glass liner, circa 1890, just under 1½" high

4214—Sterling, hallmarked Sweden, circa 1890, excellent detail, 2" high

4215—Plated, Victorian, crackle glass insert, circa 1877, 4¼" high

4216—Plated, Victorian, crackle glass insert, gold top edge, fox heads of top of legs, circa 1877, 2½" high

4217—Plated, Victorian, marked Meriden Co., circa 1877, just under 4½" high

STERLING & PLATED

4218—Sterling 830, South American, circa 1940, just over 1½" high

4219—Plated, marked WMM, origin unknown, circa 1900, 1¼" high

4220—Sterling, hallmarked Tiffany & Co., new in 1970, salt bowl on top with small bowl for pepper underneath, matching spoon with ornate lion head as on salt, 3¼" high

4221—Sterling, Chinese salt & pepper set, salt is hanging on tree branch, age unknown, just over 3" high

4222—Sterling, hallmarked Thune, Norway or Sweden, age unknown, unusual feet with flower on top, 1¾" high, blown glass liner

4223—Sterling, unidentified hallmarks, salt is made so bowl is removable by turning screw on bottom, garlands of fruit around bowl, 1¾" high, oval

4224—Sterling, hallmarked Geo. Sharpe, circa 1855, gold wash bowl, 1¾" high plus handle

4225—Sterling, no hallmarks, American, circa 1890, 2¼" high

4226—Sterling, hallmarked Reed & Barton, gold wash bowl, circa 1890-1904, 2" high, oval

4227—Sterling trencher type, Nelson Rockefeller Foundation reproduction of Peter & William Bateman original from 1807, just over 1" high, new in 1970's

4228—Sterling 800, hallmarked Germany, circa 1894, excellent detail of mythological angels, with garlands of flowers & ribbons, 2½" high plus handle, blown glass liner

4229—Sterling 800, hallmarked Berlin, Germany, circa 1890, embossed garlands of fruit, ribbons and flowers, 2" high

4230—Sterling, hallmarked Dominick & Haff, circa 1890, embossed design around paneled bowl, 2" high

4231—Plated, hallmarked Gorham circa 1910, 1¾" high

4232—Sterling, hallmarked England, David Hannel maker, circa 1754, 1¾" high

STERLING & PLATED

4233—Sterling double, no hallmarks, circa 1880, 3½" high, purchased in Switzerland

4234—Sterling 925, no hallmarks, origin unknown, circa 1920, 3" high

4235—Black glass on brass pedestal, age & origin unknown, 1¾" high

4236—Sterling 925, no hallmarks, American, circa 1920, embossed design shows inside & out, gold wash bowl, ½" high

4237—Sterling, hallmarked MFH, American, circa 1920, 1" high

4238—Sterling, hallmarked Towle, modern design, ½" high

4239—Plated, marked Meriden, circa 1900, just under 1" high

4240—Sterling, no hallmarks, hand made with inverted top, hammered, top also serves as saucer, age & origin unknown, ¾" high

4241—Plated, hallmarked Forbes Silver Co., after 1894, 1" high, oval

4242—Sterling, hallmarked Gorham, circa 1900, all over gold wash, 1¼" high

4243—Plated, no marks, blue insert permanently attached, age & origin unknown, 1¾" high

4244—Sterling, no hallmarks, clear glass inserts, just over ½" high plus handle

4245—Plated, EPNS, combination salt & knife holder, age & origin unknown, ¾" high

4246—Sterling, hallmarked Birmingham 1899, gadroon scalloped top edge matching design at bottom, ¾" high, oval

4247—Plated, no marks, Victorian, 2" high

4248—Sterling, hallmarked Gorham, identical to #4242 except for gold wash, circa 1900, 1¼" high

4249—Sterling, hallmarked WMF Germany, blown & cut glass liner, 1" high

4250—Sterling, hallmarked Frank M. Whiting Co., before 1896, tiny scrolls and beads around top scalloped edge, ½" high

4251—Sterling, hallmarked Webster Co., circa 1900, hammered design around bottom, ¾" high

4252—Plated, marked Meriden Co., circa 1877, excellent detail on ram's heads, just under 2" high

4253—Plated, no hallmarks, American circa 1850, 3 griffins around bowl, heavy, 1½" high

4254—Plated, no hallmarks, American circa 1850, Gorham type, King Tut figures around bowl with hammered design at top and garlands of flowers mid bowl, 1¾" high

4255—Sterling unidentified hallmarks, European origin, circa 1860, gold wash bowl, 1" high in back section to show more detail, Fig. 4724

STERLING & PLATED NOVELTY TYPES

4256—Pewter-type viking ship, probably new, seen locally in tourist shops 1½" high

4257—Pewter-type viking ship, origin and age unknown, 1¾" high

4258—Pewter-type, origin and age unknown, note paddle spoon, 2¾" high

4259—Sterling, modern viking type, hallmarked Shreve & Co., circa 1930, just over 2" high

4260—Sterling 830, Norway age unknown, 1½" high

4261—Sterling 830, Norway, age unknown 1¼" high

4262—Pewter-type, new from Norway, 1¼" high

4263—Sterling, hallmarked Sweden, circa 1937, just under 2" high

4264—Pewter, age & origin unknown, 1¾" high

4265—Plated, no hallmarks, ½ acorn, age & origin unknown, 1" high

4266—Plated, apple on twigs, no hallmarks, 1½" high

4267—Plated, no hallmarks, strawberry on leaf, age & origin unknown, just over 1" high, gold wash bowl

4268—Plated, no hallmarks, english walnut on twigs, age & origin unknown, just over 1" high, gold wash bowl. Figs. 4267-4268 appear to be from the same set.

4269—Sterling, hallmarked Victor Co., circa 1890, shell on shell-shape base, 1" high

4270—Brass, no marks, half english walnut with twigs & leaves, age & origin unknown, 2¼" high

4271—Plated, no hallmarks, english walnut, age & origin unknown, 1½" high

4272—Sterling, unmarked, half brazil nut on twig pedestal, gold wash bowl, age & origin unknown, ¾" high

4273—Plated, no marks, half nut on twig pedestal, age & origin unknown, just over ½" high

4274—Plated, no marks, Victorian, circa 1890, 1¼" high

4275—Sterling, no hallmarks, thistle pattern indicates Scotland, age unknown, 1¼" high

4276—Sterling, no hallmarks, cabbage head on leaf with matching spoon, unusual design, excellent detail, age & origin unknown, 1¼" high

4277—Plated, marked Simpson Hall Miller, circa 1890, 1¼" high

4278—Plated, no hallmarks, shell with dolphin legs, age & origin unknown, 1¼" high

4279—Sterling, no hallmarks, age & origin unknown, ball feet, just under 1" high

4280—Plated, EPNS, Made in England, circa 1920, ball feet, just over 1" high

4281—Sterling, hallmarked Gorham, very delicate detail of oyster shell with matching spoon, no date marks, just under 1" high

4282—Plated, no hallmarks, heavier weight than Fig. 4278, dolphin legs, 1½" high

4283—Plated, no hallmarks, gold wash bowl, draped babies holding garlands of flowers divided by triangular shields, 2½" high

4284—Plated, marked Meriden, circa 1877-1898, baby chick breaking out of shell on wishbone, 1½" high

4285—Sterling, hallmarked England, circa 1883, just under 2" high

4286—Sterling, hallmarked Germany and dated 1822, gold wash bowl, mermaids holding baskets of fruit on either side, note tails curling around base, salt comes apart for cleaning, purchased in Copenhagen

STERLING & PLATED ANIMALS

4287—Sterling 835, hallmarked Belgium, Cut glass body, age unknown, 3" high, wings spread to reveal double salt

4288—Plated, no hallmarks, pressed glass body with pattern of wings & short tail on the glass, 3" high, definitely old

4289—Sterling, no hallmarks, pressed glass body, European, old, 3¼" high

4290—Plated with pressed glass body, detail on neck & wings identical to Fig. 4287, this one not old, 3½" high

4291—Plated, pressed glass body, age & origin unknown, but old, just under 3" high

4292—Pewter-type swan with frosted glass liner, origin unknown, just over 2" high, not old

4293—Sterling, French hallmark unidentified, pressed glass body with polished bottom, detail on glass same as on Fig. 4288, 3" high, old

4294—Sterling, hallmarked Germany, circa 1891, blown frosted glass liner, 2" high

4295—Brass neck & head, pressed glass body, age & origin unknown, 2½" high

4296—Same as Fig. 4292

4297—Same as Fig. 4294

4298—Sterling, hallmarked Germany 800, just under 2" high, circa 1890

4299—Sterling, hallmarked Germany 800, circa 1890, pressed glass liner, just under 2" high

4300—Sterling, hallmarked Germany 800, after 1890, just under 2" high

4301—Plated, WMF (white metal filled), Germany, after 1884, just under 2" high, blown glass liner

4302—Copper with brass filigree overlay, marked China, age unknown, 2¾" high

4303—Sterling 835, European origin, age unknown, cut glass body, wings do not open, matching spoon, red eyes,

saucer has base of swimming fish with flowers and scrolls around top edge, 2" high

4304—Plated, not old, just over 2" high

4305—Plated, marked EPNS Australia, age unknown, just over 1¼" high

4306—Plated, marked J. A. Babcock, circa 1894, pail has chain fastened on back side, just under 2" high

4307—Sterling, hallmarked Chester, England, circa 1906, matching spoon makes feathered tail, (not shown), very unusual, 1¾" high

4308—Sterling, perhaps Egyptian, age unknown, unidentified hallmarks, bird on top, 2½" high

4309—Plated, no hallmarks, cover has disc for moisture, blue glass eyes, not old, from Florence, Italy, just over 1¼" high

4310—Brass, red glass eyes, from Argentina, not old, 2½" high

4311—Plated, same hallmarks as Fig. 4301, after 1884, 1¾" high

STERLING & PLATED— ANIMALS & PEOPLE

4312—Plated, no hallmarks, American, circa 1890, 4½" high

4313—Plated, South American, not old, Llama on side, 1¾" high

4314—Plated, no hallmarks, European, circa 1940, 3¼" high

4315—Sterling, European hallmarks unidentified, age unknown, just over 2" high

4316—Sterling, unidentified European hallmarks, age unknown, 2½" high

4317—Sterling, hallmarked Sheffield-Foreign, may be Dutch, 2" high

4318—Bronze elephant, not old, 1½" high

4319—Sterling, hallmarked Italy or Portugal, age unknown, just over 2" high

4320—Sterling, no hallmarks, purchased in France—new in the 70's, cobalt inserts, four horses, floral garlands on coach, matching spoons, just over 1½" high

4321—Plated, no hallmarks, not old, frosted glass permanently affixed, 2½" high, also available new in sterling from Germany

4322—Plated, marked Meriden, circa 1877, wolf dogs, note tails laying on base, also comes apart for cleaning, 2¼" high

4323—Plated, marked "Made in Japan", age unknown, just over 1½" high

4324—Sterling, hallmarked Tiffany & Co, Italy, note matching spoon, extremely heavy, salt & spoon together weigh 5 oz, gold wash bowl, just over ½" high, solid silver, age undetermined

4325—Pewter, age & origin unknown, 1¾" high

4326—Plated, age & origin unknown, not new, just over 2¼" high

4327—Plated, no hallmarks, American, circa 1850, three griffins around bowl, heavy 1½" high

4328—Sterling, no hallmarks, South American, 3 llamas holding salt by their tails, age unknown, 1½" high

4329—Sterling, hallmarks showing Belgium import marks, detail on lion legs exquisite, the lion tails (not shown in picture) are complete and are beneath the bowl of the salt. Detail on top edge showing 3 groups of angels holding 3 different crests and these are separated by masked character faces, circa 1880

ORIENTAL—STERLING

4330—Open flower scrolls, 3 feet, blown glass liner, 1½" high, origin unknown

4331—Unmarked, Thailand origin, matching salt & pepper age unknown, salt is 1¼" high

4332—Unmarked, engraved etched design around bowl, engraving includes buildings not shown in picture, 1¾" high, from Indonesia

4333—Marked with oriental markings on bottom, 3" high, age unknown

4334—Marked sterling, 2¼" high, glass insert

4335—Marked sterling, salt & pepper condiment, glass insert for salt, 1" high, plus pepper & handle, age unknown

4336—Marked sterling, salt & pepper condiment, glass insert, 1¼" high

4337—Marked China, probably a candle holder, 1½" high

4338—Marked sterling, 1¼" high plus tabs

4339—Marked China, double wall, 1½" high

4340—Marked 950 silver, has dragon etched around bowl, just under 1" high

4341—Brass, double wall, probably Chinese, applied vine & leaves around bowl, 1" high

4342—Marked ZEEWC and an oriental mark signature, just over 1¼" high

4343—Unmarked double wall, probably Chinese, just under 1" high

4344—Open branch & flower design, oriental character marks on bottom, could have been candle holder, just over 1¼" high

4345—Marked with character marks on the bottom, 6 different fruits applied around bowl, 1" high, glass liner

4346—Marked with oriental characters on bottom, applied symbols around bowl, 1½" high, blown glass liner

4347—Unmarked sterling, handmade, gold wash bowl, snake handle, another snake around the top of the bowl, carved detail, origin unknown, 2¼" to top of handle

4348—Hallmarked TC, origin unknown, sterling applied dragon around bowl, just under 1¼" high, blown glass liner

4349—Design similar to Fig. 4345, 1" high, blown glass liner

4350—Unmarked, stippled design on every other panel, just over 1" high, blown glass liner

4351—Brass—double wall, probably Chinese, applied flower garlands around bowl, 1" high

4352—Oriental character marks on the bottom, could be part of a child's set, ½" high

4353—No marks, etched trees and flowers, opening for spoon at top, 1" high

4354—Character marks on the bottom, tiny hammered design on each panel, just over 1" high

4355—Unmarked fish basket, could be part of the condiment sets as seen with the coolie pulling a jinrikisha, just over 1" high

4356—Unmarked basket in heavy silver, solid inside, with applied/wicker basket design, 2" high

4357—Oriental character marks on bottom, Thailand designs, 2 piece set, together 2" high

4358—Turkish hallmarks from circa 1923, has had semi-precious stones inset around bowl, 1½" high

4359—No marks, double wall cat, embossed floral design on blanket, probably Chinese, 1½" high

ORIENTAL—STERLING

4360—Open salt & pepper shaker, Japanese Torii for the pepper and a miniature lily pot for the salt, note matching spoon, salt is 1¼" high

4361—Marked sterling 950, teapot pepper sitting on charcoal brazier, glass lined, 2" high plus handle

4362—Numerous character marks, the pail being the salt (glass lined) water can is the pepper, salt is 1¾" high plus handle

4363—Character marks on the bottom, matching salt & pepper with applied dragon design, salt is 1¼" high

4364—Character marks on the bottom of the sedan chair, roof lifts to reveal the glass lined salt, 2¼" high

4365—Matching open salt & pepper, the Foo dog being the pepper, salt is 1½" high plus tabs

4366-4368—All marked sterling, salt & pepper condiment sets with glass liners and removable peppers, 1¼" high

4369—Sterling mark, tea pot pepper over glass lined salt, note how spoon handle is inserted, 2¼" high plus handle. Door on front slides for pouring.

4370—Matching salt & pepper thongs, glass lined, ½" high, Thailand

4371—Salt & pepper set, the pegoda being the pepper, salt is 1¾" high

4372—Chinese sampan pepper, the holes are under the roof line, the junk is the salt, 2½" high

4373—Plated knife rest with a koi fish and shell salt, character marks on the bottom, 1" high at top of shell

4374—Plated, 4 half ball feet, combination salt, toothpick & knife rest, 1½" high at top of toothpick holder

4375—Marked silver 950, CPO in a triangle, diamond cut & etched bamboo pattern on front of holder, holder is 1¼" high plus handle

4376—Marked sterling, has teapot for top (not shown), note door on front for pouring salt, glass lined, 2¼" high

4377—Sterling, no marks, llama holding double salts, probably South American, age unknown, 2½" high to top of head

4378—Sterling 4-pc condiment set from Siam, age unknown, handmade, stippled design, salt is 1½" high when sitting on tray

STERLING & PLATED

4379—Sterling, hallmarked Austria, circa 1880, excellent detail on the swan and the squirrel, just over 4" high

4380—Sterling double, European origin, circa 1860, just over 4" high

4381—Sterling, European origin, cupid straddling dolphin, detail excellent, circa 1880, 4½" high

4382—Plated, hallmarked Pairpoint, gold wash bowl, circa 1880, 3¾" high

4383—Sterling, hallmarked Austria-Hungary, circa 1850, a combination of cut-back overlay art glass and sterling popular in this period, 3½" high

4384—Plated matching salt & pepper, hallmarked Derby Silver Co., circa 1890, salt is 1¼" high

4385—Sterling, hallmarked Steiff, circa 1918, chased in high relief pattern, salt is 1½" high, pepper 5" high

4386—Sterling, hallmarked Germany, circa 1760 cast, pattern of masked men, flying birds, flowers & animal feet. The beaded top edge has three butterflies, very unusual & rare

4387—Sterling, hallmarked Gorham, circa 1894, embossed floral pattern, the beading around the top has three vertical dots within each inverted bead, the whole band is applied, 1½" high

4388—Sterling, hallmarked Birmingham, circa 1843, highly chased floral pattern, ribbed scalloped top edge, 1½" high

PEWTER & MISCELLANEOUS

4389—Pewter, porcelain cobalt permanently affixed liner, no marks, age & origin unknown, but old, 2" high

4390—Pewter, unidentified American mark, just over 2" high, age unknown

4391—Pewter, marked Stieff Pewter, Williamsburg Restoration, age unknown, 2¼" high

4392—Copper with enamel scrolls and border, age & origin unknown, just over 1" high

4393—Pewter with glass cobalt liner, no marks, age & origin unknown, 2" high

4394—Pewter, no marks, age & origin unknown, 1" high

4395—Pewter, unidentified mark, age & origin unknown, under 1" high

4396—Pewter, marked Peltho, hammered design, age & origin unknown, 1¼" high, oval

4397—Plated, no marks, circa 1880. maker unknown, 1¼" high

4398—Pewter, signed "Handmade", age & origin unknown, 1" high

4399—Pewter, foreign type symbol, age & origin unknown, 1" high

4400—Pewter, signed "AE Chanal", age & origin unknown, over ½" high

4401—Pewter, no marks, age & origin unknown, ½" high

4402—Pewter, unidentified mark, 1½" high, oval

4403—Coin silver, American, circa 1870, 1¼" high

4404—Sterling, Chinese, age unknown, 1¼" high plus handles, blown liner

4405—Sterling, Chinese, age unknown, 1½" high, plus handles, blown liner

4406—Sterling, Chinese, cut out designs of sacred animals and buildings, dolphin feet, 1¼" high, china liner may not be original

4407—Sterling, oriental, etched bamboo design, blown glass liner, 1½" high plus handles

4408—Sterling, carved vine design, oriental, 1¼" high, blown glass liner

4409—Maria pottery, black on black unsigned, just over 1" high

4410—Same, signed "Romona Tapia, Santa Clara", 1¼" high

4411—Indian pottery, artist signed, 1½" high, not old

4412—Maria Indian pottery, artist signed, 1½" high

4413—Pottery, English type, brown outside, gray inside, age unknown, 1" high

4414—Sterling, hallmarked London 1774, made by Hester Bateman, hoof feet, 1¼" high

4415—Pewter, hammered design, no marks, age & origin unknown, 1½" high

4416—Pewter, hammered design, Sheffield Craftman Pewter, age unknown, identical to Fig. 4415 except height & signature, just under 1½" high

4417—Sterling 800, hallmarked Fezler, European, age & origin unknown, blown & cut liner, 1" high

4418—Sterling, hallmarked Taxco, Mexico, applied leaf design around pedestal, 1" high

MILK GLASS, MERCURY, FROSTED

4419—Silvered or Mercury Glass pedestalled salt, circa 1855 to 1880's, process of blown glass with applied silver coating on a hollowed double-walled interior was patented in 1855 by William Leighton of the New England Glass Co., this type of glass was also made in other countries, 2½" high, 2⅛" diam.

4420—Lovely French satin glass, much like the popular Lalique of the 1920's, age and maker unknown, 3⅛" high, 2⅞" diam. at top

4421—Two-face china oval salt, undecorated white, incised mark, European, circa 1910-20, 2⅞" high, 2⅝" long

4422—Pedestalled "Mercury Glass" salt, see notes Fig. 4419, 2½" diam., 2⅝" high

4423—Decorated ENGLISH HOB-NAIL salt by Westmoreland, circa 1900-1910, lengthy production life, 2¼" diam. round

4424—Westmoreland's LOTUS salt in milk glass, circa 1920's, also found with decoration and in colors, 1¾" diam.

4425—Clambroth opal-type melon-ribbed salt or patch box, Italian import, not old, 2" diam.

4426—"Octagon" salt in milk glass, probably McKee, but made by several companies, 2" long, 1½" diam.

4427—Milk glass melon-ribbed salt with cupped top rim, probably French, circa 1900, 2" diam. round

4428-4431—Pictured here are four different versions of the No. 400 THREE FACE individual salt shown in the Duncan Reprint D, circa 1885-95. Ruth Webb Lee reports the pattern was introduced as early as 1872. However, the more realistic date of production is the 1880's. When U.S. Glass took over the Duncan factory, some of the molds remained in limited production. Without question, this is one of the hardest patterns to determine the difference between the old and the reproductions. This includes the tiny salt dip. The reproductions are from new molds (not the originals) commissioned by L.G. Wright Glass Co., and just recently the salt has been trademarked with an underlined W-in-a-Circle. To the best of my knowledge, the old salt has 37 "squared" beads around the top, the new have 34 rounded beads around the top. The old have sharp prominent chins, the new have smooth rounded chins. THREE FACE has been reproduced for many years, so there appears to be more than one version of reproduction. The new have seriously affected the value of the old. Note the differences on each example pictured. The original salt has a shallow bowl, the reproductions have deeper bowls. Figures 4430 and 4431 are from the same mold, but the finish is more satiny on 4430, rough and grainy on 4431, 4428 & 29 are original.

4432—Frosted and cut, thick threaded

crystal, frosted bottom, bought in Finland, circa 1960, 1¾" diam.

4433—Frosted pressed glass salt, panelled exterior, probably foreign, circa 1915, 1⅞" diam.

4434—Milk glass melon-ribbed salt with flared rim, same origin as Fig. 4427, 2¾" diam.

4435—Decorated milk glass, American, circa 1900, maker unknown, 2¾" long rectangular

4436—DOUBLE DOT SCROLL pattern (1000TPH, Fig. 382), Gillinder & Sons, circa 1901, actually a small ash receiver, 2⅜" diam. round

4437—Milk Glass basketweave which originally had a handle (ground off); made by Co-Operative Flint as a double salt, made by Imperial as a holder for salt/pepper shakers, circa 1910-1930, also made in clear & color-stained glass, 4" long, 1½" high

4438-4441—Four more silvered or mercury glass salts, blown into different shapes with pedestal or applied feet, circa 1855-1885, probably American, 1½" to 2¾" diameters, Fig. 4438-thick, Fig. 4440-black base

4442—Milk glass pressed salt, probably English, circa 1885-95, opaline quality, 2¾" diam. round

4443—Signed Lalique figural salt or candle-holder, recent production, heavy frosted crystal, 2½" diam.

4444—Another new signed Lalique salt from the 1970's, frosted and cut, 3" long oval

4445—Plain pedestal-based Mercury glass salt, similar to Figs. 3768 & 3787, 1¾" diam.

4446—Fiery opalescent double salt, finely ribbed design, French or English, circa 1900, 4½" long across

MORE MILK GLASS

4447—Decorated double of two hens, signed S.V., old from France, 6" long, 2¾" high

4448—Toy condiment set by Westmoreland Glass (Reprint W), circa 1910-1930, with some reproductions known, ENGLISH HOBNAIL pattern, also in clear and color, nmt

4449—Old milk glass BIRD & BERRY salt, most opaque versions are Boyd or Degenhart, but this one is early McKee, circa 1900-10, 3" long, 1¾" high

4450—French double salt with tiny bird handle, circa 1900, 5½" long

4451—Squirrel on a stump, maker unknown, circa 1900, massively reproduced by Bennet (Guernsey Glass) with a hard-to-find "B" in the stump's bark, 3" long, 2¼" high

4452—Milk Glass WILLIAMSBURG #308 by U.S. Glass at Tiffin, Ohio, circa 1926, with additional production in the 1950's, called a "3 inch 2-handle Comport" in company catalogue (BTG2, 156), not a salt, but probably was used as one with the service, 2¼" high

4453—Decorated horseshoe, different from O'Hara version, probably a novelty, 3" long, more often seen with a lip designating an ash tray

4454—Top to Westmoreland sugar bowl, frequently found in salt collections, possibly deliberately designed to serve this double purpose, 3¾" long

4455—FAN-FOOTED SCROLL, maker unknown, similar to DOUBLE-DOT SCROLL by Gillinder (Fig. 4436), also known in blue milk glass, probably an ind. ash receiver to smoke set, 2¼" diam. round

4456—French opaline with enamel decoration, circa 1890, 3" long oval

4457—Another decorated French opaline, boat-shaped, 3¾" long oval, circa 1890

4458—Duplicate of Fig. 4476, later production, thicker glass less color

4459—Horse and cart in milk glass, much-copied and reproduced, age and origin unknown, 4½" long

4460—Decorated early white opaline French salt, circa 1840-50, Neal #HN-18A, very rare, claw feet, also known in clear, 3" across

4461—Appears to be a salt but was originally used to tighten and lift lids from bottles and jars, patent dates all over the piece, for 1875, 1876, 1880 and 1886, see also a second mold shape Fig. 4487, no measurements taken

4462—Clambroth colored crystal, pedestal-based with touch of gold decoration, probably European, circa 1900, 2½" diam. round

4463—BLACKBERRY pattern in scarce milk glass, made by Hobbs, Brockunier, circa 1880, see Fig. 3557 for better detail of pattern, 2¾" diam.

MORE MILK GLASS

4464—Figural fish in decorated milk glass by Challinor, Taylor & Co., circa 1890, scarce in purple slag (mosaic), 4¼" long

4465—Early lacy pressed salt by New England Glass, circa 1840, Neal #NE-1, opaline quality, 2" high, 2⅜" long, rectangular, very rare

4466—Early basketweave master salt by Atterbury, also made in ind. size (Fig. 4482), circa 1870's, 2¾" diam. round

4467—Block design appears to be one by O'Hara, circa 1890, also known in syrup pitcher, other forms not documented, 1¾" diam. round

4468—Unusual example with embossed figures of children, similar to DUTCH KIDS (1000TPH, Fig. 258), maker unknown, circa 1900-10, 1⅝" diam. round

4469—Another duplicate—see Fig. 4424 for notes

4470—Really unusual decorated salt with four feet at corners, choice, maker unknown, circa 1900, 1⅞" square

4471—Plain square salt with no pattern, maker unknown, circa 1900, 1¾" square

4472—Rectangular salt marked "J.M. & Co.", possibly an advertising giveaway, circa 1905, 1⁷⁄₁₆" long, ⅞" wide

4473—Tree Stump salt reportedly made by Portland Glass, circa 1870, also made in clear, rare in milk glass, 3" long

4474—Fostoria bird salt from the 1940's, made in clear and other colors, 3" long

4475—Charming turtle figural, maker unknown, circa 1900-10, 2¾" long, bowl is 1¾" diam.

4476—Westmoreland's ENGLISH HOBNAIL, circa 1920's with lengthy production, made in other colors, has been reproduced, 3" long, 2" high

4477—Faceted honeycomb pressed salt, maker uncertain, circa 1900, 2" diam. round

4478—Tiny pressed round hobnail salt, English, circa 1910, octagonal shape at top, 1⅞" diam.

4479—Moonstone color shell-shaped salt or ash tray, may be Jefferson or Fenton, circa 1925-35, 2¼" long

4480-81—Fostoria's GRAPE LEAF salt in decorated and plain milk glass, slight differences in mold detail, possibly different production periods, orig. made in 1940's with continued production, 2⅜" long

4482—Ind. size basketweave salt by Atterbury, circa 1875, patented June 30, 1874, 1¾" diam. round

4483—Early pressed thumbprint design, usually found in clear, scarce in milk, maker unknown, circa 1880's, 1¾" diam.

4484—Plain faceted pattern, maker unknown, circa 1890-1900, 1¾" diam.

4485—Westmoreland's LACY DAISY, circa 1910-1930, primarily found in clear, 2¼" diam.

4486—Westmoreland's ENGLISH HOBNAIL small ind. salt to condiment set (Fig. 4448), circa 1920's with continued production, 1¾" diam. round

4487—Looks like a salt but this is actually used to remove lids from bottles, patented November 30, 1880, slightly different mold from Fig. 4461, maker unknown, 1⅜" high, 2½" diam. round

4488—Pedestal-based swirl design by Baccarrat (France), circa 1900, 1¾" high, 2⅜" diam. round

4489—Figural turtle, also known in amber, probably French, appears to be recent, 4" long head to tail, still hard to find

4490—BEWARE! This is a cut-off toothpick holder in VERMONT pattern, no salt ever produced in this pattern, originally made by U.S. Glass, circa 1900, 1¾" high on this fake

WHITE CHINA

4491—Signed Vienna Austria, circa 1890, gold trim, 3 ball feet, just under 1" high

4492—Signed Bavaria, circa 1890, gold trim & monogram, 3 ball feet, 1¼" high

4493—Signed "Made in Germany," circa 1900, one foot only, pink & gold trim around top, 1¾" high

4494—No marks, Japanese, not old, 3 wide scallops & 3 tab handles, just under 1" high

4495—No marks, different mold design on opposite sides, gold fleck trim on opposite corners, circa 1890, 1" high

4496—New, probably Japan, 1" high

4497—Signed Cobert, 5 scallops around, age & origin unknown, 1" high

4498—No marks, European type, circa 1900, 1" high

4499—No marks, tab handles, gold trim & decoration, European origin, circa 1890, ¾" high

4500—No marks, ribbed melon shape, circa 1890, 1¼" high

4501—Signed Meissen, potty shape, circa 1920, 1" high

4502—Signed Royal Austria, 6 sided—no trim, 1" high, circa 1910

4503—No marks, age & origin unknown, just over 1" high

4504—No marks, Bavarian mold, gold trim, 1" high, circa 1890

4505—Signed Bavaria, plain white, 3 scroll feet, circa 1890, 1" high

4506—No marks, pearlized inside, 8 scallops around top, 4 around bottom pedestal, Austrian mold, circa 1900, just under 1" high

4507—Signed Haviland France, open tab handles, gold trim, circa 1890, just under 1" high

4508—Signed CFH over GDM (France), age unknown, 1" high

4509—Unglazed china with embossed flowers around, age & origin unknown, perhaps a studio piece, initials BMR incised on bottom, just over 1" high

4510—Signed Lenox green mark, circa 1906-1952, off-white Belleek color, just over 1" high

4511—No marks, Bavarian mold, circa 1890, 3 feet, just over 1" high

4512—Signed Belleek green mark, not old, 2 shell feet, 1¼" high

4513—Unglazed china with embossed design, age & origin unknown, 1¼" high

4514—Marked Lenox, not old, gold mark, 2¼" high

4515—No marks, age & origin unknown, old, just over 2" high

4516—No marks, Belleek type fish, age & origin unknown, 1" high

4517—Marked Lenox, green wreath mark, 1¼" high, circa 1906-1952

4518—No marks, delicate shell china pig, age & origin unknown, but old, 1¼" high

4519—No marks, unusual round shape with tab handles, age & origin unknown, 1" high

4520—Marked Bavaria, 3 small ball feet, circa 1890, just under 1" high

4521—Marked Lenox, green wreath mark, circa 1906-1952, just over 1½" high

4522—Marked France, circa 1920, ¼" high

4523—No marks, salt glaze, rabbits holding hands & dancing around bowl, age & origin unknown, just over 1½" high

MISCELLANEOUS CHINA, POTTERY & SILVER

4524—Plated open salt & pepper with matching sterling spoon, marked R. Wallace & Sons, circa 1898, embossed scroll pattern around bowl with scalloped top edge, salt is 1" high

4525—China, pepper sitting on top of salt with matching spoon or oar, marked Made in Japan, hand painted in blues, green & yellow, circa 1930's, 4" high

4526—Heavy porcelain, top rim plated over copper, matching salt & pepper in royal blue on the salt and black added on the pepper, circa 1940, salt is 1½" high

4527—China matching salt & pepper, marked with the Lenox green wreath mark, circa 1906-1952, salt is under 2" high

4528—China, artist signed, delicate pink roses painted on a green background, top edge trimmed in gold, circa 1890, origin unknown, 1½" high

4529—Signed Wedgewood, blue & white, dated 1956, just over 2" high

4530—China, matching salt & pepper clown in greens with black trim, marked Japan, circa 1930's, salt is 1" high

4531—China, gaudy blues & yellow with black trim on white background, European origin, circa 1930, 1½" high

4532—China, gaudy with purple, teal, orange & blue colors on white background, European origin, circa 1930, 1" high

4533—China, 6 pointed star, delicate green garlands & pink roses on white background, incised 6-point star pattern on bottom, origin unknown, circa 1890, just under 1" high

4534—China, unusual Nippon shape, brown tones with pink flowers, TN mark, circa 1920, just over ½" high

4535—China, Austrian mold, delicate orange color with gold beading, circa 1890, just over 1" high

4536—China, marked Bavarian, oval bowl on oval pedestal, pink roses & garlands around top blue edge, white background, circa 1890, just over 1" high

4537—China, signed Belleek, gold scrolls & enamel beading, circa 1890, just over ½" high

4538—China, unsigned, appears to be Nippon, delicate lavender & purple flowers on green background with a pink band thru the center, circa 1900, 1" high plus tabs

4539—China, unusual Dresder with lamb mark, matching spoon, pale yellow with gold trim, 4 legs, circa 1887, just over 1" high

4540—China, signed Silesia (Germany), circa 1920, 1" high

4541—Plated shell on dolphin feet with puppy holding spoon, no trademarks, origin unknown, circa 1900, 2¾" to top of head

4542—China, signed Wedgewood D&P, circa 1880, garlands of Christmas holly, red beading around the oval bowl, diamond shaped pedestal, distorted shape on bowl, 1¾" high

4543—Hand carved, Asian people under palm trees, sterling lining, just under 2" high, age & origin unknown, but old

4544—China, signed RS Prussia, brown background with white to pink roses & green leafs, outside colors blended, short pedestal, circa 1880, 1¼" high

4545—Pottery double, incised pattern and painted flowers, signed Fournisseur Brevet de SAS LE Prince—de Monoco, label reads the same, 2" high to top of toothpick

4546—China, European origin, circa 1920, tiny pink roses with a green border around the top & gold handle, 1½" high plus handle

MISCELLANEOUS POTTERY & CHINA

4547—Pottery, English seaweed mocha ware, circa 1800, in brown and beige tones, just over 2" high

4548—Pottery, unglazed slag carmel coloring with applied silver coloring known as Lester Bromley ware, American, circa 1850, 3½" high

4549—Pottery, marked "Made in Italy," cobalt blue band around the top, yellow stripes, green & red trim on creme colored background, circa 1940, 3¼" high

4550—English Staffordshire creamware, transfer print, gray on white background, circa 1850, 2¼" high

4551—Pottery, royal blue with black top edge, marked "Made in England," circa 1940, 1¼" high

4552—China, signed Lenox green wreath mark, circa 1906-1952, 1" high

4553—China, signed Belleek, third black mark, circa 1895, 1¼" high, also available with the green mark (new) 1¼" high

4554—China, signed Belleek, green mark (new) 1¼" high

4555—China, signed Belleek, green mark (new), diamond shape, 1" high

4556—China, signed Belleek, third black mark, circa 1893, star shape,

also available in new. The ribbing on the old is much more distinct & the new is pale yellow on the inside, 1" high

4557—China, marked Lenox, green wreath mark, 1¼" high, circa 1906-1952 ,

4558—China, signed Belleek, green mark (new), teardrop shape, 1" high

4559—China, signed RC Nippon, delicate pink & blue flowers with green leaves, gold beading and trim, circa 1900, ¾" high

4560—China, signed "Record, Germany," circa 1900, just over 1" high

4561—China, artist signed, pale green outside & orange inside, Austrian mold, circa 1890, just under 1" high

4562—China, marked Germany, circa 1890, unusual pedestal extending to 3 feet, 1" high, gold trim on white background

4563—Pottery, signed Moorcroft, circa 1913, deep cobalt coloring with a red flower on the inside, 1¼" high

4564—Pottery, Weller type, incised pattern of trees in tan & brown tones, the rest in various shades of blue, artist signed, 1½" high

4565—Pottery, cobalt blue, hollow underneath, not old, origin unknown, 1¼" high

4566—Pottery, aqua tones with black colors running through, age & origin unknown, 1½" high

4567—Pottery, signed Quimper (France), tin enamel glaze ware, circa 1920, 1¼" high, pink, blue & green on an off-white background

4568—Pottery, signed Quimper (France), tin enamel glaze ware, circa 1920, blue, green & orange on an off-white background, 1½" high

4569—Jasper with sterling rim, no marks, circa 1850, just over 1" high

4570—Pottery, light green with green crackle glass bottom inside, age & origin unknown, 1" high

4571—Pottery tree trunk with grass & blue flowers, marked "Keetman Giftware, England," circa 1940, 1" high

4572—Pottery, oriental, top & bottom showing masked devil face, the two "legs" are horns, black & gold inside and outside rim, facial colors

MISCELLANEOUS CHINA

4573—Signed Belleek, 3 twig feet, circa 1920, 1¾" high

4574—Brass holder with cobalt blue decoration on white background, European origin, circa 1880, 4¼" high

4575—Staffordshire, blue on white transfer decoration, could also be part of a child's set, the bowl is lopsided from the base, just under 2" high, circa 1820

4576—Minature china salt box with hole for hanging, white background, pink roses, just over 3" high, circa 1930

4577—Staffordshire, blue decoration on tan background, circa 1840, 2¼" high

4578—China, marked RS Prussia, hand painted, pink & green flowers on light green background, white outside, gold trim, circa 1900, 1" high

4579—China, marked "Princess Louise, Austria," circa 1900, pink flowers on white background, gold trim, 1" high

4580—Copper Luster, pink & green flowers on tan background, circa 1880, just over 2" high

4581—China, marked Royal Copenhagen, circa 1923, oval, blue decor on white background, 1½" high

4582—China, marked Austria, "Littleport Church", circa 1883, ¾" high

4583—Pottery, signed Babbacombe Pottery, Torquay, England, circa 1950, 1¾" high, incised pattern in brown & green on tan background

4584—Pottery, signed Enock-Woods, Wood & Sons, England, circa 1917, pink decor on white background, 1" high

4586—Heavy porcelain, Chinese Canton, medium blue decor on white background, circa 1860, 1¼" high

4587-4588—Studio type, signed Pabrowski, New Hampton, MT, off-white outside, light green inside to a glossy dark green center, Horn-of-plenty with flowers on either side, master with 6 individuals, master is 1¾" high, individuals ½" high

4589-4590—China, Austrian molds, pink with gold decoration

MISTAKEN IDENTITIES

4591—Plated with cobalt liner, portion of tea strainer

4592—Flint glass, with hole in side for pouring

4593—Green & clear glass candle holder from Japan

4594—Cambridge green glass cigarette holder

4595—Shot glass (?)

4596—Tiddly wink jar

4597—Frosted jar—should have lid

4598-99—Tiddly wink jars

4600—Jar of some type

4601-4603—Individual candle holders

4604—Dentist jar for mixing fillings

4605—Glass

4606—Jar

4607—Tiddly wink jar

4608—Marked Wedgewood, holder for cigarette lighter

4609—Amber ashtray with lip removed, also known in green

4610—Chair castor

4611—Cut off salt or perfume

4612—Milk glass cucumber, could be a salt

4613—Glass pin tray

4614-4617—Cut off & polished to look like salts, watch for dull edges

MISCELLANEOUS SALTS

4619—Outstanding art glass, blue opaline with applied canary rigaree, engraved spray of ivy along upper rim, tiny blue enamel dots at edge, English, circa 1890, about 2¼" diam.

4620—Blue-green opaque bristol with delicate enamel decoration, English, circa 1885, maker unknown, exceptional quality, slightly over 2" diam. round

4621—Beautiful and rare blue opalescent pressed salt by Davidson (Reprint AA), plain oval salt, about 2½" long, circa 1880's

4622—Rare cased ribbon swirl with applied crystal rigaree, English art glass, circa 1890-1900, unique, approx. 2¾" diam. round

4623—Two different blown crystal ind. salts with applied reeded "shell" rigaree, tiny egg-shell blue glass beads, this one is pedestalled, about 2" high

4624—Same technique of applied decoration as Fig. 4623, this one is "bubbled" heavy thick crystal, round shape, approx. 2½" diam.

4625—No silver markings were noted when this unusual salt with deep purple slag insert was seen in a private collection, definitely English, circa 1890, about 3" handle to handle

4626—Ornate handled salt or mustard pot, plated frame, cobalt insert, 3" long not incl. handle, circa 1895

4627—Sowerby's No. 1560 pedestal salt in purple slag, circa 1880's, see Reprint II, about 3" diam. round, just under 3" high

4628—Sowerby's No. 1216 master salt in rare green slag, see also Reprint II, round with tapered columns, 3" diam.

4629—Sowerby's No. 1350½ ind. salt in ivory-colored custard, circa 1880's, also in larger table size, about 2¼" diam., design of peacocks in a garden, see Reprint GG

4630—Sowerby's No. 1329 salt with garlands embossed around side, tripod feet, in opaque ivory color, see Reprint II, about 2¼" diam. round

4631—Outstanding cased glass crimped salt with an outside coating of deep cranberry, inner layer of custard color, combining together to give the glass an orange coloration, may be Webb or Richardson, circa 1890, very rare, about 2" diam. round

4632—Blown swirl salt with lightly crimped top, applied rigaree in crystal, iridescent marigold color at top, clear at base, polished pontil, circa 1900, about 2½" long, also made in many other shapes

4633—Pedestal-based purple slag master double with divider in center of bowl, probably Sowerby, circa 1890, about 3" diam. round

4634—Sowerby's smallest DAISY BLOCK rowboat, made in four other sizes, registered 1886 with lengthy production, deep purple slag

MISCELLANEOUS LATE ADDITIONS

4635—Unusual decorated milk glass ind. salt, stained pink with ornate medallions in powder blue, maker unknown, circa 1900, about 2¼" diam. round

4636—Very rare signed Quezal salt in feathered design, colors of greens, golds and a touch of white along top, golden interior, round shape, just over 2" diam.

4637—Unsigned but definitely Nakara by C.F. Monroe, makers of Wavecrest ware, the same mold is found mounted on a metal framework as a toothpick or match holder, I believe when they are seen without frames they were meant to be salt dips, beautiful enamel decoration, about 2" diam. round

4638—Rare flow-blue china star-shaped salt, salts in flow-blue are very hard to find and highly sought after, markings not noted, about 2" diam.

4639—French blue opaline salt with plated frame, very ornate Victoriana, circa 1890, oval shape, 2½" long

4640—Melon-ribbed clambroth covered mustard, frequently found without lid as salt dip, metal parts marked Made in Italy, early 1900's, about 1¾" diam.

4641—Pressed glass salt marked R. LALIQUE in block letters, rows of beading, small ind. size, round, about 1½" diam., circa 1920

4642—Gorham Silver with ivory-colored glass blown into frame, see notes Figures 2034 & 2035, about 2" diam. round

4643—White opalescent example matches green one, see notes Fig. #2090, 2" high

4644—MARDIS GRAS example here should have been shown in color, as this is a rare amber or yellow-stained example of the pattern, tiny touches of color along top, Duncan & Miller's No. 42 pattern, circa 1900-15, also made oval shape, about 1¾" diam.

4645—Rare pressed salt in olive-green color, almost amber, with lightly impressed cornsilk design, marked E. Galle, ind. size, French, after 1900, about 1¾" high, 1¾" long, rectangular

4646—Popularly known as the "Honeycomb Salt" to collectors of chocolate glass, this is actually the THOUSAND EYE BAND pattern (Metz 2, 130), also made in large table size (Fig. 2071), ind. size, 1⅞" diam. round, VERY rare

4647—Delicate light metal with thick glazed egg-shell color coating, giving it the appearance of fine bisque, quite unusual and rare, 3" high

4648—Interesting bronze tree trunks on marble bases with natural shells as holders, alligators along base, signed France, may be master salts, more likely are decorative soapball holders for bathroom, not very old, 6½" high

4649—Blown Venetian glass in opalescent crystal, gold flecks in crystal stem, 6" high, 2½" long from tip to tip, oval bowl at top, circa 1900

4650—Complete egg cup set with table size double salt in center, maker uncertain, circa 1910-20, also known in deep blue milk, embossed swirl design with stippled leaf, goofus gold trim, salt is 2½" high, 2¾" diam.

4651—Set of "intaglio" salts in brass-plated holder, Czechoslovakia signed on frame, 5½" high, 5½" wide, butterfly imprint is sometimes referred to incorrectly as a Webb signature on these salts or ash trays, all inserts are clear crystal, circa 1920

4652—Another brass-plated holder signed Czechoslovakia with intaglio crystal inserts, 5½" wide, frame encrusted with jewels, may be a double salt as inserts are permanently affixed, confirming the theory that these were designed to be used as either salts or ind. ash trays, circa 1920-30

MISCELLANEOUS LATE ADDITIONS

4653—See notes Figure 3528, shown here with the rare cover on a Lily-of-the-Valley mustard, sometimes called a covered salt, no measurements taken

4654—RIBBED IVY covered mustard or salt (Lee lists this as a salt), Boston & Sandwich Glass, circa 1850's, flint glass, very rare, 4½" high to top of finial

4655—Beautiful blown green stemmed salt with acid finish in unusual effect, definitely European, circa 1910-20, crimped top rim, light and delicate, about 2½" high, 2¼" diam.

4656—Ruth Webb Lee attributes this rare FROSTED LEAF salt to Portland Glass, circa 1863-73, no other maker known, flint glass, 3" high, 2½" diam. at top

4657-4660—Four different early pressed glass salts which are not shown in the Neal book on lacy salts (except Fig. 4659, Neal BS family, all were in amber or deep emerald, pictured at a Minneapolis antique show, American, circa 1840-50, no measurements taken

4661—European cut glass with top rim cupped down, early, circa 1880, 4" high, 4" diam. at top

4662—Clear lacy pressed salt by Boston & Sandwich, circa 1840-50, Neal #EE-3B, pg. 62, 2" high, 3" long rectangular

4663-Very rare powder blue opaque salt with chariot scene, Neal #CT-1A, circa 1840's, made by Boston & Sandwich Glass Co., photographed at antique show, no measurements taken

4664—Rare LOOP & DART WITH DIAMOND ORNAMENTS by Richards & Hartley, circa 1870 (patented in 1869), a similar pattern with round ornaments was made by Portland Glass, 2½" high, 2½" diam. round

4665-4667—See notes page 226

4668—Emerald green figural wheelbarrow, similar to one by Greentown, but without basketweave, maker unknown, circa 1905-10, reproduced, 3½" long, bowl is 2" long oval

4669-4670—Old Greentown wheelbarrow in clear next to a reproduction by St. Clair in cobalt blue, note the differences, each 3¼" long, old bowl is 2¼" long, new 2⅛" long

4671—Amber squirrel & stump, definitely old, the bottom is larger and the glass much heavier than Figs. #929-930, age & origin unknown

4672-4673—Reproduction MOON & STAR salt in blue next to an old example in clear, almost impossible to tell molds apart, remember—the pattern was never made in color originally, although a few pieces are known in ruby-stain, U.S. Glass (Adams), circa 1890's

4674—SPRIG IN SNOW in rare blue color, see notes Fig. 2966

4675—Very rare EMPRESS pattern salt in emerald green with gold, almost never found gold decorated, made by Riverside, see notes Fig. #2938

4676—See Notes Fig. #993 for this rare figural turtle

4677—Unusual crystal figural duck, maker unknown, probably foreign, circa 1920's, 2¾" long

4678—Amber shoe, maker unknown, circa 1900-10, 3½" long, opening 2¼" long oval

4679—Milk glass cart or wheelbarrow by Challinor, Taylor (U.S. Glass) circa 1890, shown in catalogue reprints, scarce, 2" high, 4½" long including metal wheel

4680—Unusual foreign glass condiment set with a fish scale pattern, 10½" long, salt dips extend ⅞" above the plated holder, no markings

4681—Engraved Mercury glass salt with gold wash bowl, circa 1855-85, probably American, 2¼" high x 2½" round

4682—Same process used on Mercury Glass, except this is gold coated, just over 1" high, 1¾" diam.

4683—Heavy glass in Silvered treatment, signed "Thomson's London, Patent", circa 1850's, 2¾" high x 3" diam.

4684—Recently produced wooden salt with wooden spoon in crate-box, little burlap bag of salt included, box measures 5¼" long, 3½" wide

4685—Gift set from Westmoreland Sterling, glass made by Cambridge, "George & Martha" pattern on the spoon, made in 1940's, box measures 2½" by 3½" long

4686—Another gift set from Westmoreland Sterling, this one with matching pepper shaker (Cambridge), sterling spoon in same pattern, box is 2" by 3¼", circa 1940

4687—Plated ornate oval lily holder with light blue opaque molded liner, may be English, 2¼" high, 3¼" long, circa 1880

4688—Marked ALPACCA (German silver) duck with molded liner and saucer, 2" high to top of head, 3" long plus saucer, circa 1910

4689—Plated with molded cobalt liner, unusual half-ball feet, round on the outside and flat on the inside, very heavy metal, purchased in Australia, 1½" high x 2" round at the top

4690—Marked Germany 800, oval basket with molded glass liner, stationary handle, delicate ribbing and garlands of flowers around, oval for monogramming, gold washed, 1½" high plus handle, 2¾" long, circa 1895

4691—Sterling, European origin, has permanently affixed black glass liner, 1¾" diam. at top, circa 1920

4692—Silver filigree basket with clear blown glass liner, European origin, 3" high including handle, age unknown

4693—Marked Germany 800, cut glass liner, 1¼" high plus handle, circa 1888-1914

4694—Marked sterling 915, Wm. Gale & Son, circa 1850-1860, 2" high and 3¼" diam. all over gold wash

4695—Unmarked sterling with gold wash inside, pressed glass liner, 1½" high, 2¼" long at top, oval, European origin, circa 1880

4696—Pressed and polished glass with silver deposit, triangular shape with slightly rounded sides measuring 2" each side, ¾" high, circa 1920

4697—Unmarked sterling with gold wash inside, unusual foot design, 1" high, x 2¼" diam., round

4698—Sterling, marked Tiffany & Co., circa 1870-75, embossed dots around the lower half of the bowl, 1¼" high x 2" diam., round

4699—Marked Germany 800 with gold wash inside, blown glass liner, after 1891, 1¼" high and 2" long, oval

4700—Hallmarked France, circa 1838-1845, molded & cut liner, 1¼" high, 2¼" long, oval

4701—Hallmarked Germany 800, molded glass liner, circa 1891, 1¼" high, 2¼" long, oval

4702—Hallmarked Germany 800, elegant flower & leaf design, molded and frosted glass liner with clear scalloped top rim, circa 1890, 1½" high x 2¼" long, oval

4703—Marked 935 sterling, either French or Canadian, circa 1880, 1½" high, 2½" long, oval

4704—Marked sterling 999 fine, makers mark blurred, American, photo is almost exact size of this tiny salt, under 1" high and 1½" diam., circa 1890

4705—Hallmarked France, circa 1838-1845, molded glass liner, 1½" high and just under 2" long, oval

4706—Hallmarked France, circa 1841-1865, molded liner with protruding serrated top edge, 2" high, 2¾" long, oval

4707—Triangular shape cobalt with silver deposit, ¾" high, 2" long each side, circa 1920

4708—Art Deco salt with light green insert on plated frame, English, 2" high, 1½" wide and 2¼" long

4709—Hallmarked Germany Nuremburg, circa 1850-1860, mythological characters in the three corners with a rabbit, doe & lion, one on each scallop, just under 1" high, 2" diam. on bowl plus corners and scallops

4710—Plated NS ornate holder with cranberry insert, 8 feet and 8 sided, English, 2" high and 2¼" diam., circa 1880

4711-4712—Sterling, hallmarked Russia, circa 1884, 1" high and 1½" diam., at the top

4713—Plated, from England, probably had liner, shield design for monogram, 1¼" high & 2" diam., at the top, circa 1890

4714—Plated, hallmarked Industria Argentina, cobalt liner, age unknown, 1¼" high x 2¼" diam

4715—Sterling, hallmarked Austria-Hungary, circa 1850, blown ruby glass top with gold trim, 3" high & 3½" diam

4716—Sterling holder with blown glass liner, individual size, no other information available

4717—Marked Gorham coin silver, circa 1848-1865, spoon has matching flowers and scrolls, 1¼" high & 2½" diam

4718—Hallmarked, possibly Polish, circa 1845, hand made, note unusual design at the waist, just over 2" high and 3½" long, oval

4719—English art deco with cobalt liner, heavy plated frame, 1¾" high, 1¾" diam. at the top, glass has embossed signature of a rooster head within a wreath and a double triangle below

4720—Plated, marked Pairpoint, circa 1890, engraved floral design, 1" high, 1½" diam. at the top

4721—Plated, ribbed ball feet, American, circa 1890, 1" high, 1¾" diam

4722—Marked Wilcox Silver Plate, circa 1869, 1¼" high, 2½" diam.

4723—Sterling, hallmarked Geo. Jensen Denmark, circa 1950, blown glass liner, ½" high, 1½" diam. plus handle

4724—Another view of no. 4255 showing the side detail on this exceptional salt

4725—Marked sterling, Gorham, circa 1920, 1" high, 2½" long, oval

4726—European continental sterling (800), gold wash inside, blown and cut glass liner, 1" high, 1½" diam. at the top

4727—Sterling, hallmarked Austria Hungary, circa 1850, 1¼" high, 1¾" diam. at the top

4728—Marked sterling, Gorham, circa 1894, 1" high, 3" diam. including rim

4729—Sterling, hallmarked Chester England, circa 1915, cobalt molded liner, 1½" high, 1¾" diam.

4730—Hallmarked Denmark, circa 1835, gold over silver, 1¾" high, 2¾" long, oval

4731—Plated, marked Meridan, circa 1880, 4 bands of stippling around this unusual salt, 2" high, 2¼" diam. at the top

4732—Sterling, hallmarked Austria-Hungary, circa 1850, 2¼" high, 3¼" long, oval

4733—Marked sterling, Mauser, N.Y., circa 1887, 1¾" high, 3½" long, 3" wide, almost round

4734—Sterling, hallmarked London with registry mark, circa 1892, cobalt liner and matching spoon, all over gold wash, 2½" high, 1¾" square plus handles

MISCELLANEOUS LATE ADDITIONS

4735-4737—3 Russian salt chairs, all very rare and unusual, #4735 in all over gold wash in 3 different colors of gold and inscribed with a very popular Russian phrase "Without bread and salt the dinner is only half a feast," #4735 measure 3" high, the salt box measures 1¾" square, shown with the lid up, also has a back. Figures 4736 & 4747 shown with the lids down, same measurements and all date from the 1880's

4738-4740—All novelty condiment sets of Chinese jinrickshaws. The 3-piece sets measure 6" long, the 4-piece set 9" long. Some of these will be sterling and marked, others a lesser type metal resembling silver. Figure 4739 is sterling and marked Hong Kong

4741—Marked sterling, Japanese hut on stilts in a farm yard scene. The roof opens up to reveal a glass lined salt, note the spoon laying to the left by the stilts, very unusual

4742—Marked sterling, unique oriental chest with an open salt drawer and pepper shaker in the other drawer, very unusual, measures just over 2" wide

4743—Very unusual oriental hut with the pepper shaker on the side, the roof holds a glass lined salt, measures 3½" long

4744—Marked sterling, salt & pepper set, see Figs. 4330-4378

4745-4746—Marked sterling, see Figs. 4330-4378

4747—Marked sterling, see Figs. 4366-4368

4748—Sterling, European origin, 5" long, bowl is 1½" high and oval

4749—Ivory carved turtle with matching spoon, age & origin unknown, could be Alaskan, 1" high, 2¼" long, 2½" wide

4750—Sterling, European origin, circa 1850, bowl is sitting on the rim held by three warriors and is removable, 2" high, 2" diam. at the top

MISCELLANEOUS LATE ADDITIONS

4751—European sterling (illustrated on the cover) cranberry salts, Austria-Hungary, circa 1850, 7" high, 7" wide, the bottom is velvet covered

4752—European sterling, circa 1850, 4½" high, 5" wide

4753—Duplication of Fig. 751, sterling, Vienna, Austria, circa 1880, round cobalt glass salts with pepper shaker on the top, 6½" high, and 8½" wide

4754—Sterling with blue bristol salt bowls, French origin, circa 1850. Note the next photo showing the messenger with a letter behind his back, most unusual, 7" high, 6" wide

4755—Plated art nouveau with blown & cut glass liners, European origin, 6" high and 6½" wide, exceptional

4756—Plated WMF, Germany, circa 1897, cut glass liners, 3½" high, 5" long, exceptional

4757—Sterling holder with blown glass salts decorated in a gold floral design, European origin, circa 1880, 6" high

4758—Hallmarked Germany 830S, molded & polished cobalt liners, leaf & berry design, 1" high/plus handle, 5" wide, circa 1891

4759-4760—China matching doubles, incised numbers on the bottom indicating Germany, both have a white background with touches of burgundy, blue & yellow, gold trim, each 2¾" high, 5" long. Set also has matching toothpick holder

4761—China, signed Conte & Boehme (English), circa 1880-1891, the canoe is 1¼" high, the light house is a removable pepper shaker and is 4" high

4762—German Jasperware condiment set in EPNS holder and trim, holder is 6" high, salt is 1¼" high, 2¼" long, oval, circa 1880

4763—Plated salt and pepper on leaf with twigs, marked Meridan Company circa 1880, insert in salt is metal, to top of salt 3", to top of twig 4½"

4764—Very delicate medium blue china with dark blue pineapple design embossing, incised numbers indicate Germany, 2" high, 3½" long

4765—Milk glass double, small for this type, measures 2½" high to the head of the chicken, 4½" long, European origin, circa 1890

BOXED PRESENTATION SETS

4766—Pressed glass with silver deposit, spoons are marked Alvin Co., circa 1920, see Fig. 3871 for detail of salt. The box is 7½" square in green on green brocade and velvet lined. Inside in gold marked Leo M. Schiller, San Diego, Cal.

4767—Complete set of 12 pressed glass, See Fig. 2512 for detail of salt. Box is orange velvet outside and lined with orange satin, with a purple braid trim in box, measures 7" x 10"

4768—Cut glass, two ind. and two masters, Sterling rim hallmarked London 1909, matching spoons, salts measure 1" x just under 1½" and 1¼" x just under 2". Box is dark red with purple satin and velvet interior and measures 5" square

4769—Threaded & cut with diamond pattern, Hallmarked Birmingham, England, 1890, on sterling rim, salt is 2¼" diam. at widest. Box is navy blue leather covered, navy satin and velvet inside, measures 3½" x 7¼"

4770—Sterling with enamel inside, Hallmarked Denmark circa 1940, matching spoons, diam. at top is 2". Box is navy leather covered and white satin inside, measures 4" x 5¾"

4771—Pressed glass with clear liner, see Fig. 651 for detail, spoons are marked sterling, taffeta covered box, 5" x 9", inside marked Sterling Silver 925-1000 fine, circa 1900-1905

4772—Sterling lattice holders with Lenox china inserts, circa 1900, salts are 1⅝" diam., the spoons are not original with set. Box is green cloth covered and lined with green satin and velvet, measures 5½" x 8¾"

BOXED PRESENTATION SETS

4773—Gold plated over metal, marked Ellis-Barker Silver Co., Birmingham, England, salts are 5" high, note figurals on pedestals of salts and tops of peppers. The set could date anywhere from 1925-1940.

4774—Silver plated unmarked, English Victorian circa 1880, salts are 1" by just over 3" including handles, matching spoons. Box is black outside and dark red satin and velvet inside, measures 5½" by 8"

4775—Plated, outlined panels embossed florals and circles in alternating series, matching spoons marked W.H. & S, American, circa 1880, salts are 2¼" diam. Box measures 8" diam., maroon leather covered with maroon satin and velvet lining

4776—Very ornate sterling with matching spoons, Hallmarked Mappin & Webb, Sheffield 1896, salts are just over 2¼" square with scalloped corners. Box is maroon leather covered, matching satin and velvet inside, 6¼" square

4777—Plated Tureen shape with chippendale handles on an oval pedestal, matching spoons, no marks, probably English, circa 1890, salts are 2½" high at top of handle and 4½" long handle to handle. Box is leather covered in brown, with deep blue velvet and satin inside, oval, 7" wide and 10½" long, 3" high

4778—Shiny black on the inside and dull black on the outside, over metal, salts are 2¼" diam. at top. Box is marked Andante Salt Cellars, Exemplar Paul Revere 1763, box is cardboard and measures 5" square, circa 1930

4779—Plated oval shape shells, no marks, probably English, circa 1880, 1" high x just under 3" long. Brown covered box with violet satin and velvet inside, measures 5½" by 8¾"

BOXED PRESENTATION SETS

4780—Plated flower on a lily leaf, set is badly damaged although probably never used. Marked Meridan B. Company, circa 1890, salts are 1¼" high. Box is leather lined with brown, purple satin in top of box and brown velvet under salts—measures 5¼" x 7¼". Another set of identical salts (set of 12) marked with a Smith-New Haven Co. Gold lettering on the box "Alice E. Stilson", box measures 7½" x 9½"

4781—Very elegant French sterling salts, hallmark 1838-1845, salts are oval with blown and cut clear glass liners, 1½" high, matching spoons. Salts are set in suede covered contoured boxes. The box is green leather outside with white satin and white suede inside, box is 10½" by 11" and 3" high

4782—Signed LCT, Tiffany salts in white leather covered box, salts are 1½" high, see Fig. 1 for detail, box is 6" square and signed Tiffany Studios, New York

4783—Carved jade in green leather covered box with white satin lining, salts are 2½" diam. across top, age uncertain, box signed Styrian Jade Ltd.

4784—Marked Sterling, 2" round at the top, has Kirk or Tiffany type flowers around top edge, dated as a gift on the bottom 1903, box is white leather covered and white fabric inside, measures 4" x 7½"

4785—Most interesting set of German sterling with each salt different. All buildings in Munchen. Box & salts signed Theodor Heiden, Munchen. Box is dark red and measures 3¾" by 6¾", dark red velvet and satin lining.

4786—Same salts as Fig. 4585, shown in different positions to reflect the detail, each measures 1½" high, 1½" diam. at top

BOXED PRESENTATION SETS

4787—Silver plated by maker R. G. Webster & Son, circa 1886-1928, 4 scroll type feet, 1¾" high, 2" diam. plus handles. This is shown in the 1908 Sears Catalog, page 340, price $1.90, postage $.12 with spoons, "A Handsome Wedding Gift", box is blue velvet and blue satin lined, measures 3" by 7"

4788—Oval sterling salts with EPNS spoons, hallmarked Birmingham, circa 1900, black leather covered box, velvet & satin lined, salts are ½" high, 2¼" long, box 3" by 6½"

4789—Sterling gold wash shells with three ball feet, matching spoons, hallmarked Birmingham, circa 1927, 2" diam., box is black leather covered, blue velvet and white satin inside, measures 3" by 6½"

4790—Plated condiment set, marked "Made in England", EPNS, Regis Plate, spoons are missing, salt & mustard have cobalt liners, salt is 1" high and just over 2" long, rectangular. Box is black leather covered, white satin and black velvet inside, 4" by 8½"

4791—Sterling shells, three ball feet, hallmarked Birmingham, circa 1896, 1¾" diam. Box is black leather covered with red satin and velvet lining, measures 2½" by 6"

4792—Plated marked Gorham, circa 1880, 2½" diam. at top, tiny decorative border around the bottom, box is green leather covered, with light green satin inside, measures 3¼" x 6". Box designed for napkin rings not original.

BOXED PRESENTATION SETS

4793—Sterling oval with dark green molded & polished liners, marked C.F. Rudolph, Wilmington, Delaware on liner of box, 1¼" by 3" long, matching spoons, box is lined with white and measures 4½" by 8½"

4794—Sterling, Hallmarked Birmingham 1884, 1½" diam., cobalt liners, three curved hoof feet, apostle spoons hallmarked and date from 1840. Black leather covered box with deep red satin & velvet lining, measures 3½" by 7¼"

4795—Sterling, 6 sided, hallmarked Birmingham, circa 1901, ½" by 2". Box is black outside with white satin and blue velvet inside, measures 2½" by 6"

4796—Sterling, embossed floral pattern, three ball feet, hallmarked Birmingham, 1887, not original spoons (marked Germany), widest diam. 2¼", box is oval, black leather covered and deep red inside in satin and velvet, 3½" wide, 7½" long

4797—Heavy china marked Limoges, brass rim, circa 1920, floral paintings in pink and green with black outlining, cardboard box, fabric lined, measures 3½" by 6½"

4798—Sterling, 3¼" round at top, ¾" high, Hallmarked London, circa 1937, black box, gray & light blue velvet & satin inside, box measures 5" to point and 8" long

4800—COINS, (Illustrated on the back cover). This magnificent set of hand made sterling salts was made by Geo. C. Shreve & Co., San Francisco and all the coins date from 1764 to 1891. No two coins match and are from many different countries. The coins on the salts, saucers and sides of the pepper shakers are all the size of our silver dollars. The pedestals on the peppers are quarter size and the spoon ladles—dime size.

The set was custom made and probably one of a kind. It appears to never have been used. The box is deep red velvet with a blue gray satin lining and measures 25" by 13" by 3" high.

The spoon coins are herein listed:

10 cents, Hong Kong	1885
10 cents, Hong Kong	1886
50 centavos, Italy	1867
10 cents, Italy	1871
10 cents, Straits Settlement Malaysia	1885
6 pence, Great Britain	1883
6 pence, Great Britain	1874
50 cents, France	1866
50 cents, France	1867
Peru, (2 coins)	1866
British India	1862
Sugar tongs, 24 Einer, Saxony Germany	1764
Handle ⅓ thaier, Saxony Germany	1792

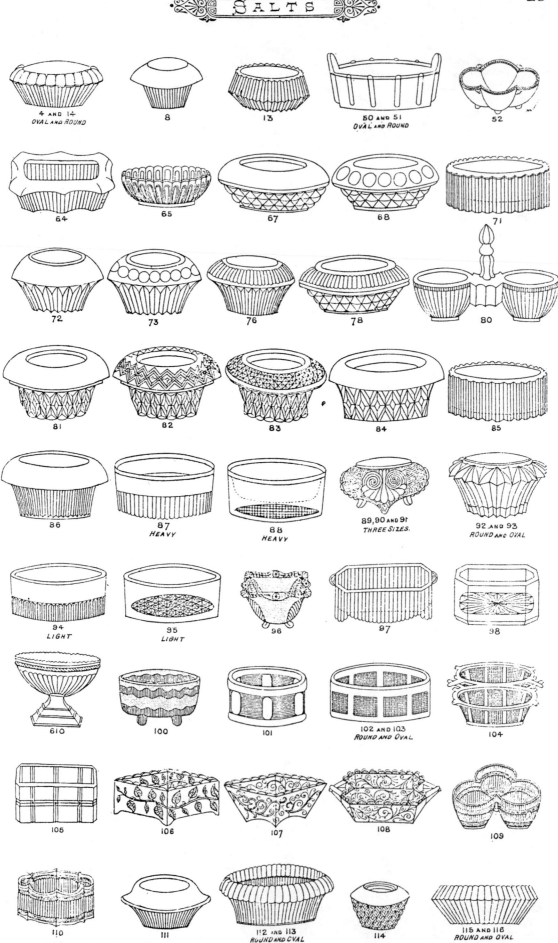

(Reprint AA) Assortment of salts from George Davidson & Co., Teams Glass Works, Gateshead-On-Tyne, England, circa 1870 (Courtesy National Arts Library, Victoria & Albert Museum, London)

(REPRINT BB) Several pages of salts from 1888 Sowerby catalogue, both pressed and cut illustrated (Courtesy Inch & Blicque)

1921
Moulded Salt.
Round.

1921½
Moulded Salt.
Round.

1922
Round.

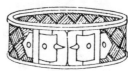

1922½
Oval.

1943
Round.

1943½
Moulded, Oval.

1945¾
Moulded Round.

1949

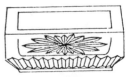

1968
Moulded, Oblong

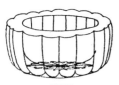

1971
Moulded, Round.

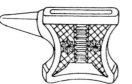

1976
Moulded, Anvil Salt.
2 Sizes.

2012
Round.

2040
Round.

2077
Round.

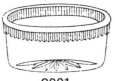

8001
Oval.

8002
Round.

8003
Oval.

8004
Round.

CUT SALTS, OBLONG, OVAL, ROUND & SQUARE.

1 / 1660
Oblong,

2 / 1660
Oblong,

V 1866
2 Sizes.
Square.

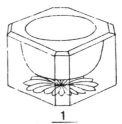

1 / 1866
2 Sizes, Square.

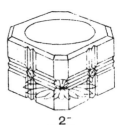

2 / 1866
2 Sizes, Square.

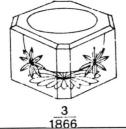

3 / 1866

1 / 1867

1 / 1879

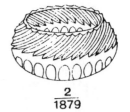

2 / 1879

(Reprint CC) Assorted pressed and cut glass salts by Sowerby & Co., Ellison Glass Works, Gateshead-On-Tyne, England, circa 1892 (Courtesy Inch & Blicque)

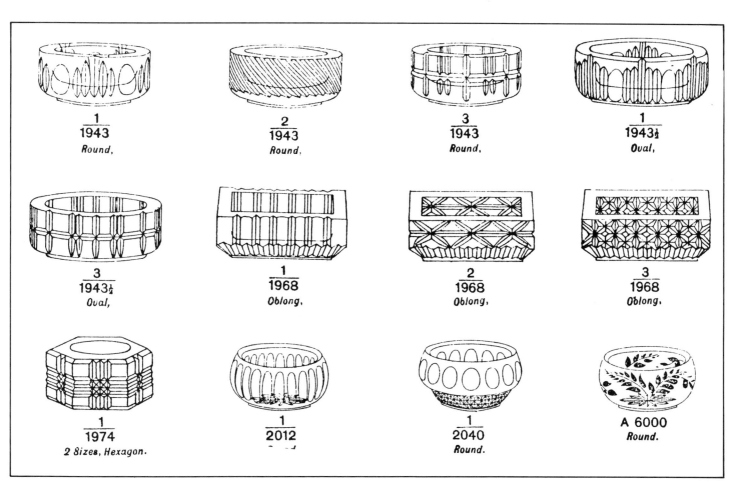

(Reprint DD) Additional cut salts from same 1892 Sowerby catalogue

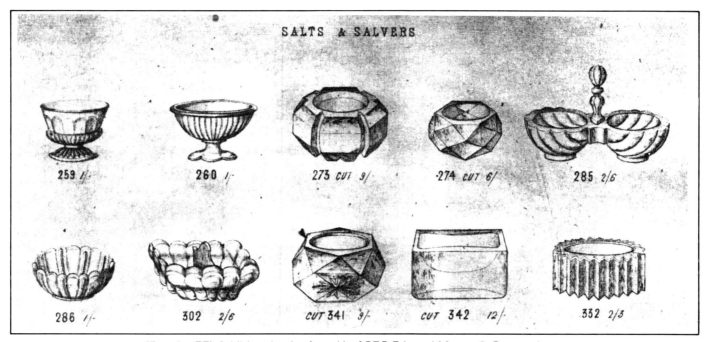

(Reprint EE) Additional salts found in 1870 Edward Moore & Co. catalogue

227

228

1030

1035

1040
Oval.
2 Sizes.

1040½
Round. 3
2 Sizes.

1071

1150

1573½ *Oval.*
1573 *Round.*

1832
Round. *2 Sizes.*
Also 1790
Oval. *2 Sizes.*

1860
Round.

1866
Square.
2 Sizes.

1867
Round.

1943
Round.
Also 1943½ *Oval.*

1974
Hexagon.
2 Sizes.

2012
Round.

8002
Round.

8003
Oval.

8004
Round.

8015
Oval.
Also 8016 *Round.*

$\frac{1}{1040 \text{ S}}$
Cut.

$\frac{1}{2012}$
Cut.

$\frac{1}{1660}$
Cut.

(Reprint FF) Assortment of salts from another Sowerby catalogue, circa 1900, with a few duplications from earlier catalogue (Courtesy Inch & Blicque)

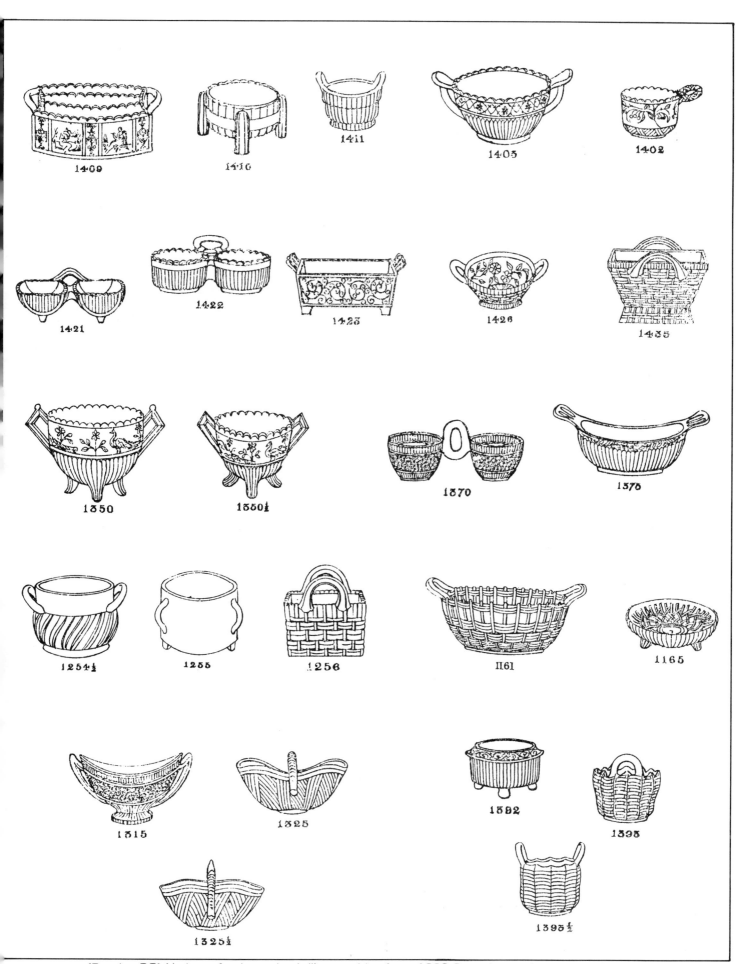

1409
1410
1411
1405
1402

1421
1422
1423
1426
1435

1350
1350½
1370
1375

1254½
1255
1256
1161
1165

1315
1325
1392
1395

1325½
1395½

(Reprint GG) Variety of salts and salt-like novelties from 1882 Sowerby catalogue, most found in opaque and opalescent colors

(REPRINT HH) Assortment of "Salt Cellars" by Edward Moore & Co., Tyne Flint Glass Works, South Shields, England, circa 1870 (Courtesy Corning Museum of Glass)

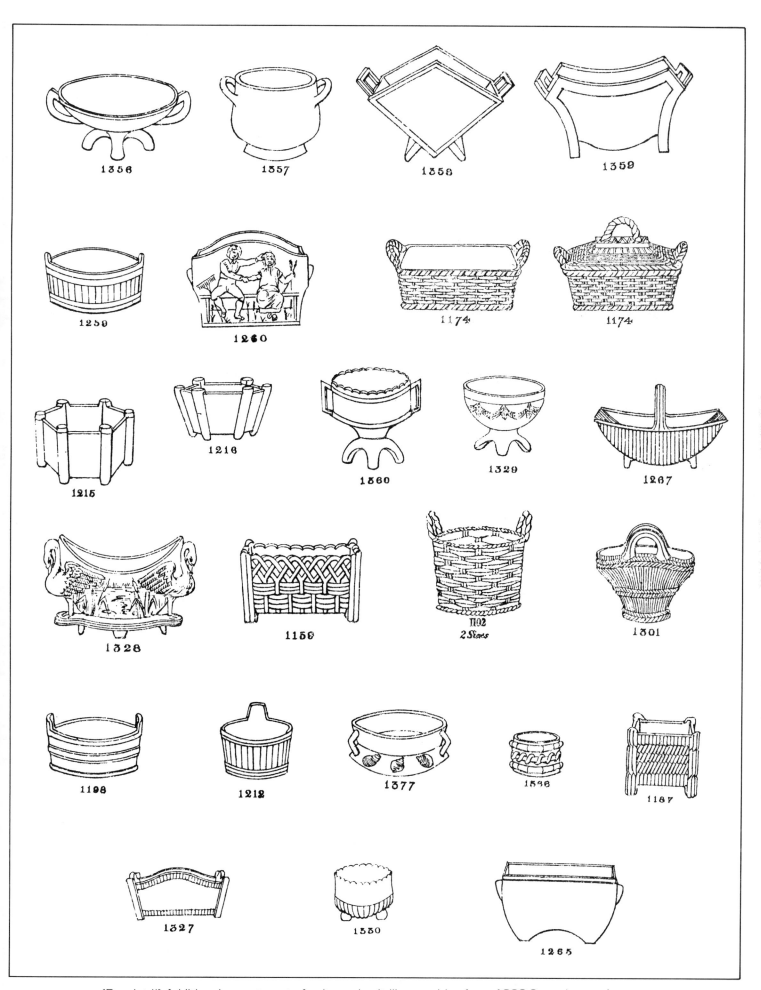

(Reprint II) Additional assortment of salts and salt-like novelties from 1882 Sowerby catalogue

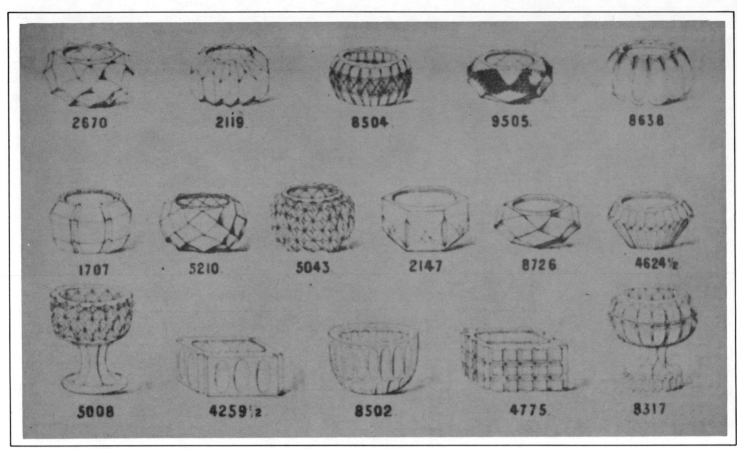

(Reprint JJ) Assortment of salts in early (circa 1870) catalogue by Joseph Webb, Coalborn Hill Glassworks, Stourbridge, England (Courtesy The Corning Museum of Glass)

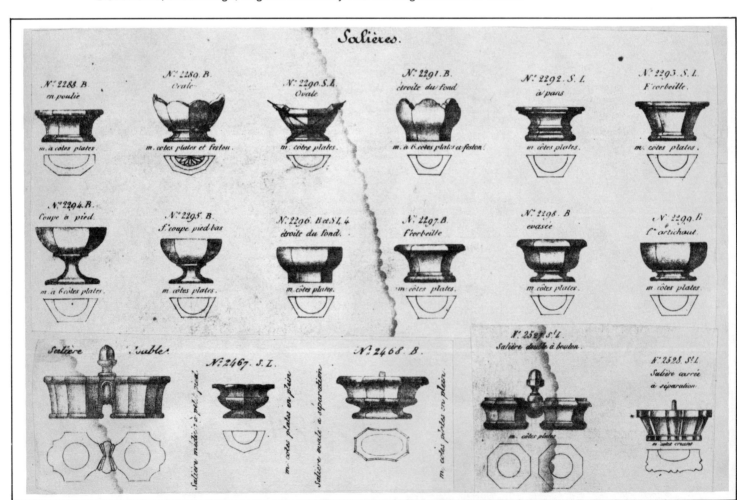

(REPRINT KK) Assortment of simpler pressed salts from circa 1842 French wholesale catalogue (Courtesy The Corning Museum of Glass)

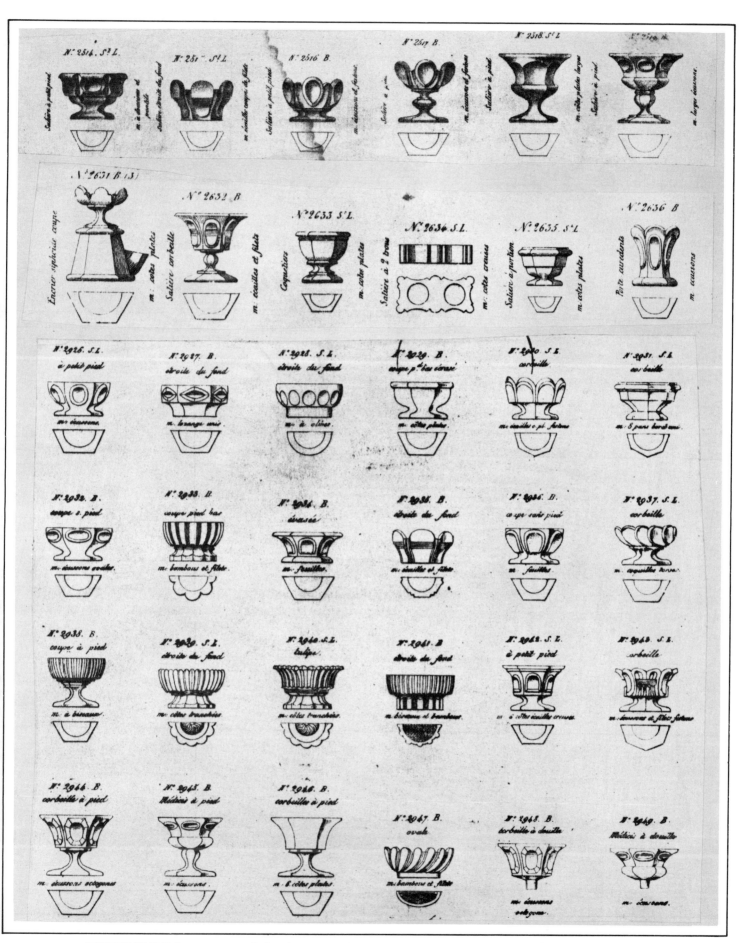

(REPRINT KK) Assortment of simpler pressed salts from circa 1842 French wholesale catalogue
(Courtesy The Corning Museum of Glass)

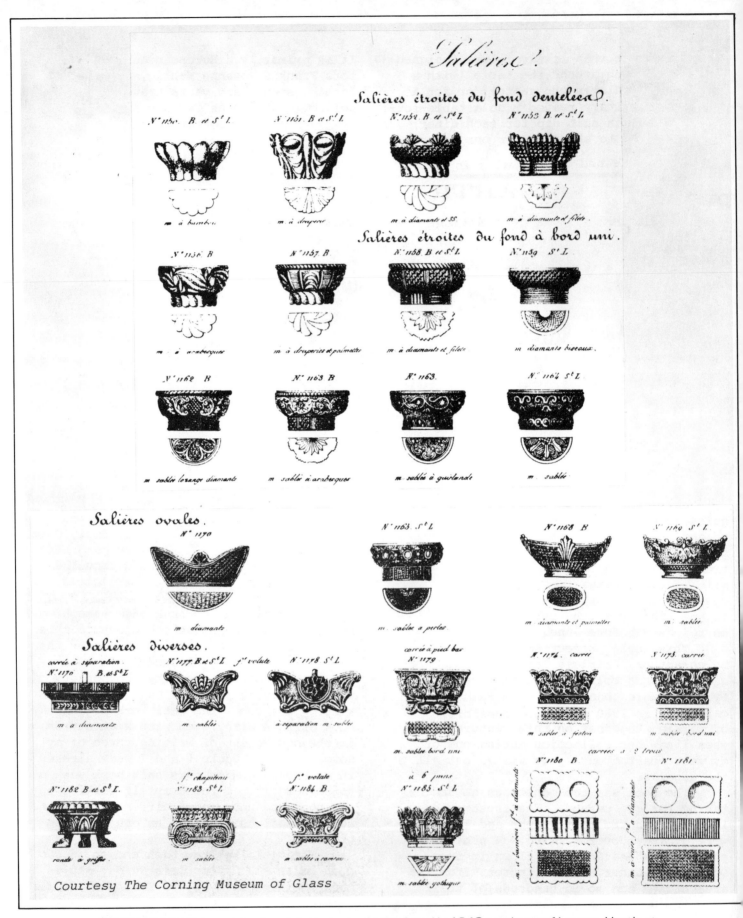

Salières

(REPRINT LL) Wide variety of early lacy pressed salts found in 1840 catalogue of Launay, Hautin et Cie, a French company distributing the glass of Baccarat, St. Louis and other lesser known glass houses. Many of these salts are similar to known American production. (Courtesy The Corning Museum of Glass)

(REPRINT MM) Assorted pedestal-based table salts offered by Launay, Hautin et Cie in 1840 catalogue (Courtesy The Corning Museum of Glass)

Moulures
Salières, Moutardiers.

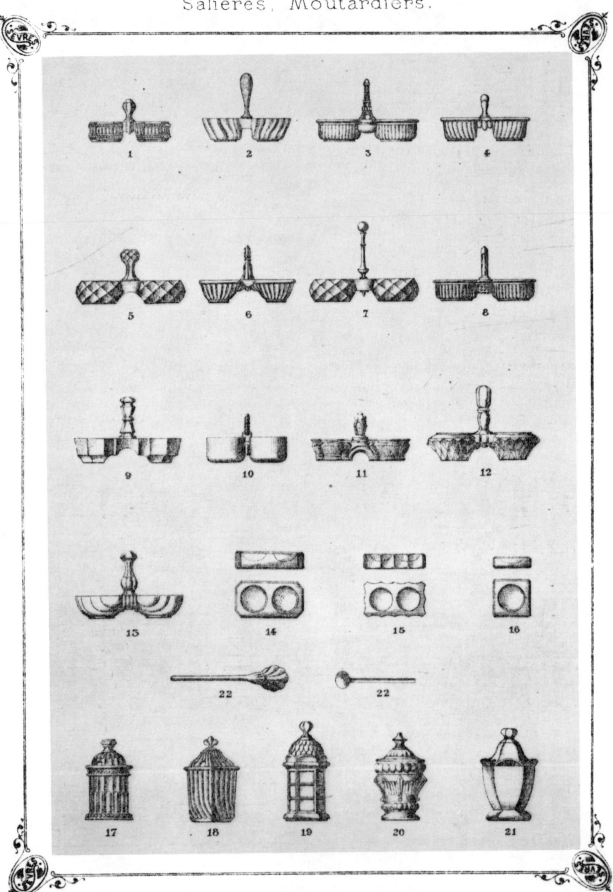

(REPRINT NN) Variety of double salts by Cristallies de Sevres (Anciennes Verreries Royales) et Clichy Reunie, circa 1888 French catalogue (Courtesy National Art Library, London)

ARTICLES DIVERS de TABLE
SALIÈRES

Modèles déposés

TARIFICATION *page 136*

Il existe un modèle de Salière à pied dans chacun de nos Services de Table
Voir Album & Tarification d'autre part.

(REPRINT PP) Variety of double salts from circa 1904 Baccarat catalogue, as well as a few individuals (Courtesy The Corning Museum of Glass)

ARTICLES DIVERS

SALIÈRES ET PORTE-SALIÈRES

Voir tarification page 35

SALIÈRES SIMPLES

648

649

650

651

652

653

654

656

657

658

659

SALIÈRES DOUBLES

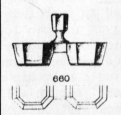
660

661

662

663

664

665

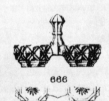
666

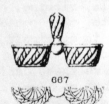
667

668

669

670

671

PORTE-SALIÈRES

672

673

674

675

(REPRINT QQ) Assortment of individual and double salts from 1908 St. Louis catalogue, French (Courtesy The Corning Museum of Glass)

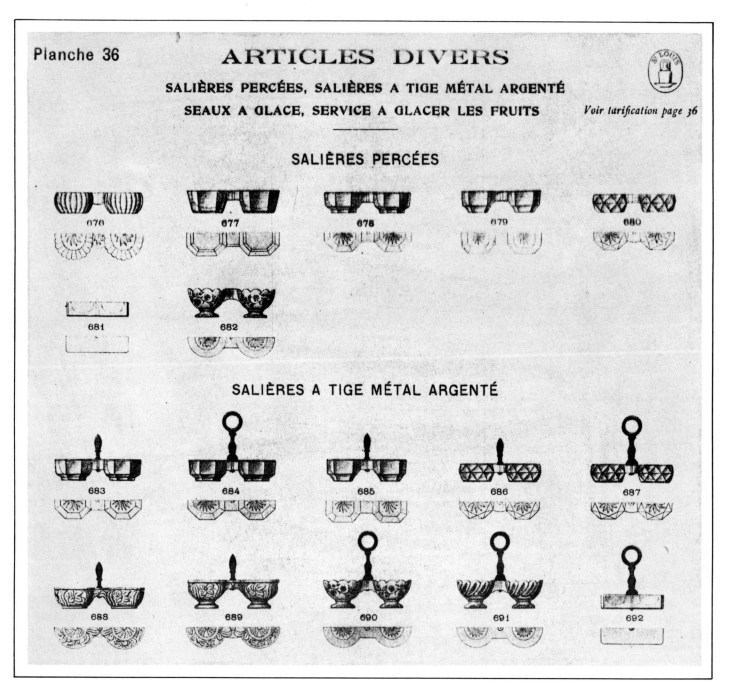

(REPRINT QQ) Assortment of individual and double salts from 1908 St. Louis catalogue, French
(Courtesy The Corning Museum of Glass)

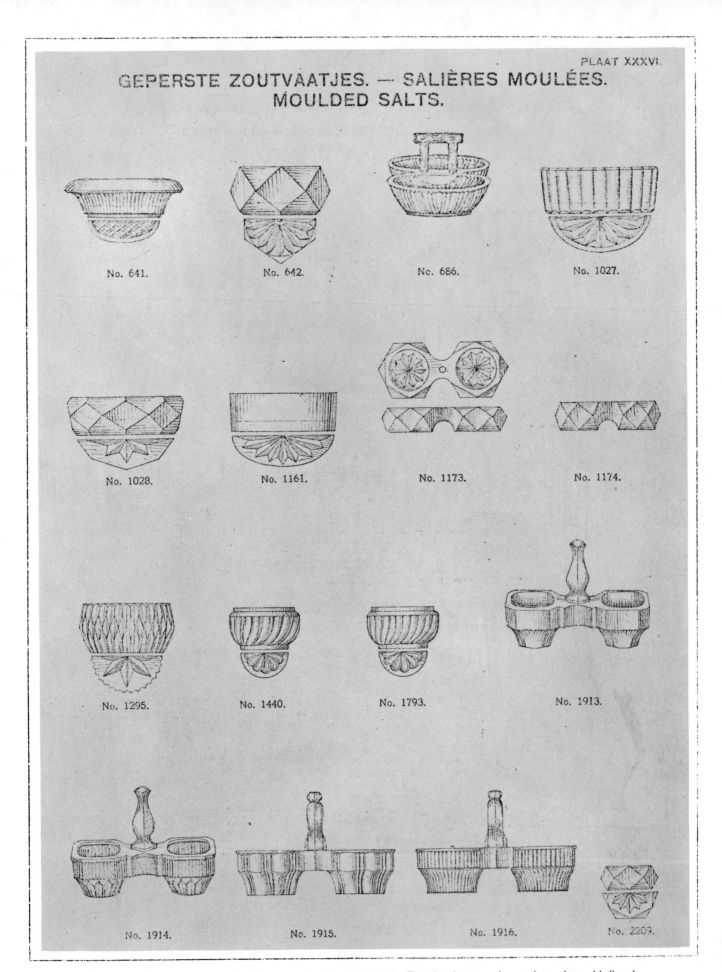

GEPERSTE ZOUTVAATJES. — SALIÈRES MOULÉES.
MOULDED SALTS.

No. 641.

No. 642.

No. 686.

No. 1027.

No. 1028.

No. 1161.

No. 1173.

No. 1174.

No. 1295.

No. 1440.

No. 1793.

No. 1913.

No. 1914.

No. 1915.

No. 1916.

No. 2209.

(REPRINT RR) Variety of singles and doubles from the Dutch glassworks at Leerdam, Holland, circa 1906 (Courtesy The National Art Library, London)

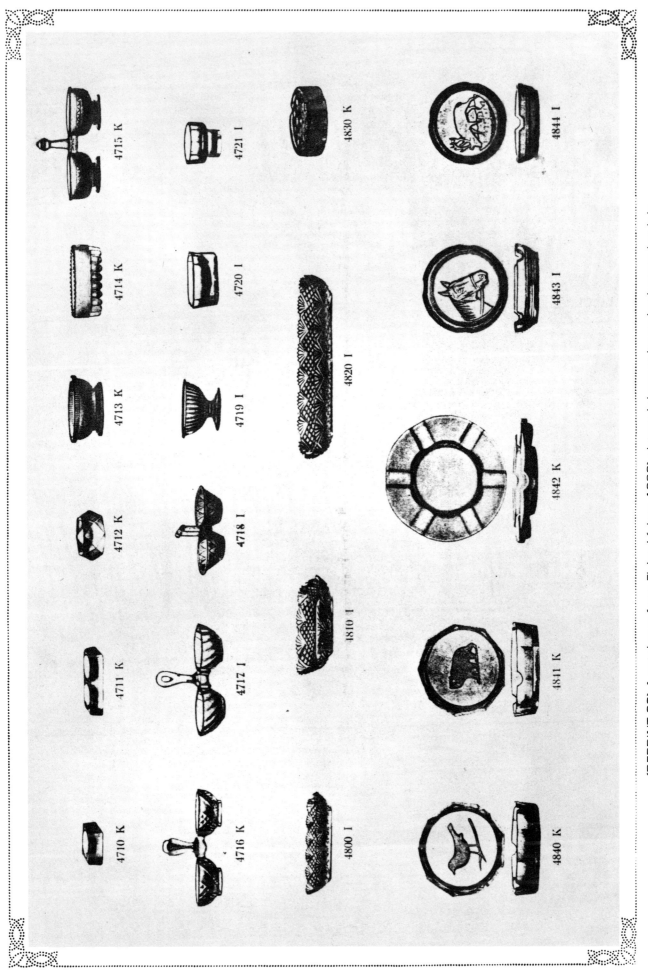

(REPRINT SS) A catalogue from Finland (circa 1920) pictured these salts and ash trays but it is unknown if the items were produced in this or another European country (Courtesy The Corning Museum of Glass)

MISCELLANEOUS SALTS FROM ORIGINAL CATALOGUES

No. 10—Ind Salt

No. 12—Individual Salt

No. 100-Sponge Cup
Small and Large

No. 11—Individual Salt

No. 401—Individual Salt
or Celery Dip

No. 205-–Individual Salt

Assorted Salts from Paden City Glass Catalogue, circa 1920 (courtesy Jerry Barnett)

SALTS.

OCTAGON. IND.   CINCINNATI, IND.   CABLE, IND.   BIRD, TABLE   ROPE.
                                        ALSO CABLE, TABLE.   AND IND.

DIAMOND, IND.   TOMATO.   CONCAVE.   TWIN.   STEADMAN.

Assorted Salts from McKee Glass Catalogue, circa 1889 (courtesy Vicki Harmon)

93 Individual Salt.
Packed 8½ gro. in bbl.

95 Individual Salt.
Packed 8⅓ gro. in bbl.

112 Individual Salt.
Packed 14 gro. in bbl.

Assorted Fostoria Glass Company Salts, circa 1900

Ind. Sailor Hat Salt.

Ind. Hat Salt
Patented.

Little German Band Cap.
Patented

Earl Ind. Boat

Ind. Salt.

Square Table Salt.

77 Ind. Salt.
Eng'd 177

27 Ind. Salt.

Individual Salt.

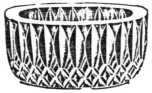

27 Table Salt. Ta

Heavy Salt.

Pavonia Table Salt.

SALT

Pavonia Ind. Salt

IND. SALT

Assorted Salts from 1891 U.S. Glass Company Catalogue

No. T785 Individual Salt
No. T786 Individual Salt
Full Cut

No.	Dozen in Bbl.	Approx. Gr. Wt.	Bbl. Price Per Dz.	Less Bbl. Price Per Dz.
T785	80	180	$1.25	$1.40
T786	80	180	$8.75	$10.00

No. T787 Individual Salt

No.	Dozen in Bbl.	Approx. Gr. Wt.	Bbl. Price Per Dz.	Less Bbl. Price Per Dz.
T787	60	145	$.60	$.75

No. T788 Celery Dip

No.	Dozen in Bbl.	Approx. Gr. Wt.	Bbl. Price Per Dz.	Less Bbl. Price Per Dz.
T788	80	180	$.75	$.90

No. T43 Salted Almond
3 inches

No.	Dozen in Bbl.	Approx. Gr. Wt.	Bbl. Price Per Dz.	Less Bbl. Price Per Dz.
T43	24	100	$1.85	$2.10

No. T784 Individual Salt

No.	Dozen in Bbl.	Approx. Gr. Wt.	Bbl. Price Per Dz.	Less Bbl. Price Per Dz.
T784	60	145	$1.10	$1.20

Assorted Chippendale pattern salts from Central Glass Works Catalogue, circa 1925.

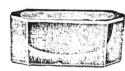

99 Table Salt
25 dozen in barrel
Price per dozen 72 cents

103 Individual Salt
140 dozen in barrel
Price per gross $3.30

103 Table Salt
25 dozen in barrel
Price per dozen 66 cents

76 Table Salt
25 dozen in barrel
Price per dozen 80 cents

98 Plain Square Individual
140 dozen in barrel
Price per gross $3.30

Assorted Salts from 1910 U.S. Glass Company Catalogue

322 Salt and Pepper Set. Not Fire Polished.
Packed 1 gro. in bbl.

Individual Salt & Pepper Set by Fostoria, circa 1900.

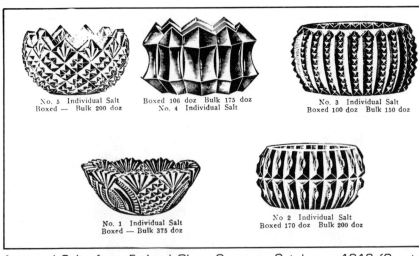

No. 5 Individual Salt
Boxed — Bulk 200 doz

Boxed 106 doz   Bulk 175 doz
No. 4 Individual Salt

No. 3 Individual Salt
Boxed 100 doz   Bulk 150 doz

No. 1 Individual Salt
Boxed — Bulk 375 doz

No 2 Individual Salt
Boxed 170 doz   Bulk 200 doz

Assorted Salts from Federal Glass Company Catalogue, 1913 (Courtesy Fred Bickenheuser)

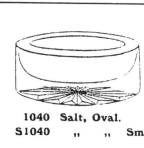
1040 Salt, Oval.
S1040   „   „   Smaller.

2012   Salt, Round.

2280   Salt. Oval

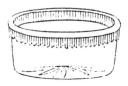
2127   Salt, Oval.

2232   Salt.

2246   Salt, Oval.
2246½   „   Round.

2303   Salt, Oval.

Assorted Salts from 1930's Sowerby Catalogue (courtesy Inch & Blicque)

NOTES

BIBLIOGRAPHY

CHINA, POTTERY & SILVER

AMERICAN SILVER MANUFACTURERS, Dorothy T. Rainwater, Crown Publishers, Inc., N.Y., 1975

THE BOOK OF OLD SILVER, Seymour B.'Wyler, Crown Publishers, Inc., N.Y., 1937

A DICTIONARY OF MARKS, Editor, Margaret Macdonald Taylor, Hawthorne Books, N.Y., 1953

A DICTIONARY OF AMERICAN SILVER, PEWTER & SILVER PLATE, Ralph & Terry Kovel, Crown Publishers, Inc., N.Y., 1961

DICTIONARY OF MARKS—POTTERY & PORCELAIN, Ralph & Terry Kovel, Crown Publishers, N.Y., 1953

ENCYCLOPEDIA OF BRITISH POTTERY & PORCELAIN MARKS, Geoffrey A. Godden, Bonanza Books, N.Y.

GUIDE TO MARKS OF ORIGIN ON BRITISH & IRISH SILVER PLATE, Frederick Bradbury, J.W. Northend, Ltd., England, 1964

MARKS & MONOGRAMS ON EUROPEAN & ORIENTAL POTTERY & PORCELAIN, William Chaffers, Borden Publishing, Alhambra, CA, 14th revised edition

POCKET BOOK ON GERMAN CERAMIC MARKS, J.P. Cushion, Faber & Faber, London, 1961

LES POINCONS, d' Argent, Published in French by Tardy, 11th Edition 1975

GLASS

AMERICAN BRILLANT CUT GLASS, Bill & Louise Boggess, Crown Publishers, N.Y., 1977

AMERICAN GLASS, Reprint of articles from Antiques Magazine, various authors, Weathervane Books, N.Y., 1974

AMERICAN GLASS, George P. & Helen McKearin, Crown Publishers, New York 23rd printing 1973

AMERICAN HISTORICAL GLASS, Bessie M. Lindsey, Charles E. Tuttle Co., Rutland, VT., Third Printing, 1972

AMERICAN PRESSED GLASS & FIGURE BOTTLES, Albert C. Revi, Thomas Nelson, Inc., N.Y., Fourth Printing, 1972

BEAUTY OF ALBANY GLASS, THE, Marcelle Bond, privately published, 1972

CAMBRIDGE GLASS COMPANY, THE, BOOKS 1 & 2, Catalogue reprints, Mary, Lyle & Lynn Welker, privately published, 1970 & 1974

CAMBRIDGE GLASS COMPANY, Reprint of 1930-34 catalogues, Collector Books, Paducah, KY, 1976

CATALOGUE OF THE CAMBRIDGE GLASS COMPANY, reprint of 1903 catalogue, Harold & Judy Bennett, 1976

COLLECTIBLE GLASS, Books 1-4, Ted & Vi Lagerberg, privately published, 1963-69

COLORED GLASSWARE OF THE DEPRESSION ERA, Hazel Marie Weatherman, Glassbooks, Springfield, MO., 1974

COMPLETE BOOK OF MCKEE GLASS, Sandra McPhee Stout, Trojan Press, North Kansas City, MO., 1972

EARLY AMERICAN PATTERN GLASS, Alice Hulett Metz, revised second edition, privately published, 1977

EARLY AMERICAN PRESSED GLASS, Ruth Webb Lee, Lee Publications, 4th edition, 1960

ENGLISH 19TH-CENTURY PRESS-MOLDED GLASS, Colin R. Latimore, Barrie & Jenkins, Ltd., London, England, 1979

ENGLISH, SCOTTISH AND IRISH TABLE GLASS, G. Bernard Hughes, Bramhall House, N.Y., 1955

ENCYCLOPEDIA OF VICTORIAN COLORED PATTERN GLASS, William Heacock, Antique Publications, Marietta, OH., Volumes 1-6, 1974-1981

FINDLAY PATTERN GLASS, Don E. Smith, privately published, 1970

FOSTORIA—ITS FIRST FIFTY YEARS, Hazel Marie Weatherman, privately published, 1972

GLASS PATENTS & PATTERNS, Arthur G. Peterson, privately published, 1973

GLASS SALT SHAKERS, Arthur G. Peterson, second printing, Wallace-Homestead Book Co., Des Moines, IA, 1970

GOBLETS 1 & 2, S.T. Millard, second printing, Wallace-Homestead Book Co., Des Moines, IA, 1975

GREENTOWN GLASS, James Measell, privately published by Grand Rapids Public Museum, Grand Rapids, MI, 1979

A GUIDE TO REPRODUCTIONS OF GREENTOWN GLASS, Brenda & James Measell, The Printing Press, Tulsa, OK, 1974

HEISEY GLASS COMPANY CATALOGUE REPRINTS, Books 1-4, Clarence Vogel, privately published

HEISEY'S GLASSWARE OF DISTINCTION, Mary Louise Burns, privately published, 1976

HISTORY OF FOSTORIA, OHIO GLASS (1887-1920), Melvin L. Murray, privately published, 1972

AN ILLUSTRATED DICTIONARY OF GLASS, Harold Newman, Thames & Hudson, Ltd., London, 1977

KAMM EIGHT BOOKS ON PATTERN GLASS, 8 volumes, Minnie Watson Kamm, Kamm Publications, Grosse Pointe Farms, MI., 1939-54 (latest editions)

McKEE VICTORIAN GLASS, catalogue reprints from 1859-1871, Corning Museum of Glass, Dover Publications, N.Y., 1981

MORE EARLY AMERICAN PATTERN GLASS, Alice Hulett Metz, privately published, latest edition, 1976

THE NEW MARTINSVILLE GLASS STORY, Everett & Addie Miller, privately published, 1972

NINETEENTH CENTURY GLASS, Albert C. Revi, Galahad Books, N.Y., revised edition, 1967

1000 TOOTHPICK HOLDERS — A COLLECTOR'S GUIDE, William Heacock, Antique Publications, Marietta, OH, 1977

PADEN CITY, THE COLOR COMPANY, Jerry Barnett, privately published, 1978

PENNSYLVANIA GLASSWARE, 1870-1904, various catalogue reprints, The Pyne Press, Princeton, 1972

PITTSBURGH GLASS — 1797-1891, Lowell Innes, Houghton Mifflin Co., Boston, 1976

PRESSED GLASS SALTS OF THE LACY PERIOD 1825-1850, L.W. & D.B. Neal, privately printed, 1962

SANDWICH GLASS, Ruth Webb Lee, second edition, privately published, 1947

VICTORIAN GLASS, Ruth Webb Lee, thirteenth edition, privately published, 1944

YEARS OF DUNCAN, THE, Gail Krause, privately published, 1980

CROSS-REFERENCE TO THE CLASSICS

Listed here is a reference to some of the major books on old glass, and the page numbers on which salt dips can be found. Also listed are catalogue reprints, ad reprints shown in the Kamm series, and other general bits of important information.

BARNETT, JERRY
Paden City, The Color Company (1978 Privately Printed) Out-of-Print
1. Page 41, No. 205 Colonial, made from old Higbee molds
2. Page 75, No. 11 and No. 12 individual salts
3. Page 75, No. 100 sponge cup which could be confused for a salt
4. Page 84, No. 401 Colonial (N.I.)
5. Page 94, No. 10 individual, same as No. 11 without the thumbprints

BENNETT, HAROLD & JUDY
1903 Catalogue of Cambridge Glass Company (1976, Privately Printed)
1. Page 12, master and individual in No. 2577 Ada pattern (made earlier by Ohio Flint Glass Co., 1898)
2. Page 16, ind. salt in Deep File (No. 2502) made earlier by Dalzell, Gilmore & Leighton, Findlay, Oh. (circa 1898)
3. Page 19, ind. salt in Josephine's Fan (No. 2504) made earlier by Robinson Glass Co., Zanesville, Oh. (circa 1900)
4. Page 31, master salt in No. 2615
5. Page 33, master and ind. salts, rectangular with waffle design in bottom

INNES, LOWELL
Pittsburgh Glass, 1797-1891 (1976, Houghton Mifflin Co., Boston)
Page 287, 16 different salts from the lacy period
Page 300 — Fascinating reprint from French catalogue, circa 1840, showing 40 lacey period salts frequently confused for American
Page 309 — Five early salts shown in 1860 Ringwalt catalogue (Lyons)
Page 318 — One ind. salt from 1864 McKee catalogue
Page 336 — 26 different salts by King Glass Co., circa 1875
Page 366 — Pedestalled salt in King's Gothic, circa 1875 (N.I.)
Page 340 — Two different salts in Bleeding Heart by King, 1875

KAMM, MINNIE
A Seventh Pattern Glass Book (1953, Kamm Publications)
Plate 12 — Ind. and Master salt in Doyle #250 (Clear Block) circa 1885
Plate 27 — Ind. and covered salt in R&H Peerless (Lady Hamilton) 1875
Plate 71 — Ind. salt in Cambridge Glass Co. Stratford (1906)

KAMM, MINNIE
An Eight Pattern Glass Book (1954, Kamm Publications)
Plate 14 — Master salt in O'Hara Diamond pattern, from 1891 U.S. Glass catalogue
Plate 19 — Oval and square ind. salts in Homestead pattern by Bryce, Higbee & Co., circa 1875
Plate 65 — Five salts by Brilliant and Greensburg Glass, circa 1885
Plate 111 — Barrow figural salt by Adams & Co. (U.S.) circa 1891